The Interpretation of
St. Luke's Gospel
12–24

R. C. H. LENSKI

Augsburg Fortress
Minneapolis

THE INTERPRETATION OF ST. LUKE'S GOSPEL 12–24
Commentary on the New Testament series

First paperback edition 2008

Copyright ©1946, 2008 Augsburg Fortress. All rights reserved. Except for brief quotations in critical articles or reviews, no part of this book may be reproduced in any manner without prior written permission from the publisher. Visit http://www.augsburgfortress.org/copyrights/contact.asp or write to Permissions, Augsburg Fortress, Box 1209, Minneapolis, MN 55440.

Richard C. H. Lenski's commentaries on the New Testament were published in the 1940s after the author's death. This volume was published in 1946 by the Wartburg Press and assigned in 1961 to the Augsburg Publishing House.

ISBN 978-0-8066-8088-0

The paper used in this publication meets the minimum requirements of American National Standard for Information Sciences—Permanence of Paper for Printed Library Materials, ANSI Z329.48-1984.

Manufactured in the U.S.A.

To
MATTHIAS LOY
My Teacher

ABBREVIATIONS

R. = A Grammar of the Greek New Testament in the Light of Historical Research, by A. T. Robertson, fourth edition.

B.-D. = Friedrich Blass' Grammatik des neutestamentlichen Griechisch, vierte, voellig neugearbeitete Auflage besorgt von Albert Debrunner.

C.-K. = Biblisch-theologisches Woerterbuch der Neutestamentlichen Graezitaet von D. Dr. Hermann Cremer, zehnte, etc., Auflage, herausgegeben von D. Dr. Julius Koegel.

B.-P. = Griechisch-Deutsches Woerterbuch zu den Schriften des Neuen Testaments, etc., von D. Walter Bauer, zweite, etc., Auflage zu Erwin Preuschens Vollstaendigem Griechisch-Deutschem Handwoerterbuch, etc.

M.-M. = The Vocabulary of the Greek Testament, Illustrated from the Papyri and other Non-Literary Sources, by James Hope Moulton and George Milligan.

R., W. P. = Word Pictures in the New Testament by Archibald Thomas Robertson.

R., Tr. = A Translation of Luke's Gospel, etc., by A. T. Robertson.

NOTE: — The translation in this volume is intended only as an aid in understanding the Greek.

INTRODUCTION

Paul mentions Luke three times in his letters: first in two epistles of the first imprisonment (Col. 4:14; Philemon 24) and then in one epistle of the second imprisonment (II Tim. 4:11). We see at once that Luke is in closest association with the great apostle to the Gentiles. Paul regards him as one of his "fellow laborers" (Philemon 24), and in sending Luke's greetings to the Colossians (4:11) he calls him "the beloved physician." During Paul's first imprisonment in Rome, when in his own hired house he was able to do a great deal of work (Acts 28:30, 31), Luke must have been working with him and was greatly endeared to the apostle. When Paul was again imprisoned in Rome and was this time held in close confinement and expected to be condemned to death, we have the pathetic statement from his pen: "Only Luke is with me." Luke alone is supporting Paul in this last severe ordeal. No gospel work is possible at this time. The pathos is greater when we note that Demas, who, during the first imprisonment, sent greetings to the Colossians together with Luke, has now, when Paul, in his second imprisonment, is facing death, forsaken the apostle and turned again to the world (II Tim. 4:10). Demas, too, should have stood with Paul, but only faithful Luke remained.

A valuable point in these passages is often overlooked, namely Luke's connection with Mark. Philemon 24 shows us that Luke and Mark were together in the work with Paul in Rome. These two Gospel writers were at the same time under Paul's influence and were in closest association with each other. Had Luke already written his Gospel—as some suppose, in Cæsarea, during Paul's imprisonment there, before he was transferred to Rome? That would have given Luke a distinction beyond any of Paul's fellow laborers. Yet in the list of persons who are sending greetings to the Colossians (4:10-14) it is Epaphras who receives the highest praise, and several others are distinguished above Luke. Mark, too, is mentioned as about to make the journey to Colossæ.

Luke and Mark, who were in contact with each other during the first imprisonment of Paul, are found to be so again at the time of the second imprisonment. When Paul says that Luke alone is with him he at once begs Timothy (II Tim. 4:10) to be sure and bring Mark with him when Timothy, at Paul's request, hastens to come to him at Rome. There is no reason to assume that Mark did not come; and both Luke and Mark were most likely with Paul when he laid his head upon the executioner's block. Neither Mark nor Luke had as yet written a Gospel; but both, as Paul's last mention of them shows, are most beloved of him and were thus close friends of each other. It is fair to conclude that whoever of them was the first to write his Gospel, the other must have promptly heard of it, secured a copy, and used it for his own writing.

We learn more from Luke himself. In the so-called "we sections" of the Acts Luke indicates his own presence in the incidents there recorded. The first of these in Codex D and its companions occurs in Acts 11:28. The genitive absolute συνεστραμμένων ἡμῶν is inserted, which describes a congregational meeting at Antioch at which prophets from Jerusalem appeared, and at which one of them, Agabus, foretold a great famine. The genitive absolute states that Luke was present at this meeting. Paul, too, was at this time working at Antioch together with Barnabas and was thus also present at this meeting. This valuable reading plainly implies that Luke lived in Antioch at this time, which agrees with the tradition that he was a native of this

Introduction

city. He was now a Christian and a member of the congregation. He was in touch with Paul, for Barnabas had brought Paul to Antioch, and the two had worked there for a whole year (Acts 11:25, 26). At Antioch Luke could easily have secured his medical and literary education, a famous medical school being located there.

All that can be said about the conversion of Luke is based on Acts 11:20, 21. After the first persecution of the church in Jerusalem some Christians fled to Antioch (v. 19). Among them were "men of Cyprus and Cyrene" who preached "the Lord Jesus" to the Grecians. Among these Greeks was Luke who thus came to the faith directly from paganism without first becoming a Jewish proselyte. He was converted before Barnabas brought Paul to Antioch. Paul calls Timothy his "son" because he had converted him, but no intimation to this effect is given by Paul concerning his beloved Luke. The fact that Luke was a native of Antioch appears incidentally in the Acts. In 6:5 only Nicholas is described by an addition to his name; Luke knew that he was from Antioch. Since he was well acquainted with Antioch, Luke also shows special interest in this congregation's affairs. The fact that Luke was a Gentile appears in Col. 4:10-14 where Luke and Demas are distinguished from three others "who are of the circumcision." We may note incidentally that about one-fourth of the New Testament was written by a former pagan.

The next "we section," Acts 16:10, etc., shows us Luke in company with Paul at Troas on the apostle's second missionary journey. He is now one of Paul's chosen companions and assistants in the work. This "we" stops with the visit to Philippi and permits the conclusion that Luke, who for some reason had not been arrested with Paul and Silas, was left behind to superintend the work in Philippi. The next "we," in Acts 20:6, etc., shows Luke joining Paul and his company (v. 4) at the end of the third missionary journey. This "we" takes Luke to Jerusalem with Paul (Acts 21:17, 18). Paul is now under arrest and is quickly transferred to Cæsarea. Among the "acquaintance" who were allowed to minister unto him there (Acts 24:23) we gladly place also Luke. It is quite probable that Luke remained near Paul in Cæsarea during the entire time of the imprisonment, for in Acts 27:1 he accompanies Paul on the long and dangerous journey to Rome for his confinement there until the emperor should hear his case. Luke remained with Paul in Rome as is shown above by Col. 4:14.

Luke does not obtrude his professional medical learning in his writings. In this he shows good taste as well as proper balance. This question has been thoroughly considered in recent years. In 1882 W. K. Hobart's, *The Medical Language of St. Luke*, cited the Greek physicians Hippocrates, Diascorades, Aratæus, and Galen to show to what extent Luke used medical language; Zahn, Harnack, Moffatt, and others accepted most of his findings. But Henry J. Cadbury's, *The Style and Literary Method of Luke, I, The Diction of Luke and Acts*, Harvard Theological Studies VI, 1919 and 1920, controverted Hobart most decidedly and was aided by George F. Moore, a contributor to the Harvard Studies. A sample is the term κραιπάλη used in Luke 21:34, which Hobart, Zahn, Harnack, and Moffatt regarded as a technical medical term, but which Moore proves to be nothing but the common Greek word for the *Katzenjammer* ("hang-over") after too much wine. The upshot of the study is that in Luke's time medical science had not developed specialized foreign terms but used the ordinary Greek world language. Luke did not parade his medical learning before his reader. What he did was to write with exactness about diseases and medical matters. Only in a quiet and a refined way does Luke prove himself a physician.

* * *

Introduction

The fact that Luke wrote the third Gospel as well as the Acts is solidly attested by the ancient tradition. Justin Martyr, born in Samaria about the year 100, quotes Luke's Gospel repeatedly. Irenæus (115-190) says in his book against heresy (3, 1): "Luke, the follower of Paul, preserved in a book the gospel which that apostle preached." He also gives an account (3, 14) of the contents of this gospel, which shows that he refers to the book we now know as Luke's Gospel. Tertullian (150 or 160—220 or 240) says that his teacher Cerdon received only Luke's Gospel. Tatian, some time after 150, includes Luke in his *Diatessaron*, a harmony of all four Gospels. The pagan Celsus, about 178, knows Luke's Gospel and directs his attacks against it. The Muratorian Canon (last quarter of the second century) attests Luke's writing. Eusebius (260 or 270—340) in his *Church History*, 3:4, speaks, without doubting, of both the Gospel and the Acts as being written by Luke.

Among the attestations to Luke's Gospel is that of the gnostic Marcion. He rejected everything Jewish from what he considered to be the real "gospel." He thus discarded the entire Old Testament and all of the New except Paul's Epistles and Luke's Gospel. He mutilated and worked over the latter to suit his own purpose. The point of this is that Marcion did not assail the authorship of Luke; he had no theory to the effect that Luke worked over and spoiled the genuine work of an earlier writer. Marcion came to Rome in 139; his gnosticism follows this date.

Considerable controversy has been carried on among German scholars regarding Marcion and Luke's Gospel. The claim was made that both Marcion's and Luke's works were based on an earlier original. This was advanced to the claim that Marcion's was the original. This again to the claim that Marcion's work was the original Gospel composed by Luke, this Gospel having been worked over by a later hand. But the whole controversy has been brought to an issue. Marcion's work has been restored sufficiently to show that he indeed mutilated, abridged, and altered the canonical Luke because he considered this the easiest of the four Gospels to handle for his purpose. Thus Marcion's testimony stands. All that he left of Luke's name in the epistles is the fact that Paul sends Luke's greetings and Luke's name is coupled with that of the renegade Demas. He thus casts an evil light on the man whose book he misused.

The caption Κατὰ Λουκᾶν, which is also extended to something like Τὸ Κατὰ Λουκᾶν Ἅγιον Εὐαγγέλιον, must be regarded as one of the ancient attestations to the fact that the third Gospel is from Luke's hand. Each of the four Gospel manuscript rolls was marked by such a κατά phrase which named that Gospel's writer. No one tries to say how far back these captions go, but they very likely reach back to the earliest days. The manuscript rolls were placed in a holder or were laid in a drawer, and some mark was needed to distinguish them. Thus the κατά phrase was written on the outside of the roll and at the top of the first column of the writing. These phrases are stronger attestations than those of the individual church fathers, for they represent the conviction of the churches in general, wherever these rolls were used in public worship, that the evangelist named on each wrote what it contained.

The preposition was not ὑπό so that we cannot translate "by Luke," etc., which would express authorship in the most direct way. For the Gospels, as Luke's shows so clearly, were not original compositions. The "gospel" contained in them did not originate with the writer whose name was placed at the head of the roll. The preposition κατά was more exact, for it obviated such a notion and yet included the idea that the person named wrote the book. *Secundum*, "according to," means that the version of the "gospel" or glad news was not invented by Luke (Matthew, etc.) but was by him recorded in the book he wrote. Luke names the source from which he drew (1:1-4). John was an eyewitness to the events, Matthew to most of them and drew the rest of them from others like Mark and Luke. It is in this specific way that the κατά captions are of such great importance.

* * *

Luke wrote both of his books for a certain Theophilus, concerning whom, unfortunately, we know next to nothing. The address κράτιστε, which may be rendered "Your Excellency," indicates knighthood, official position, or great wealth and prominence, it is uncertain just which. But we have no information concerning the contact between Luke and Theophilus, where the latter resided, and just why Luke wanted to write to him to give him the certainty that he ought to have. Some feel certain that this Theophilus was already a Christian, but this was not the case. In the Gospel Luke addresses him as κράτιστε, not so in the Acts. In all Christian literature, however, no brother Christian is ever addressed by such a title of earthly distinction. Hence when Luke wrote his Gospel to Theophilus, this distinguished man was not yet a Christian but was greatly interested in things Christian; but when Luke sent the Acts to him, Theophilus had become a convert. This conclusion is safe and not the other which is based on κατηχήθης in 1:4 and interprets this verb as if it meant that Theophilus had already been instructed in the Christian doctrine.

Something more should be added. Theophilus must have come into contact with Luke in later years, not so very long before the Gospel was written for him. Those who suppose that he lived in Antioch overlook the fact that Luke left this city to join Paul on his journeys and in his work and, as far as we know, never went back to his native town. After the death of Paul in Rome Luke went, not to Antioch, but to Greece if the old tradition is to be trusted. Now it is not fair to assume, even if the date of the Gospel is made as early as possible, that Theophilus, who lived in Antioch and had known Luke, should have remained in uncertainty about the great gospel events and facts until Luke finally brought him certainty after many years. Luke's contact with Theophilus must have occurred at a far later time. Somewhere, possibly in Rome, these two met with the result that not long after this time Luke wrote twice to his important friend.

As far as the dates are concerned, it was in the year 43 that Paul came to Antioch and found Luke in the church. Luke joined Paul to become one of his assistants in Troas in the year 52 or 53. It is a fair conclusion that Luke had left Antioch and was now living in Troas. In 58 Luke goes with Paul on his journey to Jerusalem and remains with him until they reached Rome in the year 60, after that to the end of the first imprisonment in 62, and again to the death of Paul in 66. The Gospel was not written earlier than this date. Theophilus cannot have lived in Antioch all these years and remained uncertain about the great facts of Christianity. All these years would also have lessened the personal tie between the two men. Why should Luke, after such a long separation, write two such notable works to Theophilus?

It is guessing to regard Luke as having originally been a slave in the house of Theophilus—slaves sometimes practiced medicine; it is surmising to add that Luke became a freedman and was thus able to go where he pleased. Luke is too highly educated for anything such as this. Admitting that these guesses are correct, how would this former slave come to write thus to his former master in these late years? The improbabilities are too great. They go beyond the bounds of the probable when ten years are added as those assume who think that Luke did not write his Gospel until after the destruction of Jerusalem, about the year 75 if not later than that. As far as Luke's standing is concerned, it is a far better guess to say that, like Paul, he, too, was a Roman citizen.

All the probabilities lie in the direction that Luke became acquainted with Theophilus at a later time, probably in Rome, most likely during Luke's last stay in Rome, and that Luke wrote his books to him shortly after that. The late date of composition is out of the question also for other weighty reasons.

It is Theophilus who occasioned Luke's writing. Other New Testament writings had a similar personal prompting. Only a few writers note God's hand back of these personal promptings. It was he who used individual needs and situations for providing his church of all ages with the inspired records it needed. In the case of Luke's writings we may admit that Theophilus, prominent and wealthy as he was, was expected to publish them. It was a custom of those times to dedicate books to such personages and to request that they make them available to others who would be interested. But Luke's two introductory statements (Gospel and Acts) are really not dedications and do not even hint at publication. Luke wrote most directly for the personal spiritual benefit of Theophilus. The other Gospels were written directly for the church; their publication was attended to accordingly. Mark's and John's Gospels were written even by request. Luke simply committed his writings to Theophilus. We cannot assume that the latter had requested them, for Luke would then have stated in his introductory word to the Gospel that he was complying with that request. Luke knew the value of what he sent to Theophilus, and we may assume that he thought Theophilus would recognize that value and thus publish these writings. It nevertheless remains highly dignified on Luke's part not even to hint in this direction.

* * *

Two ways of arriving at the approximate date of Luke's writing are quite unsound, for both of them are based on hypothetical evidence. The one is very old and operates with the way in which Luke breaks off his record in the Acts by leaving Paul confined in Rome and saying not a word about the outcome of his trial before the emperor. The assumption is that Luke did not know the outcome when he wrote, that the Acts were consequently written right there in Rome in the year 60 or 61, while Paul was still a prisoner. Since the Gospel antedates the Acts, it is assumed that it was written during Paul's imprisonment in Cæsarea between 58 and 60. There are those who still hold this view. The trouble is that it rests entirely on the supposed reason as to why Luke closes the Acts as he does.

The other view is less acceptable, for it assails the character of Luke. It is claimed that Luke wrote the prophecy recorded in 21:20-24 as a substitute for Matt. 24:15-28 and Mark 13:14-23, and that Luke wrote with such clearness about the siege of Jerusalem, the destruction of the Temple, and the fate of the Jews because all these things had already happened when he wrote. Luke is charged with "departure from strict historical accuracy" such as Matthew and Mark maintain. But this is a serious charge, namely that the prophecies of Jesus are recorded by Luke as if they were made *post eventum*. Anyone can prophesy in that way. What becomes of Luke's own statement that he, too, after having carefully traced everything from the eyewitnesses, writes this Gospel of his? It is not true that Luke altered the prophecies about Jerusalem to make them more like the events that occurred later. To charge this exact historian with such manipulation of his sources is to assail his character of truthfulness. But this assault is made chiefly for one reason: to get a date for Luke's books that is later than the year seventy.

There is nothing to contradict the old tradition that the Gospels were written in the order in which we now have them in the New Testament, specifically that Luke was the third to write. This is the testimony of Irenæus in the *Church History* of Eusebius (5, 8, 2), and likewise of Origen (6, 25, 3), and of the first sixteen lines of the Muratorian canon. When the Gospels were collected and arranged, our present order became fixed. In this connection we may remember that the four manuscript rolls could be placed in a holder or laid in a drawer in any order, each being taken out as needed. When they were at last written in a codex, in book form, this was a different matter; then the order had to remain fixed. In Egypt John was placed first, the other three followed in their order; yet this in no way affected the tradition as to the order in which the Gospels were written and, of course, eventually yielded to the order we now have. The dates of the first three Gospels thus depend on each other. The later Matthew is placed, the later Mark and Luke must be placed; in the same way the date of Mark controls that of Luke. This would amount to nothing as regards Luke if Luke wrote as late as the year 75 to 80; the interval would be so long that the order of writing would hardly come in question as is the case with the late date of John's Gospel.

Only a Greek legend tells us that Luke remained unmarried, that he wrote his Gospel in Achaia later than Matthew and Mark, and that he died in Bithynia at the age of 74 or 84. Another report is that he died in Hellas at the age of 80. Although they are supported by no weighty authority, these may be the facts. But neither the exact date nor the place of Luke's writing can be ascertained thereby. That he wrote while Paul was alive is altogether unlikely. As Mark wrote after Peter's death, so, it seems, Luke wrote after Paul's. But the view that Luke put off writing until near the end of his life is just as improbable if not more so. The points to be noted are these. Luke did not let Theophilus wait too long. Unless he came in contact with Theophilus long after Paul's death (66) he wrote near that time. All Luke's investigations with regard to the eyewitnesses were made during the years prior to Paul's death. Little could be obtained by Luke after that time when we consider the various and conflicting reports about him after he finally left Rome.

* * *

Luke thus wrote shortly after Mark; where, is wholly uncertain.

In this connection it is well to remember the contact of Luke with Mark. He met Mark in Antioch in the early forties, and Mark and Luke were Paul's companions during the first and most likely during the last part of the second imprisonments. Any Gospel that had been written by Mark would thus quickly come into Luke's hands. But Mark's association with Peter in Rome up to the latter's death in 64 may mean even more for Luke. Where was Luke between Paul's two imprisonments? He could have remained only in Rome. Then he must have seen Peter and Mark, must have consulted Peter as an eyewitness, heard the same things that Mark heard; so that even if Mark's Gospel did not reach Luke promptly, Luke had received from Peter directly what Mark's Gospel contained. Luke would never have let the opportunity to consult Peter pass by, especially at a time as late as this (62-64).

Zahn contends that Luke had no knowledge of Matthew's Gospel. He claims that Luke did not know Aramaic, and that Matthew's Gospel, being written in Hebrew, was unintelligible to Luke. But how about the **agreements between Luke and Matthew where both vary from Mark?** Zahn answers that these are due to the Greek translator of Matthew who used both Mark and Luke. The hypothesis is that Mark wrote in 66, Luke in 75, and that the translator prepared the Greek Matthew in 80. But this view is not maintainable. Matthew did not write his Gospel in Hebrew, all he wrote in that language were his so-called "logia," about which no one knows anything further; this entire matter is discussed in the introduction to the author's commentary on Matthew. We have no reason to hesitate regarding Luke's use of Matthew's Gospel, which was written in no other language than Greek.

As the authorities on which his Gospel rests Luke names the original eyewitnesses of the gospel events. Even if Matthew had never written a line, the probabilities are that Luke met him and consulted him just as he consulted others of the Twelve. This might explain how Luke agrees so markedly with Matthew in some passages: He had preserved what Matthew told him, he used these data when he wrote. But we are entitled to go much farther. When Luke states in his prologue that "many" wrote detailed narratives on the basis of what had been handed down to them by the eyewitnesses, Matthew himself is one of these "many." The objection is raised that he could not be included among these because he was himself an eyewitness. But Matthew was not called by Jesus and did not join him until quite late (Matt. 9:9). How did Matthew obtain a knowledge of all that preceded this date? Just as Luke did—from others. This explains incidentally why Luke's account of the birth and the childhood of Jesus is wholly uninfluenced by that of Matthew. Both were equally dependent upon others, and so Matthew told the story from Joseph's angle, Luke from Mary's.

Luke made an accurate examination of all the gospel facts before he wrote. He must have begun this investigation long before he wrote. It was natural that he should want to know all the gospel facts at firsthand. As an educated man he would embrace the golden opportunities that came his way. There was added to his own spiritual interest the urge of his gospel work under Paul's direction; for this he needed to know all he possibly could concerning the life of Jesus. Finally there came his contact with Theophilus and the latter's need. This induced Luke to write. If this is the human side of it, we know another—the divine. The Holy Spirit selected Luke for the great task in the interest of the church of all ages and enabled him with divine help to write the two books that constitute such a fountain of saving truth for us today.

The effort is made to show from Luke's prologue that he intended from the beginning to write more than the Gospel (he is said to have planned three books). But the phrase περὶ τῶν πεπληροφορημένων ἐν ἡμῖν πραγμάτων, which is made the basis of this view, does not imply such an extended plan on Luke's part for the simple reason that it refers to the writers who preceded Luke—they were the ones who have undertaken to draw up a narrative "concerning the matters that have been brought to completion among us," i.e., the matters pertaining to Jesus and his redemptive work. Now the "many" did not set out to write books such as the Acts, they wrote only Gospels. These gospel matters were also the ones regarding which Theophilus needed full assurance in order to bring him to faith.

But why did Luke not simply send Mark's Gospel or Matthew's or both of them to Theophilus to furnish him the certainty he needed? Many of these questions are easier asked than answered. Matthew's great Gospel was written for Jewish Christians, and Luke might thus have preferred to send something else. Mark's Gospel might have served for Theophilus and met his need directly as a Gentile. But Luke perhaps desired to send more than Mark contained. Beyond this lies the personal element, which is often the most important of all. An account from Luke's own pen would have a greater effect upon this aristocrat.

* * *

Luke may, after all, have known Aramaic and Hebrew. This would best explain the first chapters of his Gospel although their Aramaic cast is generally explained as being due to the source from which he drew. He knew the LXX and drew his Old Testament quotations from this translation. This may have been done chiefly because Theophilus could verify them there. Luke, however, intentionally cultivates the LXX's sacred style in the narratives that have their scene in Palestine. We also see that he follows the diction of his sources in many places where he could have refined the language. Then again, as in the preface and in a few other places, he writes the highest type of literary Koine. The opening sentence of the Gospel has often been compared to the prefaces of Thucydides, Herodotus, and other skilful writers, except that "his modesty is an offset to their vainglory," Schaff.

All this makes Luke's style varied. Luke writes like a historian and always makes the most of his material. He remains popular but gives the impression of culture and writes with a cosmopolitan outlook. His vocabulary is extensive, for he uses 750 (851 counting double readings) words that are not found elsewhere in the New Testament, some of them are still hapaxlegomena (R. 121). Of the 851 words used 312 occur in the Gospel and 478 in the Acts. Luke does not follow the chronological order of events except in certain sections and especially where this is necessary because of the nature of what is recorded. This appears in the opening narrative of the body of his work (4:16-32) which belongs chronologically to a later time.

The ancients tried to find in Luke's Gospel that of Paul. Many have understood Paul's expression "according to my gospel" to refer to Luke's book, but Luke wrote after Paul was dead. The influence of Paul on Luke's writing is only a general one. This appears from the fact that the two statements of Jesus that are preserved by Paul alone (Acts 20:35; I Thess. 4:15) were not used by Luke in his Gospel. So also Luke made no use of Paul's letters in the Acts. Luke's Gospel is Pauline in its tone and tendency. Whether direct contacts with expressions that were used by Paul in his letters can be verified or not makes little difference. As far as Luke's use of the two preceding Gospels is concerned, an independence on Luke's part must be noted. He had the fullest firsthand information with which to begin and was thus bound to follow no other writer. While he certainly knew what the "many" (1:1) had written he did not depend on any of these documents (not even on Matthew's and Mark's) but altogether on the testimony of the eyewitnesses.

* * *

Like the other Gospels, Luke's has been variously divided, and not always in an obvious way. The proper way to divide is to seek Luke's own division of marks and not to impose a division of our own upon his book. Two parts are so plainly marked as to be obvious to all, namely the first and the last. The former takes in the first three chapters and ends with the genealogy. Some would extend this first part to 4:15, which is a rather minor matter. The genealogy indicates so plain a division point that it ought to be generally recognized. So also the last three chapters belong together, recounting, as they do, the actual Passion and the resurrection. The eighteen chapters that lie between are the ones that are variously divided. But careful reading will show two division points, one in 9:51 where Jesus steadfastly sets his face to go to Jerusalem, and the other in 18:31 where he makes the announcement: "Behold, we go up to Jerusalem!" Accepting these division points as they are furnished by Luke himself, his Gospel appears to be composed of five main parts. The formulation of captions for them is a minor matter, one that exercises the skill of the commentator. We venture the following:

**The Certainty
Concerning the Matters Brought
to Completion Among Us**

I. *The Beginning, chapters 1 to 3.*

II. *While Jesus was in Galilee, chapter 4 to 9:50.*

III. *When Jesus faced Jerusalem, 9:51 to 18:30.*

IV. *When Jesus actually entered Jerusalem, 18:31 to 21:38.*

V. *The Consummation, chapter 22 to 24.*

It remains to be said that the structure of Luke's Gospel is simple and serviceable but shows far less skill than the more elaborate plans of the other three Gospels. Mark, for instance, is far more beautifully arranged.

CHAPTER XII

1) In connection with which things, the myriads of the multitude having been gathered together unto him so that they were treading on each other, he began to say to his disciples first, Beware of the leaven of the Pharisees, which is hypocrisy.

To begin a new paragraph with a relative clause is classical. It is not temporal (our versions and others) but states that what is now reported stands in vital connection with what precedes. But this connection is not restricted to 11:53, 54, because these two verses are only on a summary of what the scribes and the Pharisees did during the next days. The connection is all that precedes, at least from 11:37 onward, and we are inclined to say from 11:14 onward. The connection, too, is obvious, for after speaking to the Pharisees Jesus now speaks of them. In fact, the connection is so close that it seems that what is now reported followed shortly after Jesus left the Pharisee's house (11:37). The meal broke up, Jesus walked out. The multitudes mentioned in 11:29 were now gathered thickly about him. Luke speaks of "the myriads of the multitude," which is hyperbolic for an exceedingly great number; the article should not be overlooked: "the myriads," not merely "myriads," because these are "the multitudes" mentioned in v. 29. They kept treading on each other because they were not in the open country but in a city, jammed together in a street.

The entire chapter is a consecutive whole. The great crowd is packed about Jesus, his disciples are closest to him, and the discourse is addressed to one or to the other group as Luke indicates (v. 1, 13, 22, 41, 54). The impression made by the text is that Jesus went to the Pharisee's house alone and is now again surrounded by his disciples. He speaks to them first.

R., W. P., explains, "beware": προσέχετε (νοῦν understood) put your mind, ἑαυτοῖς (dative) for yourselves, ἀπό (with the ablative) and avoid. The figure of the leaven refers to secret, penetrating power. It is thus that hypocrisy penetrates and vitiates everything in the Pharisees. They were archhypocrites, and it was this vice that proved so fatal to them. The very preposition in the word (ὑπό) intimates that they were "under" a mask like play actors, without sincerity, acting a part, given to pretense. Jesus in public, before the great crowd, warns his own disciples against this moral perversion. He brands the Pharisees, all are to hear it; but his disciples are not to think that they are immune — remember Judas; all people are to hear this warning which is addressed to Jesus' own followers.

2) Everything that hypocrisy tries to hide and cover up shall be exposed with absolute certainty. **Now there is nothing that has been covered up that shall not be revealed, and secret that shall not be known, wherefore, whatever things you spoke in the darkness shall be heard in the light; and what thing you uttered for the ear in the secret rooms shall be heralded on the housetops.**

Note the rhythmic parallelism of the clauses in both verses. This is the utter futility of hypocrisy. We regard the perfect participle συγκεκαλυμμένον, "having been and thus now still being covered up completely," exactly as we regard the adjective κρυπτόν, as the predicate of the copula and not as the participle in a periphrastic perfect. Whether it is actually covered up most carefully (σύν) and kept so or profoundly secret in the first place, whatever the thing may be, it will be uncovered and revealed, it will be known everywhere. The statement is general and is to be applied in general, it is without exception. In Matt. 10:26 Jesus used it with a different application; it here refers to the futility of all hypocritical ways.

Luke 12:3, 4

3) Ἀνθ ὧν is like ἐν οἷς, a relative clause at the head of a sentence. The clause is idiomatic in the sense of "wherefore" and bases two specifications on the general rule of v. 2; and not the reverse, R., *Tr.*: "because," which would base the rule on two examples under the rule. In Matt. 10:27 the examples refer to what Jesus says and to what the disciples hear him say in secret. But the examples cited here refer to what the hypocrites say and imagine will never be known.

First the plural ὅσα, "what things," then the singular ὅ, "what thing." First, εἴπατε, declaring a thought, then ἐλαλήσατε, making a mere utterance, the opposite of keeping silence. So also the corresponding verbs, the declaration "shall be heard"; although it is made "in the darkness" where no one but the intended person was supposed to hear it, it shall suddenly be heard "in the light" where the whole world can hear it. The utterance is made "for the ear," whispered "in the secret rooms," like storerooms, where no one is present but the two who go there to whisper some secret to each other; suddenly the thing "shall be heralded" to all the world "on the housetops," the flat Oriental roofs, the whole street being full of people who are listening to the herald's voice. Confounding to every hypocrite will be this exposure of everything this hypocrisy sought to hide. It will, in fact, be a million times worse than Jesus says. In this life the secrets of hypocrisies are not always exposed; but the day is coming when God shall judge "the secrets of men" before the whole universe (Rom. 2:16), and the Lord "will bring to light the hidden things of darkness" (I Cor. 4:5).

4) **Moreover, I say to you, my friends: Fear not those that kill the body and after this do not have a thing further to do. But I will show you whom you shall fear. Fear him who, after killing, has authority to cast into the Gehenna. Yes, I say to you, this one fear!**

The connection is close-knit. Fear may cause disciples to dissemble before men, to act the hypocrite, to deny Jesus before men in order to stand in with them, to pretend to be faithful to Jesus while secretly denying him (v. 8, 9). Δέ adds the new injunction as being something that is somewhat different from the preceding but belongs to it. The noteworthy point is that Jesus now calls the disciples "my friends," φίλοι. This word should be taken in a passive sense: "whom Jesus made his friends," not in an active sense: "who are making Jesus their friend or themselves friends of Jesus." In John 15:14, 15 Jesus calls the Eleven his friends because he confides everything to them as one does to a friend; there, too, he is the agent, the Eleven the recipients. In the present connection "friends" is used because of the value that Jesus sets on them and the protection he accords them. Having a friend like Jesus, they are foolish to fear men and to act the hypocrite because of such fear.

We twice have the aorist subjunctive: φοβηθῆτε, and twice the aorist imperative φοβήθητε, note the accents. This repetition of the verb hammers in the idea that the disciples must not fear. It is plain, too, that all four aorists should be regarded as referring to the same time; they are constative, and the first cannot be made different from the rest and regarded as ingressive (R., W. P., and Tr.). The negative command "fear not" requires the aorist subjunctive, but the two positive commands "fear" require the aorist imperative. The indirect deliberative question "whom you shall fear" has the deliberative subjunctive. R. 577 calls the construction with ἀπό a "translation-Hebraism" which expresses that the fear causes one to flee "from" those who are feared.

Why are the disciples never to be afraid of men? Because all that they can do is to kill the body, and they have not "a thing further or beyond that to do." Killing the body is their absolute limit. When the martyr lies dead, they are done. Jesus speaks with utmost plainness. He himself, as he has said (9:22, 44), will be killed thus, and very soon. He is not telling others not to fear death while no death threatens him. He certainly does not want his disciples to underrate such a death; we see in the case of Stephen (Acts 7:58-60) and in the case of James (Acts 12:2) what this means. There is danger that they will overrate it. The two present participles express enduring qualities; even one killing makes these men permanently killers; the same is true with regard to "not having." Μετὰ ταῦτα is used freely for "after one thing" or "after more," R. 704.

5) But Jesus knows that it is not enough for so many who are of little faith to point only to the causelessness of fear; he must apply stronger medicine and by *the fear of God* drive out *the fear of men*. In ὑποδείκνυμι the preposition ὑπό lends the verb the idea of secrecy: "I will show you in confidence a secret I want you to know," namely, when it comes to fearing, "whom you shall fear." By "him who, after killing, has authority (the right and the power) to cast into Gehenna" Jesus certainly cannot mean the devil who is only one of the foes not to be feared but only to be resisted, when he will also flee from us, I Pet. 5:9. God is referred to, God in his omnipotent power and absolute justice. And the imperative "fear" has the same meaning throughout: "to be afraid of."

This is not intended to be childlike fear, the motive of filial obedience, but the terrifying fear of God's holy, burning wrath which would have to strike us if we yielded to the fear of men and denied his Word and his will. Think of Ps. 2:12, "when his wrath is kindled but a little"; Ps. 90:11; Matt. 3:7. This is the fear that really belongs to the enemies of God and of Christ, the fear from which they try to hide by their self-deceptions, which will yet overwhelm them at last. It is really not to touch the disciple's heart at all save as a last extremity when nothing else will keep him true. What Jesus says is this: "If the disciple is going to yield to the low motive of fear, then let him be scared, not of the minor, negligible danger, but of the supreme, fatal danger." The sound sense and logic of this word are beyond question.

South of the walls of Jerusalem there lay the valley that had been desecrated by Moloch worship, in which children were burned alive (Jer. 2:23; 7:31; II Chron. 28:3; 33:6). Josiah declared the place unclean (II Kings 23:10), and it was then used as a place for the disposal of offal (Jer. 7:32, etc.; 31:40). Thus *ge ben-Hinnom*, "the valley of the sons of Hinnom," furnished γέεννα, "Gehenna," as one of the designations for hell, the place of the damned. The fact that in the present connection Gehenna means hell is rather beyond question. God is to be feared more than men. Man may kill and send a soul into the hereafter; the great plus predicated of God must be that "he is able to destroy both soul and body in hell" (Matt. 10:28), "Gehenna" being understood in this sense.

It is, of course, impossible to refer the eleven passages in which Gehenna occurs to the actual valley near Jerusalem. We have absolutely no evidence for the supposition that the Jews ever burned criminals alive, or that the bodies of dead criminals were dragged out to this valley, or that constant fires were kept going there. The name "Gehenna" or anything else in Scripture that is used to establish more than two places in the hereafter, one for the blessed and one for the damned, is not used in the Scriptural sense. The confirmation "yea" and the terse repetition of the command: "I say to you, this one fear!" are used to intensify this command. Both are still needed by the disciples.

6) God's special providence which watches over the disciples of Jesus is another reason they should not fear men. **Are not five sparrows sold for two**

as? And one of them has not been forgotten in the sight of God. Yea, even the hairs of your head have all been numbered. Have no fear! You excel many sparrows.

Of course, sparrows are that cheap, five "little sparrows" cost "two little as," both words being diminutives. They were caught to be used as food. Matt. 10:29 agrees regarding the price, two for one as; an extra one if you spent two as. The value of this little coin varied greatly, it was generally considered a tenth of a drachma, but it ranged between one and twelve cents in value. The lower value is in place here, two are two cents. The periphrastic perfect tense has its present implication: "Not one of them has been forgotten (and is thus now not forgotten) in the sight of God." So vast are his providence and care that they include every cheap, little sparrow and all that ever happens to it.

7) Is this wonderful? The sparrows fly over our heads, the hairs of our head are a part of us and vastly smaller and individually quite insignificant. The human head has about 140,000 hairs. Jesus says that each hair is not only counted as one but has its own individual number and is thus individually known and distinguished. So if any one hair is removed, God knows precisely which one it is (21:18; Acts 27:34). These two illustrations exemplify the infinite extent of God's provident care. The smaller the objects are in our eyes, and the less the value, the greater is the force of the argument when God's own children are now mentioned. 'Αλλά is not adversative ("but") but copulative, and it is best to translate it "yea" or "now," R. 1186.

So the injunction is re-enforced: "Have no fear!" i. e., at any time, durative present. Robertson's translation: "Cease being afraid!" according to his explanations in R. 851, etc., would be in place only if the disciples were in fear when Jesus spoke, which was not the case. If God keeps such close track of every sparrow he will much more look after us who vastly excel many sparrows, yea, all of them.

8) **Moreover (δέ as in v. 4), I say to you: Everyone whoever shall confess me in front of men, also the Son of man will confess him in front of the angels of God. But he that denied me in front of men shall be denied in front of the angels of God.**

From the idea of fear and its causes Jesus advances to its results, namely, denial of him before men. The confession of Christ (the aorist subjunctive is constative, including all confession) is the cardinal act in the life of every disciple, and Jesus has it in mind from the start. The ἐν with ὁμολογεῖν is due to the Aramaic *b*ᵉ with *'odi*, R. 108, 475. The verb really means "to say the same thing" as another, to voice agreement with him, and thus to acknowledge and to confess him. "In front of men" emphasizes the public character of this confession; and ἐν ἐμοί should not be reduced in any way since it includes Christ in the fullest sense, him with all that pertains to his person, his work, and the teaching and doctrine that present both. The fact that on through life this confession will cost something, in some cases the very life itself, has been already fully indicated, and "in front of men" again touches this point.

Whoever (ὃς ἄν) confesses Christ and thus identifies himself with him, with that man Christ will also identify himself by confessing him. The fact that this is no mere even exchange is at once brought out by the Messianic title which Jesus uses to designate himself, "the Son of man," man and yet infinitely more than man (see 5:24). When the benefactor identifies himself with the beggar, the advantage is entirely on one side. Note the contrast that accords with this onesidedness: "in front of men" — "in front of the angels of God." Nothing but men who are on earth for a little while — the world of angels in the heavenly glory at the last day. Who would trade the acclaim of angels at that day for the pittance of the approval of men here for a few days? See how Jesus sets forth the realities so simply and so clearly that no sane mind can help but draw the correct conclusion. What a prospect to see Jesus calling my name and confessing me as his very own before the eternal angel world! Shall any persecution by men in this transient life ever make me forget that prospect?

9) Yet the reverse must be added although it is already implied in the positive statement. Jesus uses the substantivized aorist participle to designate the man who denied him; and this aorist is not past in time but constative, summing up into one the life course of the denier. And we should remember that Jesus is speaking in particular of a disciple who should have confessed but ended up in denying the blessed Son of man. Peter denied Jesus through fear of men and might have ended thus. During the ten great pagan persecutions in the early church many denied by sacrificing to idols or to Caesar because they feared the threats of the authorities. Many fear to lose the favor of men and the profits and the advantages men offer them. Self-deception veils the secret motive in thousands of cases, for the heart is deceitful above all things.

The consequences are terrible beyond words. In Matt. 7:23 we have the very words with which Jesus will in turn deny those who denied him. The agent is not indicated in the passive "shall be denied" (which is, therefore, futuristic, not volitive), but it will be Jesus (Matt. 10:33). Confusion, dismay, consternation, eternal terror will overwhelm them. Would to God that the warning might strike home to all disciples and doubly to the pastors who are to lead others!

10) **And everyone who shall say a word against the Son of man, it shall be remitted for him; but to him who blasphemed against the Holy Spirit it shall not be remitted.**

Luke records this word about the sin against the Holy Ghost in its briefest form. When the Lord spoke it in warning to the Pharisees themselves who were on the verge of committing this sin, his statement was fuller, Matt. 12:31, 32. He here speaks to the disciples, evidently not as though they needed a warning against this the most extreme sin but, as the connection with v. 8, 9, and v. 11, 12 indicates, to point out to what extreme men would go in their opposition to him and to his saving Word. The disciples had already heard the Pharisees and scribes say a blasphemous word against the Son of man (5:24) when they charged that Jesus worked in league with Beelzebul (11:14, etc.).

"To say a word against the Son of man" is meant in the sense of uttering blasphemy against him as this is evident from Matt. 12:31 where all blasphemies except those against the Holy Spirit are pronounced forgivable. "It shall be remitted to him" is not absolute but conditioned on repentance. But in the case of the blasphemy against the Holy Spirit no condition is possible because of the nature of this sin. The verb ἀφίημι means "to send away," to remove the sin from the sinner so that he is free of it, and so that the sin can never be found and charged against him before the judgment bar of God. This verb and its noun ἄφεσις, "sending away," "remission," are the most blessed terms in the Scriptures for the sinner. The agent in the two passives is God who alone remits. The future tenses are merely predictive; see R. 873 who discusses their translation by "shall" or "will."

In the present connection we have no intimation as to why remission is utterly impossible for those who blaspheme against the Holy Spirit since Jesus is here not warning against this sin and therefore adds no elucidation. But by comparing all parallel passages we see that this sin cannot be pardoned because it shuts out the very possibility of repentance. Other sins and other blasphemies do not render repentance impossible.

It is the Spirit who works repentance, and to blaspheme him bars out him and his work. The point to be noted, however, is that, as far as the symptom of blasphemy is concerned, this need not name the Spirit in its vicious utterance, it may name only Jesus and yet be against the Spirit.

We are unable to judge which blasphemer has gone too far and placed himself beyond remission already in this life; all we can say is that he who fears that he has committed this sin by that very fear furnishes evidence that he has not done so. This sin cannot be committed inadvertently or unconsciously. Its commission is possible only where the Spirit has come upon a man through the Word and has been recognized as God's Spirit with his divine grace and power to save. When a man deliberately answers him with blasphemy he puts himself forever beyond the Spirit's reach, into the unalterable condition of the devils and of the damned in hell. This sin thus constitutes his *character indelebilis*.

11) Moreover, whenever they bring you up to the synagogues and the ruling powers and the authorities, do not be distracted as to how or what you shall make defense, or what you shall say; for the Holy Spirit shall teach you in that very hour what it is necessary to say.

This is the final assurance to fortify the disciples against hypocrisy and the fear of men. In three different connections and with strong variations Jesus states this effective assurance (in Matt. 10:17-20; here; and in Luke 21:11-14). Jesus cites the very worst situations in which his disciples will find themselves; they will be arrested and brought to trial before various courts. In the synagogues the local Jewish courts of twenty-three judges tried cases and could decree scourging with rods as a penalty, which was always carried out at once in the synagogue where the court sat (Acts 22:19; 26:11; II Cor. 11:24). The next two terms are abstract nouns, used for concrete powers such as exercise rule (rulers) and authority (authorities). Although each term has the article, the three are not exclusive of each other but are only viewed separately (R. 787). What rulerships and what authoritative courts Jesus has in mind is left indefinite, but both are superior to the synagogue and decree severer penalties. This formulation shows clearly that this statement was spoken exactly as it is recorded and in this very connection and is not transferred from some other time and connection.

The textual authority is in favor of the reading πῶς ἢ τί although the verb is without the passive idea (R. 334): "as to how or as to what" you shall offer defense. The aorist imperative may be ingressive: "do not grow distracted" (the same verb that was used in 10:41). To be arrested and to be haled before judges low or high are enough to upset anyone. Aside from the shame, fear, and other conflicting emotions, the trial itself, with both the manner and the matter of the defense, would tend to cause terrible anxiety: how and on what point (indirect deliberative questions) shall the defense be made; or what shall they say, i. e., formulate their defense before the court? The idea is not that the disciples may defend themselves in such a way as to escape the infliction of penalties, but that they may defend themselves in such a manner as to cast no dishonor on Christ and the gospel by their mental confusion, by mistakes, by weakness, ignorance, or other handicaps, and thus injure the Lord's cause. After a sleepless night or more in a foul cell, perhaps, in what condition would they be to do justice to the gospel? "Do not be distracted!" contemplates and meets this situation. And the aorist is peremptory: "Drop all worry completely!" They are not to debate with a divided mind whether to center on this or on that, and whether to say it thus or otherwise.

12) Does this sound foolhardy? Ought they not to plan most carefully how to meet every eventuality? Yes, if they were alone and making their defense themselves. But this is not at all the case; the Holy Spirit, the great Paraclete and Advocate, is at their side: "he shall teach you in that very hour what things it is necessary to say." The promise is unqualified. Without previous thinking, planning, imagining the apostles will in their trials at court receive directly from the Spirit just exactly what they must say to make the defense which God wants them to make. Δεῖ is used to indicate every kind of necessity, here the one that is brought on by the trial. They will make no mistakes and after the trial have no regrets on that score.

This is direct, miraculous aid; and when the Spirit gives a man what he is to say, the proper name for this act is inspiration, verbal inspiration, than which no other exists. And the argument is quite invincible that, if God's Spirit inspired the disciples when they were subjected to court trials he was certainly able to inspire those whom he desired when it came to the far greater interest of supplying God's Word to all ages. That he did so is attested in II Tim. 3:16; II Pet. 1:19-21; by the long list of διά phrases in Isa. 59:21; Hos. 12:11; Ezek. 3:27, and beginning with Matt. 1:22 on through the New Testament. It is most tremendously attested by the result, the Bible itself, its every page being a product that is beyond human ability. Valuable also is the unconscious negative testimony of the critics and the modernists who go to no such trouble in trying to discredit any other book.

It is unwarranted to call what Jesus promises here mere "presence of mind" at court trials; what Jesus promises is vastly more. The claim that inerrancy is not included is equally specious; or does the Holy Spirit teach the disciples falsities, mistakes, errors in these critical situations? See the further discussion in connection with the more elaborate passage, Matt. 10:17-20; also Mark 13:11.

13) Now one of the multitude said to him, Teacher, tell my brother to divide the inheritance with me. But he said to him, Man, who constituted me a judge or divider over you?
The preceding discourse is a complete unit, so it seems that Jesus paused a moment, and that this man in the multitude, who had probably worked his way up near to Jesus, took advantage of that pause to shout out his request. The subject on which Jesus spoke does not seem to have been interrupted, for he does not return to it. This man's personal affair was the supreme thing for him and not the teaching of Jesus. As lawyers the rabbis assumed authority to judge and to adjudicate in disputes of the kind here presented, so this man wanted to use the authority of Jesus to his interest by bringing him into the dispute with his brother. Whether his brother was holding the entire inheritance for himself or was curtailing his brother's portion cannot be determined; nor can we say how just his claims were.

14) Jesus offers an indignant refusal as the way in which he addresses him and as the self-answering question of the reply indicate. If this man thought that he was honoring Jesus by appealing to his authority he was really doing the opposite, trying to draw Jesus into an affair that was no concern of his. The Jews had rightful judges for disputes about property. Jesus had no appointment of that kind, his office and his work were vastly higher, and he was the last person to interfere with the secular authorities.

15) But this man's appeal leads Jesus to speak on the subject it suggests to his present audience: **Moreover, he said to them, See to it and guard yourselves against all covetousness because when there is abundance for someone, his life is not due to his possessions.**

The man's eagerness to secure his part of the inheritance results in the warning against "all covetousness," the greedy desire to have and to hold earthly possessions for ourselves, *amor scleratus habendi*. Whatever form it may take, we must keep clear of it. The καί between the imperatives, R. 1083 thinks, is like the Hebrew v^e with the force of ὅτι or ἵνα: "see to it that you guard yourselves," the Koine innovation of ὅπως with the future indicative (R. 933). One striking reason for the futility of all covetousness is the simple fact that a man's ζωή, the actual life in him, the life principle (not βίος, the life one lives) is not drawn from his earthly possessions. He will not have a bit more of actual life when he has much or a bit less of that life when he has little. As the parable shows, the possession of life depends on God. We leave ἐν τῷ with the durative infinitive in the ordinary temporal sense in which Luke uses it so often: "when there is abundance for someone" (not the idea of content, R. 979). To have life man must look to something else than abundance and extensive possessions.

16) **Moreover, he spoke a parable to them, saying: A certain rich man's ground bore well; and he began reasoning with himself, saying, What shall I do, because I have not where I shall gather together my crops? And he said, This will I do: I will pull down my storehouses and greater will I build and gather together there all my grain and good things. And I will say to my soul, Soul, thou hast many good things laid by for many years; continue to rest; eat, drink, continue to be of good cheer!**

The antecedent of αὐτούς, "them," here and in v. 15, is found in v. 1: the disciples (the Twelve, the Seventy, and others) who were surrounded by a packed crowd. In v. 22 the discourse again turns to the disciples. The whole account is thus linked together. The word about covetousness is not at once grasped in its fulness. So Jesus, as he did at other times, makes it vivid by means of a parable which is a comparison and an illustration of his meaning and at the same time the full truth of what he says about covetousness.

No name is given; rich men of this sort have no record in heaven, no names worthy to be remembered. All that could be said for him and of him was that he was rich. "Rich man" — that sounds important among worldly men; great deference is paid to "rich men"; money talks — poor men do not count. It sounds good to hear Jesus drop all this false show and present this man to us as he really is, nothing but "a certain rich man."

There is, of course, no odium attached to his riches as such. It is no crime to be rich; Abraham was rich, but he was far more than "a certain rich man." There was no hint of wrongful, ill-gotten riches; rather the contrary — the man owns a fine farm which was probably inherited or rightfully purchased. He is not pictured as an extortioner, an oppressor of poor laborers. He was honest, a man of standing and highly respected in the community; many envied him. His wealth had greatly increased; his land had produced well, so well that his place could not accommodate the new crop.

This is a parable on covetousness and on this deadly vice in its most innocent-looking form. The man is thus painted in fair colors, and we may expand the picture as much as we like. Even his covetousness has nothing repulsive about it. He just lived for these earthly things; they and they alone filled his life and his soul. That was all. The world has any number of duplicates.

17) As the substantial and progressive man that he is, he sits down and considers the matter, the descriptive imperfect διελογίζετο picturing him as doing so. The aorist subjunctive in τί ποιήσω is deliberative, and the aorist does not refer to a line of action, which would require a present tense, but to a definite measure,

what he is to do about storing this grain and produce. And we should at once note the "I" and "my" that run through this conversation with himself and his soul; there are just twelve in these few words of his. They intend to mark the man's selfishness, and this is his type of covetousness — a type that is repeated endlessly. He is in trouble; he has no place where to store this tremendous harvest. He does not thank God for this abundant gift — God is far from his thoughts. And he really only acts as though this was a trouble for him; secretly he is full of elation at his increase of wealth. When the selfish rich complain about the worry their growing riches cause them, the complaint is always hollow; not for one moment would they exchange places with the poorer man to whom such worry does not come.

18) All the verbs are volitive subjunctives. The deliberation is at an end, the decision is reached, and Jesus lets this man state it in full: "This will I do," etc.; καθελῶ is from καθαιρέω. He feels that his decision is a wise one. It is certainly progressive to replace the old storehouses with new and greater ones — how people will remark about that! And we see that he has far more than just grain (σῖτος, wheat and barley), he has τὰ ἀγαθά, "good things" of all kinds, all that belongs to a wealthy farm.

The French painter Eugene Burnaud brings out the inwardness of what is conveyed by Jesus. He paints the rich man as he has come to his decision. He has carefully recounted his gold and his silver, setting aside one sack after another. A certain amount that is to be used for other purposes is placed on a shelf above his head. The money that is to be used for the new buildings is stacked on the table before him. Now he leans back — furrows of thought on his forehead, a faraway look in his eyes — he is thinking of the great change the replacement will make, the money and the work it will mean, and the picture it will make, all the new, fine, grand storehouses, full to overflowing with "all my grain and good things." What a picture! But turn the page. There is the same man, cold in death, his hands crossed on his breast!

19) This is a parable, and parables present men as they really are. You and I may be afraid to talk aloud to our souls as this man did, but the silent language of our acts may be the same. It will not do to say that Jesus said *nephesh* in the Aramaic, and that this was used as a reflexive pronoun: "I will say to myself" (the future indicative this time); for the Greek does not use the reflexive pronoun here but ψυχή, *nephesh* in the sense of "soul." Delitzsch (*Biblische Psychologie*, 104) thinks that the stronger and more masculine part of man, his spirit, spoke to "the weaker vessel, the soul." But this is not the language of the spirit, nor do we need such refinement. Man's consciousness of himself as a person enables him to think of himself and to speak to himself. That suffices here.

Ψυχή is exactly the proper term since it is the immaterial part of our being which animates the body and makes it alive. Compare further, also on the distinction between ψυχή and πνεῦμα, the notes on 1:46. The English "soul" says a little too much since it is used like our "spirit" to designate our immaterial part as being capable of receiving impressions from God. In the Greek the lower sense prevails so that the adjective ψυχικός means "carnal." This man addressed his soul life in its dependence on material things and thus speaks of such things only and as if they constituted the whole of life. His πνεῦμα was foreign territory to him.

It is thus that the man boasts to his *psyche* that it has many good things laid by for years many (the present participle κείμενα being used as a perfect, R. 902) and bids his *psyche* to take its ease, to eat, to drink, and to keep happy. We see that he knows only this lower, material side of his being, and that he has no higher concern. In this respect he is like millions of men. What he says sounds sensible up to a certain point. He did have the things for this life in great abundance. But he overlooked the fact that even this life of his was dependent, not on his many possessions (v. 15), but on the will of God. The thought is not that this man would venture to deny God, his presence and his power in this respect; quite the contrary, he may even have acknowledged the bounties of God. What he failed to do was to take God into vital account. The omission seemed slight, but it was nonetheless fatal. The first and the fourth imperatives are present tenses that state conditions, the other two are aorists to denote simple acts.

20) **But God said to him: Fool! This very night thy soul they are demanding from thee! And what things thou didst get ready, for whom will they be? Thus he that treasures up for himself and is not rich in God.**

Why regard God's speaking in this case as an act? This speaking precedes the act. God is able to express his thoughts by words as well as by acts; take Ps. 2:5 as an example. In this case the terrible thing is that God's speaking is entirely at variance with this man's speaking. Woe to the man whose thoughts concerning himself run counter to God's thoughts. What a contrast: "years many" — "this very night"! "Boast not thyself of tomorrow," Prov. 27:1. This man had taken for granted the indefinite stay of his soul in his body, and that stay was now already at an end. All his plans had been made on a false basis; he had left the most vital figure out of his calculation.

"Fool!" is the proper name, the nominative form for the vocative. R. 464. The adjective which is used as a noun means devoid of sense, without mind or reason. Wise in his own conceit, his wisdom was blank folly. The world is full of these wise fools. The proof for this judgment is given in one keen, decisive stroke, which leaves no room for argument or evasion: "This very night thy soul they are demanding from thee!" "This very night" is placed forward for the sake of emphasis. Here, too, ψυχή is the proper word, the man's immaterial part that animates his body, to which the man had just spoken. This night it would cease to animate his body and would pass into another world.

The tense is present: "they are demanding from thee," because of the immanence, not future (A. V.). The plural, which in a way serves as a passive (R. V.), is also listed as being impersonal, as hiding the identity of those meant, or as a plural of category. But the solution of Trench is better, who refers to Job 33:22. "Yea, his soul draweth near unto the grave, and his life *to the destroyers*"; it is the reverse of Luke 16:23: "carried by the angels into Abraham's bosom." "Like pitiless exactors of tribute, terrible angels shall require thy soul from thee unwilling and through love of life resisting. For from the righteous his soul is not *required*, but he commits it to God and the Father of spirits, pleased and rejoicing, nor finds it hard to lay it down, for the body lies upon it as a light burden. But the sinner who has enfleshed his soul and embodied it and made it earthly has prepared to render its divulsion from the body most hard; wherefore it is said *to be required* of him as a disobedient debtor that is delivered to pitiless exactors." Theophylact. He went to bed as he did on any other night, with never another thought — alas, even this night — with never another thought!

"What things thou didst prepare" (English idiom: hast prepared) is emphatic by position and includes all the man's wealth plus the ripening harvest. Yes, he prepared it, and it took his time, thought, effort, strength and filled his life to the exclusion of everything that was higher. And now, when his life is closing: "for whom shall they be?" Not his, that is plain. Laughing heirs will divide what he leaves behind or will quarrel over it like the two brothers mentioned in v. 13. Is this what he worked for and deceived even his own soul? So are all the possessions of the covetous (selfish) even while they hold them in their hands — not true possessions at all though they seem so real and loom so large and grand. Even our earthly life does not, in the last analysis, rest on things such as this. The man who came to Jesus about his inheritance would live whether he got his part of it or not; but in either case, if his heart knew no higher wealth, he would be — only another "fool."

21) The parable is like a photograph, at the bottom of which Jesus now signs the man's name. Look closely whether this is perhaps *your name*. "Thus," οὕτως, does not mean that every man of this kind is in all outward respects like this man in the parable. He may not die so suddenly, and he may die in the possession of less or of greater wealth. But in every case the inner details will fit and combine, just as they do here, to form the picture of what is a "fool" in God's eyes. The two points are these: he is one "treasuring for himself and not being rich in God," two present substantivized participles describe the man's character. A man generally succeeds when he sets himself to laying up earthly treasures; but it is the effort itself, when this sums up his life, which marks him as a "fool." This is true because all such treasures, however abundant they may be in any man's possession, do not enrich but impoverish his soul. Death shows that fact only too clearly. Not one bit of all the wealth remains for that soul. He laid it up "for himself," but "for whom" is it at last?

The negation, "and is not rich in God," is not intended as the complete negation of gathering earthly treasures so that we are to gather no wealth except the spiritual. The negative qualifies the preceding positive; our gathering of earthly treasures is never to bar us from gathering the true riches. But this subordination does not lie in the use of μή instead of οὐ with the participle. The former is the regular negative with the participle (R. 1136-9 at length), and even if the latter were used, the sense would be the same. The thought itself shows how the two participles, which are joined merely by "and," belong together, and that is both sufficient and clear. Whoever is rich in God will not make earthly riches his concern in life as though even his earthly life could live in them.

Our versions translate "toward God," understanding εἰς to imply direction or even motion. This blurs the sense and often leads to false interpretations. This εἰς is static as all the newer grammars show. All motion must be indicated in the verb, it never lies in the preposition, and there is neither direction nor motion in being rich. This removes the view of wealth that is devoted to (toward) God or of spiritual excellences that are held out "toward" God for his approval. To be rich in God is to have the wealth that is found in God. This wealth consists of pardon, peace, and salvation in union with God, and "in God" signifies faith. That individual is rich in God who has the saving gifts which God gives him and holds them with gratitude by faith as his own. Such a man is truly rich, however little he may have of earthly goods; nor will earthly possessions interfere with his true wealth since he will treat them as Abraham, David, and others did by making them wholly subservient to God. Thus linguistic and doctrinal soundness go together.

22) **Moreover, he said to his disciples: For this reason I say to you, Be not distracted for your life, what you shall eat; nor for your body, what you shall put on. For the life is more than the nourishment, and the body more than what is put on.**

Διὰ τοῦτο makes it certain that the scene is the same. Jesus again (v. 1) turns to his disciples in particular; the two αὐτούς occurring in v. 15, 16 refer to both the disciples and the very great multitude. So also the thought presented continues what Jesus has been saying though it is now applied to the disciples. "For this reason" means that after covetousness has been removed there should go with it also all worry regarding our daily sustenance. The two are not identical but closely related. "I say to you" is the voice of divine authority.

The negative present imperative often means to stop an action already begun, and this may be the case here; yet previous distraction has not been indicated, and we may also translate: "be not distracted," marking out a course of action. The verb is the same as it was in 10:41, "to be distracted," with divided thoughts running this way and that. We again have ψυχή, the dative of advantage, R. 538. The distraction is regarding the keeping of our immaterial part in our body, and the translation "for your life" conveys the sense better than "for your soul," the article being equal to the possessive "your." Jesus used this word in Matt. 6:25; he here leaves out "drink." The two indirect questions have the deliberative subjunctive, which is retained from the direct, and only change the first person to the second. Food is needed daily and is thus placed first, clothes last longer and are thus mentioned last.

23) "For" (γάρ) states the reason the disciples should not be distracted about their life and their body. The argument is from the greater to the less. Will he who gave us our life and our body fail to add the little food and the clothing we need? The most elementary logic ought to put every disciple above worry on that score. In πλεῖον the abstract idea of thing is expressed: "a greater thing than."

24) **Carefully consider the ravens, that they do not sow or reap, who have neither storeroom (v. 3) nor granary (v. 18); and God nourishes them. By how much do you excel the birds?**

The argument is now reversed, it is from the greater to the less (πόσῳ μᾶλλον, "by how much do you excel?"). Look at distraction in either way, either way shuts out distraction and worry for the disciples. Διαφέρω means literally "to bear apart" and thus to differ, i. e., advantageously, "to excel." In Matt. 6:26 we have only the general "the birds of the heaven," here "the ravens" are referred to as being the most useless type of birds; sparrows could be eaten (v. 6). Like all others, these birds, too, are without our advantages, cannot produce their food by sowing and by reaping, cannot store it up for later use, must live from hand to mouth at all seasons. Do they starve? "God nourishes them," καί, as often, co-ordinating an adversative thought. Will God nourish ravens and forget the disciples of Jesus?

25) **Moreover, who of you by being distracted is able to add to his lifetime a single half-yard? If, therefore, you cannot do even a very little thing, why are you distracted about the rest?**

Although ἡλικία refers to stature it may refer also to length of life. We have no reason whatever to think of stature here, for this produces a ridiculous thought. Who except a child or a dwarf would want to be half a yard taller? Nor does πῆχυς, the length of a forearm, about 18 inches, compel us to think of bodily height. Ps. 39:5 speaks of the length of life as being "a handbreadth," a few inches. Other examples have been found where linear measure is used to designate time. Worry does not lengthen life, it usually shortens life. The participle indicates means: "by means of being distracted."

26) The argument is from the least to the far greater. If one cannot lengthen his lifetime by as much as 18 inches, why should he think of distracting himself about all the rest that concerns his earthly life? In conditions of reality οὐ is the negative; and ἐλάχιστον

is a true superlative but is used in an elative sense: "the very least" (R. 670).

27) Carefully consider the lilies, how they grow. They do not toil, nor do they spin, yet I say to you, Even Solomon in all his glory did not robe himself as one of these.

Jesus turns from food to clothing. These are the common lilies that grow wild in Palestine. Again there is no effort; they just grow and come to bloom without wearisome labor, without spinning the garment of their bloom, and its beauty exceeds anything that Solomon ever enrobed himself with at the height of his glorious reign. There is here a comparison between two superlatives. To the Jew, Solomon shone in the extreme of royal splendor, yet the wild, untended lilies exceed the texture and the delicate beauty of his finest robes.

28) But if the grass in a field, which today exists and tomorrow is thrown into an oven, God thus enrobes, how much more you, men of little faith?

The lilies of which Jesus speaks have a grassy foliage and are thus called χόρτος like all plants of this type. Some think that actual grass is referred to, the lilies growing in a grassy field and thus decorating the grass. But this is shut out by the verb ἀμφιέννυσι, "to clothe round about," which refers to the flowers and not to ordinary grass. Both the designation "grass" for the little lily plants and the description of their brief life and beauty heighten the contrast with the disciples who are destined for eternal life. In a country where fuel was scarce dried grass and stalks of all kinds were used to heat ovens for baking. The appeal is here from the greater to the less. If God enrobes the lowly and ephemeral lilies so *gorgeously* he will surely give *common* garments to his far higher creatures. The apodosis needs no verb and is thus more incisive: "how much more you?" Ὀλιγόπιστοι is a distinctive New Testament term; it is found four times in Matthew, only this one time in Luke: "men of little trust." This term grants the trust of the disciples yet reproves the littleness of this trust as it is evidenced by the worry which the disciples still have at times. Our trust ought to make all worry impossible.

29) And you on your part do not be seeking what you shall eat and what you shall drink; and be not in suspense. For these things all the Gentiles of the world seek after; but your Father knows that you have need of these things.

The admonition given in v. 22 is repeated, the present imperative is to be understood in the same sense; and an argument is now added, not from our constitution (v. 23), nor from nature (v. 24-28), but from a comparison with "all the Gentiles of the world." Hence we have the emphatic ὑμεῖς, "you on your part," to impress that contrast. "What you shall drink" is added because in the hot climate of Palestine and in its rugged and dry sections water was a vital element and often hard to obtain. Μετεωρίζεσθε is passive; from it we have "meteor," and in its metaphorical use it is best translated "be not in suspense," i .e., about where food and drink are to be obtained.

30) Worry about supplying earthly needs is the outstanding mark of "all the Gentiles of the world," of all the pagan nations who know not God and the Father of the disciples (11:2). Do the disciples want to descend to their abominable level? In speaking to Jews this comparison with the Gentiles is highly effective. Pagan people imagine that they themselves must provide for their needs, hence their seeking is bent upon (ἐπί in the verb) "these things all." The disciples live in a higher world, they have one who is "your very own (ὑμῶν emphatic by position) Father." As such "he knows that you have need of these things" ("before you ask him," Matt. 6:8). He is omniscient and almighty, full of love especially for his children, and will always act accordingly. Knowing that and trusting him, all worry and suspense will disappear.

31) **But be seeking his kingdom, and these things will be added unto you.**

This supreme seeking is described as hunger and thirst in Matt. 5:6, and it is the distinctive mark of all true disciples. The present imperative commands constant seeking. The desire for the kingdom (see 1:33) is constantly satisfied, for what we seek is given to us by grace; and yet the seeking is always to continue, for the object of our desire can always be more fully attained. This seeking is, of course, in no sense synergistic but the desire of the regenerate and believing heart to enter ever more fully into union with God. Grace kindles the desire and keeps it ever active in this life. There follows the promise that it is to remove finally and down to the very roots every kind of earthly worry: "and these things will be added to you," they will be thrown in for good measure with the gift of the kingdom. He who gives us all the divine blessings of the kingdom will regard as nothing the addition of "these things" for our short earthly life.

32) **Have no fear, little flock, because it did please your Father to give to you the kingdom.**

Luke alone reports this assurance. Jesus called the disciples his "friends" in v. 4 when he bade them not to fear men; here, when he again bids them not to fear, he speaks as their Shepherd and calls them "little flock" (the article is often used with vocatives). They are a little band, but as Jesus' flock they need have no fear. The word "flock" recalls Matt. 9:36; 10:6; 15:24, passages in which Jesus describes the Jews, not as a flock, but as shepherdless and sadly scattered sheep. His disciples he had gathered as a flock under his shepherd care so that we recall John 10:14. "Little" is, therefore, not in comparison with the Gentile nations (v. 30) but in comparison with the Jewish nation. And the injunction not to fear (durative like all the previous present imperatives) is broad and general and forbids all fear whatsoever. This is an advance beyond v. 4

and not a repetition; and certainly an advance beyond v. 22, etc., and not a repetition of those injunctions. The little flock is completely under Jesus' care.

In v. 32 Jesus tells the disciples to seek the kingdom, here he assures them that it was the Father's good pleasure to give it to them. On the εὐδοκία of God see 10:21; and on the verb 3:22 and Matt. 17:5. "The good pleasure of God" is his will of grace. The tense of the verb in all three passages is the aorist and not the present as our versions translate it. "It did please God" in his counsel of grace to bestow the kingdom upon "the little flock" and upon it alone. God knew all who would be won for this flock by Jesus in all the ages. While Jesus is addressing "the little flock" which was at that time assembled around him, it is evident that his word applies to all who would in afteryears be joined to that flock. The aorist reaches back to eternity, and thus the aorist infinitive δοῦναι is constative, all the giving to all the flock in all the ages is summed up into one comprehensive act. The idea that either in v. 31 or here "the kingdom" means only the kingdom of glory in the eschatological sense is an unwarranted restriction. No one receives the kingdom of glory save by way of the kingdom of grace. "To give" denotes pure grace through Christ and for Christ's sake. They who are receiving this gift are simply to rejoice and to have no fear of any kind.

33) **Sell your possessions and give alms! Make for yourselves purses that age not, a treasure unfailing in the heavens, where a thief does not come near, nor a moth destroy. For where is your treasure, there also your heart will be.**

Jesus does not say, "Sell *all* your possessions, give *everything* as alms," although he has been understood to say just that. If this were put into practice, all believers would in short order themselves need alms. The parable recorded in v. 13-21 presents a man who covetously and selfishly kept everything for himself;

the disciple will do the opposite. "As God hath prospered him" (I Cor. 16:2) he will dispense alms, especially "in ministering to the saints" (II Cor. 8:4) after the example of the women mentioned in 8:3. This is no *consilium evangelicum* for meritorious poverty; nor is this a special command only to the apostles, that they give away all their property because of their office, for the words are addressed also to the Seventy and to other disciples before the great multitude as is shown in v. 1.

We cannot place the "purses that age not" in heaven, nor identify their contents with the "treasure unfailing in the heavens." Whereas one verb is used with both, this verb merely combines what the disciples are to do with their earthly wealth, and what they are at the same time to secure in heaven. By the way in which the rich fool in the parable treated his wealth he made himself a purse that soon grew old, worn, having holes, out of which all his wealth dropped. Zahn says aptly of him: *Wie gewonnen, so zerronnen,* and all his new structures remained air castles. Not so the disciples and their purse that ages not. The figure of the purse refers to the way in which they view and treat their earthly wealth, be it small or great. Instead of becoming its slave they remain its master and apply it as their divine Master bids them do. So it is not lost but made to serve them in their calling as disciples on the way to heaven.

Strange confusion results when the "treasure" is placed in the "purses," the latter in heaven like the former, and the "treasure" is turned into merit of some kind that is acquired by the disciples by almsgiving or by voluntary poverty. This treasure is ἀνέκλειπτος, it never gives out as did that of the rich fool "that night." No thief can even get near it as is the case with earthly treasures; no moth can spoil it as was the case with even Solomon's fine garments. The moth is added because of v. 27, 28. This marvelous treasure is the one we are bidden to seek in v. 31, hence also ποιήσατε is used regarding it. The idea is not that the verb means that we are to create this treasure; the verb is used in a zeugmatic way for both "purses" and "treasure." We make for ourselves a treasure in heaven when our heart is in the kingdom, yea, in heaven, to which grace leads.

34) Hence we have the striking final statement that where our heart is, there our treasure will be. In Biblical language the heart is the center of our personality. If that is where the rich fool's was, our treasure will be only on earth and will slip through our fingers at death. If our heart is in the kingdom, we shall not only use our possessions aright, our treasure will be in the kingdom, safe forever, for this kingdom's consummation is in the glory of heaven. What a treasure! Who would exchange it for that of the rich fool?

35) When their hearts are in the kingdom, the disciples will constantly look for and be ready for its consummation. **Let your loins be as having been girded, and the lamps burning, and you on your part like men expecting their own lord when he may depart from the wedding in order that, on his having come and knocked, they at once may open to him. Blessed those slaves whom the lord, on coming, shall find watching. Amen, I say to you, that he will gird himself and will make them recline at table and, having come, will wait on them. And if in the second, and if in the third watch he shall come and shall find it thus, blessed are those!**

This virtual parable turns from the second person and the direct address to the disciples to the third person and continues thus to the close. The key to the parable is thus furnished at once and not withheld till the end. The disciples are pictured by these slaves, and this lord is Jesus himself. The first is a periphrastic perfect imperative, the copula with the long ending σαν instead of ν: "having been, let them continue to be girded." By adding a present participle to the copula a second periphrastic imperative results which is present and simply durative: and "let the lamps be burning."

"Your" is emphatic: *your* loins must be girded, whatever others think or do. Besides, the loins are theirs whereas the lamps are a part of the palace and are not called "your" lamps. The Oriental dress consisted of a long, loose, flowing robe. This was in the way when quick action became necessary and was either laid aside altogether as when the witnesses against Stephen "laid down their clothes" at Saul's feet while they proceeded to stone this martyr, or was girded up by a belt about the waist as when the Israelites ate their first Passover in haste, ready for instant departure from Egypt. So when they were travelling men girded up their loins, and men who were serving at table where quick movement was necessary also did so. The λύχνοι were, no doubt, grander than the ordinary lamps and consisted of a bowl for oil with a snout or nozzle for the wick; the conception is one of a great palace.

It is fanciful to seek special meanings such as that all temporal possessions and gifts are the long robes, and truth is the girdle (Eph. 6:14), and faith the burning lamps. All these constitute one image only, namely constant readiness for the return of the Lord on into the night.

36) "And you on your part (emphatic ὑμεῖς, matching ὑμῶν in v. 35) like men expecting their own (proper) lord" brings out the fact that Jesus is presenting a parable about his disciples and himself as their divine Lord to whom they belong as his slaves. The key word is the participle "expecting": the disciples meet the will of Jesus when, after his leaving them, they live in constant hope and expectant readiness for his great return. So the parable is completed

by explaining how this expecting comes to be. The lord of these slaves has gone to οἱ γάμοι, "the wedding" (for which the plural as well as the singular is used). We need not change the word to mean "the feast" since nothing would be gained; nor need we see in "the wedding" some other kind of feast, a celebration that would hold the guests a longer time; for the point of the parable is the complete uncertainty in regard to the hour of the return. The article should be noted: "the wedding," and this would remain if we made it "the feast." What is meant is clear: the celebration and the jubilation in heaven to which Jesus ascended over the glorious redemption which he worked out for the world. This may be compared to a wedding as well as to a feast in general. In either case it is *the celebration* appointed unto Jesus on his return to the Father. It is now in progress. This marriage feast of the Lamb began with the ascension and will continue forever. We need not make it start at the last day. Ἀναλύω is derived from breaking camp or loosing the moorings of a ship and thus means "to depart."

The expectation has in it the purpose that the slaves may open to him the moment their lord returns and knocks. The two aorist participles are genitive absolutes, aorists to indicate momentary acts as also the opening act is an aorist. The stress is on εὐθέως, "at once." But this is no ordinary man returning to his house at night. He would then need only one servant to sit up for him, to unlock the door, and to let him in. This lord has the grandest palace with a host of slaves, and on his return with his retinue (Jesus returns with his angels) he is to be received in state with great ceremony. The greatness and the grandness are required not only to image the gloriousness of Jesus when he comes back to earth but also to give proper weight and value to his condescension when he makes his slaves lords and himself their slave. So, too, the parable stops with the thought of these slaves' opening the door for their lord and is not expanded to their making another feast or wedding for him.

37) The wonder of this parable begins right here when Jesus exclaims: "Blessed those slaves," etc. Why, it was the ordinary duty of these slaves to be thus watching and ready ($\gamma\rho\eta\gamma o\rho\epsilon\omega$=to be awake and thus to watch), no matter how long their lord delayed his return. We are right, there is no merit or worthiness on the part of these slaves (17:10); and the Lord's verdict "blessed" is in no way based on what these slaves have done but altogether on what their returned lord now does for them. No wonder Jesus exclaims once more: "Amen, I say to you" (see 4:24), verity and authority seal his statement.

Jesus takes the human imagery of a great lord's returning to his palace and his slaves' receiving him back in state at night and gives it a turn that is unheard of among earthly lords and grandees. He does the same in other parables. This lord does not seek his ease and retire for the night. He changes his slaves into lords, he makes as grand a feast for them as was the one from which he came, he has them recline to dine and—wonder of wonders!—he does not order other slaves to serve them but makes himself their slave and "ministers" to them. Many waiters and helpers are needed at a great feast, but this lord needs none. This lets the reality peep through that this is the almighty, heavenly Lord himself.

One should collect all the beatitudes of the Scriptures; they are all different like the many facets of a diamond that yet belong to one stone. In this instance the blessedness consists of the joys and the glories of heaven. "As no Israelite dared to see the ark of the covenant uncovered, so no one ought to look at this passage without first having wrapped himself entirely in the blanket of humility" (quoted by Besser). Yet, in a way, this heavenly act need not surprise us. Did Christ not humble himself unto death for us (Phil. 2:7, 8)? So, then, without laying aside his divine glory he will gird himself and serve us. What this really means is reserved for us to learn when the great hour comes. Then Ps. 126:1-3 will be fulfilled in a new way; also Ps. 23:5. Chiliasts bring in their millennial views. The pagan participation of slaves in the Saturnalian feasts was far from Jesus' mind; and even his washing the disciples' feet the night before his death in no way foreshadowed this heavenly act.

38) The beatitude is so great that Jesus repeats it together with the point that is essential for us: "if he shall come and shall find it thus," i. e., that we are watching; for all depends on that. It is true faith that keeps disciples watching, faith in the Lord and in his promise of return; when the watching ceases, faith will be gone, and the blessedness will be lost. But Jesus adds: "if in the second, and if in the third watch" and regards the night of twelve hours as being divided into four three-hour periods. Jesus does not intend to say that he will not come in the first or in the fourth watch. For that matter, he could have named the first and the fourth watch just as well as the other two. As far as the reality is concerned, the imagery of the watches intimates only one thing, the complete uncertainty regarding the actual time of the Lord's return. And that is the point in regard to watching and preparedness; he may come at any moment, and our readiness must be constant.

39) **Moreover, this realize, that if the houselord had known in what watch the thief comes he would not have let his house be broken through. And you on your part be ready because in what hour you do not think the Son of man comes.**

The connection is obvious: in the first parable Jesus seeks to make his disciples watchful by holding before them a great promise; in this added illustration he warns them against failure to watch. The positive is thus rounded out by having the negative placed beside it. This negative also sounds the note of judgment for him who does not watch. The illustration operates with the contrary: a houseowner had failed to watch only for the reason that he did not know in which of the four watches the thief would appear of whose coming he had had a general warning. The result was that he slept, and the thief broke through a door or a window and stole what he wanted. Jesus puts this into the condition of past unreality: "if he had known he would not have let," etc., (εἰ with the aorist indicative, followed by the aorist indicative with ἄν). Some texts add as they do in Matt. 24:43: "he would have watched." The past perfect ᾔδει, which is so often used as an imperfect, in the protasis leads some to think that the condition is mixed: "if he knew (present unreality) he would not have let," etc., (past unreality), a strange mixture. But the imperfect and not always the aorist is also found in past unreality, and this quite plainly (as in the case of the present verb) where the aorist is not in use. In the Greek the direct discourse: "in what watch the thief comes," is retained with the tense remaining unchanged when it is made indirect after a past tense of the verb.

40) The disciples are not to repeat this houselord's mistake; ὑμεῖς, emphatic: "you on your part." The present imperative with its durative sense means "be ever ready." The reason (ὅτι) for this only sane and safe course is that in the very hour (period, ὥρα) you feel sure he is not coming, in that very hour he will come. That is the astonishing thing about the uncertainty regarding the time. Even those who are constantly on the watch will be completely surprised, for in their watching they feel sure that at this or at that time he will not come, and one such time will be chosen

for his coming. One may state it paradoxically: when we expect him least we must expect him most. This does not, of course, say that the disciples will not be watching when they think he is not coming, but that in all their watching they will occasionally have this thought. "The Son of man" (see 5:24), he who is man and yet vastly more than man, fits both the promise and the warning of the Lord's coming. On the comparison with a thief note Rev. 3:3; 16:15; I Thess. 5:2; II Pet. 3:10, all illustrating the unexpected manner of the Lord's coming. What Jesus said here and in the following he repeated in the great discourse recorded in Matt. 24 (42, etc.).

41) **Now Peter said, Lord** (see 7:13), **art thou saying this parable to us or also to all?**

We see at once that Peter's question is explained by v. 1. Here the Twelve plus the Seventy and other disciples are surrounded by a closely packed multitude; in Matt. 24:45 no such question could have been asked, for there Jesus is alone with the Twelve, sitting on the Mount of Olives. As he does so often, Peter speaks up, and his question is natural enough. What Peter asks is whether these urgings and warnings of Jesus were intended only for the disciples as the ones who alone will sit at the heavenly table, or whether also others from the great multitude about them might apply these words to themselves and thus also come to that heavenly blessedness. The answer of Jesus is given in his usual manner. He explains more fully so that Peter is able to find his answer and able to find it in a way that is especially necessary for himself. The answer is briefly: The parable is for all, but let each one look well to himself in the station assigned to him in the Master's house.

42) **And the Lord said: Who, then, is the trustworthy, the sensible steward-slave, whom the lord shall set over his service to be giving at proper time**

the due portion? Blessed that slave whom, on coming, his lord shall find doing so. Truly I say to you, over all his possessions he will set him.

The connection with ἄρα indicates the correspondence with v. 40: "according to" the unexpectedness of the coming of the Son of man. The οἰκονόμος was usually a slave or a freedman (here the former) who was placed in charge of an entire estate or of an entire θεραπεία, "service" or "service-body" which was composed of all the other slaves, *Gesinde, Dienerschaft*. He superintends everything and gives out the stores for the running of the place as these are needed: σιτομέτριον, literally, "measure of grain," the article denoting the due amount.

Jesus first asks about "the trustworthy" slave-manager and adds "sensible" with a second article like an apposition and a kind of climax (R. 776). Jesus merely asks who this slave is and lets Peter and the others each think of himself, whether he fills this specification. Jesus evidently has in mind the ministers and pastors of his church, whose obligation is a double one, including that of the household that is committed to them. It is a great distinction to be taken from the common ranks of the slaves and to be made the manager over all the rest. The trust thus imposed ought to act as a strong incentive to be "trustworthy" in return and "sensible" in managing the entire trust perfectly.

43) Instead of describing this head slave any further Jesus exclaims because of his blessedness. This "blessed" is the same verdict as that pronounced in v. 37, 38. Note the emphatic forward position of ἐλθών, for this blessedness is one that is fully revealed at the coming of his lord. The idea of this lord's leaving his house for some time lies in his appointing this slave as the manager. The idea of v. 36 is repeated, but it is now modified so that our attention is fixed only on the one slave. Jesus and Paul, too, often place the plural

and the singular side by side, or vice versa. Watchfulness is one thing (v. 36, etc.), but it includes faithfulness and sensibleness: "doing so" as the lord has bidden him. This applies to all disciples, whatever their station and their responsibility may be, but especially to those who hold office in the church.

44) This is the blessedness that Jesus assures such a slave, and he adds his seal of verity and of authority, "truly I say to you": "over all his possessions (forward for the sake of emphasis) he will set him." His lord will elevate him from managing only the "service" in the one estate to managing the entire estate with all that belongs to it. The reality referred to is pictured only dimly and goes beyond our conception in this life; compare Matt. 25:21, 23; Luke 19:17, 19.

45) And now the opposite. **But if that base slave shall say in his heart, Delay doth my lord to come! and shall begin to beat the menservants and the maidservants, to eat also and to drink and to get drunk, come shall the lord of that slave in a day in which he does not expect and in an hour in which he does not realize and shall cut him in two, and his portion he shall place together with the faithless.**

The picture is extreme, purposely so, and is thus intended to include all lesser cases of unfaithfulness. This is the Scriptural way which is clearly illustrated in Matt. 5:21 (murder includes anger, etc.) and 5:27 (adultery includes lustful looks). Alas, the condition is one of expectancy, Jesus thinks that such cases may occur. One adjective suffices to describe this slave who is also made slave-manager, κακός, "base," *nichtswuerdig*, good for nothing; ἐκεῖνος designates the fellow Jesus has in mind. "To say in the heart" is to think without betraying oneself, and this base slave's thought is: "Delay doth my lord!" the emphasis being on the verb. He accepted his lord's trust, he promised faithful and competent service, and now see what his secret thought reveals—base hypocrisy (v. 1).

Since his lord is gone, he casts off restraint and lets out the baseness of his inner nature, which has been only hidden hitherto. He plays the tyrant by abusing all the slaves under him, even with blows. Is this a picture of the ministers in the church who play the pope? He gives rein to his passions which were held in restraint while his lord was present. He now carouses by eating, drinking, and getting drunk. Is this a picture of the ministers who are self-seekers and also indulge their flesh, even its basest side, when they think they can do so with safety?

46) What will happen? He will be caught in his folly. "Come shall the lord of that slave (the verb is placed forward for the sake of emphasis) in a day in which he does not expect (and Jesus adds for the sake of emphasis) and in an hour in which he does not realize," (the Greek needs no objects, "hour" is to be understood in the wider sense of "time"). Many have thought themselves shrewd enough to indulge their wickedness and have imagined that they could call a halt in time and thus escape. But every yielding to indulgence blinds the moral sense and helps only to make a greater fool. His end will be his execution, he will be cut in two (II Sam. 12:31; I Chron. 20:3) with a horrible saw, and thus his portion placed with the faithless, i. e., he will have the same portion the unbelievers have.

47) **Now that slave who knows the will of his Lord and does not prepare and do according to his will shall be flayed with many lashes; but he that knows not and does things worthy of lashes shall be flayed with few. Moreover, to everyone to whom much was given, from him much will be sought; and with whom they deposit much, more will they ask of him.**

To be cut in two (executed, put to death) and to have one's portion assigned among the unbelievers are evidently to land in hell. But Jesus now brings out the thought that this is by no means all for such a slave. There are great differences even in hell. Jesus thus describes two servants that end in hell. The one knew his lord's will but never made ready (i. e., for his lord's coming), never did his will. The emphatic ἐκεῖνος points forward to what is said about this slave and not backward to v. 45. The aorist participles are timeless and state merely the fact of the acts, R. 1114; this should be held fast however we translate, whether with past or present tenses. This slave "shall be flayed (or hided) with many lashes," πολλάς (supply πληγάς), the accusative after a passive verb (R. 485), an analogous cognate (R. 479). The language is figurative and refers to times of slavery when the slaves received lashes for their disobedience; it is a continuation of the figure that was used in "cut in two," the cruel form of executing criminal slaves in more ancient times; the Romans crucified slaves. But this figurative excessive lashing refers to the hereafter, the punishment in hell. The characterization of this slave is transparent: any disciples who knew Christ's will and did not prepare for his return did not do his will.

48) Now the other, who did not know (supply his lord's will). There is no need to add that because of his ignorance he did not prepare; it is enough to say that he, too, did things that were worthy of lashes. He, too, shall certainly receive them, but they shall certainly be in just proportion, only few, ὀλίγας (πληγάς). As regards the final fate of these two and the number of their lashes compare 10:12-15; 11:31, 32.

The justice that lies back of this fate of the two slaves is made clear by two axiomatic statements which are universally acted on by men themselves. "To everyone to whom much is given, much will be sought from him." Παντί brings out the universality. The point is that the person receives a free and generous gift; he is highly favored in being so blessed. The result is that he is to act accordingly. To the degree that he has been blessed, to that degree he ought to be grateful, use what has been given him according to the nature of the gift and according to the giver's gracious will. For him to be ungrateful, act as if this was not a gracious gift, abuse it, etc., is abominable and contrary to every proper human expectation. The antecedent of παρ' αὐτοῦ is left in the dative that is required by ἐδόθη. What applies universally among men and is right and true naturally, applies also when grace showers its gifts upon a disciple and perhaps makes him an apostle like Peter. But the two πολύ may vary in quantity. Not all are given as much as the Twelve received; in ordinary life some have less. But in every case the measure of what one receives is and must be the measure of what is expected of him. In all cases the gift will be "much."

But another side must be shown. "With whom they deposit much, more will they ask of him." The indefinite plurals are only a variant of the preceding passive singulars. This statement, too, is of universal application as the plurals show: people always act on it, and rightly so. The best commentary is found in 19:15-19 and in Matt. 25:20-23. The idea in παρέθεντο is that of a capital which is deposited with someone in order that he may do business therewith, and in αἰτήσουσιν that the return of this capital together with the proper interest on it are rightfully asked. Hence we have πολύ and περισσότερον; more than was deposited is to be returned. The original sum may, of course, vary and accordingly also the increase that is rightfully asked. But for one to take a trust fund like this, squander and waste it, or even to let it lie idle (19:20-24; Matt. 25:24-30) is universally condemned and entails guilt in proportion.

What this means for the disciples is plain. They receive not only gifts that are to be used with due gratitude according to the intent of the Giver; they receive from the Lord a capital deposit to invest and to do business with in order that they may increase that capital and return it to the Lord with his increase. They receive all their spiritual gifts as a precious and an honoring trust and must administer them accordingly. And there will be an accounting of the gift and the deposit. Blessed is he who can meet that accounting joyfully, but woe to him who proves faithless.

So Peter has his answer. What Jesus says applies not only to the apostles and the ministers but to all the disciples down to the humblest and even to all men (v. 48, first statement). Even this is not all. Peter and the rest must know that all that Jesus has said will not move along smoothly in this world until the day of his return but will move through the worst disturbances, beginning with Jesus himself and by him brought also upon his disciples in the entire world.

49) **A fire came I to throw upon the earth; and how I wish it were already kindled! And a baptism have I to be baptized with; and how I am straitened until it be finished!**

The two exclamatory statements are due to the intense feeling with which they were uttered, and they are thus by no means an indication that this paragraph was inserted here by Luke from some other connection; for how would Luke introduce a foreign section that begins with strong exclamations without a word of explanation? The two statements about the fire and the baptism are worded alike, which should have helped in the translation. It was not understood that $τί$ as well as $πῶς$ are exclamatory (R. 1193, and 739) and the former not an interrogative (R. 1176); and one does not see why R. 302 and W. P. add a doubt. So also εἰ after θέλω is not "if" or anything of that nature but merely introduces the thing toward which the wish or desire is directed.

"A fire," like "a baptism," is placed forward for the sake of emphasis. The aorist "I came" includes the entire mission of Jesus and not merely his incarnation. Jesus is now in the midst of that mission, and its severest part is still before him. The great purpose of that mission is to throw fire upon the earth, and when no new subject is introduced for the infinitive, its subject is necessarily the same as that of the main verb. Jesus is not commanding or praying that God shall throw this fire on the earth, but his own hand throws this fire. The mission of Jesus did start a conflagration on earth, one that has never subsided and will burn on until the end of time. It was not yet kindled (ἀνάπτω) when Jesus spoke, and he says that he desired that it were already kindled.

It seems strange that, when the fire is now burning all around us, some are content to say that what Jesus means is not clear, or that what the fire signifies is to be left indefinite, while others misconceive this fire as being one that is intended to burn up everything that is contrary to God and leave only the real substance—forgetting that the whole world lies in wickedness and has no fireproof substance in it. Why separate the fire from the baptism when Jesus combined them by the parallel wording and made the fire clear by means of the baptism? Fortunately, we have unanimity regarding the latter; it describes the passion and the death of Jesus. And it thus brings out what the fire and its moment of kindling are, namely this death on the cross. It is the offense of the cross that has set the world ablaze, that has started the division and the strife. We may also define the fire as the gospel of the cross. But it is not enough to say just the gospel in general, or the Holy Spirit, or the purifying power of the Word, or the testing fire of persecution, or merely dissension under the figure of fire. When the cross is viewed as fire, we should note that this illustrates just one function of the cross and no more. That cross and its gospel are also the power of salvation, and a number of figures are required to reveal it fully.

50) The figures are opposites: fire—baptism (water). It is the height of paradox to have a baptism kindle a fire, and yet this is not strange at all in the realities. Christ's death on the cross kindled the fire of the offense of the cross. The figure of baptism to denote the suffering and the death of Jesus has been traced back to Jesus' baptism by John in the Jordan. By placing himself alongside of sinners and asking for John's baptism Jesus did signify that he would take up the load that was resting on these sinners and remove it forever. Yet it may be questioned whether it is for this reason that Jesus here and in Matt. 20:22, 23 (Mark 10:38) likens his sufferings and his death to a "baptism." The figure would hold true even if John had never baptized Jesus. Any water that is poured upon Jesus would picture the sufferings and the death that were poured out upon him.

It ought to be plain that this baptism of blood, as the fathers called it, was not an immersion, and that Jesus never said, "An immersion have I to be immersed with." Jesus was only stained with blood; the wrath was only poured out upon him; the blows, stripes, etc., were only laid on him; our iniquities likewise. We only spoil the figure by saying that Jesus was immersed in suffering. Here again those who would insist on immersion as being the only meaning of "baptism" and "to baptize" find the water too deep.

Συνέχομαι is passive, and the translation "how am I straitened," pressed upon, distressed and troubled, gives us the sense. Jesus longs to see the fire kindled, but the severity of his coming baptism makes him exclaim and wish it were finished, τελέω in the passive, the same word that was uttered triumphantly on the cross. Yet Jesus did not hesitate because of the severity. The stereotyped phrase ἕως ὅπου means literally "until which time."

51) **Do not think that I came to give peace on the earth; no, I tell you, nothing but** (B. D. 448, 8) **division!**

In the dramatic question and answer form Jesus proceeds to make plain what he means by his mission to throw fire on the earth. The implication is that one would suppose that Jesus came to bring peace, just peace on the earth. Is he not the Prince of peace, his church the haven of peace, his greeting, "Peace to you!" and that of his apostles, "Grace and peace"? All this is true, indeed. But "on the earth" takes in the world of men, and the effect of Christ's mission on the earth in general is quite the opposite of peace, namely division, or, as Jesus expressed it in Matt. 10:34, "a sword," symbolizing war.

This contrast shows that "peace" is meant in the sense of harmony and an undisturbed condition. The idea is that, if Jesus had not come, the earth would have gone on undisturbed in its sin and guilt until the day of its doom. But he came to take away that sin and guilt by the cross. There was at once division, many refused to have their sin and their guilt removed by the cross. In Matthew's word there was war, men fought the cross, there came to be two hostile camps. Jesus foresaw it. He declares emphatically that this is exactly what he came to give on the earth: division. It is better that some accept the cross than that all the earth should perish in its sin.

52) Jesus specifies with γάρ and helps to make the matter still clearer: **For there shall be from now**

on five in one house as having been divided, three against two and two against three. There shall be divided father against son and son against father; mother against daughter and daughter against the mother; mother-in-law against the daughter-in-law and daughter-in-law against the mother-in-law.

This is a sample of the worst division that Jesus brought, the rending of intimate family ties. Few seem to ask why Jesus mentioned just five in one house. Jesus takes one of the smallest Jewish families which consisted of father, mother, married son and his wife, and one unmarried daughter. According to Oriental custom the son brings his wife to live in his father's house. The daughter who is still at home is unmarried, for after marrying she would live with her husband's people and no longer be at home. These are split into two parties, three against two, and two against three, since the mother is on one side and both the daughter and the daughter-in-law on the other. Jesus does not indicate whether the three or the two are on his side —the case may be either way; nor are we able to say that the three young people stand against the two older ones. All this is immaterial. In Matt. 10:35 the sides are marked. All that Jesus brings out is the bad division. We decline to regard the perfect participle as being joined with the copula to form a periphrastic perfect (R. 375); this participle is predicative to "five"; "as having been divided."

53) The verb is placed forward because it is emphatic, and it appears here for the third time. Here and in v. 52 the future tenses refer to what shall occur after Jesus has undergone the baptism of blood; the cross shall divide in this manner. The details: "father against son," etc., are added in full in order to bring out the complete painfulness of the division. No member of this family is neutral, which is, of course, intended to be only typical.

54) Every effort to prove that these verses were not spoken on this occasion but on some other and were inserted by Luke for inner reasons is unfounded. Thickly packed crowds were assembled about the disciples in v. 1. Luke again mentions these as being now especially addressed. Καί shows that Jesus speaks "also" to the multitudes after having spoken to the disciples in what precedes. Also the inner connection proves that these verses were not inserted. The time for the great division was fast approaching, but these people "do not discern the time," they live on like the blind rich fool (v. 16, etc.).

Moreover, he went on to say to the multitudes: Whenever you see a cloud rising in the west, immediately you say, A shower is coming. And so it happens. And whenever a south wind blowing, you say, There will be a hot wave. And it happens. Hypocrites! The face of the earth and of the heaven you know how to test, but this season of time how do you not know to test? Moreover, why do you not also of yourselves judge the right thing?

The fact that Jesus should refer to the weather signs that were current in Palestine more than once in his discourses goes without saying; in Matt. 16:2 he uses the morning and the evening signs but here the signs for rain and for hot waves.

In Palestine the rain comes from the west, from the Mediterranean. The desert on the east and the south and the mountain ranges to the north furnish no rain. So it required little wisdom to know that a shower was coming when a cloudbank began to rise in the west, ἐπὶ δυσμῶν, the plural is usually found in this phrase, the word means "setting" or "going down."

55) The same was true regarding the wind, especially that coming from the south, coming over the hot southern desert. It took little wisdom to prognosticate that there would be καύσων, "burning heat," a hot wave.

56) This reference to two outstanding weather signs is the more appropriate for the purpose of Jesus since the weather, rain and hot waves, are beyond man's control. All that men are able to do to this day is to watch the weather indications, and they do that assiduously. They are concerned only with what affects their superficial lives. Hence the judgment of Jesus: "Hypocrites!" show actors, dissemblers, pretenders. But why? Because they know how to test the face of the earth and of the sky and to tell what the signs mean, and what weather is on the way and to act as though this were all that they needed to concern themselves about. But since this season of time, καιρός, in which they are now living is so plainly marked as it is, "how do you not know to test?" as coins were tested to prove their genuineness and their quality, δοκιμάζειν.

Jesus is not scoring the inability of these Jews to test the time in which they were living. They knew how to test the weather signs means that they did test them; the question that they knew not to test the signs of the times means that they could just as easily have done so but did not do so. Every means and every aid were given them that were just as plain as the cloud in the west and the wind from the south. There were the baptism and the preaching of John; there were the wonderful person of Jesus, his preaching, and his miracles. Yet they knew not how to test these. This was pretense—they knew well enough but would not act on their knowledge.

Jesus chose the two weather signs to match the two great signs of that time, and the underlying thought is that, as easy as it is to judge the former, so easy is it to judge the latter. These men could see the beneficent shower coming, and it did come; but here was the rain of grace in the Messiah himself, and could they not see that? Πῶς marks the question of surprise. These men **knew** the blasting effects of the southern simoon even before the effects arrived; but why was it that they could not see, as they pretended, the presaged judgment of God in the rejection of their nation because they would not see his grace? Jesus saw through them completely and tells them what he saw.

57) What the question asked in v. 56 means is plainly brought out by the added question: "Moreover (on top of what I thus ask), why do you not also of yourselves judge the right thing?" The emphasis is on the phrase "of yourselves." The implied contrast is not: apart from the signs of the times; for Jesus means the contrary: to judge the right thing in connection with what they see at this time. So also the verb used is κρίνειν, to pronounce a verdict on what is so plainly the right thing, τὸ δίκαιον, a verdict that shall stand for them, and on which they will act. Jesus does not mean "of your own ability," for he is thinking of what God is doing for them through him. "Of yourselves" is in contrast to others, in particular to the wicked Pharisees apart from their coaching. God was giving them the clear truth so that under its influence and its power they could of themselves decide the right thing to do, namely to believe in his grace and to flee from the wrath to come since the heavens of their time were full of the signs of both. Why did they not judge the right thing?—yes, why? They could, but they would not. They remained as they were, unsoftened by grace, unmoved by the approaching judgment. These were sharp words, but they still contained the call of grace if only these people would at last hear.

58) Jesus warns his hearers with another illustration as to what "the right thing" is that they should do in view of "this season of time" in which they live. Instead of living on thoughtlessly like the Rich Fool (v. 16, etc.), considering only the weather indications and not the equally easily tested signs of grace and of judgment to come, let them be like the

man who, while it is still time, gets rid of his opponent at law and escapes the prison where he would have to languish hopelessly.

When, for instance, thou art going with thy opponent at law before a ruler, on the way take pains to be wholly rid of him lest he hale thee before the judge, and the judge turn thee over to the court officer, and the court officer throw thee into prison. I tell thee, in no way shalt thou come out thence until thou hand over the last lepton.

The use of ὡς is temporal, and γάρ introduces an example: "for instance." The case of these Jews is like that of this man who is on the way to the ruler with his opponent at law (ἀντίδικος). Jesus advises him to do his best (δὸς ἐργασίαν, a Latinism, *da operam*, B.-D. 5, 3, which is now fully established as such and is so translated in the old Latin versions) to be fully rid of him (the perfect passive ἀπηλλάχθαι, not to express antecedence, as R. 909 views it, but a state of completion, R., W. P.). The Jews knew "of themselves" (v. 57) that a judgment awaited them, and Jesus points out to them what they had better do before it is too late, namely do diligence to get rid of their accuser before the ruler and judge is reached, namely God. Among the Jews the ruler acted also as a judge.

Jesus implies that the Jews can get rid of their accuser and of the debt they owe. The very imperative δός, an aorist, indicates this. The way to this riddance is not stated here, Jesus has pointed it out often enough, and his disciples have found that way, all their debt is gone. Otherwise, as the law takes its course in the case of a penniless debtor, so will judgment descend upon them. The πράκτωρ is the executor who carried out the judge's orders. After μήποτε we have first a subjunctive and then two future tenses; this construction occurs often in the Koine.

59) The prison points to hell. Roman Catholicism fastens on the clause: "until thou hand over the last *lepton*," ⅛ of a cent, compare 21:2; meaning the last particle of the debt. This clause refers the prison to purgatory and suggests ways and means for paying off our guilt and being released from purgatory. The Catholic contention is that ἕως οὗ (ἕως ἄν in Matt. 5:26) always introduces something that is expected to happen and often does happen. This should no longer be contested, not even on the basis of Matt. 18:30, 34, which are like the present clause. It is true, many a common debtor who was thrown into prison has somehow managed to pay his debts, even to the last *lepton*, this Greek word being used also by the Jews. But this possibility pertains only to the figurative language of Jesus. It pictures no actual possibility for a sinner to find escape after death and judgment because the Scriptures know of no such possibility. The clause raises the question: "But how will he pay at all in the prison to which God will remand him, to say nothing of paying down to the last *lepton?*" The only answer of the Scriptures is: "Any and all payment will there be impossible."

Jesus uses these last verses to illustrate a different admonition in Matt. 5:25, 26.

CHAPTER XIII

1) Now there were some present at that very season reporting to him concerning the Galileans whose blood Pilate mingled with their sacrifices.

Καιρός is more than just time; it denotes a brief period that is marked and distinguished in some way, here, the period that is marked by what the twelfth chapter reports. A little later a number of people arrive with the report about the murdered Galileans. The imperfect παρῆσαν means that they had come and were now present; but the present participle does not say that they had come in order to report to Jesus, it only reports the fact that they did so. These men had probably just been in Jerusalem and brought this report as a piece of terrible news. Although Luke does not mention the presence of even the Twelve, the answer of Jesus which is addressed to "all" (in both v. 3 and 5) implies that the usual crowd is assembled and is, of course, excited because of this shocking news.

All that we know about it is what Luke has preserved about this crime of Pilate's. Luke's interest lies in the answer that Jesus gave, hence he does not record the crime in detail. These unfortunate men were Galileans, which is mentioned as being of interest to Jesus who came from Galilee and seems to imply also that Jesus was now not in Galilee; he was, in fact, in Perea. Pilate mingled (the aorist to express the fact only; we should use the past perfect) the blood of these Galileans with their sacrifices.

Ordinarily, only the priests were allowed in the court of the priests which extended about the Sanctuary and had in it the great altar and the brass laver; but certain sacrifices required that the laymen who brought them had to enter this priests' court for laying the hands on the sacrifice, for slaughtering, and for waving. While they were thus engaged, Pilate had his soldiers rush in and cut down these Galileans, thus literally mingling their blood with that of their θυσίαι or slaughter sacrifices. This was a typical act of Pilate's who perpetrated many outrages during his ten years in office.

Gentiles were forbidden to enter any but the great court of the Gentiles under penalty of death, and inscriptions to that effect were put up in warning. In Acts 21:28 Luke reports the riot that ensued on the false report that Paul had brought Greeks into the sacred courts and had thus polluted the Temple. Pilate ruthlessly violated the sanctities of the Jews. The report was made to Jesus, not because of this deed of Pilate's, but because of the violent death of these Galileans under the assumption that these men must have committed some great sin for which God sent this signal punishment upon them through Pilate. Their sin was, of course, secret, but this penalty was assumed to be incontrovertible evidence that such a sin had been committed by these men.

2) **And answering (1:19) he said to them: Do you think that these Galileans got to be sinners beyond all the Galileans because they had suffered these things? No, I tell you; but unless you repent you will all perish likewise!**

Jesus denies, as he does in John 9:1-3, that these victims of Pilate's rage were to be regarded as being guilty of some secret, heinous sin just because they had suffered as they did. He denies that their fate proved them to be sinners beyond all other Galileans. As far as such a comparison is concerned, other Galileans may be even greater sinners in God's eyes — think of some of the Galilean Pharisees and their vicious hostility toward Jesus. Yet we should not go too far in the other direction. Sins sometimes do receive signal punishment, and God intends that we are to see the open connection between the two; consider, for instance, Acts 12:20-23. But, as a rule, divine providence works in secret ways that are too mysterious for us to unravel. Stephen is stoned, James dies by the sword.

3) "No, I tell you!" makes the denial of the Jewish assumption emphatic. Ἀλλά reverses the idea of such a deduction. The terrible death of these Galileans is to make "all," whether they are Galileans or not, think, not of the sins of Pilate's victims, but of their own sins and of how they may be delivered from them before death, in whatever way divine providence may send it, overtakes them. The way of escape is repentance, μετανοεῖν (see 3:3). The present tense and its durative idea are used because of the subject "all," one after another repents as the call and the warning come to them.

"You will all perish likewise" does not mean that all the impenitent shall suffer a like violent death. What Jesus says is that, as these Galileans were swept away by death while in their impenitent state and thus perished forever, so all other impenitent men, no matter what the manner of their death may be, would "likewise perish" forever. The matter that Jesus warns his hearers against is not some form of cruel death but the danger of perishing in death.

4) Now he himself adds another case of violent death which occurred without a human agent like Pilate who might be blamed. **Or those ten and eight on whom fell the tower of Siloam and killed them, do you think that they got to be debtors beyond all the men that are dwelling in Jerusalem? No, I tell you; but unless you repent you will all perish the same way!**

This is another case of recent occurrence that was already known to Jesus and to all present. Neh. 3:15 speaks of "the wall of the pool of Shiloh by the king's garden"; Josephus, *Wars*, 5, 4, 2 of "the wall's bend to the south above the fountain of Siloam"; compare also Neh. 3:26. So this tower seems to have been connected with the city wall near the pool of Siloam and, most likely, collapsed because of disrepair and age and buried eighteen men. Sudden, unforeseen, and calamitous accidents are always occurring. Jesus presents this accident in Jerusalem as being even a plainer case than the one that had been reported to him. "Debtors" is used in the sense of sinners, it is analogous to Matt. 6:12. The idea cannot be entertained that these 18 men were greater sinners than all other men in Jerusalem, and that this was evidenced by the accident that swept them away. .

5) Jesus makes the same emphatic denial, utters the same call to repent, and adds the same warning about perishing. The wording is purposely identical with that in v. 3, only the adverbs are slightly different. Every calamity that sweeps men away is a divine call to repent and a divine warning to escape perishing forever by repenting in time. Sin is the cause of all evil in this world, and when it works out in striking ways as it did in these calamities it warns against itself and its eternal effects, but does so only because God, through Christ, has made a way of escape through repentance.

6) **Moreover, he went on to say** (for the imperfect see 3:7) **this parable. One had a fig tree planted in his vineyard; and he came seeking fruit in it and did not find.**

The connection with the foregoing is close so that the claim that Jesus spoke this parable at some other time and some other place is unfounded. Jesus does not solve the mysteries of the providence that lets Pilate and a falling tower kill people but points out the call to repentance that lies in such occurrences and now elaborates by showing us how God spares us so that we may have full time for repentance and at the same time warning us if we should let that time pass in impenitence.

The fact that the owner of this vineyard and fig tree pictures God is at once evident; but only some see what is imaged by the vineyard and the fig tree. The fact that a fig tree was at times planted in a vineyard shows only that the imagery Jesus used was natural but neither interprets nor shows that interpretation is not required. A point to be noted is that the vineyard and the fig tree are intended to go together. The tree "has been planted" in the vineyard, the perfect participle implying that it is now growing there as a result. This is "his" vineyard, the owner's, who, by planting the tree there, has combined the two. This was not a wild tree that was ownerless in some wild place; nor was it planted in some orchard of fig, palm, or other trees. When this is noted, we shall see that the usual interpretation is untenable: vineyard = the world; fig tree = Israel. These two would be opposites, have nothing in common, and be the reverse of what is pictured.

This is made still plainer by the extension of the parable to the "vinedresser," the owner, too, being one who owns a vineyard. To be sure, the vinedresser is shown as helping to deal with the fig tree, but he is not called an orchardist or a tender of fig trees, his work is that of dressing vines. Now where do the Scriptures call the world a vineyard? What would Jesus do in the world as a vinedresser? His personal ministration was only to the lost sheep of the house of Israel, and when his relation to the world is spoken of it is never that of one tending the world's vines — that world is a wilderness, a jungle, and must first be converted into a vineyard. All this points to the solution that the vineyard is Israel, and the fig tree is Israel's center of worship, Jerusalem.

The parable thus connects directly with the incident that Jesus himself brought forward (v. 4, 5) when he spoke of "all the men that are dwelling at Jerusalem." Jerusalem, too, is often singled out in a special way as is done in Matt. 23:37; 24:2. But the fig tree that is planted in the vineyard belongs to this vineyard. So from the Galileans that Pilate slew Jesus turned to all Galileans, from the 18 Jerusalemites to all that inhabit Jerusalem. Whereas in the parable the attention centers on the fig tree, what is said about it and done with it extends to the whole vineyard. The fate of Jerusalem speaks to all Israel, yea, to the Israel of all time.

It is precisely because the owner planted this fig tree in his own vineyard that he had every right to expect it to bear fruit. The tree had grown to full maturity in the very best of places. Jerusalem was not the capital of some pagan nation; one would then know that fruit was out of the question. So this owner comes seeking fruit of the fig tree — had come on earlier occasions. It is not said that he comes to gather the fruit but just to see whether there is fruit, whatever its stage of development. "And he did not find" tells the sad story. Since no fruit was present, finding was impossible. Where was the trouble? Not with the owner or with the vinedresser or with the vineyard. This was apparently a good-for-nothing tree. Whether it was permanently and hopelessly so was the point now to be determined — this is the point on which the parable turns. Nor are we left to guess at what "fruit" means; Jesus has already told us in v. 3 and 5: true *repentance* with all that this includes. See 3:3 on the term. "He found not"=Matt. 23:37.

7) **And he said to the vinedresser: Lo, three years since I came seeking fruit in this fig tree, and I find none. Cut it down! To what purpose does it also take up the ground?**

What is meant by the "three years"? These do not, of course, mean merely three times. Fig trees bear during many months. The accusative "three years" denotes length of time. Just how often the owner had inspected the tree is not indicated and is immaterial;

he had now waited so long a time in vain. Commentators have noted that some relation exists between "three years" and the following "this year also" of which the vinedresser speaks, but their interpretations are not always clear. Some give up the point entirely, the three years, etc., mean nothing. Some think that they include the whole time before Christ. Nor does the "three" denote completeness, i. e., a sufficient time to prove the tree definitely unfruitful; Jesus would then have said ten years, for that number stands for completeness; moreover, the question of permanent fruitlessness is yet to be determined, the vinedresser still has hope for the tree.

"Three years" or "for three years" is literal as is also "this year," which is intended to help to interpret the parable. But we should not think of three years of Christ's ministry to which a full fourth year is to be added. His ministry extended little, if any, beyond three years. On this account this interpretation is usually dropped although it is so near the truth. We should note that twice and in a most emphatic way Jesus had used the exact words of the Baptist: "except you repent," in v. 3 and 5, and here in the parable we again have the Baptist's imagery of the ax "cutting out" this unfruitful tree, ἐκ, out of the vineyard. These three years start with the Baptist's work when he first cried, "Repent!" Note how carefully Luke fixed that date in 3:1-3. Three years have now passed. Jerusalem has stood for a long time already, but God sent the Baptist and Jesus during these three years, and it is during this time that he most certainly expected and came to seek the fruit of repentance. It should have been there already in the Baptist's day but most certainly now that Jesus had helped and three full years had been spent on Jerusalem. But there was no fruit: "Jerusalem, Jerusalem . . . ye would not!"

"This year also" was the final work of Jesus and does not necessarily mean twelve full months but the time that was still left to Jesus when he spoke this parable just as the Jews count a part of a day as another day. Jesus was not as yet done with Jerusalem. He was now on his way to this city for his last effort. Jerusalem was meet for judgment already at this time, but grace is so wonderful that it extends itself to the absolute utmost. "This year also" extends from now on until the death and the glorification of Jesus.

"Cut it out!" is the peremptory aorist to indicate the one dire act. It may seem as though there is a disagreement between God and Jesus when we hear the owner give this order and the vinedresser urge delay. That this is not the case becomes apparent when the owner at once consents to this delay. This, too, is the constant teaching of Scripture which extends God's longsuffering to the utmost. Basil of old already wrote: "This is peculiar to the clemency of God toward men that he does not bring in punishment silently and secretly but by his threatenings first proclaims them to be at hand, thus inviting sinners to repentance." The ax is first laid to the root of the tree, Matt. 3:10, as a final call to repentance; the final warnings are issued, 19:41-44; Isa. 5:5, 6; Matt. 7:19 while judgment still holds back.

"To what purpose," ἱνατί (supply γένηται) means: "what good can it do?" whereas διατί would ask for the reason. The present tense καταργεῖ means "continue to take up the ground" which might be devoted to a far better purpose. Hence we also have καί (omitted in the A. V.): besides being unfruitful this tree prevents the ground from growing something else that will yield fruit. When God bestows his grace and care upon any man and gives him a favored position, by remaining unfruitful he also prevents that grace and that position from being used to far better effect upon someone else. It is only right that he should be removed and another take his place, Acts 1:20, 25.

8) **But he answering says** (this participle is used with the present λέγει just as with the aorist εἶπε) : **Lord, leave it also this year until I dig around it and throw dung. And if it shall make fruit soon after—; but if not, thou shalt cut it out.**

This vinedresser is undoubtedly Christ. The idea is not that the Father is severe, that Jesus alone is merciful, for the Father accepts the intercession, and Jesus the cutting down. We should not erase the wrath by the mercy, nor lose sight of the mercy because of the wrath. Both are real, and neither is absolute. Jesus is the Mediator, I John 2:1, 2; Rom. 8:34; I Tim. 2:5, 6; Heb. 7:25; 9:24. The basis of Jesus' intercession is his atoning sacrifice which is by no means only an assurance for *us* of God's disposition toward us but first of all and most vitally a propitiation and satisfaction that is rendered unto *God* by which our sins are expiated. This sacrifice and satisfaction necessarily occurred at a definite time, namely when Jesus bore our sins here on earth, but in the mind and the purpose of God it was a reality from all eternity. Hence Jesus is called "the Lamb slain from the foundation of the world," Rev. 13:8, "foreordained before the foundation of the world," I Pet. 1:20. It is thus that our Mediator and Intercessor Jesus speaks in the parable, and the Father accepts the intercession. It is told us in a simple, human way in order that we may grasp it; but the essential is vividly brought out that God's grace toward us is mediated wholly through his Son, our Savior, as our great and effectual Mediator.

Jesus came to do his Father's will and is thus pictured as the caretaker of the vineyard, who as such addressed the owner as "lord." But this vinedresser does not act and speak as a hired servant who merely carries out orders, for he is as much concerned about the tree as is the owner, and the owner, too, treats him accordingly. For the impenitent the intercession asks an extension of time, that grace may do its utmost to win repentance. The tree is not only to have more time, it is to receive the vinedresser's intensive care: "till I dig around it and throw dung," aerate and enrich the soil. Nothing that is possible is left undone to bring the sinner to the fruit of repentance. And we should note that, as it is the vinedresser who asks for the time, so it is *he* who will apply dung. It is Jesus who uses every means of grace; we only receive and by receiving come to the fruitage of repentance and a new life. The verbs "dig" and "throw" are subjunctives (there is no need to regard them as futures), and as aorists point to this work as being fully and properly done.

9) "And if it shall make fruit soon after" is broken off for effect and displays the vinedresser's emotion at the prospect of securing fruit at last. We have only the protasis, no apodosis, and none should be supplied by us, for that would remove this emotional touch and thus change the sense. We may call this an ellipsis or more pretentiously an aposiopesis, R. 1202, 1023. And we should note that the condition is one of expectancy; the vinedresser goes at his work hopefully, looking for the good result, not halfheartedly, pessimistically, thinking that there is no use. Jesus is an optimist when it comes to working upon sinners.

The phrase εἰς τὸ μέλλον, with the present neuter participle of μέλλω, is not merely the indefinite "thenceforth" (R. V., omitted in A. V.) or "for the future" (R. *Tr.*), for the idea is that of something that is about to occur, hence we translate "soon after," for the effect of the digging and the dunging ought to appear promptly. This shows also that "this year" does not mean another entire year; it will require only a short time to determine for good and all whether the tree is hopeless.

Jesus is, however, not a blind, foolish optimist. As "soon after" show, this final trial is to be brief. So even before it is made Jesus reckons also with failure and provides for it in advance. Note the delicate balance of μέν and δέ, which it is beyond the English to reproduce. Εἰ μήγε is stereotyped and is always used without a verb: "if not." It is in fact a condition of reality: Jesus considers what shall be done if the tree, Jerusalem, actually proves hopeless. All conditional sentences present only the way in which the speaker (or writer) looks at the matter for the moment. Jesus here looks at the repentance of Jerusalem, first as something that may well happen (κἄν = καὶ ἐάν with the subjunctive), then as something that, after all, did not happen (εἰ μήγε, the indicative verb is omitted). If the final effort proves hopeless, "thou shalt cut it out" of the vineyard, the future tense being volitive. The vinedresser does not say, "I will cut it out," for he has already received this order. God judges us, but he has committed all judgment to the Son. In the parable the Son honors the Father by thus referring the cutting out to him though the Son will perform the act.

It is a fact that judgment is often preceded by an intensification of grace. Trench points to Noah, the "preacher of righteousness" in the days just before the flood; Jeremiah and other prophets just before the captivity; Jesus himself before Jerusalem's doom. The impenitent may misunderstand this and treat the abundance of grace presumptuously and make their judgment only the more severe. But we should look at this from God's angle. This supreme effort of grace cuts off every shadow of excuse; Isa. 5:3-5, "What could have been done more to my vineyard, that I have not done in it?" Rom. 10:21. In the end the sinner himself sees this, is compelled to admit it, and his complete self-blame makes his punishment the keener.

The question is left open: "Did the tree at last bear or did it, after all, remain unfruitful?" The answer is purposely withheld. The parable, both in its form and its purpose, is complete as it stands. We know what Jerusalem did. But we should not inject the synergistic fallacy of Trench and others: "The free will of man is recognized and respected." There is no "free" will but only a bound and enslaved will in man's natural state. We reject every idea of man's liberty to decide between God and Satan, fruit and unfruitfulness. Man has already decided and holds to that decision. But the grace of God is brought to bear upon him with power from on high in order to release his will from its bondage and wicked decision and to produce power by this and by it alone a totally different decision. But man may nullify every effort of that liberating, saving power and wilfully cast it from him for good and all. His doom is then sealed, and sealed by himself. But if the power of saving grace succeeds in freeing him, not he or any free decision of his will is the decisive factor or even a helping factor in his freeing; the work is wholly one of grace, and the glory of it belongs to that grace alone.

10) **Now he was engaged in teaching in one of the synagogues on the Sabbath. And lo, a woman having a spirit of weakness for ten and eight years and was bent together and utterly unable to bend back.**

The periphrastic imperfect reveals Jesus as busily teaching. The tense is descriptive and also intimates that something happened in connection with this teaching. The time and the locality are not specified since they are not material to the event itself, and Luke has already placed us in Perea on Jesus' last journey to Jerusalem. To find Jesus in the local synagogue on the Sabbath, engaged in teaching, is only what we expect after 4:15, 44 and the single incidents of this teaching recorded in previous accounts.

The Greek uses the plural as well as the singular form for Sabbath after the analogy of the neuter plural designation for festivals. It is material to the account that it occurred on the Sabbath. The following miracle is not reported as an illustration of the mercy of Jesus but as exhibiting his renewed clash with the Jewish leaders regarding their human traditions and regulations, here those regarding the Sabbath, which they regarded as being more sacred than God's own law, which Jesus was, therefore, bound to antagonize. Luke has recorded this and other accounts as revealing the growing hostility toward Jesus, which soon brought him to the cross.

11) The exclamation "lo" shuts out the idea that this woman was in the synagogue from the start and presents her as slowly and painfully making her way in to it while Jesus was in the midst of his teaching. Because of her great infirmity she probably went to the synagogue only occasionally and on this occasion came only after hearing that Jesus would be there. She must have been just an ordinary person, but a Jewess (v. 16) and not a Gentile of this section which was inhabited by a mixed population. "A woman," etc., needs no verb, the exclamation merely points to her. The two following periphrastic imperfects describe her condition: "she was bent together and was utterly (εἰς τὸ παντελές) unable to bend back" (κύπτω in both verbs), doubled up thus for no less than 18 years, the accusative of duration.

Luke writes: "having a spirit of weakness" (which is probably to be listed as an attributive genitive, R. 496). It is Luke, the physician, who writes "spirit" just as he does in other cases of demoniacal possession and thereby clearly distinguishes such cases from all other and ordinary ailments, of which he also mentions many. These cases of possession varied greatly and often, as here, inflicted only one or the other kind of physical hurt. The supposition that this woman was only hysterical or neurasthenic is even medically too weak, granting that we may disregard Luke's "spirit." Why not, then, say that she suffered from some injury to her spine? But even this is barred out by Luke's word "spirit." Like the woman mentioned in 8:43, this poor mortal had no doubt tried many a remedy—all in vain; and as the years went on, she resigned herself to her helpless condition.

12) **Now when Jesus saw her he called her to him and said to her, Woman, thou hast been loosed from thy weakness! And he placed the hands upon her. And forthwith she was straightened up and began glorifying God.**

There is no question that Jesus at once recognized the true nature of this woman's trouble. He stops his teaching, calls the woman to him (πρός in the verb), at once utters the words of deliverance, and at the same time lays his hands upon her. He was sitting cross-legged on the platform while teaching and could easily lay his hands on the woman's head or her shoulders. The perfect passive "thou hast been loosed from thy weakness" does not reach back into the past but starts only from the moment when Jesus willed her release and extends indefinitely into the future.

Varied interpretations are given to Luke's brief wording. Some think that this woman believed before she was freed and thus support their view that no healing was possible without faith. But Luke says nothing about the faith of this woman, and that view is contradicted by clear examples in which no faith could be present before the miracle. The miracle was always dependent upon the will of Jesus alone and never on the beneficiary's faith. Jesus certainly wanted faith, but often only as a result of the miracle. Moreover, this is a case in which, as so often, the miracle was wrought chiefly for the sake of the witnesses, as a sign for them.

Because Jesus uses only the passive and addresses the woman is not reason for concluding that her ailment was not caused by a demon. This, too, sets up a wrong view, namely, that unless the demon is directly addressed, no demon is involved.

13) Luke first records the words of Jesus and then the fact that he laid his hands on the woman. The

word and the act went together with no interval between them that is worth mentioning. Yet the two are separated by the commentators, and for rather strange reasons. One is that the woman was to attribute no magical powers to the hands of Jesus. But if there was danger of this kind, why did Jesus use his hands? He would evidently then not have touched her.

Another reason advanced is that, when the woman heard the words, she did not have the courage to straighten up, and that she found that courage only when Jesus placed his hands upon her. But the verb is passive: "she was straightened up," the divine power of Jesus straightened her body just as the cruel power of the spirit had held her bent double. The laying on of hands is always only symbolical and, like the words of Jesus, the expression of his gracious will in bestowing the divine benefaction. That omnipotent will works the miracle.

The effect of Jesus' word and touch was instantaneous—the woman was straightened up before the eyes of all, the aorist stating the fact. The ingressive imperfect then adds that she began to glorify God. This is, of course, not meant as detracting from Jesus. All the works of Jesus were done to glorify God. When God's power and mercy were recognized in what Jesus did, men connected Jesus with God, began to acknowledge his mission from God, and were thus in a fair way to discover and to believe that he was, indeed, the Messiah sent from God. So a mighty impression of God's working in Jesus was here made upon the assembly in the synagogue. But there now follows an effort in the opposite direction.

14) **But answering, the synagogue ruler, being indignant that Jesus healed on the Sabbath, went on to say to the multitude: Six days there are in which it is necessary to work. In them, therefore, by coming be healed and not on the day of the Sabbath.**

Ἀποκριθείς is used with the imperfect, as here, and with the present as well as with the aorist and is in place when something is said in response to a deed or to a situation as is the case in this instance. Luke's brevity leads us to wonder that Jesus was allowed to teach in this synagogue when this synagogue ruler and other opponents (v. 17) were present. So he speaks only of this one ruler, evidently because he spoke up and the other rulers deferred to him. Though Jesus was allowed to teach, these synagogue rulers remained in charge of the service. This man failed utterly to appreciate what he saw this day. He was probably a Pharisee, certainly thoroughly Pharisaic in his thinking, particularly in regard to the Sabbath. All he saw was a Sabbath desecration, and this made him indignant so that he could no longer contain himself.

But he was unable to find anything flagrant in Jesus' conduct. Jesus had spoken only a word and used the liturgical act of laying on hands, which even the casuistic Pharisee could not condemn as a Sabbath desecration. The ruler thus had to attack the miracle itself, the act of healing as such, and could not assail some feature of the act. He is indignant with Jesus but dares not attack Jesus in person and so directs his objection to the multitude that crowded the synagogue. This indirection seems to be a part of his hypocrisy. In a commanding tone he announces that six days are ordered for doing work, Deut. 5:13, etc. Δεῖ, "must," "it is necessary," brings out the fact that God commanded to work on these days. And, accordingly, this ruler orders the people to come and to have their healing done during those days and not on the Sabbath (the Greek is here singular).

This ruler speaks as though this woman came to the synagogue to be healed and thus attacks her, too, although Luke reports nothing of the kind, his previous narrative implies rather the contrary. This ruler perhaps feared that others might be induced to come and might help further to desecrate the Sabbath. This ruler's exegesis intends to strike at Jesus. He did the healing, and that the ruler regards as "doing work," something that is forbidden on the Sabbath. The people would be involved in this work by coming and obtaining the healing. This ruler perhaps thought himself shrewd in thus delivering an indirect attack upon Jesus, one that is fortified by a divine commandment and a strong exegesis. But the man was blind both as far as the commandment and the miracle he had just witnessed were concerned and promptly receives his crushing answer.

15) **But the Lord answered him and said** (both verbs are finite, both carry full weight) : **Hypocrites! Does not each one of you on the Sabbath loose his ox or his ass from the manger and, having led him away, give him drink? But this woman, being a daughter of Abraham, whom Satan bound, lo, for ten and eight years, was it not necessary that she be loosed from this bond on the day of Sabbath?**

The Lord certainly answered "him" although he uses the plural "hypocrites" and thus at the same time answers any and all present who sided with this ruler; there were such as v. 17 indicates. The A. V. has the singular "hypocrite," but the correct reading is that of the R. V., a plural. Here, too, the term is a judgment; and it is not left unsupported but is at once fully proved as being true. Luke writes "the Lord" and lets us feel the full authority which meets this man's presumptuous charge; see 7:13.

Jesus asks two questions, the answers to which are beyond question. These questions are far stronger than assertions would have been, for they compel all present, also the ruler and other opponents of Jesus, to give the answer themselves. "Does not each one of you on the Sabbath (forward for the sake of emphasis) loose his ox or ass from the manger (not "stall," our versions), and, having led him away, give him drink?" This is purposely an understatement and is stronger for that very reason, for many had several animals to be led to water. Was this not "work"? They untied the rope with their hands, they held the rope and led the animal out, and then they tied it up again. According to their own rabbinical casuistry this was most plainly work, and Jesus employs the *argumentum ad hominem*. The divine law did not forbid this act on the Sabbath, but these hypocrites first set up a definition of forbidden work which was not forbidden and then applied their definition against Jesus only and not against themselves. Their hypocrisy was the greater because what they called "work" in the case of Jesus was not work even by their own definition while what they did was, indeed, work according to this definition. Hypocrisy can go little farther.

16) The second question calls for the same unavoidable answer. Jesus indicates it by using the interrogatory word οὐ which expects an affirmative answer. This question brings out the application from the illustration and uses the argument from the less to the greater. The emphasis is on ταύτην, "this woman," in the accusative with the infinitive after ἔδει. This verb expresses all kinds of necessity, here the moral one which is vastly higher than watering an ox or an ass. The imperfect denotes a past necessity, one that in this instance lasted up to the moment when it was met by the miracle of Jesus, R. 919.

The argument is cumulative: the woman, a human being, over against the ox and the ass, mere brutes; a daughter of Abraham over against ordinary human beings; bound by the cruelty of Satan over against tethering to a manger with fodder; 18 years over against one day; need of being freed from a demon over against need of water. The argument is overwhelming. The charge of the ruler against Jesus recoils upon his hypocritical head with multiplied force. We see that the woman was a Jewess, one of God's children, who knew and praised God. The expression "whom Satan did bind" does not refer only to common diseases as being due to the devil. Such a view needs better support than Acts 10:38 and II Cor. 12:7 and must first explain "spirit of infirmity" used in v. 11. "Lo, for ten and eight years" is again the accusative of duration of time and not the nominative as R. 460 regards it.

17) And he saying these things, there began to be ashamed all those opposing him, and all the multitude began rejoicing over all the glorious things occurring by him.

Two opposite effects are noted, both are expressed by ingressive imperfect tenses. The ruler seems to have had many supporters "lying against" Jesus, i. e., opposing him. It is best to regard the verb as a passive since Jesus made them ashamed. They were ashamed before the people, before whom they were exposed as hypocrites, not in their own hearts of their hypocrisy. Here all the common people were again with Jesus. By the way in which Luke writes it seems that Jesus must have done many other glorious things in this locality to cause such a wave of rejoicing.

18) The observation is correct: Luke would never have inserted these two parables at this place if Jesus had not spoken them after the incident in the synagogue. The objection that neither of them deals with the Sabbath question misunderstands the connection which refers only to the great joy of the people over the glorious deeds of Jesus. This leads him to add these words about the growth and the spread of the kingdom in the future. The reading οὖν, too, is correct; the texts that changed it to δέ failed to see the connection. **He, therefore, went on to say**

(see 3:7), **To what is the kingdom of God like? and to what shall I liken it?** Luke closes the account of the miracle in the synagogue in a way that seems to imply that what Jesus said now occurred afterward; and it may be possible that he now spoke only to his disciples. "Therefore" means because of the great rejoicing of the multitude.

See 1:33 on the kingdom of God; Jesus is speaking of the rule of God's grace among men. The two questions mean the same thing, the doubling is for the sake of emphasis. Since the first has the indicative, we regard the verb in the second as also being indicative, namely the future, and not as the aorist subjunctive. These questions would naturally arouse attention although all evidence shows that Jesus never lacked attention. Jesus wanted more here, namely, that his hearers should think of the kingdom, study its nature and its characteristics, and so find some likeness of it in earthly things. Anyone who was unable to find proper comparisons would be led to see that he knows too little about the kingdom and would be stimulated to learn far more about it.

19) Jesus himself helps his hearers by offering two remarkable comparisons. He has used them before, in Matt. 13:31-33 (Mark 4:30-32); the connection is decidedly different in each instance just as are the localities where these comparisons were spoken. In Matthew and in Mark, Jesus is in Galilee, in Luke he is making his way to Jerusalem for his Passion (v. 22). This may explain also the differences. In Matthew and in Mark the contrast is between the smallness and the final greatness; but the smallness is omitted here, and we have only the great spread of the kingdom.

Like is it to a kernel of mustard, which, having taken, a man threw it into his own garden. And it grew and became a tree, and the birds of the heaven tented in its branches.

The *Sinapis nigra* is referred to, the garden variety which grows to great size. This man, too, throws the mustard kernel "into his own garden," which means Israel just as the vineyard in v. 6 is Israel. In Matthew the mustard kernel is sown "in the field" whereas Mark has "on the earth," which refers to the human race in general. Here the thought is that of salvation's coming from Israel. The size of the seed is not a part of the comparison, but *the great growth is*. Ἐγένετο εἰς δένδρον is an example of the predicative εἰς, it is like the German *wurde zum Baum*. The mustard seed is pungent and must be crushed to obtain its virtue as a condiment; but such ideas are far from the comparison in which the seed grows.

This growth is so great that "the birds of the heaven," i. e., the wild birds, "tented in its branches." We should again be content with the comparison as Jesus draws it and not have the birds eating the seed of the tree. Since this great plant is itself the kingdom, all who are in the kingdom are a part of the plant. The wild birds are not members of the kingdom; they only "tent" in it, their stay is temporary and only in the spreading branches, in superficial contact with the tree. These birds picture men in general in all lands, who enjoy some of the incidental blessings of the church.

This parable, then, pictures the *visible* growth and extension of the kingdom. A number of thoughts are necessarily implied. The kingdom is a *living* organism, and its life and its power are *undying*, for its growth extends through all time, Matt. 24:14. As long as the kingdom was present in the Old Testament believers it was confined to them; the parable describes the kingdom of *the New Testament* which is unconfined and spreads over the whole world. Vital growth is described and not outward organization which holds together great numbers (the ideal of Rome and of not a few Protestants). Being Christ's rule of grace, the kingdom is always *spiritual.* This spirituality is, however, itself power, and although it is invisible makes its presence manifest in many outward and visible ways in the world. The parable stimulates faith, encourages us in our work, and fills us with joy and hope.

20) And again he said, To whom shall I liken the kingdom of God? The force of this question is the same as that of the preceding one.

21) Like is it to leaven, which having taken, a woman hid in three measures of wheat until they were leavened completely.

We have the companion parable as we do in Matt. 13:33. Leaven or yeast (ζύμη, from ζέω, to ferment) is used extensively in an evil sense with reference to something that corrupts (12:1; I Cor. 5:7, 8; Gal. 5:9). But in this instance leaven pictures the good power of Christ's rule of grace which secretly, yet beneficiently, produces its blessed results. "Lion" is thus used once in an evil sense (I Pet. 5:8), again in a noble one (Rev. 5:5); "serpent" likewise (Rev. 20:2, as against John 3:14); "dove" (silly in Hos. 7:11; harmless in Matt. 10:16). The world has many ferments, all are decomposing and destructive; Christ and his gospel alone penetrate with beneficent power.

"A woman," just as in the other parable (Luke 15:8), cannot be the same as "a man" in v. 19. The latter is the Father, the former the church to whom the gospel of the kingdom is committed to do with it just what is here described. The view that the woman pictures the divine Wisdom mentioned in Prov. 9:1-3 or the Holy Spirit has little in its favor. It would be offensive to picture the Spirit as a woman. The participle λαβοῦσα, like its mate in v. 19, is more than "picturesque vernacular" (R. 1110); it indicates that this leaven came from elsewhere and not from this earth, and that the act of mixing it with the flour was deliberate and done with specific intent. It was not a mere impulse that caused the woman to put the yeast into the flour. The church preaches the gospel with most intelligent purpose.

Note that εἰς is static, "in." The stress is not on any mixing which the woman did just as it was not on the throwing of the man. The idea is that the yeast was hid; it disappeared completely, it works *secretly, invisibly*, as a power that is hidden from view. Christ and his gospel work mysteriously, gradually, silently spreading out. We have the record of history as to how the gospel permeated the ancient Roman world until even the emperor was a Christian. Its greater work was, however, the unseen, inner change which removed superstition, social evils, vice, and lifted all it touched to a higher plane. The church just applies the gospel, and this gospel does the leavening. This does not mean that the church is to enter the field of politics, sociology, or public reform campaigns. When this is attempted, she loses her power. The yeast does not work in that way. This seems too slow to many, and so they "take" something to hasten the leaven along and thereby only hinder its silent, steady progress.

A *saton*, Hebrew *seʾah*, the third part of an *epha*, is about 1½ pecks, and three *sata* was the quantity that was used by Sarah in Gen. 18:6. Many fancies have been attached to the number three: the three sons of Noah; the three parts of the world as then known; Greeks, Jews, Samaritans; spirit, soul, body; or simply the usual quantity of flour for an ordinary baking —the woman must have had an immense family to require a baking of over a bushel of flour! It seems best to follow Gen. 18:6; Judges 6:19; I Sam. 1:24, all of which mention the same quantity, and to combine with this mass of flour what lies in ὅλον: although the baking was no less than an entire *epha* of flour, the whole of it was wholly leavened.

The aorist "was leavened," like the last three aorists used in v. 19, is prophecy. Jesus states what shall be as having been already accomplished. The verb should not be stressed to mean that all men in the world will eventually be converted. This would confuse the woman and the flour. The parable is without chiliasm. It describes the silent, beneficent influence of the gospel in the world. We may instance many points: the overthrow of slavery, the improved status of women, the appreciation of the child, the abolition of many barbarous practices, etc. Any land in which the gospel has an opportunity to exert its influence is raised to a higher level.

The divine power is again wholly *spiritual*, and while it operates altogether *invisibly* it produces any number of tangible effects, every one of them being *wholesome*. Also, the gospel cannot but *succeed*, and the one work of the church is to preach, teach, and spread it in the world. The parable teaches faith, patience, hope, and joy.

22) **And he was traveling through city by city and village by village, teaching and making his way to Jerusalem.**

In 9:51 Luke reports that Jesus set his face to be going to Jerusalem. He now recalls this statement to his readers by describing the journey as a progress through Perea "city by city, village by village" (distributive κατά), taking in all of them along this strip of territory. Through these towns and villages he had sent the Seventy in advance (10:1), and he was now on his way through them, preaching as he went along. The descriptive διεπορεύετο thus reaches back to 9:51.

The question is asked as to why Luke inserts this summary remark at this point in his narrative. A glance at 9:51 and then at 18:31 will show us that, like these two, 13:22 is also a mark of division which cuts the section 9:51-18:30 into two parts. As such this division reminds us where Jesus is now and thus indicates the background for what follows.

23) **Now one said to him, Lord, are they few who are being saved?**

The insertion of v. 22 shows that a new incident is now being recorded. The questioner must have been one of the multitude that was at present following Jesus. The address "Lord" is not of the same value as when Luke himself, beginning with 7:13, uses this term as a designation for Jesus but is only a term of respect. Yet the man offers a grave question to Jesus as being the one who will be able to furnish him the correct answer. As is done in the LXX, so Luke, too, uses εἰ with direct questions, and the grammars debate as to the origin and the correct explanation of this idiom. It may be possible that εἰ is used only as an interrogative word which implies nothing about the answer, whether it may be yea or nay. "Few" is the predicate, "who are being saved" is the subject: "Are those being saved only few in number?" The present participle intends only to describe the persons referred to: those being saved now or at any time, namely by God's grace, delivered from sin and damnation and placed safely into God's kingdom. The only clue we have to the motive that prompted the question is found in the answer that Jesus gave, in fact, the question is introduced only because of the importance of the answer.

24) Jesus answers the man's question in his characteristic way. It must not be put in an academic but in a personal way: "Am I among those being saved, whether these are few or many?" or: "Am I, perhaps, dallying about salvation and in danger of losing it?" So the Lord answers with an admonition and a warning, which are followed by a picture of the lost and of the saved in the other world.

But he said to them: Struggle to go in through the narrow door! Because many will be seeking to go in and will not succeed from then on when the house-lord shall rise up and shut the door, and you

shall begin to stand outside and keeping knocking at the door, saying, Lord, open to us! and answering he shall say to you, I do not know you, whence you are. Then you will begin to say, We ate in thy presence and drank, and thou didst teach in our streets! And he will say, I tell you, I know not whence you are! Stand away from me, all workers of unrighteousness!

The answer of Jesus at once corrects the question and goes far beyond it even as it takes in, not only the questioner, but also all others who are present.

The question is dangerous when it is put abstractly or academically as the *Concordia Triglotta*, 1073, 33 points out when it quotes our passage in warning not to sound the abyss of God's predestination. Make the question personal, and let your concern be that *you* may be saved. Hence we have the admonition: "Struggle to go in through the narrow door!" The kingdom is conceived as a great house, entrance to which is obtained through a door, and this door is narrow. Our effort is not to be to push open the door; it is open to begin with, but it is shut and locked after a time. So we are to let nothing deter us from entering while it is open. It is readily seen why Jesus pictures the door as being narrow; this portrays the μετάνοια or repentance by which we enter Christ's kingdom. "Only bent quite low, made utterly small, disrobed of all righteousness of our own, and wholly willing to have the coat of the flesh removed from us down to the last rag, can one get through." Besser. Hence we have the strong verb "struggle," which is taken from the ancient athletic contests, from which we still have "to agonize" and "agony." The durative imperfect recalls Luther's first of the famous 95 theses that repentance is to be constant. We are to exert ourselves to the utmost to enter the kingdom by true repentance. This is the opposite of indifference, being languid or careless, or living in false security.

But does this not contradict the teaching that man is spiritually dead and cannot struggle and strive? This struggling is not one on the part of man's corrupt natural powers—they never could or would struggle to enter that narrow door. This struggling is caused by the law and the gospel when they operate upon and in the heart and move it mightily. The Scriptures are full of urgings to men who are still without faith just as the law and the gospel go out in all the world to those who are still far from God. The thought is never that man's dead powers are to move and to save him, but the very Word itself offers what it demands, bestows what it requires, brings those it calls to come. "Struggle!" says Jesus, and in the very saying of his words there was the narrow door that was open to receive and the power to produce the struggling which is called repentance. So Jesus cries, "Believe!" And by his very call he reaches out to kindle faith.

A warning follows: "Do not wait till it is too late!" "Many will be seeking and will not succeed." Note that the verb is changed, and that Jesus does not say that many "will be struggling" and will yet fail to succeed. He does not say even that many will struggle in the wrong way and thus fail. No; these "many" do not struggle, they turn a deaf ear to Jesus, let the time of grace when the narrow door is open pass by—they do not like this narrow door and entrance only by repentance. Then, when it is too late, they wake up and "seek" to enter and cannot "succeed" (ἰσχύειν) because the door is shut. Hence we have the future tenses "will seek," "will not succeed." Both point to the time when the door will be shut; and "will seek" indicates that, although they want to enter, it will even then not be by means of the struggling of repentance. Repentance, too, will then be impossible, for the gracious work of the Word will then have ceased for them.

25) Some begin a new sentence here, which would, however, require γάρ and would even then be

less clear and effective than it is to make no break. Many will be seeking and not succeeding "from then on when the house-lord shall rise up and shut the door," which is followed by the vain effort to enter. The imagery is stripped of all but the essential features, nor should we bring in a feast that is in progress or anything else. The sole idea is that, unless we get into the kingdom while we may, we shall be barred out forever. The door will, of course, be shut at the last day. But it closes also when the patience and the longsuffering of God come to an end for any nation or for any individual. This shutting of the door belongs to the secret counsel of God, to his inscrutable judgment upon the unbelief and the obduracy of men. God either removes the gospel entirely from those who despise it, or its presence only plunges them more deeply into guilt.

"The gospel has its course and runs from one city to another; today it is here, tomorrow in another place just as a downpour passes, and now rains here, now in another place, and makes the land moist and fruitful." Luther, Erl. ed., 48, 186; and 191: "This he told the Jews, but it helped nothing; and it will be the same with all the work-righteous when faith is lost. For what the Jews got, that we, too, will get. The world will not be helped, it does not believe, I am almost weary of it; but on my own account and on account of a few godly people I must preach, otherwise it is in vain. People will not believe but learn by experience. Thus, too, the Jews did. Christ, God's Son, came himself, then his apostles, and warned them; but they would not believe. So also Germany (and other countries as well) must go on and take the consequences. Thus it will come upon us, nothing will do, we want to learn by experience."

In a parable it was not necessary to bring out the difference in time between the continued judgments and the final judgment as regards shutting the door.

In the parable all is one act; and Jesus pictures what shall follow it. But now he turns in his masterly way from the third person to the second, Zahn finely combines the two: "Many—and who knows how many also of you!" The shutting of the door represents the judgment as it comes now and again and then at last. The knocking and the cry: "Lord, open!" picture the effort to evade and to reverse the judgment and to escape its doom when it is too late. Those who scorned to enter the open door can not and shall not enter the closed door. The house-lord's reply: "I do not know you, whence you are" is the seal of the judgment. "Whence you are" points to the sin of these "many." Where have they been all this time when the door was open? Elsewhere—not entering the door! They had other attractions and scorned this narrow door and the house-lord who stood there waiting to welcome them. How, then, can he know them now through the shut door? They must be *Landstreicher,* miserable tramps, yea, worse. One thing is certain, and they have made it so by scorning the open door and the house-lord's invitation —they do not belong inside.

26) Jesus now gives his figurative language a turn that strikes the Jews who are listening to him in the most direct way. This is really an extension or appendix. We prefer the reading that has the future indicative ἄρξεσθε since the variant aorist subjunctive ἄρξησθε seems to be only a mechanical repetition of this form from v. 25. Yes, of all people in the world the Jews had Jesus as none other had him: they ate before him and drank, and he taught in their streets, πλατεῖαι (ὁδοί), the ones that were wide and roomy enough. Certainly, was he not one of them, a native Jew, whose daily life was one with theirs? He surely knew them! Alas, this was all that they could say; they could not add: "and we followed thee and believed in thee," for they would then not have stood and clamored before the shut door. Jesus breaks through the figurative lan-

guage as he does also in some of his parables and adds the plain reality. His concern is to be understood, and that is what language forms are for. But on the basis of what these Jews will then say to the house-lord it becomes plain who this personage really is, namely none other than Jesus himself. They ate and drank "in thy presence"—Jesus purposely avoids saying "in company with thee"; "thou didst teach in our streets" —Jesus avoids saying "thou didst teach us," etc. The entire contact was only outward.

27) Not for a moment does this reminder change the verdict, it only intensifies it: "I tell you, I know not whence you are!" And on top of this we have the terrible command in the peremptory aorist: "Stand away from me, all workers of unrighteousness!" Matt. 7:23; 25:41. Jesus does know these men in one way, and since they insist, he tells them: they are "all workers of unrighteousness." And right here they prove it to the last: they are demanding that the righteous Judge shall act unrighteously, unjustly, break his own, oft-given word, reopen the door which he said he would shut forever, and without repentance let them in beside all the repentant. So the rich man cried even in hell, "*Nay*, father Abraham!" and demanded that a new way of salvation be invented for his five brothers and thereby secretly charged that, if something like that had been done while he lived, he, too, would not have landed in hell. They who die in unbelief remain morally as base as they were when they died. As Jesus once walked among the Jews, so in his Word he now walks among us and teaches us in the identical words—shall it again be in vain?

28) **There shall be the weeping and the gnashing of the teeth when you shall see Abraham and Isaac and Jacob and all the prophets in the kingdom of God but yourselves being thrown outside. And they shall come from east and west, and from north and south, and shall recline at table in the kingdom**

of God. And lo, there are last who shall be first, and there are first who shall be last.

This is the fate of those who are barred out; and it is presented with greater intensity because it is contrasted with the lot of the blessed. Matthew has the first statement no less than six times so that it must have been stereotyped already in Jesus' time. The figure is dropped, and the stark reality stands out. Hence it is unwarranted to stress the adverb "there" by connecting it with the door that is now locked. Only two places exist in the other world, and "there" is hell. Note the articles "the weeping," "the gnashing," both are specific because there is no weeping, etc., like this weeping. All interpreters are agreed that the weeping is the result of the complete loss of happiness, but some think of rage or helpless despair as causing the gnashing of the teeth. Both weeping and gnashing go together, both are caused by the torment in the outer darkness of hell. The damned are not annihilated; even their bodies shall be in hell. Jesus used Luke 13:28, 29, in Matt. 8:11, etc., but in a changed order and in a different connection; repetition was, indeed, justified.

Jesus says that this weeping and this gnashing of the teeth shall occur when the damned shall see Abraham, etc., ὄψησθε, which is regarded as a late aorist subjunctive, or the variant, the future indicative ὄψεσθε. The reference of this verb cannot be to the imagery of the door, for a door would prevent sight. Jesus speaks of the other world in a human way, and to stress the words in the fashion of this world is only to mislead ourselves. This is certain, the damned shall know fully about the joys of the blessed, and still worse they, too, might be in the midst of those joys. See 4:43 on the kingdom; the heavenly rule of glory is meant here although we need not think exclusively of its eschatological consummation, the joys and the glories are now **present.** The warning of Jesus is intended for Jews, hence Abraham, etc., are mentioned. The covenant was originally made with him, and he is "the father of all them that believe," Rom. 4:11, 16. The pride of the Jews in Abraham persists to this day. Isaac and Jacob are added because the three are exalted together in the covenant name "the God of Abraham, Isaac, and Jacob." Finally the prophets are added, who labored to keep Israel true to the covenant.

These were the names that made Israel glorious to every Jew. These would indeed be "in the kingdom of God," and all their descendants should be with them, especially this generation that had the promise of the covenant, the seed of Abraham, Jesus, the Messiah himself. But lo, the tragedy: "you (emphatic) being thrown out outside." The contrast is between "in" the kingdom and "out (ἐκ in the verb) outside," the adverb intensifies the verb. It is unwarranted still to think of the door and to find a lack of correspondence in the participle "being thrown out." Yet it is correct that the idea of being thrown out implies that all the Jews should be within; they even thought themselves within and in an outward way were within. The present participle is descriptive and at the same time speaks of the throwing out as it occurs throughout time.

29) But the situation will be still more poignant. The Jews took it for granted that the patriarchs and the prophets would be in heaven, but to see also hosts of Gentiles there, the people whom they utterly scorned, and themselves, the very children of Abraham, shut out, this would be the climax of their astonishment. Jesus says only that "they shall come," on the other occasion when Jesus used this statement he said "many" and added that they would all recline at table together with the patriarchs and the prophets, namely as the true children of Abraham.

This is prophecy, one that was spoken already by the prophets, yea by God to Abraham in whom all the nations of the earth were to be blessed. Jesus is only once more holding up the Old Testament vision of the covenant and the kingdom. These shall come from the four corners of the earth—from so vast a territory shall they be drawn. The Greek uses idiomatic plurals for "east and west" (the parts of the rising and of the setting) and the names of the winds for "north and south" with the Doric genitive βορρᾶ (R. 254); νότος is used for wind in 12:55.

"Shall recline at table" is not a continuation of the figure of the narrow door but an entirely new figure for the blessed joys of heaven, which reminds of the parable of the King's Son's wedding feast, Matt. 22. Heaven is too exalted to be described in direct language, hence the Scriptures condescend to our finite minds and speak of it in figures and images, but these are so rich and high that already they exceed our comprehension. What a feast as the countless millions gather! It is in progress now, and the kingdom is not yet full.

30) What Jesus says of Jews and of Gentiles he sums up in a terse *mashal* (pithy saying), one that is used repeatedly by him. "Lo" emphasizes the strangeness, the unexpected feature: "there are last," etc. The "first" and the "last" are frequently taken to be those who enter the kingdom first or last, and kindly words are written of the "latecomers." But this is a mistaken view. The play on the words by putting them first in one order then in the reverse order calls on us to mark well the sense in which they are used; and this makes them a *mashal*, its meaning being open only to those who have the key. "Last"=men who are far from the kingdom, the means of grace, etc. Yet they "shall be first," by the grace of God enter the kingdom. Humanly speaking, we should not expect it. Yet the event proves it to be a fact. "First"=men who are close to the kingdom, means of grace, etc., like the Jews, Rom. 9:4, etc. Compared with the condition of the Gentiles, the

Jews were certainly first. "First" is more favored, "last" less favored. And yet these "first shall be last" =never get into the kingdom at all, "last" now in this intensive, tragic sense. Again, who would have expected it? But the event proves the fact.

So first and last are used at one time with a present tense with reference to present conditions, having and not having the means of grace; and a second time with future verbs with reference to the eventual condition, being in or being outside the kingdom. Some people have all the means of salvation but fail to use them and are lost, others are destitute of these means in the beginning, yet the moment they get them they make full use of them and thus obtain salvation. This fact is beyond dispute, and it is used here as a warning: "It is to frighten the greatest saints," Luther. The very advantages we enjoy are to be our warning. Not because we have them shall we be saved but only because we faithfully use them. But note how Jesus places the words in this *mashal*: "There are last—there are first," some, perhaps many of each sort, but *not all*. And that leaves also this: some who are now first shall be and remain first, and some who are now last shall also be and remain last.

31) In that very hour there came forward some Pharisees, saying to him, Get thee out and be going from here because Herod wants to kill thee.

The connection with the foregoing is temporal rather than material. These Pharisees, who were always dogging the steps of Jesus, "came forward," apparently in a very friendly way to warn Jesus regarding his life. Already that should make us suspicious. They were, of course, not sent by Herod to bid Jesus to leave his territory under pain of death; they came to Jesus of their own accord. Their motive coincides with Herod's; both want Jesus out of Herod's territory, these Pharisees want him in Jerusalem. In Perea as in Galilee, both of which were ruled by Herod, the people admired Jesus, and the Pharisees accomplished little; in Jerusalem this would be different. Their motive was to scare Jesus out of Herod's territory, to get him to Jerusalem as fast as possible.

Zahn's analysis of the situation seems to be correct. Herod had no intention of killing Jesus. He had not intended to kill John but had been crowded into this act by Herodias, and we know how this act disturbed him in his superstitious mind (9:7-9). He had himself wanted to see Jesus and with his own eyes view one of his miracles (23:8). Jesus, too, who had been sent to preach the gospel, had not attacked Herod's vicious life as John had done. Yet we are not warranted to conclude from all this that these Pharisees lied to Jesus about Herod's intention to kill him if he persisted in working in Herod's domain. Jesus does not expose these Pharisees as being liars in what they tell him. We know that the Herodians had plotted together with the Pharisees to destroy Jesus (Mark 3:6), and we see these two in conjunction again in Mark 12:13 and Matt. 22:16. Herod himself was undoubtedly involved in these machinations even as Jesus was discussed in his court (9:7-9). Herod was decidedly averse to Jesus, especially to having his own people made the object of Jesus' activity, and thus uttered the threat that he would no longer tolerate that activity in his domain. He uttered the threat to kill Jesus, not because he was burning to shed his blood as he had shed John's, but with the cunning purpose of having it reported to Jesus and thus driving him out of the country.

32) **And he said to them: Having gone, tell this fox, Lo, I am casting out demons and accomplishing cures today and tomorrow, and on the third day I am at the goal. Nevertheless, it is necessary that I journey today and tomorrow and the coming day because it is not permissible that a prophet perish outside of Jerusalem.**

The *tertium comparationis* in the term fox is cunning, and by calling Herod a fox Jesus indicated both his contempt for Herod and his threat and his perception of the tricky purpose of that threat. To call a king "that fox" in public is also to defy him and any threat of his power. Jesus notifies Herod as also these Pharisees that he will not for one moment change his course because of any power of man. In the message to Herod he refers only to his miracles, but not because Herod would not understand about his teaching—its substance he did not need to understand, that teaching was Jesus' work he certainly understood—but rather because the divine power and the majesty of Jesus were revealed in his miracles, for which reason also the expulsion of demons is placed first. He who is master of demons and diseases remains serenely undisturbed by any barking of a tricky fox. "Today and tomorrow" have been taken literally, but Jesus neither died three days after he spoke these words nor ceased performing his miracles. He is merely indicating that the time left to him is short. He was, in fact, not far from the Jordan crossing which would take him into Jericho on the direct road to Jerusalem.

In many connections the active of τελειόω means "to lead to the goal" and the passive "to be led to the goal," thus in the present, "I am at the goal." Jesus is speaking of his mission, doing miracles, etc. A certain goal has been set for him, namely his death in Jerusalem (v. 33). In a short time he will attain that goal. No Herod can interfere with the program that is laid out for Jesus. On the verb see C.-K. 1049, etc.; B.-P. 1296. We reject the middle: "I finish my task." This says too little because the goal of Jesus is his death. His statement says far more than that Jesus will execute the last stroke and then call his job completed. Killing by Herod precedes, and perishing in Jerusalem follows. "I shall be perfected" (A. V.) and "I am perfected" (R. V.) understand this word in its other meaning.

The usual interpretation refers to a process that takes place in the personality of Jesus himself, which is incomplete until it is perfectly completed in his death. The entire context refutes this idea. Nor can it be introduced here from Heb. 2:10. Jesus is not speaking of the completion of a process in his person but of the goal he is about to reach. Let Herod threaten as he will, Jesus will not be killed in Herod's territory; he will be killed and in his death reach the goal set for him by God (the verb is passive) only in Jerusalem, and that soon.

33) Πλήν is always adversative (R. 1187) and here means "nevertheless," in spite of the fact that Jesus is soon reaching his goal. "It is necessary that I journey today and tomorrow and the coming day," namely just as Jesus is now doing, here, too, in Perea, despite anything that Herod may do. Δεῖ is used to indicate any kind of necessity; the context points to the necessity of doing the appointed work (casting out demons, etc.) during the time allotted him until the goal set for him is reached. The unmodified πορεύεσθαι is not the same as πορεύου ἐντεῦθεν and has nothing to do with "making his way to Jerusalem" which occurs in v. 22. All it says is that Jesus must go from place to place in his mission as he has done from the start. And so he will continue. The implication is: right here in Perea, ignoring Herod's threat. For the period of his work Jesus names "today and tomorrow and the coming day," three terms instead of two as he did in v. 32, but he has in mind the same period by both expressions, i. e., one that is thus characterized as being short.

Jesus tells us in the ὅτι clause why he goes on wholly unconcerned about Herod: "because it is not permitted that a prophet perish outside of Jerusalem," *es ist nicht zulaessig;* it would not do at all to have a prophet die outside of Jerusalem. Jerusalem has a monopoly on killing prophets. R. 1198 finds irony in this statement, and it is certainly cutting. Jesus intends to say that however long he yet lingers in Herod's territory, there is no fear of his perishing there—prophets have a place where they perish, namely Jerusalem. Some may prefer the strong translation "it is not possible." The sense is, however, not absolute, for John perished outside of Jerusalem; but in no other place were so many prophets put to death, and surely the greatest of them all (Deut. 18:15, 18) would have to perish there.

34) Jesus now exclaims in words that are nearly like those he uttered on the last Tuesday before his death, cf., Matt. 23:37-39. The time, the place, the connection, are totally different, which makes a hard problem, indeed, for those who think that this plaint was uttered only once by Jesus. It is more creditable also as far as the integrity of the two evangelists is concerned to say that Jesus uttered these sad words twice, here in Perea in the hearing of the Pharisees and again to the Twelve on the Mount of Olives.

Jerusalem, Jerusalem, that art killing the prophets and stoning those having been sent to her, how often did I will to gather thy children to me the way a bird her own brood under her wings, and you did not will. Lo, left to you is your house! Moreover I say to you, In no way shall you see me until you say, Blessed the One coming in the Lord's name!

These words are full of deepest pathos. The Pharisees are cold and hard, but the heart of Jesus is surcharged with deepest sadness because of their obduracy and the coming judgment. There is no "reverberating thunder" in the repetition "Jerusalem, Jerusalem!" All we need to do is to compare these repetitions as they are found elsewhere. Note II Sam. 18:33: "O my son Absalom, my son, my son Absalom!" and again: "O Absalom, my son, my son!" Luke 10:41: "Martha, Martha!" Acts 9:4: "Saul, Saul!" These repetitions voice tender love and concern. "Jerusalem" stands for the nation whose capital and religious citadel this city was. The distinction between "Jerusalem" to designate the rulers and "thy children" to indicate the common people is not tenable, for the very ones whom Jesus willed to gather refused to be gathered—rulers and people alike.

"Jerusalem" means "city of peace"; but what a city of peace: "killing the prophets and stoning those having been sent (commissioned) to her" by God (the agent in the passive) to bring her peace! All her guilt is summed up. The prophets are a small group to which a wider one is added by taking in all who seconded the work of the prophets. The present participles "killing" and "stoning" mark characteristic conduct and thus go beyond aorists, which would state only the past facts. "Unto her" instead of "unto thee" matches the participles, which present the subject they modify in the third person.

"How often!"—not just once but with utmost persistence did Jesus seek to save his nation until it actually stilled his voice in blood. John describes the ministry in the capital at length, but all of Jesus' ministry to the Jews is included here: "thy children," the nation. One of the features of divine love that is inexplicable to us is that, in spite of the infallible foreknowledge that all will be in vain, its call and its effort to save never cease until the very end. Judas is another example. Such knowledge would either stop us at once or make our efforts a mere pretense. God is so far above us in this that even our minds cannot follow his ways.

The verb ἠθέλησα denotes the gracious, saving will of Jesus. It is the so-called antecedent will which takes into account only our lost condition, from which it works to deliver us, and not our reaction to this will. The will which deals with this reaction is always the subsequent will, and this will is judgment for the obdurate. Determinism and other confusions result when this distinction is not known or is ignored. The gracious antecedent will and its call of grace are equal for all. To make it serious and real only for one class of men and only a pretense for another class is to attribute duplicity to God, against which all Scripture cries out, Rom. 11:32. The preaching of the Word is no *Spiegelfechten* (fencing only before a mirror, hence not in earnest), *Concordia Triglotta,* 1072. Who dares to say that Jesus willed to save even the Sanhedrists less than he willed to save the Twelve; or Judas less than Peter?

The figure of the bird and her brood is not only beautiful as a designation but especially so in the case of Jews, whose rabbis spoke of the *Shekinah* as being the gathering place of the proselytes. See the expressions in Deut. 32:11; Ps. 17:8; 61:4; Isa. 31:5. Ὄρνις is any bird and not merely a "hen." The idea of the hen has led to the bringing in of the swooping hawk. The idea is rather that the brood (τὴν νοσσιάν; in Matt. τὰ νοσσία, the fledglings) belongs to the mother bird, and that she thus gathers them together under her wings; the reflexive ἑαυτῆς is stronger than the mere possessive αὐτῆς. So this nation belonged to Jesus, and as being his very own he willed to gather it to him (ἐπί in the verb, a first aorist infinitive). This gathering is the essential thing—all these children of Jerusalem are attached to Jesus as his very own; hence we have the aorist: to gather once for all. Luke omits the verb "gathers" in the simile, and ὃν τρόπον is the adverbial accusative, the antecedents being incorporated in the relative.

Nothing is more tragic than the outcome of this gracious will of Jesus: "and you did not will." As is done so often, the adversative idea is added with a telling copulative καί. This brings out all the abnormality, the utter unnaturalness, the absolute unreasonableness of the negative. The sentence ought to close "and you, too, willed"; but it closes *"and* you willed NOT!" Only this, nothing more, is said. There is no qualification, no explanation, no addition. The one fatal thing is: "you did not will."

Despite the brevity many facts center here. Grace is not irresistible; every case of resistance proves it, notably this glaring case of the Jews. Damnation results from man's own will, which settles into permanent, obdurate, unaccountable resistance against God's will of grace. The more God draws the will with the power of grace, the more this will rejects God until grace can do no more. To bring in the omnipotence of God is to confound its attributes and to darken all saving Scripture, *Concordia Triglotta*, 1077, quoting Matt. 22:3, etc.

Why do some wills resist thus? This asks a reasonable explanation for an unreasonable act—no such explanation exists. To say that this is due to inborn sin is no explanation, for men who have the same inborn sin are won, and their wills assent under grace. Moreover, this obdurate resistance is produced only when grace operates with its power. The spring is poisonous and throws out a poisonous stream. The *gratia sufficiens* is applied to the spring and the stream with power *sufficiens* to unpoison both. Behold, *now* the spring and the stream are a hundred times more poisonous than they were before! Explain that! All we know is that the mystery of this resistance lies in the will itself and in no way in God. How could Satan fall? How could Adam sin? How can man resist grace and salvation to the end? How can a believer, whose will is changed, again turn to unbelief and be damned? It is all the same question.

"A master of music has laid all the power which his art gave him into this lament of the Messiah, and he into whose ears has once been sung 'And ye would not!' will never forget this heart-penetrating music. What? Shall the art of music do more than the voice of eternal love speaking from heaven? No; let it penetrate our hearts when Jesus calls to us: 'How often would I have gathered you even as a hen her nest under her wings—and ye would not!' Then shall we will what he wills, our salvation, and shall flee from the judgment of Jerusalem, which scorned the wings of the hen and fell into the talons of the eagle (Matt. 24:28)." Besser.

35) An exclamation may well introduce the verdict of the subsequent will which Jesus now states: "Lo, left to you is your house!" Some think that "your house" is the Temple, but the context is not so specific but points rather to Jerusalem, which, however, includes the Temple. Jerusalem is today not a Jewish city, to say no more. History tells the sad story of how the Jewish nation was driven out of its land and its capital, never to possess either again. In Matt. 23:38 ἀφίεται ὑμῖν ἔρημος (the adjective is textually assured) is simple: your house "is left to you desert"; in Luke the adjective is absent, which causes difficulty and the offer of various solutions. Zahn takes ὑμῖν in the sense of the agent: "is abandoned by you," "lost by you." But this seems forced. We take the words in the same sense they have in Matthew: your house "is left to you." God or Jesus leaves it entirely to them with the dire consequences we know. They did what they pleased with Jerusalem and the Temple; they wrecked and ruined both as Jesus told them to do with the Temple in John 2:19. They were even now desecrating their Temple and making Jerusalem anything but a city of peace.

Δέ means that Jesus has something else to say in addition, and "I say to you" is the voice of authority. "In no way shall you see me" (Jesus cannot add "from now on" as he does in Matthew) with its strong οὐ μή and the futuristic subjunctive announces the final, complete withdrawal of Jesus from the Jews. "Until you say (or shall say), Blessed the One coming in the Lord's name!" has the idea of expectancy although ἕως is without ἄν (ἐάν). In whom this expectation will be fulfilled we see in Isa. 65:8-10: "that I may not destroy them all"—"a seed," "an inheritor," "mine elect"—"that have sought me." Read the whole of Isa. 63:7-65:10. Paul answers: "a remnant"; read Rom. 10:18-11:5. A remnant of the Jewish nation which was made up of all those Jews who, beginning with the days of the apostles and continuing through the many years of history, turn to repentance and faith and greet Jesus with the Palm Sunday cry of Ps. 118:26: "Blessed the One coming," etc. Εὐλογημένος is the perfect participle with its present connotation: "has been and is thus now blessed"; ὁ ἐρχόμενος is "the One coming," a standard designation of the Messiah; "he comes" is also used with reference to him. "In the Lord's (*Yahweh's*) name" means "in connection with the revelation Jehovah has made." In all such phrases "name" is the equivalent of revelation (see 9:48). Both the psalm itself and the acclamation on Palm Sunday shut out the idea that these words could ever be applied in a double sense, willingly by believers and unwillingly by the obdurate (at the second coming of Christ). Ps. 118:26 adds as the other half of the greeting: "We have blessed you out of the house of the Lord!"

Although the words of Jesus do not declare that any or many or all Jews at any one time or era in the future will greet him as the Messiah they do express the expectation that some will do so. And Jesus says that whenever any, few or many, beginning even with his present hearers, Pharisees (v. 31) and others, do so, namely by faith, they shall see him, not, indeed, merely with the eyes of the flesh—for no Christian sees him in this manner although he is always with us—but on earth with the eyes of the spirit, as our Savior, indeed, and in heaven by direct vision.

All chiliasts refer v. 35 to the final conversion of the Jews as a nation. They also add further details: the

Jewish nation will stand at the head of all nations, will constitute the cream of Christendom, will have Jerusalem as the center of the millennial kingdom, the metropolis of the whole earth, and from Jerusalem the heathen living at the time of the millennium (!) will be converted by Jewish missionaries, etc., etc.

But ὑμῖν, ὑμῶν, ὑμῖν in this verse, together with the "you" form of the two verbs, address the Jewish hearers that are right before Jesus: your house is left *to you,* and any of *you* who acclaim Jesus as the Messiah shall see him. By natural implication this, of course, extends to any Jews of coming times who likewise accept Jesus. How can any man regard these simple pronouns and "you"-verbs with their obvious meaning as a reference to the last generation of the Jews that is living at the beginning of the millennium?

CHAPTER XIV

1) And it came to pass when he went into the house of one of the rulers of the Pharisees on a Sabbath to eat bread, they kept watching him closely.

For καὶ ἐγένετο καί see 5:12; the second καί follows farther down in the sentence. For ἐν τῷ with the infinitive see 1:8 and 3:21. Jesus is proceeding slowly through Perea (v. 22). Comparing the present narrative with that of the other visit to a Pharisee's house recorded in 11:37-52, we see that the two differ greatly. The Pharisaic hostility manifested in the present case is far less intense than that which was evidenced in the previous one. "The rulers of the Pharisees" occurs only here and means Pharisaic rulers of the synagogue. How this ruler came to invite Jesus, i. e., with what motives, is not indicated. The narrative makes the impression that, despite the Pharisaic hostility, perhaps even because of it, these men sought contact with Jesus, most likely to fan their hostility, at any rate to observe him more closely by getting him into their own midst. Jesus accepted the invitation. He had come to save also these men and, when he was in their midst was ready to show them their grave faults.

We need no article in εἰς οἶκον since the genitive makes "house" definite. See 5:17 on Pharisees. "To eat bread" means to dine, and the story shows that this was a grand meal to which also many other Pharisees and rabbis were invited. We hear nothing about the Twelve and judge that, as was the case in 11:37, etc., they were not included. This seems to have been a δεῖπνον, the main meal toward the end of the day, a dinner in our language. The Pharisees and the Jews in general made the Sabbath a day of feasting and often went to excess although no excess is reported in this instance. Παρά in the periphrastic imperfect brings out the idea that all those present watched Jesus "on the side," not enviously (R. 613), but in a covert way, and the imperfect implies constant watching.

2) **And lo, a man with dropsy was there before him!** Τίς is only our indefinite article. Luke does not say that this man was placed there in order to tempt Jesus and to find out whether he would heal on the Sabbath; hence we decline to assume, as some do, that his presence was arranged in advance. Trench draws attention to the fact that feasts such as the present one were semipublic. Outsiders could enter, stand, or sit, and watch what was going on. So the woman mentioned in 7:37 came in after the dinner was in progress, and this man apparently before it started, for Jesus presently found him right before him. Did the man have the desire and the hope that Jesus would heal him, Sabbath though it was? Or did he come in only as others did because a great person was being entertained? The point is immaterial for the narrative, and no certain deduction can be made because we have no answer to these questions.

3) **And answering Jesus said (1:19) to the lawyers (10:25) and Pharisees, saying, Is it lawful to heal on the Sabbath or not? But they were quiet. And having taken hold, he healed him and released him.** "Answering" is used in a broad sense when a situation, for instance, requires a statement. Jesus does not wait until the real point of the case is brought forward by these Pharisees but at once states it himself. He had come to help these men by freeing them from their false ideas; this was his contribution to the feast, and so he starts at once. The one article combines "lawyers and Pharisees" into one class, for Jesus addresses them as one group; in other connections they may be viewed as two groups, each will then have its own article. Not all lawyers were Phar-

isees, and many Pharisees were, of course, not lawyers. The question is simplicity itself, and men like these ought evidently to be able to answer it at once. Surely, they knew whether it was in harmony with the law or in conflict with it to heal (aorist: actually heal) on the Sabbath. "But they were quiet," which is stronger than just silent. Strange, indeed; no one spoke up, no one came forward to do so, there is no whispering even among themselves — all are motionless, their eyes are fixed on Jesus. The situation became dramatic as the Lord looked around and waited for a reply, waited until it was clear that he would get none.

4) So Jesus makes the reply himself—forthwith and before the eyes of all he heals the man. Deeds speak louder than words. This is the most decisive answer of Jesus himself: "Indeed, it is lawful to heal on the Sabbath!" The participle is not redundant but says that Jesus took hold of the man and healed him in this manner. He could have avoided that act and could have uttered only a word, but he added the act — in the case of some other Sabbath healings he did not do so — to show that the Sabbath law did not forbid even that. He sent the healed man away, who might otherwise have remained. The man was to be removed from this company to a place where he could be undisturbed and think of the miraculous blessing God had bestowed upon him through Jesus. The miracle is reported with the utmost brevity because it is told, not for its own sake, but for the sake of the explanations which Jesus made regarding the Sabbath. So it is beside the mark to ask about this man's faith as a requisite for being healed. Faith or no faith, he was healed; and the miracles justify no deduction that faith was invariably a prerequisite to healing.

5) **And he said to them, Of which of you shall a son or an ox fall into a well, and he will not draw him out at once on the day of the Sabbath? And they had no strength to reply to these things.**

The R. V. decided in favor of the reading "an ass or an ox," which would make the argument exactly the same as that employed in 13:15, from the less to the greater: if one rescues an animal on the Sabbath, much more should he deliver a human being. But the better reading seems to be "a son or an ox" — the other readings may be disregarded — and this would offer a different argument, one that is based on the divine law that we love our neighbor as we love ourselves: what we would do for our own, even for our own beast, we should do for others likewise. The φρέαρ is the shaft of the well. When one was watering cattle, an unruly ox might fall into such a shaft; yet, Sabbath though it be, what man would not at once go to the rescue, and do that without regarding it as a transgression of the Sabbath law? Jesus implies that such a deed, whatever strenuous work it required, would be perfectly lawful. Shall the same love, which requires no labor at all, be denied a fellow man?

6) To this justification of his healing act the learned *nomikoi* and the other legalists not only made no reply, they had not the strength, the ability, and the courage, to attempt one. Since Luke reports no more in regard to the attitude of these men, this was probably all there was to report. Whatever they thought, the dinner proceeded.

7) **Moreover, he went on to say a parable to those that had been invited, noting how they were choosing for themselves the chief reclining places, saying to them, etc.**

Ἔλεγε merely describes, see 3:7; also v. 12. The perfect κεκλημένους, "having been invited," implies that they were now present as such invited guests; and with ἐπέχων we supply νοῦν, "holding the mind on something," "noting." The vice of securing the prominent places at table and elsewhere was so general among the Pharisees that Jesus scored it more than once (20:46; Matt. 23:6; Mark 12:39).

The chief reclining places at table were those on the left end of each couch (not those in the center as some suppose), for the person reclining there had the fullest view of the table and the guests while those toward the right end had to bend back in order to see. There were at least three persons to a couch. When there was a number of couches, even when they were larger, the number of chief places would be increased. In the present instance the guests must have crowded and scrambled in a very unseemly way to pre-empt these coveted places. Jesus, we take it, waited to take whatever place was left or whatever place the host assigned to him.

He then spoke what Luke calls "a parable." It would, however, not be a parable if it ended with v. 10, save for εἰς γάμους (regarding which there is dispute), for the whole would then be a direct admonition to the guests regarding their table manners. It is v. 11, which announces a divine principle, that makes the preceding illustration an actual parable; compare Matt. 22: 1-14 where v. 14 brings in the point that is illustrated.

8) **Whenever thou art invited by anyone to a wedding, do not recline in the chief reclining place lest one more honored than thou have been invited by him, and he who invited thee and him, having come, shall say to thee, Give this man place! and then thou wilt begin with shame to hold the last place. But when thou art invited, having gone, drop into the last place in order that, when he that has invited thee comes, he shall say to thee, Friend, go on up higher! Then there will be honor for thee before all those reclining together with thee.**

We see no reason for having γάμοι (the plural is used in the same sense as the singular) mean "feast" instead of "wedding," for this is a parable and not a description of the present dinner. The same question was raised in 12:36. The reason for "wedding" is not, however, that at a wedding the places at table were allotted according to ranking, for a guest who himself took the lowest place without waiting to be directed to the place that was intended for him would then be acting disorderly. No; if "wedding" is chosen for any special reason it would be because many guests would be invited to such a function, and thus the chief places would be multiplied, and the difference between the highest and the lowest place would be the greater.

Among the high places one would, of course, be the highest of all, namely for the guests. Since this is a wedding, it would be the upper place on the couch that was nearest to the groom, and thus the lowest place would be the minor one on the couch that was farthest away. Since this is a parable, the illustration presents the extreme by mentioning the highest place of all and opposite to that the selection of the lowest one. When a vice is illustrated, its fullest development must be covered, and that automatically includes its minor manifestations. So murder includes anger in Matt. 5:21, etc., adultery includes lustful looks in Matt. 5:27, etc. Here the choosing as high as possible a place at table is covered by referring to the choice of the highest place.

9) Jesus describes what *may* happen and states it mildly for what *will* most likely happen. After μήποτε we have the subjunctive (the periphrastic perfect) in v. 9 and then the future indicative ἐρεῖ, a frequent construction in the Koine, R. 988. In the same way we have ἵνα ἐρεῖ in v. 10. Ordered out of the highest place, the presumptuous guest will have to take what is left, namely the lowest place, everybody else having found his place before this fellow's case is settled. He certainly also deserves his "shame."

10) So the parable bids us do the opposite: "drop back into the last or lowest place," "drop back" is a variant for "recline" occurring in v. 8. As μήποτε introduces negative purpose, so ἵνα states a positive purpose; in fact, we have two opposites throughout, even to the

words with which the host ousts the one and elevates the other guest. In this parable Jesus steps down to the level of these Pharisees by showing that, if they wanted honors at table, the way to get them was not to run for the highest place and risk being ordered to the lowest but quietly to take the lowest place in order to be conducted to the higher one. Let it be understood that the motive implied in both "lest" and "in order that" is the selfish, base one exhibited by these Pharisees and not the motive Jesus would inculcate for us at table or in our lives in general. He is making a parable out of what he sees the Pharisees doing right before him and, not without stinging irony, telling them that they ought to go about it in just about the opposite way if they intend to be greedy of empty honor; for by doing it in their way they always run the risk of getting "shame" whereas the opposite way would be almost sure to get them δόξα, "honor" or distinction — provided, of course, they are the distinguished persons they think they are.

11) All this would be little more than a sarcastic dig at the Pharisees at table with Jesus if he had not added: **Because everyone exalting his own self shall be humbled, and the one humbling his own self shall be exalted.** Compare the same dictum in 18:14 and in Matt. 23:12, and similar statements in Ps. 18:27; Prov. 29:23; James 4:6.

We now see that all that precedes is a parable, and this is the great truth it is to convey. These future passives have God as their agent. This business of putting oneself up high by rudely crowding oneself into the foremost place or getting a higher place by hypocritically dropping into the very lowest one is not just a matter regarding men, whether it succeeds in the one or the other way, but one that God takes note of. Before him all such selfish pride and arrogance, whether they are open as in the case of the rude fellow or sneaking as in the case of the hypocritical fellow, are an abomination which he will most certainly punish, perhaps already in this world, but surely in the next. With God only genuine humility counts, which neither pushes itself forward nor cunningly schemes to get itself pushed forward; and this God invariably rewards, perhaps already in this world, but surely in the next.

It was this worldly pride of the Jews, this unspiritual holiness superiority of the Pharisees especially, that made them despise a Messiah who was as humble as Jesus was. In spite of all the humiliation the Jews have suffered they to this day deem themselves the cream of the human race and attempt to come before God in this pride. And they have hosts of others who are as presumptuous and as arrogant as they are, especially over against the gospel and its way of salvation through repentance. That way may be good enough for the common herd (John 7:48, 49), it is not good enough for them. But he that exalts himself shall be humbled, and only he who humbles himself shall be exalted. And the parable shows that even men copy God in their blind way, and this may help us to see what he will do in a far more perfect way. Does not a host ask a guest who crowds into the highest seat to step down and bid him who acts humble and takes the lowest place to step up higher? Is not the one covered with shame before the company while the other is graced with honor?

12) **Moreover, he went on to say also to him who had invited him: Whenever thou makest a morning meal or an evening meal, do not keep calling thy friends or thy brothers or thy relatives or rich neighbors lest they, too, invite thee again, and there be a due return for thee; but when thou makest a banquet, be inviting poor people, maimed, lame, blind; and blessed shalt thou be because they**

have not in order to make due return to thee; for due return shall be made to thee in the resurrection of the righteous.

Jesus first served the guests, now he serves also the host. The perfect τῷ κεκληκότι parallels the perfect τοὺς κεκλημένους occurring in v. 7: "he has invited," they have been invited. With the exception of Jesus, who was probably invited as an afterthought, this was evidently one of the dinners that were exchanged by the prominent company present, it being the present ruler's (v. 1) turn. It is on this point that Jesus speaks. The ἄριστον was eaten near noon (see 11:37) and the δεῖπνον toward evening. The present tense of the imperative is important: μὴ φώνει, as is also the same tense in κάλει (v. 13): "do not make a practice of calling only thy friends"—"but make a practice of inviting poor people." Jesus by no means forbids our inviting those who will in turn invite us; nor does he demand that we invite only such as cannot invite us again. What he does is to forbid us always to invite the former and to forget all about the latter.

Note the four classes that he mentions, over against which he places four other classes. Again note that the article and the possessive "thy" are used with the three classes but are not used with the fourth, not "the rich neighbors of thine" but "neighbors (such as are) rich," not other neighbors, for they can offer no return invitation. The point is that if I invite those who will invite me again, this amounts to nothing. I have my due return (ἀντί, in return; ἀπό, due, especially when it is added to a form from δίδωμι). To this day men feast each other and spare no expense; but for charity and sacred needs — not one cent or a mere pittance.

13) Do the opposite, Jesus says. We help the poor and needy, however, not by gathering them around our rich dinner table once in a while and then imagining that this beatitude will apply to us. False literalism has led to many sad misinterpretations and mistakes.

Jesus wants genuine love and proper care for the needy, which are true fruits of faith. His pointed words are illustrative of this meaning and are thus pertinent, indeed. The δοχή is any feast.

14) "Blessed"=in the divine and thus true sense; "because they have not in order to make due return to thee." That is one of the tests of true charity. The idea is not that due return shall be made. God himself will attend to that through Christ, and how he will do this is related at length in Matt. 25:24-40. Hence we have the addition "in the resurrection of the righteous." Only the Sadducees denied the resurrection (Acts 23: 6-9; 24:15). Only "the righteous" are mentioned simply because the resurrection of the unrighteous has nothing to do with what Jesus is saying. Δίκαιος is always used in the forensic sense: he who has God's verdict in his favor; he whom God pronounces free from guilt at his judgment bar — as the Scriptures teach *in extenso*: by grace, for Christ's sake, through faith. We thus see that the love and the good works which Jesus asks are the fruits of faith and are produced by the righteous alone.

15) **Now, on hearing these things one of those reclining together at table said to him, Blessed he that shall eat bread in the kingdom of God!**

This exclamation on the part of one of the guests, who must have been a Pharisee and, perhaps, also a lawyer, comes as a surprise; but it helps to show that "these things" which Jesus was saying were not enraging the Pharisee, that some of those present were deeply impressed, and that Jesus therefore adds further instruction. What the man says is certainly true. He thought of it as the eating of bread, i. e., of dining with the saints in heaven, therefore Jesus speaks a new parable of the Great Supper which God makes for us here on earth, of which we must partake in order to dine with the saints in heaven and thus to be forever blessed.

This response on the part of Jesus shows that it is wrong to call this Pharisee's exclamation a mere Jewish platitude which anybody could utter. Jesus treated it as a serious word that was seriously meant. It is correct to say that the last statement of Jesus (v. 14) caused the exclamation, the reference to the exaltation and due return in the resurrection of the righteous. But it is sinning against the Eighth Commandment to call the man's utterance a piece of ignorance or hypocrisy, to add that the man may have meant that dining in heaven was a prerogative of the Pharisees, and may have complacently assumed that he was to be one of the blest. In exegesis, too, it is a sin to put anything but the best construction upon the utterances of men. This man's words sound like a longing for the heavenly feast — let us understand them so. Then the parable fits admirably: Jesus shows this man and the company at table with him how to become truly righteous, and how thus to come to the heavenly banquet.

16) **And he said to him: A man was making a great dinner, and he invited many. And he commissioned his slave at the hour of the dinner to tell those that had been invited, Be coming because things are already prepared!**

"To him," yet in the hearing of all. Like the two preceding parabolic presentations (v. 7-11; 12-14), this, too, refers to a dinner. "A man," has τίς like our indefinite article. The parable itself shows who he is, and he grows ever greater as the parable unfolds, for he is none other than God. We should note the imperfect ἐποίει, "he was engaged in making a great dinner," and this is not inchoative: "he was on the point of making" (R., W. P.). This imperfect tense covers the entire Old Testament preparation which culminated in Christ, his death and his resurrection, when "things are already prepared." Yet we should abide by what the parable pictures and not insert what is left out, namely the provisions made for salvation in the old

Luke 14:16, 17

covenant. Abraham, etc., (13:28) dined at the heavenly table and thus partook of the gospel feast during his earthly life; but the parable restricts itself to the time of Jesus and the ages that followed and refers to the old covenant only as the preparation for the gospel feast which was finally ready in Christ.

This is likened to a δεῖπνον (compare v. 12), but only because it designated the main meal of the day, and the old idea that it was eaten in the evening and thus pictures the end of time must be dropped. Already the fact that this *deipnon* was "great" casts its light on the "man" who was making it; his own greatness is revealed more and more fully. He naturally invited "many"; who they were appears presently already in the aorist ἐκάλεσε, "he did invite." This, too, reaches back into the past, and the Greek is content to state only that the invitation was extended some time in the past whereas the English would place this verb in relation to ἐποίει and thus use the past perfect "he had invited many."

The parable is thus seen to be historical, the "many" who were invited thus early were the Jews. They had this invitation in the old covenant and in the Old Testament; we might say that God sent them a written invitation. But we should here again abide by the parable which has in mind the Jews who were then living and their treatment of the invitation and does not intend to cover the previous generations of the Jews. While it is thus plainly historical, the parable is at the same time prophetic and reaches out to all future generations, whether of Jews or Gentiles. This appears in what follows.

17) **When the proper time came, the summons to the dinner went out.** This is not a second invitation even as καλεῖν, "to invite," is not used. In the invitation that had been extended in the past the date of the banquet was not announced, that announcement was now finally made. This procedure is said to be an ancient

custom and as such lends itself perfectly to the parable. Some challenge this alleged custom; yet, whether it can be properly verified or not, the parable is built in this fashion. And that means that we should discard the idea that the many had to be urged by a renewal of the invitation, i. e., that they treated already the original invitation with contempt. This spoils the picture; for one thing, it lowers the great Giver of this feast who would not add a second invitation to the one that had already been despised. Moreover, "he invited" in v. 16 and "to tell those that have been invited" (we should say "had been") are single acts in the parable and in the reality pictured constitute the invitation issued during the entire Old Testament, which was followed by the summons issued during the ministry of Jesus.

"The hour of the dinner" was about to begin with the redemption on the part of Jesus. It is important to note this, for the dinner of which Jesus is speaking takes place in the kingdom of grace whereas the eating of bread in the kingdom referred to in v. 15 is the feast in the kingdom of glory. It is all one kingdom, but its grace and its glory should not be confused; see 4:43. "Be coming because things are already prepared!" is the parable's language for the call of the gospel of Christ. In ἕτοιμα, "things prepared," we have the completed redemption.

Various opinions have been held regarding the δοῦλος, "slave," who appears repeatedly in this parable. Does he represent the prophets or the Baptist or the evangelists and apostles or, as Theophylact thought, Jesus, the great *Ebed Yahweh* of Isaiah, Jehovah's Servant who "took the form of a servant"? Only the latter satisfies, and does that in every respect. This "slave" was right here summoning the Pharisees to the great dinner. There is some hesitation to adopt this interpretation because of the use of the term "slave," but Phil. 2:7 ought to satisfy on that point,

Luke 14:18

where "slave" is used in nonfigurative language with reference to Jesus.

18) **And they began with one voice all to make excuse. The first said to him: I bought a field, and I am compelled, after going out, to see it. I request thee, consider me excused. And another said: I bought five yoke of oxen and am on my way to test them out. I request thee, consider me excused. And another said, I have married a wife, and because of this I cannot come.**

So many declined in the reality that is here pictured that the parable may well say, "They all began to make excuse," and that "all" is true with regard to the Jews to this day, and too many among the Gentiles followed the example of the Jews. What a strange unanimity! Ἀπὸ μιᾶς occurs only here and calls for some feminine noun like γνώμης ("with one consent"), hardly ψυχῆς ("with one soul"), we prefer φωνῆς ("with one voice"), meaning that they all talked alike and, of course, not that they sang out in unison. Παραιτεῖσθαι and its two perfect participles that follow has several meanings, here it means "to beg off," "to ask to be excused."

The parable offers three excuses as samples, and let it be understood that these are the best that were offered and are still the best that are offered today, all the many others being worse as are those recorded in the other parable, Matt. 22:6. By stressing the mildest all the rest stand condemned. All the excuses are empty, have to be, for no reason exists why a man should not save his soul by means of God's gospel of redemption but only a multiplied and tremendous reason why he should. All three present something that is perfectly legitimate in itself but use this in a fearfully illegitimate way for declining the means of salvation and thus salvation itself. All are dishonest, for they that make these excuses know that they are pretending. All merely veil the real reason the invitation is now turned down, the wicked will which says: "I will not — reason or no reason!" (13:34: "you did not will," see the comment).

The first pleads *necessity*, he is compelled to go out to see his newly bought field. It is impossible for him to put this off. He simply *cannot come*. Who has not heard this type of declination repeated again and again? But this man and the next are polite: "I request thee," etc. The use of ἔχε is a Latinism, the verb being used in the sense of *aestimo*, "consider me as having been excused," the slave is to do that for his master. R. 109, 1122.

19) The plea of the second is that he *cannot well come*. Πορεύομαι, he is already starting to test out the five yoke of oxen he had just bought; he is now on his way and cannot well change his plans as the slave should, of course, be able himself to see. This is typical of thousands. They cannot arrange to save their souls at present!

20) The third drops the politeness and is blunt. This man has married a wife (ἔγημα, perfect tense) and is thus in the married state, hence he *will not come* — it is utterly impossible: οὐ δύναμαι, "it is impossible for me to come"; and that is why he does not even ask to be excused — one does not ask to be excused for an impossible situation. Yet, though the first could not take his field or farm with him, nor the second his five yoke of oxen, this third could and should have taken his wife along. The excuses become thinner until the last even drops the show of an excuse, and any others would, of course, voice open objections to the gospel, Christ, the church, the church members, etc. The third is after the pleasures offered in his new marriage, and how many have forsaken the gospel for the pleasures of this life?

Other distinctions between the three have been sought, but they seem to be either only variations of the one indicated or mere refinements that are of little or no service. Some of the ancients allegorized: 1) priests, the ecclesiastical state, husbandmen who sow the seed of the Word; 2) rulers, the governmental state, those who drive oxen; 3) the domestic state. Or 1) pagans (*pagani*); 2) Israelites (5 yoke = 10 oxen = the Ten Commandments); 3) heretics.

21) **And having returned, the slave reported these things to his lord. Then having become angry, the housemaster said to his slave, Go out quickly into the streets and alleys of the city and the poor and crippled and blind and lame bring in here! And the slave said, Lord, it has been done what thou didst order, and still there is room. And the lord said to the slave, Go out into the roads and hedges and compel to come in in order that my house may be filled.**

In the parable it is always the same single slave, and the whole work of filling the banquet hall is his alone, and he works in closest conjunction with his lord. This certainly fits Jesus and his Father. This is different in Prov. 9:3 and in Matt. 22:3, 8. The houselord's anger pictures the wrath of God against all who despise him and his salvation, and all attempts to erase this from the Scriptures are in vain. See 13:26 on πλατεῖαι; these were the wide streets, the opposite of the narrow alleys (a city has no "lanes"). The naming of the two together makes it plain that the entire city was to be scoured for guests, and the greatness of both the feast and of its giver now begin to loom up. Any and all are to be brought in. There will, of course, be left only the four classes mentioned already in v. 13, which are now grouped under one article as a single immense class.

All these have nothing whereas the others have wealth, one to buy a field, the other to buy so many oxen, the third to support a wife. This new class is composed entirely of beggars. The descriptions refer to spiritual states — any other interpretation is untenable. The transient values of the earth satisfy so many (12:16, etc.), but they who have learned to despair of them may be won for the eternal values. These are "the poor, crippled," etc. But note, they are "in the streets and alleys of the city," still in the city (Israel) but practically homeless there. By these Jesus pictures the publicans, sinners, harlots (Matt. 21:31, 32) and many others who were little esteemed by the haughty Sadducees, lawyers, scribes, and Pharisees who were taken up entirely with their wealth of false religious ideas and practices.

22) The parable does not need to say that these homeless and destitute and injured ones were brought in; "there is still room" implies that. The idea is never that, if those who were first summoned had come, the banquet would have been filled, and there would have been no room for others. All the others would also have been brought in. The parable is, however, not hypothetical, it sticks to the historical facts and aims to picture only these. Theoretically all the Jews should have come at Jesus' call, but the mass of leaders were the very ones who refused; this is illustrated and no more. So it is unwarranted to speak of two calls for the Jews and of a third for the Gentiles. Yes, "there is still room" — God made the banquet of gospel grace so great that there was ample room for even the Gentiles, and these together with not a few Jews are still being called.

23) It is the same δοῦλος who is now ordered to go outside the city (Israel) "into the roads and hedges or hedgerows," where wanderers and homeless wayfarers stray (like gypsies, Trench). Paul characterizes them: "being aliens from the commonwealth of Israel, and strangers from the covenants of promise, having no hope, and without God in the world," Eph. 2:12, 19. The new order is: "Compel them to come in!" and we need not soften the verb to mean "constrain" (R. V.)

Yes, this is the text for the persecutor and the inquisitor who would compel with brute force and claim that he is doing this by order of Jesus. We answer at once that Jesus has in mind the compulsion of grace, its spiritual drawing power, and may point to any and all of the strong gospel commands even as Paul said: God "now commandeth all men everywhere to repent." But this order to compel appears only here in the parable and has its appropriate place only here; for those outside of the city, who are roaming around far from it, need especial assurance and urging so that they may believe that this invitation really and truly includes also them. Something like that was needed, we may say, already for the poor, etc., in the city although, being in the city, they could know about this feast that was to be prepared in the fulness of time. The Gentiles could not know, it was all new to them. Thus "compel" does not mean to overcome hostile resistance but to remove the fear that so gracious and wonderful a feast could not be intended for them.

"In order that my house may be filled" means that it will indeed be filled — no place shall be left vacant, and no one shall come and find no place for him. It does not mean that God takes miserable wretches and outcasts because he cannot get the grand people, the aristocracy; read I Cor. 1:26-29. This purpose of God that his house must be filled is uttered here because Jesus is speaking to lawyers and Pharisees who reject the invitation and refuse to take their places at the banquet; they are to understand that despite their outrageous absence every place shall be full, and nobody will even notice that they are not there.

The effort is made to confine the whole parable to only two parts, both of which treat only of the Jews, by combining v. 21-23. The effort to exclude the Gentiles from the parable appears arbitrary, for it skims over v. 22, 23 and says practically nothing that could be considered an interpretation so that one feels that Jesus should have omitted these two verses.

24) For I say to you, That not one of those men that had been invited shall taste my dinner.

Some interpreters contend that this final word is not a part of the parable but is an addition that presents its cardinal point. It does do the latter, but the imagery of the parable is continued without a break. According to this view ὑμῖν would refer to the lawyers and Pharisees present. And this is the real reason for this view. For if the house-lord is still speaking, whom does he address with ὑμῖν? It will not do to say the "slave," for ὑμῖν is plural. Some think that this pronoun refers to all the guests at table, others think of his numerous household, for a host such as this certainly had many servants about him. It is hard to decide because the parable itself offers no hint.

Ἄνδρες is more in keeping with the parable than ἄνθρωποι would be, "men," not "human beings" in general. After a verb of tasting we have the genitive (R. 473), and not to taste the dinner means not to partake of it. Luther brings out the sense of this main point: "They who are most certain and want to taste the supper. But why, dear Lord, seeing they have done nothing wicked? Why, this is the cause, that they refused faith." Indeed, unbelief is back of every refusal of the gospel invitation. Therefore they are called "those men that have been invited" — yes, "those," now speaking of them as being far, far away.

25) Now great multitudes were going along with him; and having turned, he said to them: If one comes to me and does not hate his own father and mother and wife and children and brothers and sisters and even also his own life he cannot be my disciple. Whoever does not bear his own cross and come after me cannot be my disciple.

Luke records no more than is necessary for the purpose of the discourse that follows. Jesus is journeying slowly on toward Jerusalem, he is far down in Perea (v. 22). The great crowds that were following

Luke 14:26

him may have consisted in part of pilgrims who were also traveling slowly to Jerusalem for the coming Passover. Judging from what Jesus tells them, some must have wanted to become his disciples. The imperfect pictures the great crowds as moving along with Jesus; he turns about, a general halt ensues, and he speaks as follows.

26) The condition is one of reality, i. e., Jesus thinks and speaks of somebody who really wants to be a disciple of his. "Comes to me" means: with the desire to attach himself to me as disciples attach themselves to a master or rabbi. If such a man does not "hate" his own father and all other relatives, plus even his own life, Jesus tells him right out that he is not able to be his disciple.

Much ingenuity has been expended on the verb "hate," to little or no effect. Instead of leaving μισεῖν in its true sense "to hate," it is generally reduced, even "watered down till the point is gone." All we need to remember is that this hating is the same as that which was exercised by God: "Thou hatest all workers of iniquity," Ps. 5:5; 45:7; Heb. 1:9; the same hate that is voiced by the saints as in Ps. 101:3 and in other passages. The startling thing lies, not in the verb "to hate," but in the objects to be hated, one's own father, etc., with the still more startling climax: and even also (ἔτι τε καί) his own life, ψυχή, that which animates the body and is thus inclined to become ψυχικός, "carnal." This is nothing but a repetition of 12:49-53, father against son, etc. Despite all of this hate in God his love ἀγάπη remains, and the two are entirely compatible (see 6:27), each even to the highest degree of intensity.

So the hate required for discipleship goes together with our love (ἀγάπη) to our parents, etc., that love which understands any evil in them and would, with the help of Jesus, remove it. Jesus is speaking of the father who is not a disciple, or, if he be a disciple, would in his blindness hinder his son in his discipleship.

Even our natural affection for all our relatives and for our own life is left untouched by this hating, for our very φιλία toward them will keep us from yielding to any desire of theirs which is in conflict with our discipleship.

It is thus that we are to do this hating, μισεῖν, which is not to be reduced and softened in any way but is to be understood in the fullest sense of the word even as it is required by ἀγαπᾶν and even by φιλεῖν. For this we have Jesus' own example in Matt. 12:48-50. When Jesus says: "is not able to be my disciple," we should remember that a μαθητής (from μανθάνω) is one who has learned and imbibed, at least to a degree, and is endeavoring to learn to the fullest degree through the teaching and the example of Jesus the latter's very own spirit so that as a disciple he may be like his teacher, Matt. 10:25; Luke 6:40. When this is noted, it is at once apparent that Jesus asks only that any and every disciple of his must be copying him as his Master in this hating. Jesus naturally had to state this requirement of true discipleship many times; a few of them are on record: Matt. 10:37; 19:29; Luke 18:29.

27) This requirement, too, is repeated as it is in 9:23; Matt. 16:24; Mark 8:34 (II Tim. 3:12). The form is again negative and shows who cannot be regarded as a "disciple" in the sense just indicated. Coming "after me" is only a variant of the preceding expression coming "to me." But in coming to him we turn from others, and in coming after him we share what is his. And that is the cross. Each disciple will have to bear "his own cross," only in this way can he "come after Jesus" and be his disciple, truly copy Jesus as his Master. On the word "cross" see in full 9:23. Since there is no escape from some suffering for Christ's and the gospel's sake, it is impossible for anyone to be a true disciple without carrying this cross, whatever it be that is allotted to him.

28-30) **For who of you, wanting to build a tower, does not first, after sitting down, calculate the cost, whether he has it for the completion lest perhaps, when he has laid a foundation and is not able to finish, all who behold begin to make fun of him, saying, This man began to build and was not able to finish!**

Two illustrations elucidate (γάρ) the point of the two preceding negative statements that discipleship demands much from which the natural man is bound to shrink, a certain hate of what the natural man counts most dear, and a certain love for what the natural man always hates (the cross in its true sense). So the two illustrations are properly negative: ἵνα μήποτε, "lest perhaps," and εἰ δὲ μήγε, "but if not." The object of the entire presentation is, however, not merely a warning against a hasty decision to become a disciple. These negatives involve a positive: not with a hasty but with a deliberative and thoroughly considered decision resolve to become a disciple.

Discipleship is no small thing. Jesus magnifies it when he describes it as undertaking to build no less than a grand tower — not merely an ordinary house or shed. He magnifies it again when he describes it as a great war campaign, fighting a king with an army that is twice the size of our own. The psychology involved is altogether true: an appeal to do great things. To build a Christian-like life is like erecting a mighty tower (positive), also like conquering an enemy who is twice our strength (negative). Such things certainly cannot be done by blindly, inconsiderately rushing in. As to the tower, any sensible man would first calmly sit down and calculate the cost lest he become a joke to everybody, unable to lay more than a foundation, a lasting monument of his folly. In ἐκτελέσαι the preposition signifies to carry "out" to the very end; and ἐμπαίζειν means to have fun as with a child (παῖς).

The great point to be noted is that Jesus does not say that this man should not build the tower. That is the usual interpretation, but it is not even by implication contained in Jesus' words. Jesus wants us to become disciples, the man ought to build the grand tower. But no man can do this by his own natural ability; to attempt it thus is utter folly. He could never get beyond the foundation, mere outward profession of faith, mere outward attachment to Jesus. Where, then, is the money to come from to build this tower? Grace furnishes us all that discipleship needs, grace alone.

31, 32) Or what king, going to clash with another king in war, will not, after sitting down, deliberate whether he is able with ten thousand to meet him who is coming with twenty thousand against him? And if not, while he is still far off, by sending an embassy, he inquires for the terms of peace.

The middle βουλεύσεται means to deliberate with himself; εἰ δὲ μήγε is a fixed phrase which is always used without a verb: "and if not," "otherwise"; ἐρωτᾶ is dignified, as one king dealing with another; συμβαλεῖν, "to throw together" as armies are thrown in battle, the aorist to designate the one decisive clash. The added point of this second illustration is the negative one of overcoming an enemy, which is placed beside the positive idea of erecting a tower. Discipleship builds up something grand in us and strikes down something hostile outside of us. It builds faith and a new life — a glorious tower, indeed; and it overcomes the devil and all his assaults—a glorious victory, indeed.

Again Jesus does not say: "Go, inquire for the things toward peace (τὰ πρὸς εἰρήνην)" with the idea of accepting the terms that are imposed by the mighty enemy in abject and permanent surrender. The king would have to do that if he depended on his own unaided strength; every man would have to do that if he depended on himself alone in fighting the devil and trying to be a disciple. The king would have ignominy either way, whether he surrendered or whether he fought in defeat. We should not insert the thought that this king should not in the first place have allowed things to come to the point of war. This war is inevitable the moment one decides to be a disciple; it is the devil that will not have such a decision. Only by never attempting such a decision, by quietly remaining under Satan, can we escape war with him.

Jesus wants disciples, he wants this war, and he therefore warns us not to enter it with our inadequate strength, for we should then be doomed. That means that we take the armor of grace (Eph. 6:10-17) and so, like Paul, fight the good fight of faith.

33) The fact that this is the burden of these illustrations comes to full view in the application that is now marked as such by both οὕτως and οὖν, the one drawing the point of comparison, the other indicating a deduction. Both are needed for a correct understanding. Since everything that precedes is negative, this deduction is properly so also. **Thus, therefore, everyone of you who does not renounce all his own possessions cannot be my disciple.**

It would be a mistake to think that Jesus adds renunciation of earthly wealth and property. If that were meant, this dictum would have to precede v. 26. Here, after the illustrations, it would be worse than an anticlimax. Nor is this a mere repetition, "all his own possessions" merely summing up those mentioned in v. 26; this view overlooks the intervening illustrations and "thus, therefore." Nor should this statement be divided into two sentences by making: "thus, therefore, everyone of you!" a sentence by itself. How can anyone think that Jesus is telling these people: "Do not build the tower!" "Do not enter this war!" i. e., "Do not try even to become my disciples!" No; the present statement links right into the two illustrations which, of course, illustrate v. 26, 27. And Jesus now tells his hearers to renounce everything, literally everything they have in and of themselves, because it will all, however much of it there may be, never get beyond the foundation of a tower, beyond 10,000 against 20,000 troops. They must get what will take them through, clean through from start to finish in the case of the tower; clean through from the first clash to a complete victory in the war. When they come to Jesus absolutely empty of anything in and of themselves, then they can truly be his disciples; then he can fill them with his possessions, and with them the tower can and will be built, the battle can and will be won.

This is not synergism as if to the funds in hand Jesus would add enough to build the tower and to the 10,000 soldiers add enough re-enforcements to make an army that is greater than 20,000. He supplies all the funds, the entire army: "Renounce all your own possessions!" Discipleship and salvation are so great things that nothing of our own can avail in securing them. The two illustrations should not be extended beyond the *tertium* they are intended to illustrate: the vanity of all that lies in and of ourselves. And the deduction is: "Abandon all that is your own!"

34, 35) So the last point is reached. **Excellent, therefore, the salt! But if even the salt become insipid, with what shall it be seasoned? Neither for land nor manure is it fit; out they throw it. He who has ears for hearing, let him be hearing!**

The figure of the salt that loses its saltiness was used repeatedly by Jesus (Matt. 5:13; Mark 9:50), and each time in a distinctive way. Much has been said about the use of "salt" in Jewish sacrifices, Lev. 2:13; Ezek. 43:24; Mark 9:49; in binding covenants, Num. 18:19; II Chron. 13:5; in Elisha's purifying the water of Jericho, II Kings 2:21; about a pinch of salt being placed in the child's mouth at baptism in the old church; about the Arab considering him inviolate with whom he had eaten salt. In any figurative use of salt the *tertium comparationis* must be that which was used by Jesus; it is the quality of checking corruption, and we should not add the other of rendering food palatable.

When Jesus uses ἐάν he speaks of salt at times becoming saltless, μωρανθῇ, becoming μωρόν or tasteless, insipid, ἄναλον in Mark 9:50, unsalty. Cases are cited to show that in olden times when natural salt was procured in an impure state and mixed with other chemicals it might actually lose its power and become unsalty. This proof is deemed necessary on the assumption that Jesus would not draw a figure from what does not actually occur in nature. But the assumption is unwarranted—Jesus does use such figures. Who ever lights a lamp and clamps a peck measure over it? Who ever goes out to gather figs from thistles? What father would ever send his son as did the one mentioned in Matt. 21:37 does? Where is the lord who would reward his slaves as does the one mentioned in the parable of the Talents and in that of the Pounds?

These impossible figures bring out most strikingly the astounding realities that Jesus intends to picture. The use that Jesus makes of figures is beyond the mastery of "the good writers." The very idea of salt losing its saltiness! But that is exactly what happens in the reality which Jesus portrays. The fact that Jesus is using as a figure something that is impossible in nature is shown by the question: "With what shall it be seasoned?" i. e., made salty again. "There is no salt of salt," Jansen. Once the saltness is gone out of salt, nothing can restore the saltness to that salt again. Both ideas are beyond nature—salt losing its saltness and having it restored. Yet Jesus speaks of both as if men had found the former and had tried the latter.

With οὖν Jesus connects the new, strongly figurative statement as a further deduction from the foregoing. Beyond question, "excellent is salt." The entire connection from v. 26 onward shows that by salt Jesus means "being my disciple" (μου εἶναι μαθητής, three times). To be rid of all false loves (v. 26), heroically to bear the cross (v. 27), actually to build the tower and to triumph over the foes, and doing this by renouncing all the things of self as being utterly useless, yes, this is καλόν, spiritually excellent to a high degree.

But what if this excellent salt should turn μωρόν, insipid? By using the condition of expectancy (ἐάν with the subjunctive) Jesus says that such cases may be expected. One may return to the old love, refuse to bear the cross, again trust in his old possessions. It would, of course, be just as unnatural as salt losing its saltness. Salt is better than some disciples; it ever stays salty, but some disciples become renegades. And they are then hopeless (Heb. 10:26, 27); saltless salt — "with what shall it be seasoned" so as to restore its saltness? It is good for nothing. After its chemical action has been dissipated, it would be useless for the cultivated land or for the manure pile, the lowest possible use for salt. "Out they throw it" into the street where men tread it under their feet (Matt. 5:13), and this pictures judgment. The renegade disciple is worse and meets a worse fate than the pagan.

The call to use one's ears was used frequently by Jesus. His immortal figures naturally stick to the mind. Let their meaning sink in. Let them keep sounding in your ears, not only while you hear them, but also ever after. That is why God put ears on sinners.

CHAPTER XV

This chapter and the next one are Luke's two immortal parable chapters which are filled (with the exception of one brief section) with parables, none of which have found a place in the other Gospels, the entire group being arranged in an obviously natural order, in the order in which Jesus spoke them.

1) **Now there kept drawing near to him all the publicans and the open sinners to hear him. And there were murmuring both the Pharisees and the scribes, saying, This fellow keeps receiving open sinners and eating with them!**

Luke again offers only enough information to indicate how Jesus was prompted to utter the following parables. The time, the place, and the other circumstances are immaterial. Once before, in 5:30, the same class of men raised the same objection. See 3:12 on the publicans; the ἁμαρτωλοί were classed with them, being notorious sinners of various kinds in a society that was very different from ours, in which the Pharisaic, ostentatious type of holiness dominated the public and by contrast made men like these tax collectors, etc., practically outcasts.

One of the marked features of Jesus' ministry was the attraction of these outcasts to him. The Pharisees and the scribes only scorned and damned them, but the holy Jesus had a way of salvation open for them, one that, indeed, condemned their sins in no uncertain terms but at the same time opened the divine way of remission for all sins. So they drew near to him in numbers (πάντες) and did this continuously at the present time as the periphrastic imperfect states. They kept drinking in his words eagerly, therefore we have the durative present infinitive.

2) As was done in v. 1, the verb is again placed forward for the sake of emphasis, it is again an imperfect to indicate duration (it is not merely ingressive). The two actions, drawing near and murmuring back and forth (διά in the verb), are parallel. As the one class drew near, so the other stood off and found fault. These latter were the Pharisees and the scribes, see 5:17; many were both Pharisees and scribes although the articles distinguish them as being two groups just as the two articles do in v. 1, but τε . . . καί combine them more closely than a mere καί would (B.-D. 444, 2).

These men were scandalized because Jesus did not treat these disreputables as they did. In their holiness they scrupulously kept their skirts clean of any and all open sinners and thus clashed with Jesus on this point. They thus pointed also to Jesus in holy scorn by derisively using οὗτος, "this fellow," and thus began the infamous practice of the Jews of never uttering the name "Jesus" if they could help it; they abutted this with ἁμαρτωλούς: "this fellow — open sinners," etc. — just think! The one word is enough to include also the publicans. The two verbs, both durative presents to indicate customary action, are arranged in the order of a climax — terrible to be receiving such people, unspeakably terrible to eat with them. We learn again incidentally (as we did in 5:30) that Jesus would occasionally dine with one or another of the open sinners just as we have seen him dining with some Pharisees (11:37; 14:1).

3) In 5:30 Jesus met this complaint by pointing to himself as being the physician who necessarily treats sick people. In a somewhat similar way he answers with a pair of parables: The Savior finds the lost, and the church does likewise. **But he spoke to them this parable, saying: What man of you, having a hundred sheep and having lost one of them, does not leave behind the ninety-nine in the wilderness and go on after the lost till he finds it? And**

having found, he puts it on his shoulders, rejoicing, and having come to his house, he calls together the friends and the neighbors, saying to them, Rejoice with me, because I found my sheep, the lost one! I tell you that thus joy will be in the heaven over one open sinner repenting more than over ninety-nine righteous, such as do not have need of repentance.

"This parable," as Luke states, extends to v. 10; Jesus made the whole of it one parable. The fact that the two parts begin with questions does not prevent the whole from being a parable in the fullest sense of the word. Its appeal has always been tremendous; witness the many paintings of the Shepherd bearing home his sheep or being out seeking to find it.

The parable is simplicity itself. Jesus tells the Pharisees and the scribes that they do the same thing that he is doing, they in the case of only a lost sheep, he in the case of a lost soul. The argument is thus *ad hominem* but as justifying a right deed by one that is equally right in the case of the objector. The argument is at the same time from the less to the greater, from a sheep to a man. If a Pharisee would do for a lost sheep what is sketched here, shall Jesus not do at least the equal for a lost human being?

But the climax of the parable is reached in the joy over the finding of the lost. How natural and self-evident that would be! Jesus places this joy "in the heaven" and "before the angels of God" over against the murmuring of the Pharisees and the scribes. They look sour, in heaven the very angels sing with delight. In so masterly a way is this done that the very parable becomes a seeking and reaching out by the Shepherd Jesus after these Pharisaic lost sheep so that their joy at being found may produce still more joy in heaven among the angels. Thus through the entire parable there run in duplicate: 1) being lost, 2) the great search, 3) the happy finding, 4) the abounding joy.

This parable is sometimes treated superficially. But, on the other hand, beginning with the ancients, those who gave it full attention often went entirely too far and overloaded every statement and even every word with their extravagant fancies. Its pure, chaste simplicity was buried by astounding importations. It was made to reach from eternity to eternity; in addition to the Jews all the Gentiles were brought in; the whole Passion of Jesus was added plus his ascension to heaven; in heaven itself God, the angels, and the saints were treated; and still other things were added—all of which Jesus is to have had in mind, if not for the Pharisees and the scribes, then at least for his disciples and for us. Homiletical works of even more recent times still offer material of this kind to preachers and think that the name of Jesus is signed to it all.

This parable does not stand alone. It presents the first chapter, and three more are to follow. Here there is shown what is done for the sinner; the parable of the Prodigal Son adds the inner change and the new status of the sinner, conversion, justification, sonship; the parable of the Unjust Steward the changed sinner's new obedience; and the parable of the Rich Man and Lazarus the final chapter, the sinner's transfer to heaven. Each parable becomes clearer when it is viewed in connection with the others. It will then be seen that each treats one central thought, and that we should not introduce more.

4) "What man of you?" by addressing a direct question to each and any one of the murmuring Pharisees and scribes, a simple question about themselves and what each of them would unquestionably do under the circumstances described Jesus not only grips their attention but also appeals to whatever good sense they have left and asks them to use it in giving their own answer. Jesus often uses questions in this way. They disarm completely because they turn the whole matter

Luke 15:4

over to the opponent and leave it entirely to him as to what answer he will give.

They, however, disarm in another way, namely by generalizing the point at issue and thus clarifying the entire matter. If Jesus had asked specifically about his treatment of publicans and sinners, these Pharisees and these scribes, blinded by their self-righteous pride, would only have uttered their secret grumbling to his face. The question about a sheep is exactly the same question, but the picture of the sheep gets these men away from their pride and from any false answer it would suggest and gently leads them to the true motive, that of prizing a sheep of theirs and not wanting to let it be lost. Prompted by that right motive, the right answer is bound to be given—Jesus has no fear about it, he freely, smilingly asks: "Which one of you," etc.? — I care not who of you states the answer. Figures are ordinarily used for literary embellishment. Jesus always uses them for something that is far higher, here for bringing the truth about his work to view and for letting the Pharisees and the scribes correct their own pride and folly. Figures are powerful engines in Jesus' hands.

Now it is simply a fact that every one of these men, even if he had as many as a hundred sheep, and only one of them got lost by straying away, would never think that the one does not matter, seeing he still has as many as ninety-nine, or that the exertion of seeking and finding that one lost sheep, seeing it is only one, would be too much to undertake, considering also that despite all effort it might even after all not be found. Nothing of the kind! Invariably, as the present tenses state, in every case like that the man leaves his ninety-nine behind in the wilderness and goes after the lost till he finds it.

To be sure, it's all about sheep which were so common and numerous in the entire country, and that enables even men like these blind Pharisees and scribes to assent to the right thing. But that means that Jesus has already with the first sentence won the case against these objectors to his dealing with sinners. He turns a finger, and down they go under their own verdict. That, too, is the way with Jesus, and yet some men cannot see that it displays a wisdom that is more than human. Οὐ is the interrogative word that expects an affirmative answer. Even if these men do not say "yes," their thoughts cannot help but do so. That is enough, for the rest follows automatically and is affirmed by that first "yes"; hence the interrogative form is now dropped.

A few things should be noted. In this parable it is one out of a hundred, the value being in proportion; in the next it is one out of ten, the value rising in proportion; finally it is one out of two, the value rising to the limit. There is a tendency among interpreters to make things complex; the mastery of the parables is their simplicity. Jesus says "which man of you?" though those who are addressed were Pharisees and scribes and did not tend sheep. So the question is hypothetical: if anyone of them had a hundred sheep. That, too, makes it easier to give the correct answer as all such theoretical questions are readily answered if they are simple as this one is.

Wisely Jesus does not ask: "If *I* had so many sheep," etc. Even the word "shepherd" is not put into the parable; it is only we who use it when we interpret the parable of Jesus. For Jesus is, indeed, doing the very thing of which he speaks here, doing it by receiving sinners and eating with them. The silent "yes" of the Pharisees and the scribes regarding the lost sheep approves his course, unwittingly, indeed, but for that very reason honestly. So all skeptics, who object to God's and Christ's ways, must approve them in spite of themselves, for when they are put into clear light they stand out as being right, noble, blessed. The perfect neuter participle τὸ ἀπολωλός, "has been lost," implies "is still lost."

It is pointless to ask about the leaving of the ninety-nine in the wilderness. The ἡ ἔρημος (χώρα) was open, uninhabited country that was suitable for grazing sheep. The fact that the ninety-nine were left behind in entire safety is so obvious that Jesus did not clutter up his parable by inserting an explanation. Those that have been attempted are uncalled for. The one sheep became lost by straying from the flock. This is the least of it, it somehow got away from the eyes and the care and the control of its owner — that is the real trouble. So the sinner strays from Jesus and is then lost.

"He goes till he finds it" is sometimes exaggerated; goes a great distance over rocks and ravines, through brambles and thorns, weary and spent — all this in order to bring in the Passion and the death of Jesus. There is nothing of this in the parable. Jesus is not depicting his Passion to the Pharisees and the scribes; to do that would require other language. His receiving and eating with publicans and open sinners is what he describes by means of which he seeks to bring them to repentance by the law and the gospel (v. 7).

5) "Having found" purposely restricts the parable to this one lost sheep which is found after the search. "Till he finds it" and "having found" are purposely adjoined and repeat this important verb; the same thing is done in the second half of the parable. The two expressions do not read as though the finding took so exceedingly long. Who, too, would say that Jesus is not an expert at this work? The emphasis is on χαίρων, "he places it on his shoulders *rejoicing*." The sheep would naturally be carried on the shoulders, the idea being that it was exhausted when found. Some would change αὐτοῦ into ἑαυτοῦ, "his" into "his own shoulders," and make a point of this carrying. As far as Jesus is concerned, humanly speaking, the sinner is heavier when he lies on Jesus' heart before he is found

than when he lies on his shoulders after being found. But the subject, let us not forget, is still some one of the Pharisees and the scribes. He, too, on having his lost sheep safely on his shoulders, would be "rejoicing."

6) That this participle is the real point comes out in full in the fact of this man's calling together his friends and neighbors and bidding them to rejoice with him (second aorist passive) because he found his sheep, the lost one (the modifier being added by a second article and thus being made emphatic, R. 776). This brings out the theme of the parable: *Joy over Finding the Lost*. It stands out squarely in contrast with this murmuring against even seeking the lost. The fact that Jesus is here drawing a picture of himself goes without saying. The view that God is the owner of the sheep will find few who accept it.

This is another instance in the parables in which the imagery is strained because it is too weak to picture the reality. A man would rejoice upon recovering his lost sheep, be glad that his search was successful, but he would hardly summon friends and neighbors and make such a great event of it, and expect that they, too, would regard it as being great by helping to make a celebration. Read what is said on 14:34 about saltless salt. It is the reality that compels the imagery to be carried beyond what is ordinarily done. The divine is shining out through the human, and the human takes on a new coloring. Jesus is noted also for the way in which he handled his earthly material. It is transmuted into gold under his hands.

Who is meant by "the friends and the neighbors," and what is the difference between the two? And what is imaged by this man's house or home? If we see that the sinner who is found is found forever, found by being taken to heaven at death, i. e., that finding takes in the whole work of Jesus upon the sinner, we have our two answers: "in the heaven" (house), v. 7; "before the angels of God" (friends and neighbors in one),

v. 10. Then, too, we shall not talk about this man's leaving the ninety-nine in the wilderness while he takes the one sheep to his house. That is raising difficulties where none exist.

7) The parable is complete, and Jesus now states the reality which it illustrates and justifies. The λέγω ὑμῖν is therefore no longer a part of the parable as is λέγω γὰρ ὑμῖν in 14:24. With the voice of authority, "I tell you," Jesus declares that in the same way (οὕτως) as just pictured "joy shall be in the heaven over one open sinner repenting." Be he ever so great a sinner, whether in God's eyes only or also in men's, his repenting causes joy in the very heavens. The aorist participle would hardly do, for it might mean just coming to repentance (ingressive); the aorist is used to express several types of punctiliar action. This present participle is durative and expresses the fact that repentance goes on and on. We indeed enter heaven repenting, in the repentant state, and in none other. Luther was right when in the first of his famous ninety-five theses he declared that our entire life must be a continuous repentance. Again he said that our sins are forgiven richly and daily—because of this constant repentance. Μετανοεῖν is discussed in 3:3. The seeking and the finding of Jesus, his receiving and eating with sinners, his great Shepherd work as depicted, is his bringing poor sinners to permanent repentance.

Jesus here says "shall be joy" but "comes to be" in v. 10. Both are true. Heaven knows about us sinners here, for is not Jesus there? Are the angels not sent forth to minister unto those who shall be heirs of salvation? All the mighty works of men cause no jubilation in heaven, but one miserable sinner's repentant state does. But what if a repentant sinner again falls away? Will the joy over his temporary repentance not be kind of a mistake? Celebrating before the game is finished has often turned to grief. Dismiss the question — since sinners exist, heaven never made a single mistake.

Thus far all is simple. But how can Jesus add: "more than over ninety-nine righteous, such as (οἴτινες, causal: because they are such as) do not have need of repentance"? The key is given in ἤ, "more than" (R. 661: B.-D. 245, 3), with its plain implication that there will be joy in heaven also over the ninety-nine righteous as well as over the sinner. And the man with the hundred sheep certainly has two joys, one over the many that did not stray away, over that fact as it is vividly brought home to him by the straying sheep; and then joy over the one sheep that has been recovered after having strayed.

This corrects those explanations which refer the ninety-nine only to the legally righteous, meaning the scribes and the Pharisees; also those which consider ἤ exclusive: only over the one and not at all over the ninety-nine. These ninety-nine are thought to need no repentance in their own estimation, they are like the self-righteous Pharisees who justify themselves (16:15). But the phrase "in their own estimation" is not in the text, nor is it implied. It is barred out by the fact that there is joy in heaven over the ninety-nine who cannot therefore be self-righteous Pharisees. The view that Jesus speaks as he does of "righteous who do not need repentance" because he wants to raise the question in the minds of the Pharisees whether they are truly righteous before heaven, is misdirected because, if Jesus had meant them, his words would do the very opposite, namely make them think themselves truly righteous, men who actually did not need repentance. Jesus, indeed, wanted to jar these Pharisees in regard to their righteousness before God; and he chose the right way, namely by speaking of men who are actually righteous before God.

Since there is joy over the many as well as over the one, it becomes plain why the one needs repentance and the others do not need it—they already have it! The one needs it because he is "an open sinner"; the many have it because they are truly "righteous." That alone is why there will be joy over both.

Another point is certain: that repentance is used in the identical sense in the case of both and not in two different or modified senses. Now, too, it is easy to see why the joy over the one is greater than that over the many. There is a constant, steady joy over the many who are righteous and have this long while gone on in repentance; but when this sinner, who has lived a long time without repentance, through Christ now achieves it and joins the ranks of the righteous, he causes a sudden shout of joy in heaven, a great wave of joy such as does not resound for all who are already in the blessed state. Luther understands this rightly when he speaks of the great and sudden joy of a mother to find her sick child restored, a joy that is greater than that for all her other children who are still sound and well. We may add that the very restoration of the one brings to her mind the thought of the others and the joy that they are still well.

Δίκαιος here, as always, is used in the forensic sense, God declaring one righteous; the wrong view, too, is forensic, but according to this view the person either declares himself righteous or trusts in himself that God has declared him so (18:9); C.-K. 309 holds the latter regarding the righteous in this passage. Appeals to the older brother in the next parable as an interpretation of the righteous mentioned in this parable are beside the mark; the father had no joy in that son at all — that son, too, was lost in a different way than the other was, but just as badly lost, and the father went out to find him too, if possible.

8) **Or what woman having ten drachmas, if she shall lose one drachma, does not light a lamp and sweep the house and seek carefully till she finds it? And having found, she calls together the women friends and neighbors, saying, Rejoice with me because I found the drachma which I lost! Thus, I tell**

you, there is joy before the angels of God over one open sinner repenting.

The ἤ at the beginning marks this as being a continuation. So does the question, which is a parallel to the one asked in v. 4, which again has the interrogative word (οὐχί) that expects an affirmative answer. Any normal woman would, of course, do what is asked by Jesus. "What woman" is parallel to "what man" (v. 4) and yet marks a difference. Some decline to interpret "woman," which is an easy way of disposing of her; some see in her the Holy Spirit, which is against all Scripture analogy which never speaks of the Spirit as being a woman. If the Hebrew feminine *ruach* be pointed to, what about the Greek Πνεῦμα which is neuter? The gender of words is often merely grammatical. By this "woman" Jesus pictures the church, which is filled with the same spirit as her Lord, seeking the lost and rejoicing over the found.

We now have drachmas, ten, one of which is lost. The Greek drachma = the Roman denarius = about 16c = about a day's wage for common labor. But whereas the man does not lose the sheep, the woman is said to lose the drachma. A common interpretation is that it is not the Lord's fault but the sinner's own fault when he is lost; but that it is to a degree also the fault of the church when she loses a sinner. We question the validity of this interpretation. The sheep is animate and is therefore represented as getting lost; the coin is inanimate, hence if it is to be lost, somebody must be said to lose it. More than this, the sheep and the drachma picture one and the same sinner, and every lost sinner is lost through a fault of his own. Jesus is speaking of his true church that is moved by his own spirit, and that church is guilty of no fault that loses sinners.

Much has been made of the drachma as compared with the sheep. We find little beyond the changed proportion, one out of ten instead of one out of a hundred.

This advance, which is climaxed in the next parable with one out of two, progressively pictures the value that Christ and his church (and the Father) set upon the lost sinner. We fail to see that the motive which prompts the seeking is different in the three illustrations. Any progression in the presentation of the motive is blocked by the figure of the inanimate coin which is placed between the living sheep and the living son. This, too, disposes of all that is made of the image that is stamped upon the drachma. Jesus does not refer to the image. The drachma bore a pagan image, a crowned head of a pagan emperor, and on the other side this emperor seated and holding his insignia. Does that signify anything of the general divine image that is left in the sinner? Why, then, did Jesus, who is here speaking to Jews (v. 1), not name the Jewish half-shekel or shekel, both of which bore sacred images? So we drop that interpretation.

The church, like her Lord, does her utmost to find the lost. Both seek until they find. As far as the parable goes, both do this in the same way. There is but one way for both: to go after the sinner with the law and the gospel. It is thought that this is made specific in the case of the church, the lamp being the gospel and the sweeping broom the law, these being added to the Passion of Jesus which is found in the first part of the parable. We have dealt with the Passion and have failed to find it in the parable. Since the law and the gospel are in any case the means for recovering the sinner, be he pictured as a sheep or as a drachma, it really makes little difference how we interpret the lamp and the broom. Yet the law as well as the gospel is a lamp, for by the law is the knowledge of sin, and that rather mars the view: lamp = gospel; broom = law. Here, too, the parable restricts itself to the lost sinner who is found, and we abide by that and say nothing about sinners who are not found. The next parables deal with them; moreover, an inanimate coin is hardly an image that is suitable for this part of the story about sinners.

9) On finding the coin the woman does exactly what the man does on finding the sheep, and all that is said regarding v. 6 applies also here. We of course have the propriety that the woman calls her women friends and neighbors, and no one makes anything more of this difference in sex. "Which I did lose" only repeats this point from v. 8 and in the sense indicated.

10) In stating the application of this part of the parable Jesus repeats, abbreviates, and interprets. The repetition is obvious, and, like every such repetition, emphasizes strongly: "Thus, I tell you, there is joy!" "Is" or "occurs" (γίνεται) and its present tense add to "shall be," the future. "Shall be" at once upon the sinner's repenting and thus "is" when he repents. We may say either. "Before the angels of God" interprets "in the heaven." The interpretation usually adds also the saints in heaven. Add them; but the greatness of this joy lies in the fact that the heavenly angelic host jubilates, and the greater is named as including the less. "Over one sinner repenting" is repeated unchanged, for this is the vital point and needs emphasis. The addition found in v. 7 is omitted here, one statement of this point being enough.

This double parable, which is addressed to the Pharisees and the scribes, brought us the glaring difference between them and the angels in heaven: they murmured at the very thing that made the angels rejoice. That should have given them pause to search their hearts, where something must have been wrong. Repentance rings out in this parable; it is that which causes this astounding joy. That, too, reached at the hearts of these men. Were heaven and its angels rejoicing over them? Were they furnishing heaven the repentance that would cause such joy? Did their lack of joy over sinners who were drawn to Jesus hang together with a lack of joy over themselves in heaven?

From v. 1 it appears that the publicans and the open sinners also heard this parable and the following. From it they would have to gather that drawing near to Jesus and even dining with him were not enough, that only true repentance was sufficient. Also, that whatever these Pharisees said about them and their repenting at the call of Jesus, the angels of God and their joy were the one essential to be concerned about. Thus in this very parable Jesus was using law and gospel and seeking to save both the Pharisee and the open sinner.

11) Moreover, he said: A man had two sons. And the younger of them said to his father, Father, give me the part of the property that is falling to me. And he divided the living between them.

See the introductory remarks in v. 3. "Moreover, he said" is inserted in order to separate the parables, and δέ means that Jesus added another that is somewhat different. This is the crown of all parables, an *evangelium in evangelio*, which has no equal in all literature. The sheep and the drachma are not human, the two sons are; more intense and dramatic is the father in his relation to his sons than are the man and the woman to the sheep and the coin. The first parable brings out the truth *that* sinners are brought to the kingdom; we now see *how* they enter. We first see *the Lord and the church* going out to seek and to save; we now scan *the sinner* more closely and see the change that is wrought in him as he is saved. Doctrinally this parable presents *conversion and justification*, and does this in a form that has deep appeal. The emotions depicted in the parable are deep and strong. So brief the parable, but so stirring in every part.

"A man had two sons." This simplicity is the soul of beauty. The heavenly Father has always been recognized in this picture of the earthly father. The parable is both historical and universal in one. The older son is a picture of work-righteous Pharisees, the younger of the publicans and the open sinners, v. 1, 2. Yet the younger typifies the sinner who turns from God and runs into open worldliness whereas the older son is the type of the self-righteous sinner who is outwardly in the church, inwardly without faith. Both are lost, both must return. One did; did the other? Although it is called the parable of the Prodigal Son, this is really the parable of the Two Lost Sons.

12) The parable as such permits only the younger son to ask for his share of the estate and to leave because the older son was expected to keep the home place and to carry on. Jesus builds his parable on this ancient custom. So the younger son prepares to leave home — what a warning to youth! Inexperience, dislike of restraint, self-will, glamor of independence, all come to mind here. Why do some of the commentators say that there was nothing wrong in this younger son's demand for his portion of the inheritance? The germ of all that followed in his deplorable career was in and behind his demand. His *heart* was no longer with his father. "Father," he says in making his demand; what a different tone and meaning in the same word in v. 21! "Father," he said only to be rid of his father, his father's care, guidance, and control.

In Jewish law the oldest son received two-thirds of the inheritance, the rest was divided among the other children, the third would here go to this one younger son (Deut. 21:17). In the parable the father accedes to the younger son's demand, διεῖλε (second aorist from διαιρέω), he made the division and gave to both their part. Only the fact is stated: this father did so. It is necessary for the parable, that is all. We are not to think that younger sons had a right to do this, older ones either; no children have a right to divide the parental inheritance until after the parent's death. But God divides as is here stated, and so the parable is made to illustrate this reality. God gives without demur, even to the sinner, life, health, faculties of mind and body, earthly wealth, a thousand advantages, and among all these blessings ever some that remind the sinner strongly of the heavenly Father and of the Father's house — "not knowing that the goodness of God leadeth thee to repentance?" Rom. 2:4; Acts 14:17.

13) And after not many days, having gathered everything together, the younger son left home for a far country and there squandered his property by living prodigally.

The slight delay is a fine touch; after the inward separation there comes the outward; but only in his case and not in his brother's. This son turns his back upon his father, ἀπεδήμησεν (absent from his δῆμος), he left home to go elsewhere, away, far away from his people. Thus the sinner quits his Father's house, the church, the communion of saints. Ask sadhearted parents and pastors for the details. What can the "far country" be but the world with all that the word conveys in Scripture as in I John 2:15-17? How its glitter, its pleasure, its promise of great things attract! So the flame ever attracts the moth — only to scorch and to kill it.

Jesus' statement is brief regarding how this son fared. He now squandered all that he had gathered together at home, scattered it as chaff is made to fly in the wind. Two words suffice to say how he did it: ζῶν ἀσώτως, "living prodigally" (the adverb is derived from σῴζω: "unsaving," active; or "unsaved," passive). We need no salacious descriptions of the stage and of writers of fiction to expand the picture; they only gild the corruptions to tempt the unwary. The older brother said, "Who devoured thy living with harlots." The parable describes the limit so as to include also all that is less of this type of life.

14) More must be added. **But he having spent all, there came a strong famine throughout that land, and he began to be in want. And having gone, he attached himself to one of the citizens of that coun-**

try; and he sent him into his fields to pasture swine. And he began to desire to be filled from the carob pods which the swine were eating, and no one would give to him.

This is a parable which pictures the sinner after he has squandered God's gifts,. "he having spent all." Temporal gifts vanish at last. The satisfaction found in the creature without the Creator and the Savior comes to an end. Let us remember that this type of want often comes in the midst of many earthly possessions, namely when the vanity and the emptiness of it all fall like a blight upon the soul.

It is then that the famine sets in, one that that entire country cannot remove because it is so ἰσχυρός, "strong"; κατά with the accusative to express extent, R. 608. The prodigal began to be in want, not only because he had lost his portion, but also because he now had no inner support or stay, nothing spiritual to fall back on, no soul treasure, no comfort for the soul in affliction. When men reach this stage, the devil often reaps his harvest — they commit suicide. After money is gone, pleasures gone, friends gone, they conclude that all is gone and commit the fatal act.

15) Jesus might have introduced the prodigal's return at this point. Thank God, some do return more quickly than others. But many go a step farther, and the parable is to include all of them. What hope is there in this far country? Instead of the plenty in his father's house the prodigal has poverty; instead of the freedom in his father's house he is now in servitude; in place of the honor of a son he now has degradation and shame. In his extremity the prodigal attaches himself to "one of the citizens of that country." So there were "citizens" there, men who were completely adjusted to life apart from God. "With all his guilt the prodigal was not a citizen but a stranger in that far land." Trench. He is not wholly and permanently obdurate. There is a stage beyond which even grace can-

not reach a man any more. It is a significant part of the picture which paints this citizen as an owner of "swine," which were unclean according to the law and an abomination to the Jews.

To such a man the prodigal attached himself, ἐκολλήθη, "glued himself," the passive being used in the sense of the middle, R. 817. The thought is that the citizen did not want him, hence the labor to which he assigned him. This is the association that results from separation from God. Sin makes man a companion of swine in more ways than one. To herd and pasture swine (βόσκειν) is not merely degrading as we should regard it today, to the Jew it represented moral defilement and all the shame that this involved. It crushed pride and cut the conscience with one blow. So the fancy gilding and deception were gone, the galling disgrace, the deadly heartache alone were left. Still a mercy hides behind such bitter experience for the sinner. It is good once for all to end the deception even if the hour be late. It is good really to see and to feel the consequences of sin while repentance is yet possible, for these may bring the sinner to his knees.

16) Now the final drop in the bitter cup — not only feeding swine but feeding himself with swine's food — and lacking even that, the human being thus having sunk to the level of the beast. To this the devil would bring every man whom God intended to be in the divine image. The parable had to take in this utter extreme as already stated. The κεράτια, "little horns," are the little, sickle-like pods of the carob tree, the *Bockshornbaum*, goat's-horn tree, also called *Johannesbrodbaum*, which is still common in Palestine and around the Mediterranean. The gelatinous substance in the pods has a sweetish taste. Used as feed for hogs, these pods contain also small, shiny seed kernels. The pods were eaten by the poor but not as regular food. They here symbolize the empty, unsatisfying food that is offered to the starving souls of men by the world.

What are its shows and shams, its carousals and "good times," its religious lies and fads, its science falsely so-called, but such pods for swine, unfit for the soul?

The imperfect ἐπεθύμει, "he began to desire to be filled" from this hogfeed implied that his desire was not fulfilled, for "no one would give to him," another imperfect to express constant denial. Some texts read γεμίσαι τὴν κοιλίαν αὐτοῦ, "to pack his belly full," but χορτασθῆναι from χόρτος, "fodder," is coarse enough. If you have never reached such degradation, thank God's mercy. The parable goes that far in order to hold out the hope of help to men who are even as low as that.

17) **But having come to himself, he said: How many hired men of my father are abounding in bread while I myself am perishing here with hunger! Having arisen, I will go to my father and will say to him: Father, I did sin against the heaven and in thy sight. No longer am I worthy to be called thy son; make me as one of thy hired men.**

The heart of the parable is stated in this sentence: "He came to himself." He was converted in that instant. "He came to himself" implies that heretofore, in his whole course of sin, he was beside himself, not in his right mind, suffering from a species of insanity. And it is true, neither sense nor reason exists in sin but the very contrary. It was an insane thing for the prodigal thus to leave his father, thus to plunge into riotous living, to go on till he ended amid the swine and envied them their food.

Conversion means to become rational, right-minded, properly balanced again. It is a sound, rational act to turn from sin, its curse and doom, to God, pardon, and salvation. The real turn occurs in the depth of the soul. It comes, not without preparation, yet in an instant as is shown here in the prodigal. Much about it is mysterious, for it is like a spark of new life that has come into a dead heart, a sudden pulsebeat of vitality where all was lifeless and still before. God alone knows just how this is produced. The further description in the parable reveals the means he uses, namely law and gospel.

"How many hired men of my father are abounding in bread while I myself am perishing here with hunger!" Thus God *enlightens* the sinner; he begins to see things as they actually are. This is confession to himself: "I (emphatic in contrast with the hired men) am perishing with hunger." To his own self he admits his folly and the results of that folly. And he thinks back of his father's house with its many hired men and of the happy state of even these hired men, who are so different from himself, who is hired out to one of these citizens. The law and the gospel thus begin to work in the sinner's heart.

18) The limitations of the parable necessitate drawing apart into a kind of progress what is one in the sinner's heart. Jesus separates the elements as he sets them before us pictorially; yet in reality they all go together, there is especially no interval of time between conversion and justification. So we are shown the *contrition* in full: "Father, I did sin!" the second aorist acknowledging the whole of the terrible fact as such (the English would use the perfect "I have sinned"). Even in the resolve to go and to make this confession to his father no excuse, no extenuation are offered, nothing but the full, straight admission of guilt. Although contrition is an inward thing of the heart, its presence is always manifested by an open and sincere confession; when this is absent, we cannot be sure that contrition is present. "Against heaven" states the real essence and guilt of sin, for "heaven" includes God and all that is perfectly holy. "And in thy sight" or "before thee" implies more than that the father, as it were, saw this his son's sins; it involves that the father must adjudge his son guilty because this is his son who has sinned thus. Ps. 51:4.

19) To this full and open confession there is added the humblest kind of plea for pardon. They are laid

out side by side here, but they are found together in the heart: no right contrition without faith, no faith except with contrition. Some would add the words: "No longer am I worthy to be called thy son" to the confession, but in the parable they are to be construed with the plea: "make me as one of thy hired men," and help to characterize this plea in all its humbleness.

This humility gives up every claim of its own righteousness, every hope of being received because of anything good in self, even the past rights of sonship. This humbleness is vital to all true faith and remains in it to the very end, even after the sinner has been pardoned. But the sinner goes to the Father, still calls him "Father," dares to ask him at least to take him back to the lowest place in his house. That is *trust or faith* which is inspired by what he knows of his Father, that knowledge being derived from the gospel. Wonderful is this trust, the heart's confidence that the Father will not turn away because of the great sin. No sinner could achieve such confidence of himself, it is ever kindled only by the true knowledge of his Father, i. e., by the gracious God himself.

20) The inner change was genuine, the resolve was carried out. **And having arisen, he went to his own father. But he being still far off, his father saw him and was filled with compassion and, having run, fell upon his neck and covered him with kisses.**

In the reality of conversion to resolve to arise and to go to the Father is the same as actually doing it. The change called conversion is inward and instantaneous. The parable spreads this out because parables picture the realities. When we interpret them we should never modify the reality for the sake of the imagery but use the reality for the right understanding of the imagery. It is wrong, then, to say that between the resolve to go and the actual going there lay many hard battles, and that many never get through battling. This parable has no battles and justifies no man in preaching to sinners to produce and to prolong such battles and in keeping the sinners in prolonged agony until they finally get through battling. This method is a grave, dangerous perversion of the parable and also of the entire gospel. It belongs to the sad pathology of preaching and not to its normal and healthy functioning.

This is normal: the sinner makes an open confession and asks God's grace and pardon. An example is the malefactor: the change wrought in his heart brought to his lips the admission of his sins and his humble plea to Jesus to be remembered, and then Jesus uttered his wonderful absolution. So sinners still express their contrition and their faith and receive absolution, the sentence of pardon and justification in and through the Word.

Jesus pictures the grace of God in a wonderful manner, as being ever ready to pardon the repentant sinner. As if he were constantly watching the road, the father sees the son while he is yet in the distance — "saw him" is put forward for the sake of emphasis. The first glance fills his father's heart with compassion — ἐσπλαγχνίσθη is explained in 7:23; this compassion and this alone is the sinner's hope. This it is that lends wings to the father's feet; he runs, falls upon his son's neck, covers his face with kisses — κατεφίλησεν, *kuesste ihn ab*. The entire action displays the fact that the prodigal is already pardoned before he utters a single word of confession even as the omniscient and ever-present God pardons the sinner the moment he believes.

Jesus pictures the pardoning grace of God in such strong colors because this is highly necessary. The oppressed conscience must not doubt in the least that God really intends to pardon. This picture of the heavenly Father intends to win, to draw, to call mightily to every sinner's heart. Nothing in God could make us hesitate, only our own blindness and perversions which do injustice to God would cause us to act in that manner. The mediatorial work of Christ and his atoning sacrifice are not introduced in this parable. Only part of the story is told. No deduction is warranted that God ever pardons sinners without Christ.

21) And the son said to him, Father, I did sin against the heaven and in thy sight; no longer am I worthy to be called thy son—.

Yes, Jesus lets the sinner make his oral confession even though the pardon is assured in advance. Men may require an investigation, God never does so. But note well that the father interrupts his son's words before he can complete them. This is one of the tenderest touches in the parable. The son is spared his humiliating petition.

22) The father, however, said to his slaves: Quick, bring out a festal robe, the best, and put it on him and give him a ring for his hand and sandals for his feet; and be bringing the calf, the fattened one, slaughter it, and, eating, let us make merry because this my son was dead and came back to life; he was one that has been lost and was found. And they began to make merry.

This is the sinner's absolution, pardon, justification, adoption (reception to sonship), all rolled into one. Compare the similar act in Zech. 3:3-5. We need not ask who the "hired men" and the "slaves" are in the reality pictured; they are needed only for the human side of the parable. The στολή, *Talar*, is a long robe that was worn by the nobles on state occasions. The adjective that is added with the article after the noun is like an apposition; compare the case of the calf, R. 776. "The first" means the finest, the one that ranks first. Thus the sinner "puts on Christ," Gal. 3:27. "He hath clothed me with the garments of salvation, he hath covered me with the robe of righteousness, as a bridegroom decketh himself with ornaments, and as a bride adorneth herself with her jewels," Isa. 61:10. This is the "wedding garment," Matt. 22:11, which signifies the imputation to the sinner of the merits and the righteousness of Christ.

The ring is another mark of sonship. The same truth in another form is presented in Hosea 2:19, 20: "I will betroth thee unto me forever; yea, I will betroth thee unto me in righteousness, and in judgment, and in lovingkindness, and in mercies. I will even betroth thee unto me in faithfulness; and thou shalt know the Lord." Slaves went barefoot, not so a son. In God's pardoning reception of the sinner he gives him shoes to honor him as a son and heir but also in the confidence that he will henceforth walk worthily as a son.

23) The fatted calf contains no reference to Christ's sacrifice for us or to the Eucharist. This is the counterpart to the endings of the two halves of the previous parable, v. 7 and 10; the passive εὐφρανθῶμεν is used as a middle: "let us be merry," the subjunctive being hortative. "Thou preparest a table before me," Ps. 23:5. This feast and its rejoicing are the absolute opposite of the prodigal's sitting in rags among swine, longing for and failing to get even swine's food. Can any earthly contrast be greater? This rich table in the father's house is the preliminary of the heavenly feast (13:28, 29). In this verse there are pictured all the spiritual gifts, food, joys, and blessings that are found on the table of God's abounding grace.

24) Ὅτι states the great reason for all these jubilant orders: "Because this my son — mark the significant word! — was dead and came back to life." God's own joy at the conversion of the sinner is expressed here. "You hath he quickened, who were dead in trespasses and sins," Eph. 2:1; I John 3:14. The life away from God is spiritual death; conversion is the gaining of the true life, faith is that life. John 11:26.

So great is this reason for the joy in God that it is restated and thus emphasized: "He was one that has been lost" and, as the perfect participle states, was in that terrible condition for a long time. "Lost" refers to God: lost to him. "As sheep going astray," I Pet. 2:25; "all we like sheep have gone astray. Isa. 53:6. This parable here links into the preceding one. "And was found" with its aorist states the fact, and that is enough. "Found" by God is every converted sinner; lost to Satan. What a world of blessedness in these two simple words: "came to life" — "was found"! "And they began to make merry" — with that the scene ends.

Here, as in the other parable, Jesus puts the silent question to the Pharisees and the scribes (v. 1, 2) as to how their murmuring agrees with this rejoicing of God. He at the same time here asks the publicans and the open sinners whether God shall rejoice also over them.

25) **Now his brother, the older one, was in a field. And as, coming, he drew near to the house he heard music and dances; and having called one of the lads, he began to inquire what these things might be. And he said to him, Thy brother has come; and thy father slaughtered the calf, the fattened one, because he received him back safe and sound. But he became angry and would not go in.**

Another son is lost. His story is entirely different from that of his brother since he is lost in his own father's house. How is that possible? Because of self-righteousness. He is busy in a field with his work — the self-righteous are great workers. As he approaches the house he hears music and dances — συμφωνία (our "symphony") in the sense of several players making their instruments sound together in harmony, an orchestra, a concert; χορός is the choral dance with gestures, clapping of hands, perhaps also steps and is done by chosen performers as a spectacle for the audience. The celebration was grand, indeed.

26) We shall excuse this brother for not going right in, seeing that he came from a field and needed to wash and to dress, also that he called one of the lads and began to inquire what was going on, for all

must have seemed very unusual to him. The word παῖς is like *Bursche,* "boy," in the sense of servant. The imperfect ἐπυνθάνετο is inchoative: "he began to inquire." The optative with ἄν in the indirect question is left unchanged from the direct, and ἄν indicates perplexity (R. 940), and R. 938 adds even a deliberative element; the indeclinable τί is often used as a predicate with a plural subject which is here ταῦτα.

27) The lad is happy to tell the good news and to state the reason the celebration was great enough to include slaughtering the fatted calf. We note "thy brother" and "thy father" as if the lad meant that all that is yet needed is for this older brother to step into the house. In ἥκει we have a present form used in the perfect sense: "has come" and so "is here," R. 881. In his own homely way the lad states the reason the father ordered the celebration: "because he received him back safe and sound," ὑγιαίνοντα, present participle: "being healthy." The lad is discreet. It does not behoove him to repeat the father's words (v. 24), so he states what is obvious. This, too, is a masterly touch in the painting.

28) This brother at once "became angry" (ingressive aorist) even before the lad and "was not willing to go in," the imperfect to indicate continued unwillingness. All urging by the lad and by others was in vain. This is the exact picture of the Pharisees and the scribes (v. 2). What is veiled in v. 7 and 10 is now fully revealed. Celebrate the return of this prodigal — not for one moment!

But now behold a new mercy which is fully as great as the one we have already seen. The Father comes to seek the lost just as the Son, our Savior, does. **Moreover, his father, having come out, began to beseech him. But he answering said (1:19) to his father: Lo, for so many years I am slaving for thee and never yet transgressed thy bidding; and never yet didst thou give me a kid in order that I might make merry with my friends. But when this thy son**

who devoured thy living with harlots came, thou didst slaughter for him the fatted calf!

Someone must have gone and told the father who hastens out and, as the imperfect conveys, "begins to beseech" this son. Whereas he deserved the severest calling-down the father meets him with gentle entreaty. What a picture, the Father begging the sinner to come in! "As though God did beseech you," II Cor. 5:20.

29) But now all the blindness, perversity, and hardness of this selfish and self-righteous brother boil to the surface. As in the case of the younger son we saw a secret alienation of the heart that did not come out at once, so we do also in the case of this older one, but his is an alienation that is of far longer standing. The occasion has come for him to reveal himself as he really is. He does not once say "father" or "my brother" in his outburst, but Jesus significantly says that he answered and said "to his father" — yes, to his own father he spoke thus.

Hear the proud boast of self-righteousness. In this parable Jesus lets it speak out its real thoughts concerning itself: slaving for the father these many years — never transgressing his bidding during all this time! But see the spirit of this slaving which makes a boast to throw up to the father, to show him how he has never appreciated this wonderful son of his. Paul writes, *"Not having mine own righteousness,"* Phil. 3:9. Never once transgressing — that is this son's substitute for his confession of sin; "all these have I kept from my youth up," 18:21. Yet in this very boast the greatest of God's commandments is transgressed, that of love. This son knew nothing of such a commandment.

From boast of self he turns to blame of his father. For all of his slaving and perfect obedience — what did the father give him? Not even a kid (some texts: a little kid) to have a celebration with his friends. That is the kind of father this son has, one who is ungrateful to his son.

30) Worse than that, he is shamelessly partial and unjust: for this other son he killed the fatted calf which had been especially fattened for some great celebration. All the contrasts are intended to be vicious cuts. He the paragon of sons — this thy son, the wretch who devoured thy living with harlots; I with my good friends — he with a lot of whores; "thy son" — he will not own him as a brother; "thy living" — as if the father had made no partition; he devoured — I wanted to make merry. Could any son have a worse brother and a worse father? The picture is extreme as is that which Jesus paints of the younger son. Both types of sinners may not go so far, but any sinner of either type who goes in the two directions indicated to any degree must be classed with these.

31) **But he said to him: Child, thou art ever with me, and all mine is thine. Moreover, to make merry and to rejoice was necessary because this thy brother was dead and became alive, and one that has been lost and was found.**

Might the father not have turned upon this son in just anger, denounced his wicked words and heart, and used his right of revoking his inheritance? He does the opposite, but with firm and telling words. "Child," he addressed this son who was acting the opposite of a child. The deeper the tenderness, the more glaring the contrast to the omission since this son never once said, "father." Thus the power of love reaches out to expel all lovelessness. "Thou art ever with me," yea "with me" — what "friends" couldst thou have that would require thee to turn from *me* to make merry with *them?* He contrasted his friends with his brother's former harlot friends but failed to see that any friends that might take him from his father were really like his brother's friends. Who was his best friend but his father? Here is the proof: "All mine is thine" — kid, calf, all the house and the fields; for had it not been divided to him? More than all, *the father* and all his love were his into the bargain! So Jesus is here entreating the Pharisees to forsake their self-righteousness. To have the Father in Jesus through whom the Father speaks is to have a very heaven of love, grace, mercy, and goodness. To have all that is his as our own through the adoption of sons is more than all the world.

32) Δέ, "moreover," adds another consideration, that of a moral necessity, the imperfect ἔδει reaches from the past to the present joy, it necessitates joy. To joy no joy would be monstrous, for it means that spiritual death has been turned into everlasting life, that the soul, which was once in the condition of being lost (perfect participle of past condition reaching forward) to God, is now found by God and by grace. Will this older son refuse to rejoice? Will these Pharisees and these scribes go on murmuring? Do they now see what that means?

The parable ends abruptly, and purposely so. All who heard and who now hear and read that ending automatically ask themselves: "What did that brother do in answer to his father's appeal?" But that is the very question you must ask yourself if there is the least self-righteousness in you. What do *you* answer?

CHAPTER XVI

1) Moreover, he went on to say also to the disciples: A rich man there was who had a steward. And this man was denounced to him as squandering his possessions.

Another somewhat different one is added to the preceding parables (δέ, "moreover"); the imperfect ἔλεγε is used as it was in 3:7. Καί, which is omitted in the R. V., means that this parable, which no longer deals with finding and recovering the lost but with the life of those found, has its application to the disciples. From 15:1, 2, our present verse, and then v. 14 we gather that all the parables in these two chapters were spoken to an audience that was composed of Pharisees, scribes, publicans, open sinners, and a goodly number of disciples. Compare the further discussion under 15:3.

In his masterly way Jesus places the essentials before us with a few simple words: the rich man and the dishonest steward. This man's business was extensive; he employed a general manager with full power to handle all affairs as we see from his dealings in v. 5-7, and the values of his affairs were large. Jesus at once places us into a typically worldly atmosphere which is unlike that of the preceding parables. This steward is crooked — nothing new in managers who have powers like his. We are placed at the time of his career when somebody (hidden in the passive διεβλήθη) denounced him to his employer. R. 697 makes οὗτος anaphoric, pointing back to "steward," but the demonstrative reads as if it were spoken by the man who denounced him: "this fellow was denounced." The verb is used to indicate secret denunciation, and the efforts to give it a neutral sense in this connection seem to be misplaced. So also ὡς with a participle, which states the substance of the denunciation, is more than an allegation that is inspired by malice, an allegation that is untrue in fact (R. 1140); here the allegation is undoubtedly true, ὡς being used to express real or assumed crimes (R. 966). The sequel shows that the evidence convinced the employer, who proceeds at once to discharge his steward; and the steward makes no effort whatever to defend himself but admits his guilt. He was charged with squandering his employer's possessions. Some tone this down to mere carelessness or incompetency; but the fellow presently shows himself as being exceedingly shrewd. He was plainly crooked, that is all, was doing his crooked work at the very time when he was denounced as the present participle states. A wealthy man often used one of his own slaves as a steward (as in 12:42, etc., where the fellow is cut in two); but here the man is a freeman who is merely employed, his master only discharges him.

2) **And having called him, he said to him: How do I hear this concerning thee! Give due account of thy stewardship, for thou canst no longer be steward.**

The employer summons his man at once, exclaims because of what he hears, demands an accounting, and discharges the rascal. As regards τί, R. 1176 is right in making it adverbial, not R. 736 and 916: "What is this?" (R. V.). This is not the interrogative adverbial "why," it is the exclamatory adverbial "how" (A. V.). The employer is not asking a question, neither "what" nor "why." He knows "what" he has heard, and he knows "why" the steward did as he did; nor does the steward reply in any way. The employer exclaims because of his steward whom he thought honest and capable: "How do I hear this concerning thee!" No investigation is needed, no defense is possible; it is already a closed case. The employer demands that due accounting be made; ἀπό in the aorist imperative expresses the idea of "due." The steward must go, close up his books, and turn them in with whatever they show. The only explanation (γάρ) he receives is the announcement of his discharge: he can no longer "be stewarding."

3) **But the steward said in himself: What shall I do, seeing that my lord is taking the stewardship away from me? To dig I have not strength, to beg I am ashamed. I got what I will do, in order that, when I shall be discharged from the stewardship, they may receive me into their own houses!**

The preliminaries of the parable (v. 1, 2) are brief; the main point, the shrewdness of the steward, is elaborated at length. We are shown his reasoning, his prompt decision, and the instant execution of his shrewd plan. He did not delay, he debated at once as to what he should do. He had little time as far as turning over the accounts is concerned. If he could do anything, it had to be done at once. So he asks himself what is possible under the circumstances: "What shall I do?" ποιήσω is either the future indicative or the deliberative subjunctive (R. 935); and ὅτι is used in the consecutive sense, compare R. 1001. He at once eliminates two distasteful courses. To earn his living by digging and downright hard labor is out of the question because he has not the physical strength for that; to go begging and to eke out an existence in that way are also out of consideration because he is ashamed to come down so low after his prominence for a long time. That is straight thinking? But what else is left?

4) It is quite impossible to translate the ingressive aorist tense ἔγνων (R., W. P.) accurately since we have no tense equivalent of any kind in English. The punctiliar aorist marks the sudden arrival of the knowledge on which the man resolves to act and marks it as occurring prior even to its expression in words. We venture to translate: "I got," i. e., the knowledge or idea, "what I will do," etc. He does not state the knowledge that just flashed into his mind; we deduce it from what he promptly does while the accounts are still in his hands. But he does state what purpose he

expects his plan to serve, namely to make his employer's debtors take him into their own homes so that he can live at ease until something better turns up for him. The ποιήσω is here volitive but again ambiguous as to form (R. 935).

5) **And having called to him each one of the debtors of his lord, he went on to say to the first, How much dost thou owe to my lord? And he said, A hundred bath of oil. And he said to him, Take thy writing, and, having sat down, quickly write fifty. Thereupon he said to another, And thou, how much owest thou? And he said, A hundred cor of wheat. He says to him, Take thy writing and write eighty.**

"Each one." He deals with them individually and without witnesses. Only two are introduced as samples of the shrewd scheme, but this rich man had a number of such debtors. Until his books and his papers are turned over to his employer the steward is still in power, and, having squandered his lord's possessions heretofore, he does so once more with a special purpose. He will make "his own (ἑαυτοῦ) lord's" debtors his own debtors in another sense and live off them.

These do not seem to have been renters of land; the entire description does not suit farming. Though olive oil and wheat are mentioned, the quantities are very large, too large to be considered payment in kind, and one man owes nothing but oil, the other nothing but wheat, which seems as though they were traders, the one in the one commodity, the other in the other. This lord was a wholesaler, the creditors had bought from him and still owed him the money.

6) In reply to the question the first tells how much he owes. The steward shrewdly asks the man and makes him tell in order that the man may realize the more what a gift the steward is making him. A "bath" is an old Hebrew measure (R. V. margin and reference) which contains between eight and nine gallons. The selling of between 800 and 900 gallons of olive

oil to one customer shows the wealth that this steward handled for his lord. He has pulled the debtor's note out of the strongbox, hands it to him, and tells him to write a receipt and a note for just half the amount of oil. That was certainly making a friend of this debtor. All the transactions are in the steward's hands; he made the sale, received and kept the papers, his lord had other business to do, had employed him as his manager. So the debtor could safely accept the reduction. The matter is rushed: "quickly" the debtor must write and go. The plural τὰ γράμματα may refer to one document.

7) He proceeds in the same manner with another debtor, one who had bought a hundred "cor" of wheat, another Hebrew measure, a "cor" amounting to ten bushels, thus a thousand bushels in all. This man is told to make out papers for eighty "cor." The view that the original documents were altered is untenable. Why did the steward himself not then alter them, he being an expert scribe? But he does not say, "I will write," but makes each debtor write. Documents that had been tampered with would have been invalid, and the debtors would afterward be held liable for the entire amount. Entirely newly written obligations, which were substituted for the originals, would make the thing sure. So the debtor is also told to sit down, which would not have been necessary for a slight alteration.

Why the difference in the reductions? Surely not, as has been thought, because the steward knew each man and how much to give him. We cannot judge from the quantities but must judge from the monetary value, and fifty bath of oil may have been of no more value than twenty cor of wheat — the trouble is that we do not know how these commodities were priced at just that time.

8) So this rascally steward shrewdly provided for himself. **And the lord praised the steward of**

unrighteousness because he acted shrewdly; because the sons of this eon are shrewder beyond the sons of light in their own generation.

The shrewd way in which this conscienceless steward had feathered his nest at the very last moment became clear at last, and when his lord heard it he, too, was shrewd enough to appreciate this shrewd action and praised his steward for it. As we said at the start, the entire parable is a genuine picture of worldliness. Thus also this man is called "the steward of unrighteousness," which is usually called the qualitative genitive; it is like an adjective ("the unrighteous steward") but is always stronger. The parable has received its title from this designation: the Unjust Steward, which follows the translation of the A. V.

The usual view is that this ends the parable, and that its exposition and application now begin. But the decided: "and I myself say to you" in v. 9 brings the application so that the sentence: "Because the sons," etc., still belongs to the parable. Not, indeed, as adding to its narrative part but as putting the parable into the right light for the hearers. This last statement informs them that this parable is taken *in toto* from the shrewdness of the sons of this eon who exceed the sons of light in this respect when it comes to their own generation, i. e., to dealings with the men of their own time. They know how to gain an advantage for themselves and are not deterred by conscience and moral considerations even as the main figure in the parable, the steward, is boldly marked by the quality of unrighteousness in his entire office and at the end.

"In their own generation," i. e., for its duration, refers jointly to the sons of this eon and to the sons of light and includes the entire generation in the case of both. Some divide them: worldlings dealing only with worldlings, disciples only with disciples, the former being shrewder than the latter; and one interpreter has suggested this application in the case of the latter: "We all know how stupid Christians can be in their cooperative work"! But do worldlings not deal with Christians as well as with worldlings, and vice versa? How many Christians have not been cheated and fleeced by worldlings! It is a simple fact: in matters of their own generation worldlings are decidedly shrewder than Christians.

But, of course, only for this their generation even as Jesus calls them "the sons of this eon" and uses φρόνιμος, "sensible," "shrewd," namely in the way pictured, in earthly affairs. "This eon," ὁ αἰὼν οὗτος, has its contrast in "the eon to come," ὁ αἰὼν μέλλων, the one being the present world era, the other the heavenly world era. The term αἰών, however, means more than a vast period, it is one that has a specific character that is derived from what transpires in it, hence we have the modifiers that are always attached. "This eon" is the one that is marked by transient temporalities, sin and its effects, the coming one is marked by the blessed and perfect conditions of heaven.

The term υἱοί is sometimes overlooked. These "sons" are not only "children" (τέκνα) of this eon, for "sons" refers to legal standing as heirs; "the sons of this eon" have nothing to expect except what this eon furnishes, temporalities only. It is true, "the sons of the light" is not an exact verbal opposite, and yet "the light" is in fact the opposite of "this eon," for this eon is one that is filled with darkness. The sons of this eon continue in this darkness, but the sons of the light receive the divine light of saving truth which God sent into the world, into this eon (John 3:19). The sons of the truth thus have the inheritance that is promised in the truth, in the revelation of God. Their hearts are thus set on the treasures of this truth, the hearts of the worldlings on the treasures of this eon. No wonder, then, when it comes to dealing with men in their generation, that the latter are far shrewder than the former. It could not be otherwise, and this is by no means said in criticism of the sons of the light. The statement is made in order to bring out the fact that the parable is taken from what is usual among the sons of this eon and is to be understood in that way. The genitives "of this eon" and "of the light" are qualitative like "of unrighteousness."

9) No other parable has caused as much perplexity and has received as many interpretations as this one. Because there are so many interpretations, those who attempt a survey of them find it necessary to classify them into groups and then admit that they have not included all of them. One reads this story with depressed feelings. One interpretation alone is sound, the one Jesus himself gives. Why do only a few adopt it? Because this interpretation is derived from the parable as a whole, not from its details.

And the other point in Jesus' interpretation is the fact that it is confined only to the disciples even as Luke emphasizes this at the start (v. 1). Not until one becomes a disciple can this parable mean to him what Jesus intends it to mean. The interpretation rests on one point, namely on the picture of the unrighteous steward, the whole of it being treated as a unit. This man, as he is here portrayed, is one of millions of the sons of this eon and is typical in his complete development. The interpretation is given from the direct opposite, and that, too, in full development. Thus: *the fully developed unrighteousness* we see in this man as regards the unrighteous mammon is to help us to see and to inspire us to attain the complete contrary, *the fully developed righteousness* with which we are to handle this unrighteous mammon: first, in the use to which we put it (v. 9); second, in the estimate we put upon it, which underlies any use we make of it (v. 10-12); third, in the resistance which we offer it, this underlying both the use and the estimate (v. 13).

Many find the *tertium comparationis* in φρόνιμος, "shrewd": as the steward was shrewd in a worldly way in dealing with mammon, so we are to be shrewd in a spiritual way; instead of the *weltliche Klugheit* we are to have and to use the *geistliche Klugheit*. But it will be observed that this word is not repeated in Jesus' application (v. 9-13) whereas, resting on "unrighteousness" in "the steward of unrighteousness," we have "the mammon of unrighteousness" and then three times the concept ἄδικος, "unrighteous," and three times its opposite πιστός, plus the corresponding verb πιστεύσει, "faithful" ("trustworthy") and "will entrust." These terms put the *tertium* beyond question and also show that the comparison is one of opposites. As far as sensibleness is concerned, in the disciple this would be wisdom; but v. 9-13 do not turn on this point.

And I myself, to you I say: Make for yourselves friends by the mammon of unrighteousness in order that, when it gives out, they may receive you into the eternal tents.

This is not a simple λέγω ὑμῖν, "I say to you," which is so frequently used by Jesus, but far stronger: ἐγώ, "I myself to you," as my disciples, "to you alone" (ὑμῖν before the verb) now say. It should be accepted that the exposition begins here, and not until here. We have seen how the steward of unrighteousness used the mammon of unrighteousness in making friends for himself to take him in when he was discharged from office; Jesus orders us to do the same thing but to make our *use* quite the opposite.

The parallel is quite close, which makes the point of opposition stand out the more boldly. He is a steward — we too; he is entrusted with property and values — we too; these are the unrighteous mammon — in our case too; he makes friends with it — we too; he comes to an end — we too. The two lines run in the same direction, side by side, until in a flash the final phrase reverses the second line and makes it run in the opposite direction: "into the eternal tents." The sons of this eon care for earthly houses, the sons of light are set on entering eternal habitations, heavenly mansions. And this reverses the entire line so that the two now run like this ⇌, the one being motivated by unrighteousness, the other by its opposite, righteousness.

The aorist ποιήσατε is constative, summing up into one the doing of the entire life; and ἐκ has the idea of source: "out of the means afforded by mammon" (μαμωνᾶ, a Doric genitive). The derivation of μαμωνᾶς (which is always written with one *m* except in some minuscules) has not been determined (C.-K. 712), but its meaning is clear; it is not the name of an idol but a designation for valuable possessions; it is probably of Aramaic origin yet was current among the Greek Christians and was not translated. Luke uses it much as we ourselves still do. In v. 13 it enables Jesus to put its idea in opposition to God.

The genitive is again qualitative: "the mammon of unrighteousness," exactly as was "the steward of unrighteousness." Mammon has the very quality of unrighteousness. The explanation that it is so called because it tends to unrighteousness is too weak. The usual explanation is that money and wealth circulate among sinful men and are used in sinful ways and for sinful purposes and thus get this quality and retain it when they come into a Christian's possession. The idea of ill-gotten wealth in the hands of the publicans and of the Pharisees who are here addressed by Jesus, some of the former having become disciples, is untenable; 19:8 shows that money of that kind must be returned.

The moment we ask who it is that receives us ("welcomes" is too weak) into the eternal tents we shall see that the friends we are to make by means of mammon cannot be fellow Christians whom we have helped with charitable gifts. Those who hold this view feel constrained to add that some of these Christians preceded the donors in death. How many received the malefactor? Christ and God alone receive in heaven and not even the angels of whom some have thought and have forgotten that only by making God and Christ our friends do we make the angels our friends. Matt. 25:40 makes the matter plain: what we do for the least of our brethren we do for Christ who will receive us into the heavenly mansions. This also bars out anything like meriting heaven, for all the works enumerated in Matt. 25:35 are evidences of faith and no more. So Jesus here speaks to disciples who already have heaven by faith and by the fruits and evidences of faith must show that their faith still endures.

"When it (mammon) gives out" (eclipses) is the hour of death when even our very body will become the property of others and certainly every cent of our money. So the steward found his income suddenly gone and needed another abode. Σκηνή is not "habitation" (A. V.), and whether we translate it "tent," "booth," "tabernacle," the expression is peculiar, the noun denoting a transient structure and its adjective modifier being "eternal." The fact that heaven is meant is plain. But Jesus is not speaking of the judgment day as some suppose; "when mammon gives out" refers to the Christian's hour of death.

10) One sentence gives us the gist of the interpretation; but this involves more. Back of *the use* made of mammon is *the estimate* we put upon it. Involved in the use made by the steward was unrighteousness, involved in our use is to be trustworthiness. So Jesus adds this point. **He who is faithful in very little, also in much is he faithful; and he who in very little is unrighteous, also in much is he unrighteous. If, therefore, you did not prove to be faithful in the unrighteous mammon, the genuine thing — who will entrust it to you? And if in what is another's you do not prove faithful, what is your own — who will give it to you?**

First, the estimate. To the sons of this eon mammon is the very greatest thing, they will sell themselves into unrighteousness for it. But to the sons of light, who judge it in the light of divine truth, it is "a very little thing," yea, "the least" as compared with their eternal possessions. On this estimate there rests the axiomatic statement, the principle on which all men act: any man who is faithful in administering the littlest thing is certainly to be trusted in much more, and men readily make the venture with regard to him; and the reverse is equally true about a man, and no one will think of entrusting him with more.

Note the significant terms πιστός and ἄδικος, each being repeated twice. These are the key terms for interpreting the parable. "Least" and "much" refer to things entrusted to us; the fact that all disciples are stewards need not be said. One may think that what is "least" does not count so that he may treat it as he pleases; but no, it is quite decisive as revealing our true character. One may think that if something very great were entrusted to him, he would be faithful; men will not agree with him, they will first want to test him out with something that is very small.

11) That is the case with regard to "the unrighteous mammon" (the adjective suffices since it has been used twice just preceding this verse). For the disciples this is, indeed, "the very least" of what is entrusted to them. And Jesus draws the conclusion (οὖν) for them: if they do not prove faithful in administering this, who would ever think of entrusting to them τὸ ἀληθινόν, "the genuine thing"? Mammon is, indeed, not the genuine thing, transient, fleeting, deceptive as it is, bound presently to give out altogether (v. 9). They are fools who place that estimate upon it. "The genuine thing" is that which never gives out, never disappoints. It is left unnamed, but by analogy it is all our spiritual and heavenly wealth. Jesus uses the condition of real-

ity: εἰ with the indicative in the protasis, any tense in the apodosis.

12) "Least" and "more," "mammon" and "the genuine thing," do not exhaust the analysis of this estimate. We are stewards, and our earthly wealth is "another's," of which we must necessarily give an accounting. If it were ours, we might more easily think that we are free to do with it as we please. Therefore Jesus asks very pertinently: "If we are not faithful in what is 'another's,' for which we are accountable, who will give us 'what is our own,' which we would therefore treat as not being connected with an accounting?" "What is your own" (ὑμέτερον) is, of course, the same as "the genuine thing" (τὸ ἀληθινόν). These objects are placed forward in the questions for the sake of emphasis.

13) Back of the *use* of our earthly wealth and of the *estimate* we place upon it is the *resistance* we offer to its deceptive power. **No house servant is able to be slave to two lords; for either he will hate the one and will love the other, or he will hold to the one and will despise the other. You cannot be slaves to God and to mammon.** Compare Matt. 6:24.

Earthly wealth not only tends to unrighteousness in its use and leads us to place a false estimate upon it, it would also make us its slave and at the same time lead us to think that we could also be slaves to God. Hence the resistance needed by every disciple against both being enslaved and being deceived by mammon. The statement of Jesus is again axiomatic, self-evident. The matter is viewed from the standpoint of the slave and is more pointed here than it is in Matthew, for the specification "house servant" is added, one who would thus serve in one house only. How two masters would act in the case is not touched upon. A slave's person and his work belong only to one master. Two or more masters might jointly own a slave and might even divide his service; but this would make the owners one and thus not affect the proposition. The underlying thought is that no man is his own master; it is our very nature that our heart, will, and work are governed by another. The only question is who this shall be.

With γάρ Jesus elucidates the impossibility from the viewpoint of the slave. Suppose he did try to be a slave to two masters — not, indeed, that he could get himself two masters, but that the slave were fool enough to accept such an abnormality. Then, Jesus says, he himself will demonstrate that no slave can be a slave to two masters. He will hate the one and will love the other; or he will hold to the one and will despise the other. In other words, in his very heart and by his very thoughts he will make one of the two his real master, give him heart service, and will make the other his sham master, give him only outward service. Though it is used with regard to a slave, ἀγαπᾶν is still the love that involves a certain understanding plus corresponding purpose; more is involved than just φιλεῖν or liking. Note the contrast between ἀντί and κατά in the compound verbs: "to hold oneself face to face with" — "to think down or against someone," R. 573.

The two masters whom Jesus has in mind are God and mammon. What is never attempted in the case of other masters and lords is often attempted in the case of these, but the outcome is only as is indicated — only one can really be master and lord in our hearts. This, we may add, will never be sham service to mammon and heart service to God; the danger is always in the other direction, hiding our heart service, love, and devotion to mammon by a show of service to God. We must constantly resist the power of mammon in this direction, purge our hearts of this unrighteousness also, and serve God alone.

We have had no reason to make anything especial of "the rich man" in the parable (v. 1), either to make him picture God as some do or mammon as others do. He belongs to the essence of the parable no more than do the oil or the wheat or any difference between the two. The debate about having a rich man represent God in this parable whereas in others he represents a godless man (12:16; 16:19) is of no interest to us; also how mammon can be spent and wasted by the steward and yet be his personified god. If we abide by Jesus' own interpretations, all such difficulties are avoided.

14) **Now there were listening to all these things the Pharisees, who were money-lovers, and they turned up their noses in derision at him.**

The last parable was addressed only to the disciples (v. 1), but we see that the Pharisees, etc., were still present (15:1, 2). The two imperfect tenses are descriptive, and "all these things" is best regarded as including all that Jesus had said from 15:3 onward. The reaction of the Pharisees came to view as Jesus offered the last parable and its exposition. They, of course, resented the implications that were directed against them in the other parables but gave no sign of this until Jesus, though now speaking only to his disciples, touched their avarice and their greed (Matt. 23:14). Luke notes this when he says that they were "money-loving." They then "began to turn up their noses in derision at him," *sie ruempften die Nase*, although they ventured no reply in words. They probably thought that such talk was easy for Jesus, seeing that he himself had no property.

15) Jesus promptly takes them up. **And he said to them: You are they who are justifying your own selves in the sight of men, but God knows your hearts, seeing that the thing high among men is an abomination in the sight of God.**

The reply of Jesus to the scorn of the Pharisees takes in vastly more than the one point of their love of money and their wicked ways of getting it while they made long prayers and a great pretense of holiness. The reply strikes at their fundamental sin, namely at the hypocrisy with which they covered up their avarice and all other flagrant sins. The emphasis is on ὑμεῖς: "You, just you are the ones who keep justifying your own selves!"

The participle, like all uses of this verb and its derivatives, is strongly forensic. Every criminal likes to oust the real judge who pronounces the verdict, "Guilty!" upon him and likes to usurp the judge's seat, sit on his own case, and pronounce upon himself the verdict, "Innocent — acquitted!" That is exactly what these Pharisees did, not once, but habitually; the present participle makes this self-justification their outstanding characteristic. They condemned others without mercy as if their judgment were divine. In their own cases they ignored and set aside God and his verdict and, like a supreme court, acquitted themselves.

Jesus adds significantly "in the sight of men." Men they could and to a great extent did deceive. Men they could get to accept their self-justification. Men considered them as high and holy. But men only. "But God knows your hearts," all the baseness which your false justification covers up. He, the divine, eternal Judge, is the great Καρδιογνώστης, "Knower of hearts" (Acts 1:24; 15:8), and him they do not for one moment deceive.

"Seeing that" is intended as a translation of the ὅτι consecutivum (R. 1001); it states the point that makes the preceding statement so important. What difference does it make that God sees the hearts of these Pharisees? This — "the thing high among men, abomination is it in the sight of God." He abominates all self-exaltation, especially that of hypocritical self-justification. The thing that men thus deem high, look up to, admire, boast of in themselves, glory in, is not only low but utterly abhorrent in God's eyes. The more the Pharisees managed to get exaltation among men, the more abominable they made themselves before God. Jesus is letting these Pharisees know what God's verdict on them is; he does this in order, if possible, to move them to repentance. Why the thing high among men is abomination before God needs no explanation. Exaltation that disregards God and all true, divine exaltation by way of his grace must be crushed as an imitation of the devil's own pride.

16) What Jesus tells the Pharisees is what the eternal Word of God as well as the kingdom that is now being preached to them have long declared, and a further striking example is the Jewish contradiction of the law which is manifested in their flagrant disruptions of marriage. The connection of thought is not that Jesus justifies what he says against the charge that he is running contrary to the Old Testament with his preaching of the kingdom, which permitted the Pharisees to justify themselves for rejecting what he says. This would make these verses a defense; they are undoubtedly an attack, one which drives the matter home by pointing to God's own eternal Word which these Pharisees still claimed to obey, yea, obey perfectly, and base their self-exaltation on this very obedience.

The law and the prophets — till John; from then on the kingdom of God is being preached as good news, and everyone is energetically pressing into it. But it is easier that the heaven and the earth pass away than for one particle of a letter of the law to fall.

This is a powerful assertion of the unchanging authority of the divine Word. What Jesus has just said about the Pharisees' justifying themselves before *men* when *God* regards them as an abomination is sealed by *the Word of God*. Compare the interpretation of Matt. 11:12, 13 on v. 16.

"The law and the prophets" is a standard title for the Old Testament. This Word stood as God's authoritative revelation from Malachi onward for 430 years until God sent John. And from that time onward, during the past three to four years, God gave the Jews even more: "the kingdom of God (see 4:43) is being preached as good news" (the verb is used as it was in 1:19; 2:10; 3:18; etc.). This is the kingdom in its fullness as it is now being established by Christ. It existed in the old covenant but was to merge into the new covenant when all the promises of redemption were fulfilled. This fulfillment was now in progress, and the good news was being heralded throughout Judaism. Jesus brings to the Jews the whole of God's revelation up to the moment of his speaking: law and prophets, then John's and Jesus' preaching the promises about the kingdom as now being fulfilled. We have no comparison between law and prophets on the one hand and John, etc., on the other; not a thing of any defending the latter by an appeal to the former. The two are presented as a unit.

When Jesus adds: "and everyone is energetically pressing into it," his disciples, a goodly band of them, to whom he had just addressed the last parable, were right there as evidence of his claim; and this addition is made in order to ask the Pharisees why, when the law and the prophets to which they claimed to hold are now receiving their fulfillment in the good news of the kingdom, they, too, did not develop energy to press into it. This clause is a supplementary touch and no more. A comparison with Matt. 11:12 is helpful on the verb as that will show that the verb is not passive: "everyone is being pressed in," for which meaning there is no call here, but that it is the middle: "presses himself in." Nor need we stress the "violence" when the context is satisfied with energy, that decisiveness which is wrought by the preaching of the kingdom in all who accept it. "Everyone" is naturally restricted by the sense of the clause and includes those who enter the kingdom and those alone.

17) This preliminary statement lays the groundwork for the main thought that follows, that it is easier for heaven and earth to pass away in one sweep (παρελθεῖν, aorist) than for even the least little horn or projection on one or the other letter of the Hebrew text of the Old Testament to fall so that the sense would be changed by the falling away. Jesus does not say that every copyist of the Old Testament is infallible. Some of the Hebrew letters differ only in the presence or the absence of a little projection, and a copyist might, indeed, make a mistake. Jesus is speaking of God. In the case of God not a letter of his Word shall fall, lose its authority, be abrogated, be altered into something else.

Ὁ νόμος has the same force here as ὁ νόμος καὶ οἱ προφῆται, the entire Old Testament is designated by either expression. The idea that Jesus in v. 17 speaks only of the legal requirements of the Old Testament and not of the teaching of the prophets is a misconception. It is not because the prophets taught also the legal requirements, but because the Torah (ὁ νόμος in the stricter sense), the Pentateuch, together with the prophets taught the gospel faith which makes true children of God who alone can keep the legal requirements as God desires. Of the Old Testament in this sense Jesus says that its validity and its authority stand unalterable for all time.

"God knows your hearts" thus means not only that he sees the vices and the wickedness in the hearts of the Pharisees but their entire condition of unbelief, from which their avarice, etc., spring. He sees not only that they transgress his legal requirements but also that they scorn his gospel, that gospel which is being revealed in the entire New Testament and then still more fully in the good news that was preached by John and by Jesus. Did the Pharisees think that they could repudiate it in their hearts under a show of holiness, and repudiate it with impunity? Why, it was easier for heaven and earth to be swept away than for God to cancel one particle of the authority of his Word which damns not only this and that vice but the very source from which every vice springs, unbelief and hardness of heart. Justifying oneself before men is a farce; the only justification that avails is that on the part of God and his authoritative Word.

18) Jesus is not throwing together heterogeneous and nonpertinent thoughts when he now scores the Jewish practice of dissolving marriage *ad libitum*. Among the "open sinners" who drew near to Jesus were harlots (15: 1, 2), and some of these may have been in the present audience. But did these holy Pharisees keep the Sixth Commandment any better when they drove one wife after another away and took a new one as often as they pleased? So this statement is decidedly pertinent.

It is in order, too, because the parable and its exposition (v. 1-13) dealt with mammon, and the scorn of the Pharisees was aroused by what Jesus said on that subject (v. 14). Jesus therefore brings in this other flagrant sin of the Pharisees and exhibits likewise how they manipulate the Word of God in order to permit its open violation, their most famous teachers showing them the way. But here, too, no single letter of the Word can be abrogated, God will judge also these sins according to that authoritative Word, never according to the Pharisaic perversions of that Word. By bringing in this different group of open sins Jesus makes the Pharisees understand that he could go on and on by enumerating still other sins. To understand the wickedness of their love of money they must understand this same wickedness in its workings also in other directions. Jesus rips away their defenses and drives hard at their conscience.

Everyone having released his wife and marrying another commits adultery; and he marrying one that has been released from a husband commits adultery.

This is not an exposition on marriage and divorce; this is a charge which Jesus hurls at the Pharisees who are before him. That is why the statement is brief and summary. They were making mean remarks about Jesus (15:2) for having anything to do with open sinners like harlots. Were these Pharisees any better than harlots? No; they lived in the same open violation of the Sixth Commandment. Jesus now confronts them with that fact. What he tells them is this: You Pharisees also disregard and violate God's law of marriage by changing from one wife to another at pleasure, by marrying a discarded wife as if her having been discarded in such a way meant nothing whatever to God's law. Jesus is not expounding what is commonly called divorce but is scoring the dissolution of marriage; ἀπολύειν, "to release," "to dismiss," and thus to dissolve the marriage, this being the standard term. On at least two other occasions he fully expounded this subject, in Matt. 5:31, 32; in 19:3-9; and in Mark 10:11, 12. See the exposition of these passages for all details.

Only a charge is made here which is wide and strong and includes every transgressor. The charge is: μοιχεύει! The English translation is inadequate: "he commits adultery." The verb means *ehebrechen*, ruin marriage. In the Sixth Commandment, οὐ μοιχεύσεις (Matt. 5:27), as here in the charge against the Pharisees the verb means far more than πορνεύειν, to practice forbidden sexual intercourse; it means to do anything that destroys or helps to destroy the divine institution of marriage, the very nature of which is permanency (Mark 10:6-9). Fornication on the part of a husband or a wife, of course, does that (Matt. 5:32), but so does every Jewish dismissal of a wife for other reasons or for no special reason at all. And that is why Jesus here includes, as being equally guilty, the Jew who marries a wife who is dismissed by a Jewish husband and says of him as he says of the other: μοιχεύει, he helps to ruin the permanency of marriage. These Jews and Pharisees were all alike; none of them regarded marriage as having been made a permanent relation by God and his Word. All of them regarded marriage as being something that was to be dissolved at pleasure. The man who married a discarded wife married her only in this way, i. e., himself to discard her when he so pleased. In the very act of marrying her (γαμῶν expresses action that is simultaneous with that of μοιχεύει) he thus violated God's law of marriage.

Unless this is clearly understood, wrong deductions will be made. Jesus is scoring these Pharisaic violators of the permanency of marriage and is neither legislating concerning marriage (he never legislates) nor giving instructions to his disciples regarding marriage (that he does fully elsewhere). In both the Matthew and the Mark passages the verbs are passive (our versions, the commentaries, and some dictionaries regard them as being active); all these passages leave the discarded wife innocent of any blame; they all bring out the fact that the discarded wife is sinned *against*, and that the man who discards her sins *against himself* and sins likewise *against* the man who eventually marries the discarded wife. Those passives must stand as they are; indeed, to change them into actives has Jesus say what he cannot have said since it would not be true — that the discarded wife commits adultery by the husband's act of discarding her!

Once this is clear, no attempt will be made to alter the sense of the Matthew and the Mark passages by a reference to Luke. A discarded innocent wife (Mark says also husband) may marry again even as Paul so plainly declares in I Cor. 7:15; and the man who marries her as he should honors marriage as it was made permanent by God, condemns the man's action in breaking his own and her marriage, and commits no sin. Far otherwise any Jew or Pharisee who marries her in his way as he should not. He rejects the permanency of marriage, consents to the other man's action in breaking his marriage, is ready at any time to do so himself if he feels like it. By this very act of marrying this man, μοιχεύει, *bricht die Ehe,* exactly like the other and helps to break down the divine institution of marriage.

19) Jesus proceeds to relate a new parable without a break and after the interlude (v. 14-18), the unrighteous use of mammon, presents one who has wealth in his own right, misuses it in utter selfishness all his life, and thus ends in hell. The two parables are thus a pair, the second being an advance upon the first, which take us into the hereafter and thus exhibit God's final judgment, and do that in full. This parable presents an extreme case, necessarily so, in order to include all lesser cases in which selfishness does not come out so boldly yet is the mainspring of a man's life. This parable again strikes the rich, utterly selfish Pharisees; it delivers the final blow. In a marvelous way, as it seems at the spur of the moment, Jesus weaves in what he has just said (v. 16, 17) regarding the law and the prophets (v. 29). So this is another marvelous masterpiece.

Now there was a rich man, and he constantly put on himself purple and fine linen, making merry day by day splendidly. Moreover, a beggar, by name Lazarus, had been thrown at his portal, suffering from ulcers and longing to be filled from the things falling from the table of the rich; yea, even the dogs coming kept licking his ulcers.

Like living pictures, the two men are distinctly flashed on the screen. But this is preliminary, the main scene is to follow. We have τὶς twice which is used like our indefinite article. We construe: "A rich man there was," not: "A man was rich," although either construction is possible. His being rich is nothing that could be reckoned against him, for Abraham, too, was rich and appears in this very parable. Jesus gives this man no name; when we call him "Dives," that means

"Rich." One is struck by the fact that he appears without a name while the poor man is given one. His name was not known in heaven.

We still read discussions as to whether these were two actual men whom Jesus knew and used for this parable, or whether, as in other parables, notably in the one preceding, these were imaginary persons. The question answers itself — the main part of the parable is placed into the other world, these are figures that are used only in a parable. Nor need we disturb ourselves as to whether this is a real parable or not and puzzle about the definition of a parable.

Nor was this rich man a Sadducee, many of whom were, indeed, rich and ostentatious. Those who hold this view refer to some actual person like Caiaphas. But Sadducees denied the resurrection, and this man believed in it (v. 30). Could he have been a Pharisee when Pharisees did not live so voluptuously? And is Jesus not speaking to Pharisees so that this man ought to be one? The question is pointless, for the parable does not turn on the fact of being rich or poor but on unbelief which is exhibited in heartless selfishness in this life and in open contradiction in the hereafter.

We regard ἐνεδιδύσκετο as a middle (not as a passive), for it was his own doing that "he put on himself" (whether by the aid of a valet or not) "purple," such as kings and nobles wore, in the form of a magnificent long robe, "and byssus," the finest of linen, in a tunic next to the body. Both are named together in Esther 1:6 and Rev. 18:12. The point is that he wore such garments all the time as the imperfect states — he moved in constant splendor. Likewise, "making merry day by day (distributive κατά) splendidly" — his whole life was one gorgeous celebration. The parable concerns him, hence the fact that he had a great following of friends who admired him and basked in his favor is not added. All the parables are drawn with chaste simplicity.

20) We now have the complete opposite, but it is at once connected with the other. Πτωχός is more than "poor"; it is derived from the verb "to crouch or cringe," as a noun it means "beggar," as an adjective "beggarly," which is exactly what Lazarus was. Jesus has, however, ennobled the word (as he did in 6:20, etc.); and here, too, this "beggar" shines with a nobler splendor than the rich man.

In one of the regular ways, with the dative ὀνόματι, his name is stated: "Lazarus" (nominative). It is as if Jesus had looked into the book of life and found his name there but failed to find the other man's name. It is this naming of the beggar that leads many to think that both men were real. Although it is exceptional in a parable, this common name seems to be symbolical, "God a help." It is shortened from *Eleazaros* and, stated right at the start, marks this man as being one who put all his trust and faith in God.

And now we have the connection of these two men: "he had been thrown, dumped, at his portal," the grand, wide entrance through the wall that opened into the spacious courtyard of the rich man's palace; had been dumped and was now lying there. He could not move himself even on crutches and those who carried his diseased body just dropped it down regardless of the groan of pain they caused. Through that portal the rich man and his friends had to pass, had to see him in his wretchedness, had to hear his quavering, begging voice as he stretched out his hand. That is why he was put there — a golden opportunity for alms and for more than alms. "Disgusting!" thought the rich man. Not one of the Old Testament statements about helping the helpless even entered his mind, and his following imitated him. One word, a perfect participle, thus describing his present state, explains the dumping at this place: "suffering from ulcers," loathsome, festering, painful, untended sores.

21) The present participle ἐπιθυμῶν, "longing to be filled," etc., leaves unsaid whether his longing was satisfied or not; and many feel certain that it was not. But why did he then remain here and not seek another station? "The things falling from the table of the rich man" were, indeed, the "off-falls," waste to be thrown away into the street for the scavenger dogs to devour. Not by any desire or order on the part of the rich man did the beggar receive any of these scraps but by the kindness of some slave boy who was sent out to dispose of them.

The ἀλλά is not adversative: "but even the dogs," etc. Our versions have the correct feeling when they avoid "but" and translate "moreover" (A. V.) and "yea" (R. V.). This is the copulative ἀλλά (R. 1186) which merely carries the description forward by adding a striking detail. This is the fact that the dogs kept coming and licking the ulcers. These are the ownerless dogs that roam the city and act as general scavengers and are known in all Oriental cities where they have not been abolished.

There is a dispute as to whether this licking of the ulcers was an affliction or an alleviation. It marks the abject state of this beggar, it was so low that such dogs were his only friends. The views that they aggravated his ulcers, and that he was too weak to fend them off; or that they treated him as almost being a carcass, reveal lack of dog knowledge. These dogs licked the beggar's sores as they would have licked their own, to clean and to ease them with their soft tongues. Dogs did that, no one else would.

22) The main part of the parable begins. **Now it came to pass that the beggar died and was borne away by the angels into the bosom of Abraham; moreover, there died also the rich man and was buried.**

The accusative with the infinitives is the subject of ἐγένετο, compare 6:1. The beggar's disease killed him.

Nothing is said about his burial; his body was ignominiously dumped into an obscure grave; but his soul was borne into the bliss of heaven by God's own angels. Tissot has a wonderful painting of two glorious angels with six wings bearing the beggar's soul into the empyrean. The view that this was his body needs only to be mentioned in order to be rejected.

"Abraham's bosom" is a Jewish designation for heaven. Abraham is the father of believers who stood at the head of the old covenant. When the soul goes where he is, that means entrance into heaven. "Bosom" does not refer to a feast at which the guests recline on the left elbow on broad couches so that the person next to Abraham, on turning back, would let his head rest against Abraham's bosom. "Borne into Abraham's bosom" conveys the idea of a child being laid on Abraham's bosom and being embraced by him. The expression is figurative, not only for being in heaven where Abraham is, but as being in the most intimate association with the father of believers, accepted and acknowledged as a son of Abraham (19:9). So all true believers are borne into Abraham's bosom.

"Borne by the angels into Abraham's bosom" — these words have made an indelible impression on all Christendom, and all the interpretation of learned exegetes who try to disturb the honest faith which humbly accepts these words as they read has never succeeded in shaking it in the least. In spite of everything I truly believe that God's angels will stand around my deathbed and will carry my soul into Abraham's bosom!

We here meet the simple way in which Jesus speaks about the souls or spirits of the dead. All conceptions of time and space, succession and distance, must be removed for the other world. We know that they do not exist there. But our finite minds are inexorably fettered to these mundane concepts and are unable to think in terms of the supernatural world. Hence the Scriptures, even as Jesus here, condescend to us and use earthly terms to convey something of the heavenly realities to us. If Jesus should speak in the terms of that world, no human mind would understand a thing.

Two facts follow. We can only receive and accept what is thus told us and can do no more. It is folly to rationalize, speculate, draw conclusions with our finite minds beyond what is so inadequately conveyed to us. This extends to the spirits of the dead. Abraham has a bosom, the rich man eyes and a tongue, yet as disembodied spirits they have neither. For us on earth no other way of speaking about human or angelic spirits in the other world exists. To argue from this language that these spirits have some kind of an impalpable body is unwarranted. To go farther and to say that God creates these bodies for men as they die one by one, or that these bodies already now await us is to increase the confusion of thought.

Whether sooner or later—it makes no difference — the rich man also died. The same word is used with reference to both: each died. They were alike in this regard. "And was buried" means far otherwise than the beggar was buried. That is why the word is used — vast mourning, hundreds of friends, great display and honor. But no angels. How, then, did this man's soul get to hell? They know who get there!

23) **And in hades, having lifted up his eyes, being in torments, he sees Abraham from afar and Lazarus in his bosom. And he, calling out, says, Father Abraham, have mercy on me and send Lazarus that he may dip the tip of his finger in water and cool my tongue, because I am anguished in this flame!**

The fact that the rich man's soul went to hell needed not to be stated. It is a master touch in the parable to take that for granted. See 10:15 on the etymology of hades. The commentators are divided on this word, and especially its use in this parable. First there is a group which sees only an accommodation to the current Jewish views in all that Jesus says about the other world; then there are those who reduce everything to their conception of the Old Testament *sheol;* finally there are those who make this passage their *sedes doctrinæ* for the view that there are at least four places in the other world and regard "hades" as being the *Totenreich,* the realm of the dead which has two compartments, an upper and a lower. The latter is developed so as to make possible a conversion for those who in this life remained without the gospel, and the borders between this idea and the Catholic purgatory become very dim.

Other views are added such as that the soul of Jesus also entered this realm of the dead and remained there until his resurrection, and that his descent into hell meant that he went into this realm of the dead and released from its upper part the souls of the old covenant saints and took them with him in triumph to heaven. So this part of the realm of the dead is now vacant. The Scriptures and Jesus know nothing of this speculation but contradict it at every point.

The Biblical facts are these. *Sheol* is used in the Old Testament as a general and an indeterminate term, somewhat but not exactly like our "beyond" or "hereafter." All that makes departure from this life sad such as death, the grave, parting from the dead, etc., including also the godly dead, is thus connected with *sheol.* This broad view justifies the translation "grave" in certain connections, namely where only the general idea of removal from this life obtains. Those who deny the reality of hell use this translation for all the Old Testament passages that have *sheol;* all are referred only to "grave," and so hell as the eternal abode of the damned is erased.

But the Old Testament uses *sheol* also in a specific sense with reference to the wicked alone, who go down in terror to *sheol;* and in these passages the translation "hell" should be used. But we should keep in mind the broad meaning of *sheol,* literally, "a place into which one goes down, comparable to a belly . . . and according to Ps. 139:8, etc., the direct opposite to heaven," E. Koenig, *Hebraeisches und aramaeisches Woerterbuch* 474. Thus it is always described as "down," never as being at the borders of the world.

Neither the Greek, the English, nor the German has an exact equivalent for *sheol.* The Greek used *"hades,"* the unseen place, for *sheol* in the sense of the abode of the damned. It was the best the LXX could do. "Hades" is narrower than *sheol* but serves well enough in the New Testament with its clearer revelation about the other world and always means "hell," the abode of the damned. The linguistics regarding the term are of help only when all the contexts are considered; thus also in the New Testament the terrible descriptions of "hades," which, whatever its name, is always the same place of terror.

The Scripture and Jesus are a unit in revealing the existence of only *two places* in the other world, heaven, the abode of God and of the angels and the saints, and hell, the abode that has been especially prepared for the devil and his angels, to which also all those who follow the devil are consigned. Why the Scriptures speak of both as being places we have explained above, also why *our* ideas of space are absolutely inadequate for the understanding of the other world; look at Rev. 21:16: heaven, the Holy City, "the length and the breadth *and the height* of it are equal," "foursquare," a perfect *cube,* which is beyond mundane conception. The Scriptures speak of places, abodes ($\mu o\nu a\iota$, John 14:2), not merely of conditions, and with that we must be content in our present thinking. All speculation which claims the discovery of a third or intermediate abode treads the outworn paths of Romanism and merely modifies the Catholic views.

"And in hades (the unseen place) having lifted up his eyes, being in torments, he sees Abraham from afar," etc., is thought to mean that Abraham and Lazarus, too, were "in hades," and this statement is thus regarded a *sedes* for the intermediate place. All the dead are placed there, saints and damned; all are in hades, but this is divided into an upper and a lower part — for did the rich man not "lift up" his eyes? Although the parable does not say so, the upper place is called Paradise whereas no special name is given to the lower. This *sedes* loses its validity the moment we note that in the sentence the phrase "in hades" is removed as far as possible from "Abraham." "From afar" refers to the gulf that is mentioned in v. 26, ἀπό being idiomatic, the Greek measuring from the far place to the beholder, not as we do from the beholder to the far place. Abraham is pictured as being in heaven, the rich man as being in hell. What is gained by inventing a second kind of heaven (Paradise) and a second kind of hell and by uniting them with a gulf between them into a realm of the dead when we already have the real heaven and Paradise and the real hell, both properly divided? The entire Scripture analogy is against this alleged intermediate place.

"Being in torments" certainly states the condition of the souls in hell — or is there a difference between the torments in hell and those suffered by the rich man? The statement is made that Jesus has already placed the rich man "in hell" (realm of the dead) and must add "being in torments" in order to indicate that he is in the lower and not in the upper part of it. This is answered when we note that according to this assumption Jesus should certainly have indicated, first of all, in what part of this realm of the dead Abraham was. The rich man is in hell, the abode of the damned, and Abraham is in the heaven of God, and "being in torments" is added, not so that we may properly locate these persons in an alleged realm of the dead, but to explain what seeing Abraham and Lazarus meant to this tormented rich man. The plural κόλποι is merely idiomatic (R. 408) and is used interchangeably with the singular (v. 22).

24) The question of the propinquity of the rich man and Abraham and of the great chasm that divided them is answered when we remember that our ideas of space do not apply to the other world, and that what applies there cannot be put into human language. Thus any argument for hades as being a realm of the dead that is based on the nearness of the persons and the fact that they are in one place over against a far wider separation of heaven and hell, is met in the same way. All arguments regarding the other world that are based on our ideas of physical space are inadequate, that world is spaceless as it is timeless. The real question is whether the blessed and the damned are able to see and to speak with each other as that is here represented. The answer is negative. The conversation that is put into this parable is placed there for its own sake — so Abraham, the father of believers, (note: not Lazarus or any other saints) would answer every unbeliever in hell and justify God's judgment on the blessed and on the damned. The very frankness of the parable ought to keep us from drawing false conclusions.

Luke uses αὐτός and its plural freely as subjects with little or no emphasis. How did the rich man know Abraham when he saw him now for the first time? Exactly as Peter, James, and John knew Moses and Elijah on the Mount of Transfiguration. No introductions are needed in the other world.

Do not ask what kind of fire caused the flame by which the rich man was anguished. Physical fire as we know it on earth does not determine anything about the fire and the burning which are constantly predicated of hell beyond its power to produce the intensest pain. That fire torments the devils who have no bodies, the spirits of the damned before they are reunited with their earthly bodies, and finally also their bodies. Is that not effect enough without prying into the nature of that fire? Much is made of the fire, nothing whatever of the water into which Lazarus was to dip the tip of his finger. When Jesus speaks of things incomprehensible in comprehensible language, let us therewith rest content. It is the languague of a parent to a child about things that are beyond the child's comprehension. The parent must either be silent or descend to one-syllable baby words.

"Father Abraham!" cries he who all his life disowned Abraham. Yes, he was a physical descendant of Abraham who had no further relation to Abraham exactly as were the Jews who are mentioned in John 8:39-42. Exactly in the same sense Abraham addresses him as "child." He who knew not the quality of mercy nor its exercise when human need called out to him day after day at his own portal, now himself cries out for mercy: "mercy me," the Greek verb being transitive.

The fact that the entire conversation is intended to teach an underlying thought to the hearers of the parable and is not a report of an actual conversation should need no proof. All mercy is ended in hell. Even the least mercy as when a mere drop of water is asked for a tongue that is burned to a crisp; R. 495 makes the genitive ὕδατος one of place; C.-K. 172 regards it as being due only to the verb. This very request shows plainly that the conversation is only a vehicle for something that underlies it. He whose tongue daily tasted the finest wines and the most delectable cooling drinks now burns with ceaseless flame. Pitiless are the final judgments of God, and this is the illustration. Let men ignore them or rave against them now and say they cannot believe in such a God, the facts stand as they are depicted here.

25) **But Abraham said: Child, remember that thou didst get in full thy good things in thy life, and Lazarus likewise the bad things; but now here he is being comforted while thou art anguished. And in**

connection with all these things between us and you a great chasm has been fixed in order that those wanting to cross from here to you may not be able, nor that they may pass over from there to us.

All his life the rich man had forgotten, and he still forgets, and Abraham must tell him to remember; all his life he thought the impossible possible, that, although living the life he did, he might pass into heaven, and he still thinks impossible things possible, that Abraham might send Lazarus from heaven to hell to cool his fiery tongue. The damned do not learn even in hell.

Ἀπό in ἀπέλαβες adds the idea of getting what is "due" so that one can ask for no more; and the rich man certainly had no more coming to him. Abraham states only the facts, that the conditions of the rich man and of Lazarus are now reversed — that and no more. Why they are reversed is not stated — that comes later. Let it sink in that God's judgment so decides, and that settles the matter eternally.

It would be wrong to take this statement to mean that *because* a man has good things in this life *therefore* he is anguished in hell, and *because* a man has good-for-nothing things (κακά) in this life, *therefore* he is comforted in heaven. Abraham does not say this, nor would it be true. But when a man in hell asks for mercy, or when living men think hell ought to be changed by even a drop of water, they may think on this reminder to the rich man in hell. Hence also Abraham says *"thy* good things," those the rich man alone thought good, while he cared nothing for spiritual and heavenly treasures and showed that his life was bare of these by his lack of mercy; but not *"his* bad things," for these were only trials that were sent to Lazarus to refine his faith and to make his trust rest on God alone. Regarding good things as the rich man did, he had them all, no more were coming to him; having spurned all others, he must now do without.

Patiently taking and bearing the bad things God sent Lazarus, keeping his faith under them all and his hope in God, the good things of heaven were now his.

26) "Besides all this" renders the sense of the phrase which means literally "in connection with these things" (not: "through all these regions," Robertson's translation), i. e., in connection with the reversal which God made in his judgment he has also separated heaven and hell forever. The Greek always names the first person before the second: "between us and you"; not as we do: "you and us." The perfect passive ἐστήρικται has the present connotation of being fixed so now and ever. "Those wanting to cross from here to you" does not mean that there will be such although one may well suppose that those in hell would like to cross over to heaven. The sense of the statement is that death decides forever, it is either heaven or hell. This is not stressed by those who believe in the realm of the dead and make room for conversions in its lower part and thus a transfer into the higher part.

27) **However, he said: I then request thee, father, that thou send him to my father's house — for I have five brothers — in order that he may thoroughly testify to them lest they, too, come into this place of torment.**

The rich man is presented as seeing and dealing with Abraham and Lazarus only, and they only with him. So also the request is made of Abraham and not of Lazarus, the latter is treated as Abraham's servant who would do what Abraham ordered. All these features, plus the conversing of the rich man with Abraham, are means which the parable uses for bringing out first, the finality of the judgment at death (v. 23-26), second, the all-sufficiency of the Word. So the rich man is not presented as asking Abraham to warn the brothers but to send Lazarus; and we are not to ask whether Abraham's going to them would not have been more effective than sending only a beggar like Lazarus.

The rich man uses a respectful tone when he **says,** ἐρωτῶ, "I request," but what he requests is as bad as his complete disregard of Moses and the prophets, **yea,** also of Abraham's faith, during his earthly life. Οὖν, "then," intends to say that if the other request cannot be granted, he would ask this. He still calls Abraham "father"; the Pharisees who are listening to this parable are to note that Abraham has such "sons."

28) The rich man seems to have great concern for his five brothers since he wants them to go to heaven and not to hell. They evidently lived much as he had lived during his earthly life. But this man fails to see even in hell that his unbelief brought him to hell. He does not repent of that unbelief. He invents a new means of grace for his brothers, one that God should have applied also in his case but did not apply. His plea for his brothers is a covert accusation of God who could have prevented his arriving in hell by a simple means but failed to use that means. If the rich man had been warned as he now proposed to have his brothers warned he would not be in this place of torment. Yes, he is more concerned about his brothers than God is, knows better than God how to save them, and blames God for his terrible fate.

29) **But Abraham says: They have Moses and the prophets. Let them hear them! He, however, said: No, father Abraham! On the contrary, if one shall go to them from the dead, they will repent. But he said to him, If they do not hear Moses and the prophets, not even if one rose up from the dead will they be persuaded.**

This is the climax of the parable; for this reason the rich man and Abraham converse in the parable. Abraham knows all about Moses and the prophets who lived and labored long after Abraham was dead. Abraham is in full accord with them, for they all preached the same faith in which he lived and died. To have Moses and the prophets is to have the Old Testament Word.

Moses wrote the Torah or Pentateuch; the prophets, in the broad sense of that term, wrote all the other books of the Old Testament. This Word is the all-sufficient means of salvation. It is more, far more, than Abraham had in his life. We have Jesus and the apostles in addition.

"Moses and the prophets" takes us back to "the law and the prophets" mentioned in v. 16, "the law" being the Torah. "Moses and the prophets" contain the divine law which convicts of sin and the heavenly gospel which provides and imparts release from sin and thus saves from hell and brings to heaven. "Let them hear them" is the effective aorist: actually hear them so as to receive in the heart what they say — not merely learning and learning and never coming to a knowledge of the truth. To hear effectively is to believe. This is exactly what the rich man had not done; his heartless selfishness, his whole fleshly life were evidence of that fact.

The Jews made much of Moses, do so still, and even decorated the graves of the prophets whom their fathers had killed, and are still proud of those prophets (11:47); they neglected only one thing as Jesus pointed out already in v. 16, they did not hear them effectively. The supreme proof of that was their rejection of Jesus of whom Moses and all the prophets testified (John 5:46). It was because the rich man refused to hear Moses and the prophets that he was now in hell; the same end awaited the Pharisees who now listened to Jesus unless they heeded the warnings addressed to them.

30) Οὐχί is the sharper Greek "no." The most direct contradiction of unbelief persists even in hell: "No! father Abraham"; and the vacuous "father, father," too, persists. Abraham is contradicted in what he says, and that is a contradiction of Moses and the prophets and of their Word as the means of salvation. Although the rich man sees Abraham in heaven, knows

that Moses and the prophets are there likewise, he says "no" to all for which they stood, to all that brought them to heaven. Even the fires of hell bring no unbelievers to repentance and faith, and that is why they are in hell forever — where else could they be?

That strong "no" is re-enforced by the equally strong ἀλλά, which here, after a negative, means "on the contrary." This adversative draws a line of cancellation through the entire Old Testament as a means of salvation and substitutes a new means, one that was invented in hell instead of in heaven. The condition is that of expectancy, and ἐκ νεκρῶν, like many such phrases, is considered definite without the article (R. 791) and should be translated "from the dead." The rich man pictures one from the dead going to his wicked brothers who would then repent. A hellish repentance that would be, scaring them by a threat of the fires of hell.

He uses the verb "repent" but has no conception of its true meaning, bowing to God in contrition and accepting his pardon by faith (see 3:3). Did the rich man think of a resurrection of Lazarus like that of the actual Lazarus in Bethany whom Jesus called out of the tomb? Or of some ghostly return of only the soul of Lazarus? Decidedly the former as Abraham's reply shows: "even if one rose up from the dead." The idea that Abraham's answer overtops the rich man's assertion, that the latter spoke only of a spirit's appearance, Abraham of a complete resurrection, is without warrant in the words or in the thought.

31) Abraham does not reply that Lazarus cannot possibly rise from the dead, the ἐάν clause implies the contrary. But such a resurrection return and testimony would not accomplish anything in the case of men who constantly refuse to hear (οὐκ ἀκούουσιν, the durative present) in the sense of take to heart the divine testimony of Moses and the prophets, they would not even persuade such unbelievers. "They will not even be

persuaded" (passive), i. e., persuaded that the man has really risen from the dead. Think of the answer he would get on the part of unbelievers today. A thousand proofs would be offered that he was not dead in the first place, that someone was impersonating him if he were dead, that he must *a priori* be a fake, etc.

Was Abraham thinking of the resurrection of Jesus himself, or did Jesus place these words in Abraham's mouth as foretelling his own resurrection and its failure to persuade the Jews? This cannot be the intention because the risen Jesus never appeared to any but his own disciples as his chosen witnesses, and the parable speaks of Lazarus' going πρὸς αὐτούς, "to the five brothers." The proposition is general as it stands: "if anyone rise up from the dead," and only so does it include Jesus, not as saying in any way that he will arise. The Word is the all-sufficient and therefore the only means of salvation. God not only furnishes no other means, he had no stronger means to furnish, or, as we may surely say, he would have furnished it. They who now resort to other means produce no saving faith, in fact, intend to reach heaven without such faith.

The parable has reached its end, for the great fact it intends to teach is presented fully. It has been allegorized in what is an astonishing way. We need waste no time in presenting this allegory and in showing the impossibility of such an interpretation. The Pharisees have their warning which is complete in every way.

CHAPTER XVII

1) The view that no connection exists between the last parable and the new discourse is not tenable. The Pharisees and the scribes were causing dangerous offense to the publicans and the sinners who were inclined to believe in Jesus and were already believing in him (15:1, 2). Jesus has warned them in two chapters, and the matter is now carried a step farther. The same is true regarding the claim that the parallel utterances found in Matt. 18:6, 7 and Mark 9:42 were not recorded in their proper connection but are so recorded by Luke. A glance at Matthew and at Mark shows that this claim is untenable. Only portions of Luke are similar to those found in Matthew and in Mark, and these portions are of such a nature that they certainly permit a repetition, and the situation is decidedly different in Luke. See the question raised by the Twelve in Matt. 18:1, then note the situation in Luke. The Pharisees and the scribes who were present throughout the time when the last two chapters were spoken, for whom the parables were spoken in particular (15:1, 2; 16:14) certainly must have been glad to withdraw. Jesus is alone with "his disciples," and these include far more than the Twelve, namely all who had also listened to the parables, one of which was spoken to them (16:1). In v. 5 "the apostles" appear as a separate group.

Moreover he said to his disciples: Impossible it is for fatal traps not to come; nevertheless, woe through whom they come! It is profitable for him if a millstone has been placed around his neck and he has been pitched into the sea rather than that he fatally entrap one of these little ones.

The impossibility is due to the devilishness that is found in the world, a sample of which appears in 15:2, compare 11:52. Wicked men will always set deathtraps, especially for inexperienced believers, and will bait these traps in all kinds of ways; and some believers will be caught. Jesus knows all this and therefore pronounces this woe. See 7:25 on σκάνδαλον and the following σκανδαλίζω. The noun refers to a deathtrap which is baited so that, when the bait is touched, the stick holding the bait springs the trap. "Offenses" (A. V.) and "occasions of stumbling" (R. V.) are out of line. One gets over an offense, stubs himself in stumbling, picks himself up after falling over something, but is killed by a *skandalon*, here, of course, spiritually, thus landing in hell like the rich man. So the verb, too, means to catch and to kill in a trap. M.-M. 576. The accusative with the infinitive "for fatal traps not to come" is the subject of the sentence, it has pleonastic τοῦ which is often added to infinitives, but the genitive force of the article is lost; the infinitive is here in the nominative; see R. 1094, 1068 (B.-D. 400, 4 and other explanations are not acceptable).

Πλήν means that in spite of the fact that deathtraps will be set, woe is "nevertheless" on him through whom they are set. This "woe" is neither an accusation nor a mere exclamation of sorrow. Exactly like the "blessed" in the Beatitudes, these "woes" are verdicts, and these verdicts will be carried out inexorably.

2) In what a terrible way this will occur is indicated by the following. Both the εἰ and the ἵνα clauses are nominative subjects of λυσιτελεῖ (R. 997) ; R. 992 shows that ἵνα clauses are freely used as subjects or as objects of a sentence. The thought is plain: is would be a tremendous advantage if, before a man ruined a human soul forever, he were pitched into the sea with a great millstone around his neck. The crime is so terrible in the eyes of Jesus that he mentions an unheard-of manner of death as being vastly preferable to its commission. No human judge or court ever decreed such a death as a penalty. And this an-

swers the idea that such a penalty is to be regarded as alone befitting the crime of destroying one of God's inexperienced children. What the awful penalty for that will actually be Jesus allows his disciples to guess from the way in which he pictures its enormity.

The λίθος μυλικός is "a stone connected with a mill," and περίκειται is used as the perfect passive of περιτίθημι, "has been placed around," and thus harmonizes with the perfect ἔρριπται, "has been pitched," the tenses saying that for this to have been done with the man, thus for his body to be beyond recovery in the bottom of the sea where it could never get near to a Christian, is preferable and to be chosen "rather than" — and now an aorist subjunctive to express a single act in the future — that he fatally entrap one of these little ones. The connection makes plain whom Jesus has in mind: new and as yet inexperienced believers like those mentioned in 15:1 as well as any others. In Matt. 18 children are especially referred to.

3) **Take heed to yourselves — if thy brother commit a sin, rebuke him; and if he repent, remit it for him! And if he commit sin against thee seven times during the day and seven times turn to thee, saying, I am repentant! thou shalt dismiss it for him.**

Worldly men seek to entrap the disciples so as to kill their faith. In this matter, Jesus says, take heed to yourselves, i. e., so as to guard each other; with προσέχετε we supply τὸν νοῦν. The moment a brother commits a sin (the aorist to denote a single act of sin), he who sees and knows it is told to rebuke him by showing him that he has sinned and how deadly the guilt of that sin is. Ἁμαρτάνω, "to miss the mark" set by God's law, is the ordinary verb for "to sin"; and there is no restriction here such as "against thee," which occurs in the next verse. This is any open sin into which one of us may fall. The one aim of this rebuke is that

Luke 17:3, 4

the brother may repent (see 3:3), and the rebuke must be according.

Jesus speaks only of the case of a successful rebuke and uses the condition of expectancy, ἐάν with the subjunctive. The aorist denotes the one act of repentance, which is usually accompanied by a confession of the sin. The moment that occurs, the rebuking brother has the order: "Remit it to him," pronounce absolution upon him in Jesus' name; on ἄφεσις see 1:77. Luther has often spoken of this great and blessed function of the royal priesthood, this delivering a brother from his sin by getting him to repent of that sin and giving him God's pardon to relieve his conscience. The fact that the pardon is not pronounced by a pastor but by an ordinary brother makes no difference whatever if only the brother truly knows what he is about and acts as though he were in the sight of God. This is the first place in Luke's Gospel where "brother" is used to indicate the relation of one disciple to another. This word of Jesus is also spoken for the sinning brother; he is to know what Jesus orders others to do for him, and what his Lord expects of him, namely prompt and genuine repentance.

4) Jesus adds further instruction (καί) on this subject. The act of sin (again aorist) may be directed "against thee," against another brother. And Jesus cites the extreme case of seven different sins that are committed against a brother in a single day. We cannot think that this is merely the same sin repeated again and again because it would then be farcical for the sinning brother to say, "I repent!" In this extreme case, in which the sins are even being committed against the one brother, upon the sinning brother's sincere repentance of his sin, which is each time expressed by the sinning brother, Jesus bids the wronged brother to remit the sin time after time. "Seven times" is not intended as a limit but as what might possibly

occur during one day, τῆς ἡμέρας, the genitive to indicate the time within.

This is not an abbreviation of Matt. 18:21, etc., where no time limit such as "during the day" appears. In Matthew the remission is that of brother to brother, seventy times seven times, the moment a brother sins against another even if he never thinks of saying, "I am repentant." Never am I to hold a grudge against a brother for any sin or any number of sins. The parable recorded in Matthew makes that plain. In Luke the remission is that of God to one who sins against me. I am pronouncing God's pardon (not my own). To do that I must have the repentant confession: Μετανοῶ! Without that I, indeed, hold nothing against him but I cannot declare unto him the divine pardon.

Thus the disciples are to deal with each other, and those sinning are to know in advance about this dealing in order that no brother, whether because of some general sin or because of some sin against another brother, may remain under God's condemnation. Whereas worldly men seek to entrap our brethren, the brethren are to save each other.

5) **And the apostles said to the Lord** (the title is explained in 7:13), **Add to us faith! But the Lord said, If you have faith as a kernel of mustard, you would say to this mulberry tree, Be uprooted and be planted in the sea! and it would have obeyed you.**

Not since 9:10 does Luke write "the apostles." The term is used here in order to distinguish the Twelve from the larger body of disciples (v. 1), and it thus shows that the scene is still the same. The request, too, is in line with what precedes. One of the apostles must have voiced it, by word or by nodding the others seconded it. "Add to us faith!" is a petition for more and thus stronger faith. The apostles felt that they must have far greater faith than they had at present to beware of the *skandala* or deathtraps and to help each other and their other brethren as Jesus had just directed. They felt this as apostles who were to warn and to correct each other and others. This was, indeed, a good prayer like the one mentioned in 11:1.

6) The answer of Jesus is frequently misunderstood. It is thought that he is speaking of charismatic faith (I Cor. 13:2; 12:9), as if he said that they ought to have such faith. We are also told that the apostles ought to have answered their own prayer. But who of us would have thought that the apostles asked for charismatic faith, or that this kind of faith was needed for what Jesus had just said?

This paragraph is also removed from the preceding, and we are told that Jesus must have performed some great miracle which Luke omitted, which caused the apostles to pray for more charismatic faith. Such views are answered when we note that Jesus does two things: he encourages the faith of the apostles and thus increases it; and he shows that, despite all their works of faith, they must remain humble and claim no special merit.

The sentence is unusual because it has three types of conditions: "If you have faith" (a protasis of reality; and, indeed, you have, Jesus admits it), "you would say" (apodosis of present unreality, the imperfect with ἄν; Jesus declares that in spite of having faith they are not using it), "and it would have obeyed you" (a second apodosis, now of past unreality, the aorist with ἄν; it did and could not obey because you are not telling it to do so). It is thus that Jesus gives them more faith, namely by encouraging the faith which they have to put forth its power and thus to grow by seeing to what power it can rise.

This encouragement Jesus applies to a faith that is even as small as the very least garden seed, the tiny kernel of mustard. For faith is a vessel; its power lies, not in being a vessel, but in what it contains as a vessel. Faith embraces the divine promises, and when it makes use of these promises, its greatness and its power appear, and it can do all that Jesus asks in v. 1-4 and far more because divine grace and help are contained in the promises that are held by faith. Such faith the apostles have; let them use the promises to which it holds.

The remarkable thing that Jesus says the apostles could do — though he admits that they are not doing it — is to say to this mulberry tree, "Be uprooted and be planted in the sea!" with the effect that it would have been done but was not because even now they fail to say such a thing. Note that both of the verbs are passive in this figurative command. Neither the apostles nor their faith pretend to do such things; the agent in the passives is God, and he does things that are as astounding as that wherever we have his promise.

What Jesus says is not a mere variant of Matt. 17:20; 21:21 (Mark 11:23; compare I Cor. 13:2). Those interpretations which assume that dropping the mountain into the sea and uprooting the mulberry tree and planting it in the sea are the same, namely two illustrations of humanly impossible things, both of which are possible only to charismatic faith, have misunderstood the words of Jesus. The mountain just drops into the sea and disappears, a hindrance that it is humanly impossible to remove is nevertheless removed by charismatic faith. But here is a fruitful mulberry tree, and it is carefully taken up by the roots and as carefully planted again right in the sea, where no man can plant anything, and it stands there and keeps on bearing fruit. This is an entirely different story from having the tree pitch itself into the sea. To be sure, human impossibility is pictured by the tree as well as by the mountain, but in the case of the tree something is added that far exceeds what occurred in the case of the mountain — the tree is planted and flourishes in the sea.

Exactly this very thing the apostles would soon do over and over again, for at their word the kingdom would be transplanted, root and branch, from Israel into the Gentile world in congregation after congregation — into territory in which no man would have thought the kingdom could grow and flourish; the Jews were sure that it could not. No charismatic faith was necessary for this, for the gospel was not spread through the world by anything but the ordinary faith of its bearers. All it needs to do is to act, and in its testing of the promise concerning the gospel that faith will grow and grow. And for that reason Jesus carefully adds the promise right here: "and it would have obeyed you." So Jesus answers the prayer. Faith is living trust in the gospel, and that trust grows as it witnesses and experiences the gospel's power.

7) But as he always does, so here, too, Jesus sees all sides of a subject. The apostles are now humble and feel how small their faith is even in view of what Jesus says in v. 1-4. It must remain humble when it now steps out into the world and accomplishes wonders there. That is the point of the parable.

Moreover, who of you is there, having a slave plowing or shepherding, who on his coming in from the field will say to him, At once, having come along, recline at table! On the contrary, will he not say, Make ready what I shall dine on and, after having girded thyself, keep serving me until I finish eating and drinking, and after that then thyself shalt eat and drink? Does he thank the slave because he did the things he was ordered to do? Thus also you yourselves, when you shall finish doing all the things ordered for you, be saying, Slaves unprofitable are we; what we were under obligation to do we have done.

The interrogative form into which the parable is put makes it far stronger than if it were stated in the form of an assertion. The answers to the questions are self-evident, and the disciples themselves are bound to give these answers.

Jesus asks the apostles to put themselves into the position of a man who has a slave or bondservant, one whose entire time and labor belong to his master. This slave is out in the field working all day long, "engaged in plowing or shepherding," both participles being durative. These occupations are not selected at random but with a view to the work of the apostles. For plowing compare I Cor. 3:9: "ye are God's husbandry," meaning tillage; the figures of sowing and reaping presuppose plowing. Plowing is hard work, to be understood as such here. "Or shepherding," which, according to the constant analogy of Scripture, refers to sheep (R. V.), certainly not to cattle (A. V.). This, too, is hard work and pictures the coming task of the apostles, John 21:15, etc.

When, after such a hard day's work, the slave comes in toward evening, Jesus asks, would you, if you were his master, say to him, "At once, having come along, recline at table!" i. e., rest and refresh thyself? We construe εὐθέως with ἀνάπεσε (regular second aorist imperative and the correct reading) and not with ἐρεῖ (A. V.) or even with παρελθών (R. V.). "By and by" in the A. V. was proper when this translation was made in the seventeenth century, it was used for "immediately" but now misleads, for it now means "after a while." The Jews and the Orientals reclined at table, resting on the left elbow on broad couches. This slave's work is not yet done after all the plowing or shepherding. His labors during the entire day are not considered as being anything great at all.

8) "On the contrary," the strong ἀλλά begins the new question, this one with the interrogative word οὐχί which involves a decided affirmative answer. The master will certainly order his slave to make ready his master's dinner, the δεῖπνον, the main meal of the day that is eaten toward evening. We regard "what I shall dine on" as an indirect question with the aorist sub-

junctive and τί as the object and not as an adverb (R. 1045, "how").

More than that, the master will order that slave to keep on serving him or waiting at table (durative present imperative) "until I finish eating and drinking," this being the force of the two aorist subjunctives (not "while," R. 976, which would require present subjunctives). So all this service still goes into the slave's work; nobody expects anything else, and he himself would be the last to complain. If he were the master he would expect his bondservant to do the same thing.

"And after that thou thyself (emphatic σύ) shalt eat and drink" is a part of the master's speech, not because he would ordinarily say this, but to express the common thought about such a slave, namely that he is to eat and to drink only when all work is done. The so-called futures like πίεσαι and φάγεσαι, which are really old aorist subjunctives (R. 869), have the uncontracted personal ending -σαι.

9) To emphasize the point of the parable Jesus asks another question, this time with μή because he thinks only of a negative answer. The master has finished dining, the slave clears the table, then he himself at last proceeds to eat. Does the master, on rising from the couch, offer anything like thanks to the slave (the idiom χάριν ἔχειν = *gratiam habeo, Dank wissen*, to feel thankful, and thus to thank)? Trench would soften this and would let the slave receive some recognition; he lets his modern feeling enter a little. No; the slave gets not even a "thank you." Who, even today, is everlastingly thanking us when we do what is our ordinary work in our station of life? The addition in the A. V.: "I trow not" is an interpretative translation, an effort to show to the English reader the force of the negative answer that is assumed in the Greek form of the question. When it is so understood it may pass, for we have no interrogative word to match μή.

10) Jesus himself interprets the parable, and we should at once see that it is intended for us, for our proper attitude toward our Lord, and is not intended to bring in what he does or ought to do toward us. This is essential and clears away those criticisms of the parable which have been made when this restriction is overlooked. "Thus also you yourselves" (emphatic ὑμεῖς) is decisive on the matter. However much our faith is increased and is able to do and actually does do in the Lord's work, let no false claims of merit enter our minds. "When you shall finish doing all things ordered for you," actually finish them all (this being the force of the aorist ποιήσητε), then do not boast or set up special claims — which would only spoil it all. We need not discuss the question as to whether any servant of Jesus ever did all that was commanded him, without omission whatever. The Lord cites a case that is perfect in this respect. Even Paul feels constrained to say that, although he knows nothing against himself, he is thereby not justified (I Cor. 4:4, R. V.)

Even after having served perfectly we are to say from our inmost conviction, "Slaves unprofitable are we." The sense of ἀχρεῖοι, although "unprofitable" is not an exact translation but only the best we can do, is fortunately understood by our English Bible readers, the entire parable making it so plain. It is otherwise in the case of the commentators who labor with the etymology. Romanists even run counter to the word and in spite of it hold to works of supererogation, for which they claim the highest merit. "Unprofitable," which is defined by the parable itself, certainly does not mean *entbehrlich*, servants without whom the Lord can do, but "deserving of no special thanks" because they have no special claims on the Lord. The Lord's own interpretation is certainly lucid: we are to call ourselves "unprofitable" because "what we were under obligation to do, we have done." We thus drop all claims, for we, indeed, have none; even the most perfect servant whom the Lord ever had has none. We do not pretend in this respect and with secret hypocrisy think that the Lord owes us something.

So much for the parable and its *tertium* and its teaching. We know from other parables and from other Scripture passages that the Lord is not going to act as the master in this parable did. It will not do to interpret this parable by saying "who of you" represents God or the Lord, for the Lord will not act as is here described, wherefore also Jesus does not begin this parable by saying, "There was a man" who had a slave plowing, etc. "Who of you" pictures ourselves as we in ordinary life act toward those who are working for us. The Lord does far otherwise (19:17, 19; Matt. 25: 21, 23) and rewards even those who have not succeeded in doing "all things ordered for them," forgives them their shortcomings.

But when he so rewards, this is altogether and absolutely due to his abounding grace and generosity. It is because *of himself* and not because of *us and our work*. Once for all learn: if we think we ought to receive recognition at the Lord's hands for our service, which is imperfect and poor at best and not to be compared with that of the slave in the parable, we are doing an outrageous and utterly presumptuous thing. We are then turning his wholly undeserved grace, his glorious generosity, which is so glorious just because he gives it without the least merit on our part, into nothing more than a mere payment that is coming to us by right and justice. Can the Lord consent to such a double lie?

11) And it came to pass in going to Jerusalem he was going through between Samaria and Galilee.

On ἐγένετο καί see 5:12, and on ἐν with the infinitive 1:8; Luke often uses the unstressed αὐτός as the subject. Διὰ μέσον, which is found only here in the New Testament, does not mean "through the midst" of the two countries, first through Samaria and then through

Galilee, but between them, along the border where they meet. Luke does not keep to the chronology as we have seen hitherto. He has already brought us far on this journey to Jerusalem where Jesus was to die, as far as southern Perea, but he now reverts to the start of this journey, when, after being refused hospitality by the Samaritans (9:51, etc.), Jesus passed along the border of Samaria and Galilee to cross the Jordan into Perea. Luke, who is seldom specific about the localities of his narratives, is so here in order to explain how one of the ten lepers happened to be a Samaritan. We conclude also that Jesus is on the Galilean side of the border, for it would be hard to account for the presence of nine Jewish lepers in Samaria and much easier to have one Samaritan leper associated with nine Jewish lepers in Galilee near the border.

Luke places this incident of the lepers at this point in his Gospel as a continuation of 15:1, 2. The entire piece from 15:1-17:10 is a unit. It referred to publicans and open sinners in chapter 15, and Luke now brings in even a Samaritan, one who did not come in contact with Jesus in vain.

12) **And as he was entering into a village, there met him ten leprous men who stood far off; and they lifted the voice, saying, Jesus, Master, have mercy on us! And on seeing them he said, Having gone, show yourselves to the priests! And it came to pass while they were going they were cleansed.**

As he was on the point of entering a village near the border, ten men who were affected with the dread disease of leprosy meet Jesus. They came from the side toward the road that entered the village, for they had to live outside of the village in such huts or dwellings as they could construct for themselves and avoid all contact with people who were not leprous like themselves. These ten, one of them being even a Samaritan, had congregated to aid each other. Their misery had overcome national and religious antipathy. Being un-

Luke 17:12-14

clean (Lev. 13:46), they stood afar off lest they render others unclean also. The Greek says that they stood "from afar," for it always measures the distance from the object to the beholder, not, as we do, from ourselves to the object. The rabbis prescribed a space of at least four paces, but these lepers stood well to the side because of the crowd that was following Jesus.

On leprosy see the Bible Dictionaries and Trench, *Miracles of Our Lord*, 10, The Cleansing of the Leper. The leper was regarded as one who was already dead, unclean for this reason. No cure was known for this disease.

13) The reason the lepers lifted up their voice was to attract certain attention from the distance at which they stood. Yes, leprosy gradually destroys the voice, but the ten could still make considerable noise. Their cry does not reveal more than that they knew about the power of Jesus to heal even men like themselves. They call him by his name "Jesus" and use only the title "Master," which is equal to "Rabbi," which latter title Luke never uses (see 5:5). And the prayer: "Mercy us!" (the Greek verb being transitive) means only that Jesus is to free them from their leprosy. The most that we can deduce from this is that these lepers believed that Jesus could help them.

14) He sees them, hears their shouting, perhaps raises a hand to hush them, and then issues his command, "Having gone, (the Greek always expresses the minor action by a participle) show yourselves to the priests!" And Jesus goes on into the village and lets the lepers stand there.

Imagine their situation. They must have stood and looked at each other and then started to debate this command. They had surely expected something else. If they had news of other lepers whom Jesus had healed (5:12, etc.) they knew that Jesus had never merely ordered lepers to go to Jerusalem as if they were healed when they were not. Should they go? They decided to do so, for they told each other and, indeed, rightly that this command involved a promise, the promise that they were to be healed. The command of Jesus is terse, but it means the same as it did in 5:14 where the details of the priests' duties in reinstating healed lepers are described. Cases occurred that eventually turned out not to be leprosy.

The plural "to the priests" is used because ten lepers are involved, and the ceremonies described in 5:14 plainly show that the contention that one priest could attend to all at one time is mistaken. Did Jesus know that one of the ten was a Samaritan and, even if he desired, could not enter the Temple at Jerusalem much less offer sacrifices there? Jesus always knew all that he needs to know for his work and so did not need to wait until the Samaritan returned to learn that he was not a Jew. Did Jesus say "priests," meaning that this man should show himself to a Samaritan priest at his own sanctuary? Let us remember that Jesus was not building up Judaism, was not trying to make men Jews. We may add that the Jewish priests accepted the findings of the Samaritan priests when they pronounced a man clean of leprosy.

Jesus healed in different ways according to the condition of the sick persons. These men as yet believed only in his healing power. Jesus desired to advance that faith to something better. So he acted as he did. Leprous as they were, these men were to go to their priests like clean men to be pronounced clean. That required stronger faith than ever in Jesus' healing power. The way in which to increase even such faith is to feed it with the Word. Jesus gave these men his word. That, too, moved them to act. They would have been fools not to act on that word, to stand around only to debate and to rationalize about it. In only one way could they find out whether that word had power in it, the power of which they had heard so much: they must trust that word and go to the priests. That would show just what power was in that word.

Commentators like to call this a trial of faith to which Jesus put these men. "Trial" is not the proper word. They were not tested as to the strength of their faith, their faith was given the word that it needed to give it more strength. But the word is like food, only by eating it will it give us strength; so only by trusting Jesus' word and thus trustfully acting on it will faith grow and increase in strength.

And sure enough, while they were going, leprous as they were and holding only to that precious word from Jesus' lips, they were all at once cleansed. Did they look at their bodies, feel of them, do this to each other, and then, certain of the fact, shout with delight? Their faith was justified to the uttermost. So this is what Jesus meant! Why are we told that they gradually, very gradually lost the disease? Is that the manner in which Jesus healed? Why are we told that they had to go all the way to the priests before they were healed? The narrative makes the impression that they went only a moderate distance, and that the happy moment came then. Luke puts stress on the sentence by starting it with "and it came to pass" (see 1:8).

15) **But one of them, on seeing that he was healed, turned back, with a great voice glorifying God, and fell on his face at his feet thanking him; and he was a Samaritan. Now Jesus answering said: Were not ten cleansed? But the nine — where are they? Were there not found, having turned back to give glory to God, save this foreigner? And he said to him, Having arisen, be going! Thy faith has saved thee.**

Before the one turned back he must have debated with the others about turning back. Had Jesus not told them to go to the priests, and now, healed as they were, had they not more cause than ever to hurry to the priests? But with nine against him, left in a minority of one, this one turned back. The idea is not that he was disobeying Jesus' orders—how long would it take to return and to seek the priests after that? Whatever outward arguments this one had with the nine, the decisions were due to something inward. In the heart of the one, out of the faith that made him, too, cry to Jesus for mercy, and out of the word of Jesus that had healed him, something was born that was not born in the hearts of the others, something that drew him back to Jesus in spite of the decision of the nine to go on, something that could not draw the others because it was not born in them because they grasped only at the healing and not also at the Healer.

Majorities impress us too much. What would you have done if you had stood alone against nine? Majorities can go wrong as easily as an individual may go wrong. The decisive thing is the right, the true, and not the numbers. Luther stood against the world of his day; he stood with and for the truth. It is still true that God and one make a majority. It was right that this man should return, right that he should do so by glorifying God with a loud voice when he came back to Jesus and the crowd that was with him in the village, which now included the villagers. He praised God for healing him through Jesus even as Jesus did all his works to glorify God. By glorifying God he withheld nothing from Jesus.

16) For he prostrated himself at Jesus' feet and thanked him. That, too, was the proper thing to do. The greatness of Jesus that had been manifested in the miracle — healing ten lepers with less than ten words —overcame this man. So he lay at Jesus' feet and thanked him with all his soul. The nine had the same greatness to impress their hearts, owed the same response of prostration and gratitude to Jesus, but their hearts did not, would not respond. Whatever faith in Jesus' power had made them cry for mercy advanced

not one step to something better in spite of what Jesus had given that faith. Like a promising bud it stopped growth, then began to wilt, and finally died. They never went back to Jesus, not even after they had been to the priests; the record would have mentioned such a return, one that was made late but was vastly better than no return.

"And he was a Samaritan" — the nine Jews were absent. It was thus with the whole Jewish nation. Read Rom. 9:4, 5 regarding the Jews and John 4:22 regarding the Samaritans and then you catch Luke's meaning: "and he was a Samaritan." Then compare Luke 11:30-32.

17) The Greek "answered" (see 1:19) is used also here where Jesus responded to a situation — only one of the ten had returned. Jesus is addressing no one in particular. His questions are exclamations that all those about him are to hear. They are surcharged with feeling. Rom. 10:21. "But the nine — where?" with its longing and its pain, with its appeal in spite of all disappointment, has been echoing through the years, is calling, calling still.

18) The Greek places the negative with the verb: "were there not found," whereas we place it with the noun or subject: "were none found," etc. "To give glory to God" is meant in the same sense as it was in v. 15. The point of the question lies in the clause: "save this foreigner," ὁ ἀλλογενής, one of another race. The Samaritans were of Gentile extraction, not even partly of Jewish blood as is often supposed. The personal work of Jesus was intended for the Jews (Matt. 15:24), but here nine Jews take his blessing, and the one Samaritan who was with them breaks away from them and returns alone.

19) Jesus now tells this man to get up and to be going (durative present imperative) on the journey to the priests to be legally pronounced clean and to be reinstated in the society of men. But Jesus adds what

was so vital: "Thy faith has saved thee," the perfect tense as well as the verb itself refer to his saved condition into which one act of saving or rescue had placed him. In this and in other such statements of Jesus faith is not the *causa efficiens,* the saving power that caused the healing from leprosy, but the *causa instrumentalis,* the subjective means that connect the leper with the power of Jesus. This man was healed by trusting Jesus and by trustfully crying out to him. So, indeed, were the nine. But their faith produced nothing but that cry, then faded out even as they were now far from Jesus and remained away from him. But this man's trust remained, brought the fruit of gratitude as described, and was thus on the way to still more. That is why Jesus reminds this man of his faith. It is as though he told him: "See what thy faith in me and my power has done for thee! Keep that faith and see what it will yet do for thee!"

This was not yet soteriological faith, justifying faith that saves the soul. It was to lead to this type of faith. The power that saved from leprosy is divine, and he who has it must be able to save also the soul with the power of grace. It is thus that soteriological faith was to be born in the Samaritan; he was on a fair way to have it produced in him.

The next statement is misunderstood when Jesus' word addressed to this man is made equal to the word he spoke to the pardoned woman in 7:50. How could this man be already saved from sin? It will not do to say that Jesus had already saved him and declared that fact here. Jesus is not making an astonishing revelation to the man about his soul. The soul's salvation rests on more than had as yet come to this man's soul. But he was on the way to his salvation, and to tell him, as Jesus did, encouraged him to go on toward the greater goal of faith.

20) Luke again follows his manner of leaving the time and the place unnamed and concentrates all atten-

tion on the words that Jesus uttered as being perfectly clear without reference to the time or the place The account about the thankful Samaritan is a minor link in Luke's progress of thought — others step in where the Jews fail. The discourse on the coming of the kingdom and on its consummation (17:20-37) connects in a broad way with the last parable recorded in chapter 16 and with 17:1, etc.

Now having been requested by the Pharisees as to when the kingdom of God is coming, he answered them and said: The kingdom of God does not come accompanied by observation; neither will they say, Lo here, or there! For lo, the kingdom of God is inside you!

Neither the question nor its answer betrays an ulterior motive or purpose on the part of the Pharisees. Some find ridicule in it as if the Pharisees mean. "Thou hast talked much about the kingdom, but we have as yet seen nothing of it; when will it come?" Others find a temptation in it: "He claims to be bringing the kingdom—let us get him to tell us when he is making it arrive." But neither of these views is verifiable.

The Greek retains the tense of the direct discourse: "When comes the kingdom of God?" This question does not intend to inquire as to the date but as to the visible signs and tangible proofs for determining that the kingdom has truly come. The Jews generally looked forward with longing and hope to the arrival of the Messiah and the kingdom which he would establish But they conceived this as an outward, visible, glorious kingdom. If Jesus could have brought such a kingdom, all Jews would have flocked to his standard. That is one great reason why he was rejected — he looked, spoke, and acted like anything but such a king who was bringing the kingdom. It was a very pertinent question, this about the "when" of the kingdom.

Jesus gives a pertinent answer. These Pharisees have a complete misconception concerning the kingdom. It and therefore its coming are not like what they think. Hence Jesus must tell them: "The kingdom of God does not come (at all) accompanied with observation (with men sitting by and watching the grand spectacle of its arrival)." It is not at all a kingdom that could come in such a way.

21) Jesus explains what he means by the phrase "with observation": "neither will they say (of this kingdom when it comes), Lo here (it is — pointing a finger at it) or there (it is)!" The plural ἐροῦσιν is indefinite. The kingdom does not come like a magnificent procession with bands playing, hosts marching, a glittering king at its head. There is no "when" at all for such a coming or for any kingdom that could come in this way.

In place of the false "lo" Jesus offers the true one, and γάρ gives the brief and complete explanation. "For, lo, the kingdom is inside you!" It is wholly and altogether a *spiritual* kingdom. The phrase ἐντὸς ὑμῶν means neither *in animis vestris*, for the kingdom is certainly not in the hearts of these Pharisees, nor merely *intra vos* (R. V. margin), "among you," "in your midst," in the hearts of the believers that are scattered here and there among the Pharisees. The phrase does not locate the kingdom but states its *character* as being something internal and not, like earthly kingdoms, external. The pronoun "you" is general and does not mean "you Pharisees" or "you," any definite person. So the Pharisees sit in their observation towers in vain; the kingdom, being spiritual and internal, comes right under their noses, and with their unspiritual eyes they never see a thing of it or of its coming. See 4:43 on the kingdom. It is Luke's concern to report this word of Jesus and therefore he says nothing more about the Pharisees.

22) The Pharisees had left, or Jesus and the disciples had proceeded on their journey. The Pharisees needed to be told that the kingdom is within, is spiritual; to this the Lord adds for the sake of his disciples that, after the spiritual work of this kingdom is done, it will come suddenly, like lightning, in judgment on the world.

Moreover, he said to the disciples: There shall come days when you shall long to see one of the days of the Son of man, and you shall not see it. And they shall say to you, Lo, there! Lo, here! Do not go away or pursue after. For just as the lightning when lightning shines out of one part under the heaven unto the other part under the heaven, thus shall be the Son of man in his day.

The Jews looked for a glorious earthly kingdom; Jesus tells his disciples that depressing times constitute the immediate prospect. "There shall come days" again and again, many of them, which shall be filled with what Jesus does not need to say because their effect speaks for itself — days when you shall long to see "one of the days (just one as a breathing spell in your afflictions) of the Son of man" (on this title see 5:24). Note that "one of the days of the Son of man" is analogous to "the day of the Lord Jesus Christ" mentioned in I Cor. 1:8 and thus analogous to "his day" referred to in v. 24.

Jesus does not intend to say that times will come when the disciples will desire again to enjoy one of the happy days when he walked on earth with them, but that in future times they will long and sigh earnestly for Jesus to send, in advance of his coming, just one day of that glorious period when he shall reign in might and majesty with all his enemies under his feet. "Son of man" is the proper term, for as such he shall return to judgment, John 5:27. But all such longing must necessarily be denied: "you shall not see it." The visible, glorious consummation of the kingdom must wait *in toto* until the spiritual work has been completed.

23) This ἐροῦσιν is different from the one that is negated in v. 21, for the words "they shall say to you" betray who they are, false Christs and false prophets, compare Matt. 24:24-26 which was spoken on the Tuesday of the Passion week. The spiritual coming of the kingdom into men's hearts never interests men so that they cry, "Lo here, or there!" But it will be different in regard to the glorious coming; disregarding all that Jesus said about it, some will raise this very cry, "Lo there! Lo here!" and by that very cry demonstrate their own falseness. They will imagine that they see plain indications and signs of Christ's immediate coming. They will pose as prophets, even as manifestations and incarnations of Christ, and call the true disciples to flock to their standards "here" or "there." Jesus warns, "Do not go away or pursue after," leave not your faith in the words which Jesus has spoken, do not chase after these false leaders and the promises they make. This warning has often been disregarded, will often be so, but should not be so by us.

24) Jesus gives us the reason (γάρ): his coming and the consummation of the kingdom will occur in such a manner that we need go nowhere — it will be instantaneously visible over the whole earth just as a lightning flash lightnings out of one part of heaven and shines to the other part and lights up the entire sky. In ἐκ τῆς and εἰς τήν the articles have demonstrative force: "out of this," "unto that," and we supply the noun μερίς, "part." Not the mere suddenness or the unexpected flashing of the lightning or the brightness of its dazzling light is the point of the comparison but the universal, instantaneous visibility of it when it flashes across the sky; so shall the Son of man be in his day. Nor need the shape of the earth or its physical extent cause us one instant of doubt, for the world it-

self shall be changed, sun, moon, and stars shall be moved from their place; and grand as the simile of the lightning is it is only a faint illustration of what Christ's appearance in his day shall be, for he is greater than heaven and earth and the whole universe of created things, the glory of his countenance shall penetrate everywhere.

25) **But first it is necessary that he suffer many things and be rejected by this generation.**

What a contrast: the heavenly glory and majesty — suffering, rejection, and death! Jesus frequently linked the two together. This repeats the prophecy uttered in 9:22, 44, and has the same δεῖ of the necessity of God' saving love (see it already in 2:49), the same verbs ("suffer, be rejected" after due examination like a bad coin), the same πολλά which still veils the details. The fact that Jesus knew these "many things" through direct knowledge and not merely from the Old Testament prophecies, as some claim, is evidenced by his naming scourging, mockery, deliverance to the Gentiles, and crucifixion, all of which are not directly named by the prophets. "By this generation," ἀπό naming the agent (R. 579) "from" whom the actions come, refers to the Jewish nation then living, whose constituted authorities and great mass would, indeed, reject Jesus. — So fades the Jewish "observation" which is looking for a grand earthly Messiah and kingdom.

26) **And even as it was in the days of Noah, thus shall it be also in the days of the Son of man: they were eating, they were drinking, they were marrying, they were being married up to the day Noah went into the ark, and the deluge came and destroyed them all.**

In Matt. 24:37-39, on the Tuesday of the Passion week, Jesus repeated this illustration and parts of what follows. The way in which the people acted in the days of Noah during the 120 years when they had the warning of the flood is a sample of the way in which the world will act "in the days of the Son of man," the plural to denote the era preceding his coming, the singular is used in v. 24 to designate the day of his actual coming.

27) They disregarded absolutely all warning and lived on as though the warnings meant nothing. The four verbs which are without connectives are dramatic, all are imperfect tenses to express customary actions. It is a masterly description of that blind, secure, unbelieving, ungodly generation of Noah's day, whose successors are with us now and shall fill the world when the Son of man comes. Such was the rich man mentioned in 16:19, etc. To eat, drink, marry, be married (the passive in the case of the woman) are not wrong in themselves, but to make life nothing more, to forget the soul, God, the Word, salvation, worship, service to God, eternity — this is not only wrong and sin but the most fatal sin of all. The Scriptures tell us that in the days of Noah the people where so wicked that God could no longer tolerate them on earth, likewise that the sin of Sodom cried to heaven. Jesus does not mention this excessive wickedness, he is content to describe the soil from which it naturally grew and will always grow, namely hearts that are devoid of God and godliness, sunken in earthly, temporal, transient things.

Noah entered the ark at God's bidding, and then doom descended. Ἄχρι ἧς ἡμέρας=ἄχρι τῆς ἡμέρας ᾗ, the noun being drawn into the relative clause, the relative pronoun taking the place of the article. The word for "ark," ὁ κιβωτός, is suggestive since in Heb. 9:4 it is used for the ark of the covenant, and in Rev. 11:19 for the ark of the heavenly sanctuary; the word means a wooden chest. Impressive in its simplicity is the statement: "and came the flood and destroyed them all," the verbs being placed forward for the sake of emphasis. Jesus states nothing but the cold, terrible facts Κατακλυσμός is derived from κατακλύζω, to overflow completely (our "cataclysm"). "All" — nothing can be more complete than this masculine pronoun.

28) Here, but not in Matt. 24, Jesus adds the second illustration. **Likewise as it was in the days of Lot: they were eating, they were drinking, they were buying, they were selling, they were planting, they were building; but on the day that Lot went out from Sodom it rained fire and brimstone from heaven and destroyed them all. According to these things will it be on what day the Son of man is revealed.**

"Likewise" places the second illustration beside the first. The one intensifies the other. Both stand as the great Biblical types of the final judgment and its doom for the unbelieving which is swift, frightful, complete. We again have the same imperfects, this time six, four new ones, which include all such actions and picture lives without God.

29) Lot, like Noah, left at God's bidding, both being preachers of righteousness (II Pet. 2:5, 7) whose preaching was in vain. Then the doom descended. The first came by water, this came by fire—God orders both. "And destroyed all," the same power of brevity as in v. 27. What the once beautiful country is like to this day is described better in the Scripture than by modern travelers: "Brimstone, and salt, and burning . . . not sown, nor beareth, nor any grass groweth therein," Deut. 29:23. "Never to be inhabited, nor dwelt in from generation to generation; where neither Arab should pitch tent, nor shepherd make fold," Isa. 13:20. "No man abiding there, nor son of man dwelling in it," Jer. 49:18. "A fruitful land turned into saltness," Ps. 107:34. "Overthrown and burnt," Amos 4:11. It is only a legend that Sodom and the four other cities sank into the Dead Sea, and that traces of these cities can still be seen beneath the waters.

30) "In accord with these things," Jesus adds most impressively, "shall it be," etc. Once more we have the warning, and it is now given to the whole

world for the last time. Noah — eight souls (not even ten); Lot — four souls (not even five), these alone escaped. "In what day the Son of man is revealed," the tense is the prophetic present, the verb as it is used in II Thess. 1:7: "When the Lord Jesus shall be revealed from heaven with his mighty angels."

31) **In that day who shall be on the housetop and his utensils in the house, let him not go down to take them away; and he in the field likewise, let him not return for the things behind. Remember the wife of Lot! Whoever shall seek to preserve his life shall lose it while whoever shall lose it shall keep it alive.**

In Matt. 24:17, etc., (Mark 13:15) the word regarding the housetop and the field is used with reference to the time of the destruction of Jerusalem, when precipitate flight alone will save the Christians from being shut in by the Roman armies. In the present discourse the destruction of Jerusalem is not referred to; Luke 21:5-38 reports Matt. 24 and deals with Jerusalem in v. 20, etc. Jesus speaks of the end of the world throughout and therefore says nothing of flight, for no flight will then save any man. The thought begun in v. 26-30 is continued. Those who, like the people in Noah's and in Lot's time, cling to the things of earth alone will do so to the last. Jesus tells his disciples not to be like them in any way. When the end comes, let no one on the housetop think of any of his goods or valuables (σκεύη) down in the house and run down to take them away to safety, or anyone working out in his field run back for anything that is left behind. The phrase εἰς τὰ ὀπίσω is not the adverb "back" but means "for the things behind." They whose valuables are entirely material and earthly will think only of these. No such thought is to be in the disciples' mind.

32) "Remember the wife of Lot!" makes plain by a historical example what the warning of Jesus means. She only looked back and was lost. To have the heart set on our earthly valuables even to so slight a

degree will be fatal. To have it set only on Christ and on our eternal treasures cannot, of course, be accomplished in the last hour; we must learn this by following Christ and must live so all our lives, which is the absolute opposite of the conduct of the rich fool mentioned in 12:16, etc. For the end of the world may come at any time and does come for us who die before the end at the time we die. Read I Cor. 7:29-31.

33) The fact that Jesus is speaking of the disciples' attitude toward all earthly things for the entire period up to the end of the world appears in the new statement. It is a dictum that Jesus uttered at least four times in different connections and in different formulations, Luke 9:24 (Matt. 16:25; Mark 8:35); Matt. 10:39; John 12:25. "To seek to preserve one's ψυχή or life" means to devote all one's thought, time, and effort to getting everything for our animated body only (see 1:46), for the ψυχή is only that which makes our bodies alive. By the very act of devoting oneself only to the preservation of "the life" in this sense one simply and inevitably loses even that "life," i. e., his ψυχή. Not, indeed, by just dying, for all believers also die; but as is stated in 12:20 — the *psyche* goes to judgment. That which animated the body is damned, and when it is reunited with its body on the last day it shall enter hell.

Also the reverse is true: whoever loses his life (*psyche*) by devoting himself to his πνεῦμα or spirit, his great aim being not merely to do for that which animates his body but also being willing even to have his body die or suffer for Christ and the gospel or to lose many things the world counts dear and sweet. He it is who keeps his ψυχή, even that, alive (the verb being used in this sense in the New Testament, C.-K. 495). He, too, will, of course, die, his *psyche* will leave his body; but it will not be judged, it will be safe, saved, and reunited with the body at the great resurrection to live in heaven forever. The English has trouble with all these passages since we have no real equivalent for ψυχή, both "life" and "soul" being inexact. We must consult the original.

34) I tell you: On that night there will be two men on one bed; the one will be taken away, and the other will be left. There will be two women grinding together; the one will be taken away, but the other will be left.

The illustration is drawn more firmly than it is in Matt. 24:40, 41. "I tell you" lends the weight of authority to the double statement. The difference of which Jesus is speaking from v. 26 onward is not outward but inward. Here are people who are outwardly alike, first two men (δύο is masculine as ὁ εἷς and ὁ ἕτερος show) sleeping side by side in the same bed; yet one may be taken along, accepted, and received, the other left, abandoned, rejected. The agent in the passive verbs is left unnamed, but it is surely the Son of man (v. 24) of whose great return Jesus is speaking. Why this difference? It does not need to be stated again. The one is like Noah and Lot and the man who does the right thing for his *psyche* (v. 33); the other is like the people in Noah's and Lot's time who were out to give their *psyche* everything earthly only (v. 33). "On that night" does not mean that the Parousia will occur at night, for the next verse speaks of work that is done during the daytime. The coming is a certainty, it may occur at night or during daylight.

35) Two men, and now two women; two sleeping, and now two working, namely "grinding" the meal for the family which was a woman's task and was done with a handmill. They sit side by side, doing the same thing, each woman's hand being on the same mill, grinding the same grain, wheat or barley. Outwardly they are so alike, but inwardly there may be the greatest difference as in the case of the men, so that the one is saved, the other lost. Verse 36 about the two men in the field is plainly inserted from Matt. 24:40, where

alone it belongs. Emphasis is gained by duplication, not by triplication.

37) **And answering they say to him, Where, Lord? And he said to them, Where the body, the eagles will be gathered together.**

The response of the disciples is to ask the Lord, "Where?" i. e., where this separation, taking the one, leaving the other, is to take place. This is an answer that tells the Lord that this point is not clear to the disciples.

The Lord's reply is couched in the proverbial language which is repeated on the last Tuesday of his life when he sat on the Mount of Olives (Matt. 24:3), the changes being only verbal (Matt. 24:28), that the eagles are bound to gather together where the body is, i. e., the dead, decaying body (Matthew, the carcass). In Matthew this saying applies to Jerusalem as the carcass. The attempt to have it apply so in Luke has led to misinterpretation. Some abhorrent views have been offered: Christ is the carrion, the believers the vultures; or believers are the carrion, Christ the vultures.

'Ἀετοί are eagles; some dictionaries have the word mean "vultures" here where carrion draws them, being ignorant of the fact, it seems, that eagles, too, love to gorge themselves on carrion. The reply of Jesus means: "Neither here, nor there, nor in any particular place, but there where men are ripe for judgment." So it was in Noah's time, so in Lot's, and so it will be on the day of the final judgment. The fate of carrion that is devoured by eagles pictures the fate of all who fed only their earthly lives. The judgment is only for the ungodly who make this world their all; the godly do not come into the judgment (John 5:24: εἰς κρίσιν οὐκ ἔρχεται). Hence the word about the dead body is enough.

CHAPTER XVIII

1) **Moreover, he went on to say a parable to them for this that it is necessary that they be always praying and not losing heart, saying: A judge there was in a city, fearing not God and regarding not man. Moreover, a widow there was in that city, and she kept coming to him, saying, Vindicate me of my opponent at law! And he would not for a time. But afterward he said in himself, Though I neither fear God nor regard man, because this widow is making me trouble, I will vindicate her lest finally by coming she be knocking me out.**

Jesus continues speaking to the disciples (17:22) and on the same general topic as v. 6, 7 indicate. But the new thought is that, until the end comes, the disciples must always keep praying and never lose heart (to be κακός, inferior, good-for-nothing in this matter). Πρὸς τό with the infinitive means "with reference to," R. 1075. The impersonal δεῖν is used to indicate all types of necessity, here that which arises from the situation of the disciples in a wicked world that is ripening for judgment as a dead body begins to rot and get ready to be devoured by the eagles (17:37).

2) Note the correspondence: "A judge there was in a city," and: "Moreover, a widow there was in that city," the subjects being placed forward for the sake of emphasis, and the indefinite pronoun being used twice, as is often done in Luke, for our indefinite article "a," R. 743. The point of the parable is missed when the wickedness of this judge is reduced in any way, for the force of the parable lies in the contrast between this judge and the just and righteous God; wherefore also this wickedness of the judge is again emphasized in v. 4. He feared not God in the conduct of his high office nor all the dire threats of God against

unjust and conscienceless judges. Nor did he have "its poor and miserable substitute" (Trench), regard for man, for the opinion of the world which holds many a man and an otherwise conscienceless judge in line.

Here we have another (16:1) parable in which we cannot proceed as we did in that of the sower and find counterparts for all that the parable mentions. This judge is not God. These two are opposites, and this is the thought that makes the parable. The illustrative feature is only one and not a number of them that run through the picture, and that one point, the *tertium comparationis*, Jesus himself states in v. 6-8a; we have no right to go beyond that. We found Jesus doing the same thing in 16:9, etc.

3) A widow comes to this judge's court, and we may well suppose that she was a poor widow, without power and influence. She has an "opponent at law" (the same word that is used in Matt. 5:25) who has robbed her of the little she had. So she appeals to this judge, keeps coming again and again although he keeps putting her off; and her petition is: "Vindicate me of my opponent at law!" The verb ἐκδικέω means "to avenge or vindicate," here by making the opponent at law return his extortion and robbery and by inflicting on him the penalty he deserves.

4) But this conscienceless judge "would not for a time." The law of God and of man was on the widow's side, and that fact the judge saw; yet because she was only a lone widow, this judge would not act. But she had one weapon that made even this judge succumb. In the parable he is made to acknowledge it himself. Parables are built like that — the wicked are made to state their wicked thoughts outright in so many words. After some time (μετὰ ταῦτα), the widow persisting in coming and demanding action, this judge, yes, even one who is as base as this, who admits to himself, "Although (εἰ καί) I fear not God and regard not man," capitulates.

5) Διὰ τό with the infinitive states the reason the judge finally resolves to act, and it is certainly about as low a motive as can move any judge to act; and ἵνα μή states his purpose and aim, and it, too, is of the lowest. Not the widow's unquestioned right and her opponent's flagrant wrong against her move this judge, move him at last, but his own personal ease and peace which this widow's constant coming and pleading destroy.

Παρέχειν κόπον is idiomatic, "to furnish or make trouble"; and ὑπωπιάζω, literally, "to hit under the eye," "to give a black eye," is strong even when it is used metaphorically: "lest finally by coming she be knocking me out." It would require an aorist subjunctive to mean that the widow would finally fly into a rage and literally knock the judge under the eye with her fist — although he richly deserved it; the present subjunctive means that the woman's everlasting coming will, if it continues much longer, knock the judge out by finally moving him to give in. He sees that he cannot hold out forever, and so in order to have no more bother and to avoid yielding in the end he resolves then and there: "I will vindicate her." The moment we see that God acts in the very opposite way, the disgraceful conduct of this judge will appear in its proper light. We should also remember that Jesus paints an Oriental judge, to whom the aggrieved go without the legal red tape and the lawyers who are required in our modern courts.

6) Now the interpretation. **And the Lord said: Hear what the judge of unrighteousness says! But God, will he not work the vindication of his elect, crying to him by day and by night? and is he waiting long over them? I will tell you, that he will work their vindication with speed! Nevertheless, the Son of man, on coming, will he find the faith on the earth?**

The whole parable centers in what the judge "says," vivid present tense; all else is subsidiary. He is called "the judge of unrighteousness," which characterizes him by a qualitative genitive (which is stronger than an adjective), it is like "the steward of unrighteousness" and "the mammon of unrighteousness" occurring in 16:8, 9.

7) Fixing attention on that, Jesus brings out what we are to see. By placing ὁ δὲ Θεός before the double interrogative words οὐ μή (which involve an affirmative answer) "but God" receives strong emphasis, δέ placing him into contrast with "the judge of unrighteousness." Because this contrast culminates in the judge of unrighteousness and the God of all righteousness, it runs through the entire parable. Thus, over against the widow, in whom the judge has no interest, there are set the elect, in whom God has supreme interest. She comes to the judge from time to time; over against that there is set the crying both by day and by night (the genitives to indicate time within which something occurs; the accusatives would mean all day and all night long). The widow is not heard for a time; over against that short period there is set the long period that God waits before he acts. Over against the utterly base and selfish yielding of the judge there is set the holy, righteous, loving deed of God which he resolved to do from the start. So the contrast runs clear through.

Nothing in the parable represents the reality save the vindication — there is vindication alike in the parable and in reality; all else is opposite, and the whole force and argument lie in this cumulative opposition. Even the widow is understood wrongly if, amid these opposites, she is made *like* the elect, they being poor and helpless as she is. The elect are supremely precious to God, the widow, just because she is a widow, poor and helpless as such, is just nothing to the judge even when he at last vindicates her. On the elect compare John 10:14, 16; II Tim. 2:19; I Pet. 1:2: "elect according to the foreknowledge of God." Their cries for vindication ring through the Scriptures, Ps. 35:17; 74:10; 94:3; Rev. 6:10.

The addition to the question: καὶ μακροθυμεῖ ἐπ' αὐτοῖς, has called forth a number of interpretations. It has been termed awkward; the reading, though it is fully assured, has been changed; the verb has been regarded as an Attic future instead of the present tense; the words are separated from the question and are read as a declaration; the pronoun does not refer to the elect but to their opponents at law. One cause of this confusion is the idea that the parable calls for the wrong contrast, namely that, whereas the unjust judge delayed the widow's vindication for a time, the just God does not delay the vindication of the elect at all whereas the fact is that God delays the full vindication to the end of the world. The correct opposition is: a short time — a long time. Hence this long, long crying by day and by night.

Another mistaken view is that everything is close to the end of the world. Or, which is the same, the end of the world as the day of vindication is placed close to the time when Jesus was speaking. According to either view the period is made as short as possible with the idea that the parable requires this. On this idea of shortness rests also the view that the verb means "to be longsuffering" (R. V., for instance), i. e., that God waits patiently for the training and the development of the elect under the world's hatred until, when this is finished, he steps in with his vindication. But what about all these elects' dying, generation after generation of them? According to this view the parable and the interpretation would apply only to the generation that witnesses the end; and will all those then living, young and old, be alike fully developed by suffering?

We have neither the adversative καί (R., W. P.), "and yet," nor an aorist subjunctive (ποιήσῃ) plus a present indicative (μακροθυμεῖ) after οὐ μή (R. 1158). We have a simple second question that is added by an ordinary καί, one that has nothing to do with οὐ μή. It is a question because καί prevents us from regarding it as a declaration. The A. V. had a correct intuition, the R. V. went off on a wrong track. "But God, will he not vindicate," etc.? Absolutely, he will! "And is he waiting long," etc.? It does seem so — for the promised end is not yet. In answer to both of these rhetorical questions Jesus says with great authority: "I tell you," etc. On the meaning of the verb as used here: "to wait long," "to delay long," see C.-K. 503; and "over them" means "over vindicating them."

8) Jesus declares with all his authority that God's vindication of his elect will come ἐν τάχει, "with speed," the stress being on this phrase. Because of this assurance of speed the second question about God's delaying was added — had to be added. This is the very problem that is faced by the elect of all ages: God seems to delay and delay their final vindication whereas they are told that the vindication is coming with speed. Jesus answers that problem by once more asserting the fact of the speed. So Peter, too, understood him when he reasserted in II Pet. 3:8, 9 that God is not slack as some men count slackness; he delays in longsuffering in order to save as many people as possible; and with him a thousand years are as one day. Peter's commentary satisfies fully.

The assertion that it cannot be determined whether the sentence that is introduced by πλήν is declarative or interrogative is not well supported. Greek accents were added at a later date by fallible editors and are subject to review to this day; hence it is for us to decide whether the reading should be ἄρα, the particle expressing correspondence like our "then," or ἆρα, the interrogative particle, which is left untranslated in English and in German and admits either an affirmative or a negative answer in the speaker's mind. The fact is that the inferential ἄρα does not fit here. From the great fact that God will vindicate his elect with speed the inference does not follow that, when the Son of man (see 5:24) comes, he is sure to find the faith on the earth. The point is not that he will then find some believers, some of the elect, still among the living; for it is self-evident that God would not let the world continue without there being believers among men. The point is in regard to *"the* faith" and not faith in general, that faith which is pictured in the parable, that is so necessary for all the elect, which Jesus is working to produce and to increase, *"the"* faith that ceases not to cry by day and by night.

The question ($ἄρα$) is will *that* faith be there to greet the Son of man at his coming? Some think that the answer must be *no*, that *no* was in Jesus' mind, in fact, that all faith is negatived as far as the end is concerned. This view misunderstands the object of the question, which is not to raise speculation about what will occur at the end but is to stimulate us all to keep on crying as the elect until the Son of man appears. "Will there be this faith to welcome me when I come?" Jesus leaves the answer to us and to all the elect that follow us.

9) Moreover, also to some who had been resting their trust on themselves that they were righteous and were treating the rest with contempt he spoke this parable.

Neither the preceding parable nor the one that is now introduced deal with prayer as such; prayer is only the vehicle in both. So the connection is not from prayer to prayer. The first parable deals with the kind of faith Jesus wants the disciples to have, one that is constantly longing and asking for his return; the second parable adds the true humility of faith, of that faith which alone justifies. It may well be possible that this parable followed the other promptly. Since $εἶπε\ πρός$ is constantly used to mean "he said to" the persons who are then named, we cannot have it here mean "he said regarding" absent persons.

Those who are addressed are characterized by a perfect and a present participle: such as "have been trusting in themselves" and continue to do this and such as now "go on condemning the rest." The substance of the trust is "that they are righteous," the present tense matches the perfect participle, δίκαιοι (as always) is used in the forensic sense. These men were convinced that they had God's verdict in their favor; but the only ground on which they were resting this conviction was "themselves" (ἐφ' expresses the basis). The result of this self-righteousness was that they were considering others as nothing; in their estimation they alone amounted to something — and that just about everything — before God. Who were they? Not Pharisees although the description fits them. Luke would most likely have inserted this word. That leaves other Jews who have the Pharisaic spirit or followers of Jesus who are still infected with that spirit.

10) **Two men went up into the Temple to pray; the one a Pharisee, and the other a publican.**

This occurred at one of the regular hours for prayer, and τὸ ἱερόν is the entire Temple complex. Into the court of the men these two came for their act of prayer-worship (aorist). The Pharisees are described in 5:17; the publicans in 3:12. These two constituted the extremes in Judaism, the one stood at the pinnacle of holiness, the other was a wicked outcast. The scene is laid in the Holy City itself, in the very court of the Temple, and thus in the presence of God. Jesus is showing the men he is addressing a photograph of what they really are and a companion photograph of what they ought to be. It is a Pharisee but may just as well be anybody else who thinks like this Pharisee speaks and acts; it is a publican but this one represents, not publicans as a class, but all men who think as he speaks and acts.

11) This is a parable — we are allowed to enter with these men and to see and to hear all that

reveals them as they are. **The Pharisee took a stand and went on praying these things for himself: God, I thank thee that I am not like the rest of men, robbers, unrighteous, adulterers, or ever as this publican! I fast twice during the week; I tithe all whatever I acquire.**

The picture is not overdrawn in the least. The Jews had fixed prayers just as we teach our children to pray: "Now I lay me down to sleep," etc. But free prayers were also spoken. The point is that the parable lets this Pharisee pray the real thought of his heart. In this prayer we see what a case of full-grown self- and work-righteousness looks like. The type is Jewish, but while it is thus individualized it can easily be translated into other types. We are shown only the heart of the prayer; "he went on praying" (imperfect) means that he said much more, for the Pharisees loved to make long prayers. This man may have spoken many other words in his prayer, words from the psalms, words from the prophets, the most godly words in the world — many hypocrites and self-righteous men love to use them; but his heart is truly revealed only in words such as these which the parable puts into his mouth.

"He took a stand" right up in front, next to the stone balustrade which divided the priests' court from that of the men. Πρὸς ἑαυτόν does not mean "to himself" in the sense of "silently," "under his breath," as some think, who add even that he would not have dared to say these things out loud. He not only dared this but was admired by those who heard what he could say. The phrase is to be construed with the verb (not with the participle) and means that he prayed these things "for himself," "in favor of himself," using πρός of direction which may be either hostile ("against") or friendly or neutral; it is here the second. He boasted about himself — that was his praying. He thought that was in his favor with God.

It is held against him that he said only ὁ Θεός — the nominative with the article is used as a vocative — but everything is trimmed down in a parable, and so "God" is enough. "I thank thee" makes this prayer a thanksgiving, but only in form — it names not one thing that God has done for this man. For when he adds: "that I am not like the rest of men" and names three vicious kinds and then the publican on whom his eyes fell, his meaning is not that God's grace has made him different, but that he has made himself righteous, yea, vastly better. And he, indeed, could not thank God for what he had become, for God's grace never made him what he was, never turned out self-righteous boasters.

He thanked God that he was not like "robbers," etc., but he really had nothing to thank even himself for on that score, for the Pharisee that he had made of himself was worse in God's eyes than a robber and most certainly much harder to save as witness the publican. This man was merely what Jesus charges in 16:15. He was measuring with a wrong human rule and not with the rule of God's Word, and doing this right in God's Temple which had been dedicated to God's Word. By the ἄδικοι he refers to all such as have no righteousness in men's eyes, who cannot face an earthly judge. With καί he does not include "also" this (derogatory οὗτος, R. 697) publican but tops the pile with him as being the worst of all—glance at 3:12.

12) First, self-absolution from all sins — not one to confess to God; then, merit, even supererogation, doing even more than God had commanded. "God, see in me no sin, all pure merit!" This man keeps fasting twice a week (genitive of time within). In the Greek, both in the singular and in the plural, "Sabbath" is used for our "week" and means the group of days that is bounded by the Sabbaths. God's law prescribed only one day of fasting in the year, the Day of Atonement, Lev. 16:29, etc.; 23:27, etc. The nation itself had established four other fast days. But private fasting

had been introduced since the exile, and the Pharisees practiced this as a special mark of holiness and used Monday and Thursday for this purpose. The Jews of the present time have 28 fast days. So this Pharisee claimed high merit for his fasting but knew nothing of such fasting as Isa. 58:4-7 describes.

He also tithed every last thing he acquired (κτῶμαι, not "possess"). The emphasis is on the πάντα ὅσα, "everything whatsoever"; he did not make the common exemptions but included even that which Jesus mentions in 11:42 — more works of supererogation. On tithing for Christians compare the notes on 11:42. Jesus puts just enough into the parable to bring out its point. So he stops with a mention of these works — the Pharisees boasted of more.

13) But the publican, standing far off, would not even lift up his eyes to the heaven but was striking his breast, saying, God, let thyself be propitiated in regard to me, the open sinner!

He is the complete opposite to the Pharisee. He, too, stands as was customary in the Temple, but he has not taken a special stand. The Greek says "from afar" and measures from the object to the person; we say "far off" and measure in the opposite way. He stood as far off from the Sanctuary as he could, at the rear of the court of the men. He felt that he was too unworthy to go nearer. Nor did he have the will to lift up his eyes to heaven in the face of the Sanctuary, the imperfect ἤθελεν includes the entire time that he was in the court. He was utterly ashamed before God. Over against what he did not do ἀλλά states what he did do, strike his breast in the Oriental way of showing great sorrow like the wailing women do in 8:52, the weeping women on the *Via Dolorosa* in 23:27, and the children at play in Matt. 11:17. This act symbolizes the publican's contrition. We add his confession of sin when he calls himself ὁ ἁμαρτωλός, "the open and notorious sinner," right here in God's house. True contrition is always expressed by honest confession. R., W. P. scores a point in pointing out that the article is so often overlooked. The main point lies in the article. The Pharisee thought of others as being sinners; the publican thinks of himself alone as being the sinner and not of others. This is a mark of true contrition. It finds no comfort at all in the fact that there are many other and even greater sinners; it sees only itself before God, only itself as "the" sinner who is unable to answer to God for his sins.

The publican, too, cries only ὁ Θεός as is explained in v. 11. If blame attached to the Pharisee for saying only "God" it would extend also to the publican. But how dare a gross sinner approach God, and that right in God's Temple? Because there is forgiveness with God, his Temple is open to sinners, he has provided expiation for their sins, and this is applied to sinners in his Temple, and his Word declares all this and seals the forgiveness. This publican was a Jew who knew all this and was now acting upon it. It was this gospel provision of the old covenant that drew him in the first place. The Pharisee disregarded all gospel, made the whole Old Testament law, and thus prayed as he did. The publican knew the true law that condemns sin, came smitten and crushed by that law, but, thank God, knew also the gospel in the Old Testament, the gospel in all the sacrifices for sin in the Temple, and made his prayer thus.

The translation "be merciful to me" which is found in our version and in others is unfortunate. The verb used is not ἐλεεῖν, "to be merciful or to show mercy," which is properly translated thus in all the instances where the sick cry for help (e. g., 17:13). This translation leaves out the very essential that Jesus put into the publican's mouth, without which God cannot pardon and justify, namely the expiation for sin. So this translation is either misapplied as though God justifies without expiation, or the explanation is given that because of the limitations of parables the expiation is omitted. But this verb is the very one which shows the expiation and is used here for that very purpose: ἱλάσθητί μοι, "be propitiated in regard to me"; or, taking the passive in the middle sense: "let thyself be propitiated in regard to me."

In ἱλάσκομαι there lies ἱλασμός, "propitiation," which, where sin is involved, is an expiation or atonement. C.-K. 517-521 on the verb and the noun. The publican prays that God may let the sacrifices which he ordained for sin in the old covenant blot out his sin so that God can again extend his grace and favor to this poor sinner. Such a prayer can be made only to a gracious God, to him who has provided an expiation, and only by one who makes that expiation his sole refuge in contrition, makes it by putting all his faith and trust in this divine expiation. That is the sense of the publican's prayer. All that we need to remember is that it rests on the Old Testament sacrifices for sin, which typify the final sacrifice of Christ on the cross and have their efficacy for the old covenant in and through the promised sacrifice of Christ, Isa. 53:2-7.

14) I tell you, this one went down to his house as having been justified rather than that one; because everyone exalting himself shall be humbled, but he humbling himself shall be exalted.

It is the voice of authority which announces the verdict: "I tell you!" "Went down" to his house is proper because the Jews always regarded the going to the Temple as a going up. The Temple was not built on the highest hill of the city, yet all went up, and all came down. The perfect participle δεδικαιωμένος is predicative to οὗτος: "this one as having been justified"; and the tense states that God justified him prior to his going down to his house or home, and that this justification was valid now and indefinitely. The agent involved in the passive is "God" to whom he prayed.

But the sense of this participle is of the utmost importance. Δικαιοῦν is always *forensic*, in the LXX, etc., also in a secular sense, in the New Testament in a religious sense and only with a personal object. God acquits, as the Judge he delivers and pronounces the verdict that frees from guilt and punishment. Look at the exhaustive finding in C.-K. 317, etc.; also at the cognate terms; also at the synonymous expressions and at the antonyms. The word never means *to make righteous or just* but *always forensically to declare so*. Since justification by faith is the central doctrine of the Scriptures, the sinner's one hope of salvation, the word in which this doctrine centers must be properly understood.

The reading should be παρ' ἐκεῖνον in preference to ἢ ἐκεῖνος, and certainly not ἢ γὰρ ἐκεῖνος as a question. The sense is that the publican alone was justified by God, the Pharisee was not, namely in comparing the two with each other. The view that the one was justified more than the other is in itself impossible since no degrees are possible in justification—the judge pronounces the acquittal or refuses to pronounce it and leaves the sinner in his sin, guilt, and condemnation. Nor should we confuse the matter by bringing in the sinner's conviction or feeling of having been justified by God. The divine act takes place in heaven, outside of, apart from, and only in regard to the sinner who is on earth. His knowledge, conviction, and feeling (all of which are subjective) are derived from the Word, in which the acquittal of every repentant sinner is recorded.

The reason the publican was acquitted and the Pharisee was not is stated in the form of an axiom or self-evident proposition, one that is used repeatedly by Jesus in 14:11; Matt. 23:12, and in other forms elsewhere. He that exalts himself shall be humbled, every last one; but he that humbles himself shall be exalted —both passives have God as the agent. The Pharisee put himself up high in a totally false way and contrary to God. God had to puncture his arrogance; he could not let the lie endure, especially also since God had provided a true righteousness for sinners, and this man spurned it, manufactured a sham righteousness of his own instead, and tried to pass that off on God. The facts had to be brought to the light, and then the exaltation turned into the very opposite. But the publican humbled himself by letting God's law fill him with contrition for his sins and lead him to confess his sin to God. He turned only to God in faith and to the expiation God provided for him. God could not but lift him up on high by justifying him and accepting him as his own. How can God pour anything into a full vessel? But the one that his law empties, that his grace can and does fill.

15) **Moreover, they kept bringing to him even the babes in order that he might touch them. But having seen it, the disciples went on to rebuke them.**

The connection is chronological, this incident occurred in Perea as also Matt. 19:1 and Mark 10:1 state. In the latter two evangelists this incident with regard to babes is placed after the words regarding the permanency of marriage, an obvious connection of thought. Luke places it after the justification of the publican, a less obvious connection. Yet that parable as well as the account about the rich young ruler deals with entrance into the kingdom, the very thing that is vindicated also in the case of babes.

This scene is often placed out-of-doors, but Mark 10:10 seems to place it in a house, which also explains how the disciples could rebuke those who were bringing the children. They did this outside, and thus Jesus did not at first see it. The two imperfects "they kept bringing" and "they went on to rebuke" are, of course, descriptive, but these tenses lead us to expect something like an aorist to tell us the outcome. It seems as though these persons started bringing their babes of their own accord. Somebody conceived the idea, and others followed in a little procession. Matt. 19:13 and Mark 10:13 have παιδία, "little children," Luke more exactly τὰ βρέφη, "babies" or "sucklings," the word used in I Pet. 2:2, even for an unborn babe in Luke 1:44; he adds καί: "even the sucklings." Being so tiny, it was, of course, impossible for them to understand what was being done for them.

The scene is marred when we are told that superstition prompted these parents and others to bring their babes because they attributed some sort of magical power to the touch of Jesus' hands. If that had been their motive, Jesus would have severely rebuked them and sent them away. Verbs of touching are construed with the genitive, and the present subjunctive indicates that he touched them one by one. Matt. 19:13 describes this touching as being the laying on of hands, a symbolical act that denoted blessing, and combines it with praying, invoking divine spiritual blessings upon the babes. The disciples began to interfere, and it seems that they were succeeding and that, when no more babes were being brought to him, Jesus looked out of the house, saw what they were doing, and promptly stopped them.

16) **But Jesus called them to him, saying: Let the little children be coming to me and stop hindering them! For of such is the kingdom of God. Amen, I say to you, whoever does not receive the kingdom of God as a little child in no way shall enter into it!**

Mark adds that he then took them into his arms, laid his hands on them, and went on fervently blessing them. A cluster of people and their babes seem to have been halted by the disciples outside of the house. Mark states that this made Jesus indignant. Why did they do a thing such as this? The deeper reason we gather from what Jesus said, namely that they did not as yet realize the relation of babes to the kingdom. They may have had other reasons also such as that they did not want Jesus to be bothered by having all these babes brought to him, that they considered his time too valuable to be wasted on infants, and that they desired his time for themselves for further discussion. He called "them" to him, αὐτά (neuter) refers to the babes.

Jesus appears as the great Advocate of babes, he opens his mouth for the dumb, out of whose mouth he perfects praise. It has been well said that without these words of Jesus and his attitude toward infants the Christian Church would have been far different from what it is. The disciples stood before their Master with shamed faces. His tone is peremptory. We first have the decisive aorist imperative: "Let them be coming (continue to come) to me!" Added to this is the negative command which intensifies the positive: "and stop hindering them!" When an action has already begun, the negative present imperative orders it to stop, R. 851, etc. The implication in both commands is that babes are altogether ready to come to Jesus and need only that men put nothing in their way. And this coming has the same purpose as the coming of any adult to Jesus, namely to receive the Messianic salvation. Their affinity for Jesus lies in their need of him, which is due to their inborn sin.

These were Jewish children who were already in the old covenant of grace; yet Jesus lays no stress on this but speaks of children in general even as the church has applied his word to all children. And indeed, if Jewish children, who were already in the covenant and the kingdom, needed to be brought to Jesus in order to be blessed by him as the Messiah, how much more is this the case with reference to all other children, to whom no grace has yet been applied? Jesus once for all removes every obstacle which our blind reasoning about babes may raise against their coming to him. In the case of parents "stop hindering" means

Luke 18:16

"stop refusing to bring them," for that is the worst hindering of all.

This double command would itself be enough, but Jesus goes much farther, he adds his reason (γάρ) for this command: "For of such is the kingdom of God." He does not say τούτων, "of these," the ones who are now being brought to him or in the wider sense all little children and babes; but τῶν τοιούτων, "of such," which means far more, namely the great class to which children as such belong. Bengel says that if the kingdom is "of such," then the children must with a special right be included. They are the model example of the whole class. If we want to know the character of the class we must study the children. It is their receptivity to which Jesus refers. Sin has not yet developed in them to such a degree as to produce conscious resistance to the power of divine grace, which necessitates the convicting power of the law. See 4:43 on the kingdom of God; it is where God (Christ), the King, is with his rule and his work of grace. To be of this kingdom is to have God's grace operative in us.

If Jesus had meant that all children, merely because of their being children, are already under this operation, are already saved, it would be superfluous for children to come to him; they would already be his. But he means nothing of this kind. What is born of the flesh is flesh, John 3:6 (Gen. 5:3; Ps. 51:5). It is in vain to deny original or inborn sin, the total depravity of our race, and to call babes "innocent" in the sense of "sinless." Every babe that dies contradicts this view.

It is another groundless assumption that all children are at birth (or already when conceived) made partakers of Christ's atonement *without any means whatever*. The Scriptures contain no word to this effect. Because some were misled by such thoughts, the little ones have been left outside of the kingdom until their receptiveness for grace became jeopardized. Baptism in particular was denied them, and this sacrament itself was regarded as being a mere symbol which gives and conveys nothing but only pictures something. Baptism was made an act of obedience (so much law) which was possible only for an adult and no longer an act of the Triune God which adopts babes as his children, deeds to them a place in heaven, gives them the new birth in the Spirit. Who will count the crimes that were thus perpetrated against helpless babes even in the very name of Christ by denying them the one divine means by which they can be brought and can come to their glorified Lord?

17) Although this verse recalls Matt. 18:3, we see that it is used in a different way. With the seal of verity (amen) and of authority (I say to you), see 4:24, Jesus shows his disciples how "of such is the kingdom of God," for no one shall enter that kingdom unless he enters it as a little child. This statement is astonishing in every way. We should think as, alas, so many did and do think that a babe must receive the kingdom as an adult receives it, but absolutely the reverse is true. The child is the model, not the man. It is the unassuming humility and the unquestioning trustfulness of the child that make it a pattern for all adults. This humility and this trustfulness, when they are directed to Christ, become the very essence of saving faith. To receive the kingdom and to enter into it are not diverse when we remember what the kingdom is, namely the working of his power and his grace wherever he is present. This we receive, i. e., as a gift, God bestows his grace on us; and thus we enter the circle, the domain, where God works with his grace. By receiving the kingdom we enter into it, and by entering into it we receive it. In John 3:3, 5 seeing the kingdom is described as entering it. But the decisive point is the emphatic "as a little child."

18) We are now told of one whose love of riches was keeping him out of the kingdom. **And**

Luke 18:18   911

there inquired of him a ruler, saying, Good Teacher, by having done what will I inherit life eternal?

Luke calls him "a ruler" (τίς=our "a"), one of the officials who were managing the local synagogue; and Matthew supplies the detail that he was a νεανίσκος, a man between 24 and 40. Mark adds the details that Jesus was just going out on the road to proceed to another village when this man ran out, kneeled before Jesus, and inquired of him. Though he was a ruler and prominent in his community he humbles himself before Jesus. This fact and the address, "Good Teacher," bespeak great reverence for Jesus and the assurance on his part that Jesus will surely be able to give him the vital information he desires.

This man does not ask *how* he may obtain eternal life as though he were at a loss regarding the ways and means. On the contrary, he thinks that he knows quite well, namely by his having done something, some one good thing (Matthew), "good" being used in the sense of *heilbringend* (C.-K. 5). The aorist participle ποιήσας is punctiliar to indicate one accomplishment—a difficult performance, perhaps, but the man was ready for the undertaking. He is not thinking of a merely moral act, for he has performed many acts of this kind and yet feels that he has not won eternal life.

He asks *what* he shall do because he thinks that Jesus has discovered this thing and has acquired life eternal for himself by it. This man would like to know the recipe, would like to do the same thing. His conception of Jesus is thus much like that of the modernists: a man who has discovered the good thing and found eternal life by it. This ruler wants to be let in on this secret: "Teacher, how didst thou do it? Tell me that I may also do it!" In the question "by doing what" there lies, of course, the assumption that the questioner has the necessary ability and may easily reach the goal Jesus has reached. All he feels that he needs is to know the thing that is to be done. This idea is Pelagianism in its crassest form. The best feature about the man is that he wants eternal life and despite all his past doing has not been able to secure that treasure.

John uses ζωή thirty-four times in his writings and always in the sense of the life principle itself which makes us spiritually alive. No science has fathomed what natural life is, and the essence of spiritual life is naturally still more mysterious. But both natural and spiritual life are known and recognized by their functions and their acts. The reception of the "life" is regeneration, of which Jesus spoke to Nicodemus at length.

This life is αἰώνιος, "eternal," going on through the eons unaffected by temporal death, which only transfers this life into the heavenly world. It may be lost, and it ceases in us when we wickedly and wilfully cut ourselves off from its divine source, Christ, the Life. Just what conception the ruler had of this life which he so much desired one can guess only from the way in which he imagined that it could be acquired; he supposed that, upon his having done something, it would be his.

An issue is sometimes made of κληρονομεῖν as if *doing* and *inheriting* were a contradiction in the man's question. But Matthew interprets "inheriting" by writing "have" life eternal. The verb is often used in the sense of to obtain or to have a portion in something. It is used specifically when sonship and heirship are involved. But even so, inheriting need not exclude all idea of merit as many a last will and testament shows when a larger portion is bequeathed to a more faithful child, or when a friend, a benefactor, a person who has rendered some valuable service, is made an heir. Jesus, too, says nothing and intimates nothing about a contradiction in the question.

The picture that is thus drawn of the young ruler is really pathetic: so eager to do, so desirous of life eternal (while many young men are carried away by the world), so strongly attracted to Jesus, expecting so much of him—and yet so far from the right road to life eternal! Compare the same question as it is put by a lawyer in 10:25.

19) **But Jesus said to him: Why dost thou call me good? No one is good except one, God. The precepts thou knowest, Do not commit adultery; do not kill; do not steal; do not bear false witness; honor thy father and mother.**

Rationalism and Unitarianism point to this question of Jesus as proof positive that Jesus himself says that he is not God. But they understand the words of Jesus too superficially. When the young ruler called Jesus "good" and asked what "good thing" (Matthew) he should do to gain life, everything depended on what he meant by ἀγαθός, "good." Note that both the ruler and Jesus use only the positive "good" in an absolute sense, which is much stronger than the superlative would be (R. 661).

The question of Jesus: "Why callest thou me good?" aims to make this ruler think of what he means by the word. Jesus makes no pronouncement whatever about himself in this question but tells this ruler to pause and to consider what "good" really means. It will not do to use the word lightly with reference to Jesus. In order to show what Jesus means he points out that goodness in the real sense of that term can be predictated only of God. So far is this from denying the Godhead of Jesus that it actually asserts it for him. "Good," Jesus intends to say, if you mean that in the common sense, it is too cheap to apply to me! It is quite another thing to use good in its real meaning as it applies only to God! The man is thus led to look at Jesus in a new way, to consider that Jesus may, indeed, be God, essentially one with God as his Son.

The English translation "good" obscures this deeper meaning too much. The matter is not improved when modernists translate ἀγαθός "kind," which "good" means only in certain connections in English but never in the Greek and absolutely never in a pointed connection such as the present instance. Ἀγαθός means "beneficial," good in that respect. In this sense it may signify what is morally beneficial. Did this man mean something in the way of moral benefit by asking for the good thing (Matthew) he should do? If so, then God's own moral law had answered him long ago. But ἀγαθός means beneficial also in the sense of *heilbringend* (C.-K. 5, where our passage is fully discussed), benefiting by bestowing salvation. The ruler had asked for something that would bring him life eternal, salvation; hence the question was pertinent: "Did he think of this meaning when he called on the good Teacher to tell him what the good thing was that he should do?" It is to impress this meaning upon his mind that Jesus tells him that God alone is good.

Now a Jew needed no reminder that God is morally excellent, "The Good," its very embodiment (Matthew). This Jew needed to be reminded that God alone is *heilbringend*, good as the very source of salvation, beyond which no other exists. Was he coming to Jesus to find out what the good, the beneficent thing in this sense was, and did he mean that Jesus could bestow this good upon him? In an exceedingly simple way the ruler is thus led to look upon Jesus in the true light, as the One who bestows salvation, i. e., as himself being God.

20) After jolting the ruler's mind in regard to the real meaning of "good" in connection with salvation and thus with God, Jesus proceeds to answer his question. Luke and Mark abbreviate but agree with Matthew. "Thou knowest the precepts" means what Matthew says, that if he wills to enter into life he must guard these divine ἐντολαί or precepts. Jesus follows the proper course with this man (as he did with the lawyer in 10:26); he starts with the law in order to lead him

to the gospel. The process is very simple: the man is first to understand that he cannot obtain the life by the law; second, that all the law can do for him is to show him his sin. After this is clear, his only hope will be in the gospel.

As to the commandments which Jesus cites, all the negative ones have μή with the strong aorist subjunctive, the regular form for negative commands in the aorist; the final positive command has τίμα, the durative present imperative "be honoring," i. e., always. By using only the second table of the law Jesus takes this young ruler to the place where he is surest of himself, for these are the commandments regarding which most men imagine that they can obey them with little effort—but see Matt. 5:21, etc. Jesus shows that in quoting the commandments he is not bound by their wording or by their order in the Decalog. The evangelists also use freedom in quoting. Matthew has the sum of the second table at the end, Mark and Luke have the Fourth Commandment on honoring parents there. Mark alone has the Ninth and the Tenth which are combined in, "Do not defraud." It seems to be the object of Jesus simply to pile up the commandments into a tremendous burden and to show how exceedingly much the law requires before it grants the life as a reward.

21) **He, however, said, These all did I watch from my youth on.**

He says this to Jesus without blinking an eye. And he is perfectly sincere in what he says. This divine law has no terrors for him—he has kept it all. This is a sample of Pharisaic training which nullifies the very effect God intends his law to produce, namely contrite knowledge of sin and the *terrores conscientiae*. This young ruler is altogether self-righteous in the face of the law. He was perhaps disappointed to hear Jesus recite nothing but the old commandments which he had watched from his youth. Was this all that the good

Teacher could hold up to him? The words φυλάσσειν and τηρεῖν are synonyms like *bewachen* and *bewahren,* to watch over and keep safe and to guard and keep inviolate.

He had lived an exemplary life outwardly, he had shunned grave transgressions, aided and protected, no doubt, by both his training and his environment. Many would today be only too well satisfied with themselves if they were like him, and others would praise and perhaps envy him if they saw him in modern form. Picture him: an exemplary young man in early manhood, fine and clean morally as the phrase now goes, the son of wealthy parents but not spoiled by wealth, having a strong religious bent, an esteemed member of the church, in fact, one of its pillars, a ruler of the local synagogue who was more important than a member of the church council is in our present congregations. Where are the parents who would not be proud of such a son? Where the church that would not give him a prominent place? Where the maid that would not be attracted by his position and his personal excellence? Yet all this is worthless in the eyes of Jesus. And, in fact, the man himself is not satisfied. He is sure that the trouble is not with the old commandments, for he feels he has kept these even from the first conscious days of his youth. According to Matthew he asks what he yet lacks. In Mark and in Luke this question is implied. There was, somehow, a lack which he could not explain. What could it be? Jesus is leading him to its discovery.

22) **But having heard, Jesus said to him: Yet one thing is lacking to thee! All whatever thou hast sell and give out to poor people and thou shalt have a treasure in the heaven! And come, be following me!**

Jesus not only heard but looked upon and loved the young ruler (Mark), ἀγαπᾶν, perceived his deplorable condition and purposed to help him out of it. As the "one thing" the ruler still lacks we regard all that Jesus says; it is a unit and should not be split into two or more things. This one thing is not to be ranged alongside of others and added to them as making the measure full; it is totally different from all others, beside which none of them count. Jesus tells this man that he really needs the one essential and vital thing. He has thus far attained only an outward obedience to the law and has not discovered that this is utterly useless for salvation; he still thinks that all he needs to do is to add something to this outward obedience. The thing he lacks begins with this discovery, with the realization that all his work-righteousness is in vain, that what he needs is *a complete inward change*.

Jesus describes this change to him in detail. By telling this ruler to sell all that he has and to divide it to poor people Jesus is laying his finger on the chief sin in this man's heart, the love of his earthly possessions. Jesus is demanding no mere outward act which would be as valueless as the other acts of this man had been. The outward act is to be merely the evidence of the inner change. This change is to be, first of all, *the true sorrow of contrition*. Heretofore he has clung to his earthly possessions with his heart. What a sin against God's law! By selling and giving away everything this inward sin is to be swept out by true contrition, μετάνοια. It is a pity that so many fail to see what Jesus really demands. It is impossible to agree that Jesus is showing a way of salvation to this man that is different from the way for other sinners.

Abandoning what was hitherto his heart's treasure is only the negative side; the positive side is that "he shall have a treasure in the heavens" with his whole heart fixed on that. The future "thou shalt have" starts from the moment when his heart is separated from his earthly treasure. It is a serious misunderstanding of this word of Jesus to take it to mean that by selling and giving away his earthly wealth this man would receive this treasure in the heavens as a reward. This "treasure" is the unmerited grace and pardon of God. For the other side of the one thing the man yet lacked, the one that always goes together with contrition, is *the true and saving faith in Christ*. That is why Jesus adds the gospel call to come and follow him to the selling and the giving away. This would be the evidence of true faith on the part of the man. Δεῦρο, the adverb "hither," is sometimes used as being almost equivalent to a verb, and it is used with or without an imperative, here with ἀκολούθει, the present imperative to indicate continuous following.

Jesus does not always ask us to give up our earthly wealth. It is in vain to point to this passage as proof for the abrogation of personal ownership of wealth. Zacchaeus was not required to give all his possessions to the poor; Joseph of Arimathaea was a disciple and was rich; Ananias was free to do with his own what he would as long as he practiced no hypocrisy nor tried to deceive the Holy Spirit; St. James warns the rich only against trusting in riches instead of trusting in God. Luther is, therefore, right when he draws attention to the domestic state and its requirements of certain possessions such as a house, home, food, clothing, etc., for wife and children.

The case of this young ruler is a special one and comes under Matt. 5:29, 30; 18:8, 9; Mark 9:43. We are also by no means certain that this man was to assume voluntary poverty in order to follow Jesus and take part in the work of the gospel. This is usually assumed, but we have no intimation as to just how Jesus intended to use this new follower. Others besides the Twelve were in his following for their own persons only and certainly did not divest themselves of all their possessions. Peter had his house in Capernaum; John, too, had a home to which to take Jesus' mother; and the women disciples mentioned in 8:2, 3 who followed

Jesus had means from which to supply Jesus and the Twelve.

Catholicism considers voluntary poverty (in its monastic orders) a work of merit toward salvation; it calls this command to give all to the poor *a consilium evangelicum* that goes beyond the Decalog and the observance of such counsel an *opus supererogativum*. In Matt. 18:21 τέλειος does not mean morally perfect but "complete," as having reached the τέλος or goal, which here signifies attaining the "one thing," the essential which the ruler still lacked.

The rationalistic view is that what the ruler lacked was moral power, the energy of the moral will. Others think of the ability to sacrifice all for the sake of reaching the highest moral good, or the ability really to fulfill the second table, the law of loving one's neighbor as oneself, by which eternal life would be gained. These legalistic views are not tenable. A common sermon pattern along this line is: this man was to give up everything—what are you giving up? Life, even in the sense of heaven, is not bought with money.

23) However, on hearing these things he became very sad, for he was exceedingly rich.

The effect produced on the young man shows that Jesus had struck home, had bared the man's most vulnerable spot, the love of his great wealth. First, such enthusiasm; now, such aggrieved going away (Matthew and Mark). The fact that he was not changed on the instant need cause no surprise. A struggle began, one that might be long and severe. He, indeed, left Jesus, but Jesus' words did not leave him and may well have brought him back in the end. The synoptists leave the story at this point because their interest lies in the words of Jesus which go far beyond this one case.

24) But when Jesus saw him, he said: How with difficulty shall those having riches enter into the kingdom of God! For easier it is that a camel go

through a needle's opening than that a rich man go into the kingdom of God.

Jesus saw the aggrieved ruler leaving (Matthew and Mark), then looked around on his disciples (Mark), and then exclaimed because of the difficulty with which a rich man gets into the kingdom (4:43). What appears in the narrative about the ruler is thus more fully elucidated. God alone is able to save a rich man. The emphasis is on δυσκόλως; God can save him only "with difficulty," i. e., bring him to receive the gifts and the blessings that are bestowed by God's rule of grace in Jesus Christ; τὰ χρήματα=riches. In Mark, when Jesus notes the amazement of the disciples, he repeats and substitutes "those that have trusted in riches" for "a rich man."

25) Jesus illustrates how difficult it is by a remarkable comparison, which simply means that it is impossible for a rich man, that is, one who trusts in riches, to enter the kingdom. His false trust will most certainly keep out the true trust in God's grace. Τρῆμα= perforation; βελόνη=a sharp point as of a spear and thus a needle. The Talmud uses the elephant in the same illustration of human impossibility; elephants were not known in Palestine. The Koran has the illustration of Jesus.

Not until the fifth century was κάμηλος, "camel," changed into κάμιλος, the heavy "rope" or cable that is attached to the anchor of a ship (R. 192). This view offered no gain, for no cable can be threaded through a needle's eye. In the fifteenth century the opposite was suggested, the needle's eye was enlarged by being made to mean a small portal that was used by pedestrians when they were entering a walled city, through which a camel might squeeze after its load was removed. This turned the impossible into the possible and became attractive by suggesting that, as the camel had to leave its load and crawl on its knees, so the rich man had to shed his riches, i. e., his love for them, and humble himself on his knees and crawl into the kingdom. But as in Matt. 23:24 Jesus had in mind an actual gnat and an actual camel, so camel and needle's eye are actual here. The impossibility that is thus illustrated is without a single exception. Abraham, David, Zacchaeus, Joseph of Arimathaea are not exceptions, for Jesus himself now explains how the impossible becomes possible.

26) Now they that heard said, And who is able to be saved! But he said, The things impossible with men are possible with God.

Luke does not state how shocked the disciples were on hearing what Jesus said. Καί at the head of a reply connects with the preceding speaker's word and continues the thought but adds what the one replying should add or what must be added. So the disciples here add to what they have just heard: "And who is able to be saved!" in the sense that Jesus may as well say right out that nobody can be saved—and, surely, that cannot be true.

The disciples do not speak only of the young ruler, they go even beyond all rich men. Their τίς is unrestricted. They think of themselves (v. 28, "we") and include all men generally. Have not all men a secret desire for riches of some kind? The question is really an implied confession of sin on the part of the disciples. This is excellent. It is well that they do not shield themselves behind what Jesus once said about the poor (6:20).

But another thing is not so excellent, namely the implication that they believed that a man can and should do something toward being saved. They really say: "If the illustration of the camel is true regarding a rich man's entering the kingdom, then the rich man can do nothing toward being saved, nor can we or anybody else, who are, like the rich, afflicted with some desire for things earthly." In σώζειν there lies the idea of rescue from mortal danger and of a condition of safety that is produced by the rescue. The passive σωθῆναι leaves God as the agent, but δύναται betrays the synergistic idea that is in the disciples' minds.

27) Jesus, too, speaks with feeling (Mark and Matthew). He has elicited from the disciples the very thought he wished to correct once for all. The illustration of the camel is only too true: "The things impossible with men"—they are and ever remain so. The last door of hope on that side is shut and sealed forever. Here perish all Pelagianism, moralism, synergism; man can do absolutely nothing toward being saved by any natural powers of his own. The *Concordia Triglotta* 785, etc., and 881, etc., is most certainly right. But the more all hope in ourselves dies, whether we are rich or poor, the more our hope in God rises like the morning sun with healing in his wings: "possible with God." And why not? "For with God all things are possible," Mark 10:27. Greater assurances no man can ask. God can save even the rich, difficult though it be to eradicate trust in riches and to put trust only in God's grace in its place.

Who will measure the ability of this grace? Who will describe the miracles it is able to work? We might be inclined to think of God's omnipotence as it is revealed in the physical creation and then apply our abstract mode of reasoning and say that it is by almighty power that God saves the rich and us. But Jesus speaks of the kingdom of God, which is not physical, of this world, and of the great work of saving men, including the rich, which is a spiritual work entirely and not at all a work of omnipotence. We are not in the First Article of the Creed but in the Second and the Third. "Christ is able to save them to the uttermost," Heb. 7:25.

28) The disciples go from one extreme to the other. They first fear that, on the basis of what Jesus said, none of them can be saved; now after their fears in that direction have been allayed, they want

assurances that they will be rewarded for the sacrifices they have made. **Now Peter said, Lo, we on our part, having left our own things, did follow thee!**

It occurs to Peter that he and the Twelve had done exactly what Jesus required of the rich young ruler, and so he thinks he ought to remind Jesus of this fact. Peter thinks that their act was no small thing, hence he begins with the exclamation "lo." The emphasis is on ἡμεῖς, "we on our part," which contrasts the Twelve with the ruler who went away aggrieved. Peter does not forget to bring out to the credit of himself and the Twelve the fact that they followed Jesus even as Jesus had bidden the ruler to do. The τὰ ἴδια are all their own affairs and interests, not just their homes (R. V. margin). They had identified themselves wholly with Jesus. Both the participle and the main verb are aorists which state only the facts; note the tenses in Matthew and in Mark. Mark and Luke omit the question: "What then shall be ours?" (Matthew) as being already voiced in the tone that Peter used.

But this word of Peter's has a suspicious ring with its emphasis on what "we on our part" did. It does not intend to add: "and we have found more than satisfaction in thee"; for that strong "we" would not harmonize with such an addition. To express such an acknowledgment Peter should have said: *"Thou thyself* hast drawn us to forsake our own and to follow thee." What Peter's ear had caught was the promise to the ruler: "And thou shalt have a treasure in the heavens." But he had not caught Jesus' meaning that this would be a treasure of pure grace and not a merited reward that was earned by the ruler by giving away his wealth and then following Jesus. Peter takes the word to refer to a profitable trade to which the ruler was invited. The old spirit of work-righteousness, of human claims and merit, crops out again in Peter. The more *we* do, the more *we* earn, and the more *God* owes us.

29) Jesus, however, said to them: Amen, I say to you, that there is no one who left house, or wife, or brother, or parents, or children for the sake of the kingdom of God, who shall not duly receive back many times more in this time and in the eon that is coming life eternal.

Compare the fuller answer in Matt. 19:28-30 which is followed by the parable in 20:1-16. The generosity and the magnanimity of Jesus are so great that he could and would accept nothing from us without returning it beyond all computation (Matt. 25:21, 23; Luke 19:17, 19). The vast disproportion of what we give up and the returns already display his boundless grace, to say nothing of the gift of salvation which is made before we even begin our sacrifices. Not one shall miss his due reward.

On "amen," etc., see 4:24. Since it is sealed thus, this promise cannot fail. R. 427 thinks that the repetitions with ἤ lend solemnity, B.-D. 460, 3, the impression of greatness and fulness. "And" cannot be used as a translation because each item has its own value, and because "and" would mean that each disciple would have to leave all the items listed before the promise applied to him. We cannot, however, make any exception of any item in the whole list. On "to leave" see 14:26 and Matt. 10:37. This leaving may include the outward act of giving up and separating from the persons and the property involved, but the inward separation is often enough. Luke has the comprehensive phrase "for the sake of the kingdom of God"; Matthew, "for the sake of my name" (revelation); Mark, "for the sake of me and for the sake of the gospel." The sense is the same, which illustrates the work of divine inspiration, which does not necessarily imply the sameness of the verbal expressions but the exactness of all verbal expressions to convey just what the Spirit wants conveyed.

30) Matthew and Mark write "a hundred fold" and raise the replacement proportionately to the highest degree as is done in Matt. 13:8. Luke's neuter plural "many times more" sounds just as hyperbolical, which leads some to place the entire reward into the other world. But this is barred out by "in this season (time)" which is contrasted with "in the eon, the coming one." The reward is certain already in our earthly lives. Καιρός is a portion of time that is fit and proper for something distinctive, "a season" for it. It is rather striking for Jesus to speak of earthly time as being only "this season." The contrast with αἰών is great, for an "eon" is a vast era that is marked by what fills it. "The eon coming," i. e., now approaching closer and closer, is the heavenly eon that begins at the end of the world after the *kairos* has run its brief course. The two do not overlap. The glory of heaven that is to be ours is received fully only at the end when the body will be raised and will be reunited with the soul.

Scoffers have made sport of this promise by singling out "wife"—a hundred here on earth already and then again in heaven. This wooden way of reading Scripture must always call for pity. They would, of course, pick on wife, but why not on mothers, children, or other items in the list? Jesus has in mind the new relationships and what they involve, all these become ours already in this life, 8:19, etc.; Rom. 16:13 (John 19:27); I Tim. 1:2; 5:2; II Tim. 2:1; Philemon 10; I Pet. 5:3, and other passages; other possessions Ps. 37:16; Prov. 15:16; 16:8; I Tim. 6:6. The new riches are the divine blessings which substitute in us thankfulness for worldly anxiety and delight in imperishable treasures.

It should be noted that life eternal (referring to v. 18) is separated from the preceding and placed at the end by itself, which shows that it is not intended as a reward for forsaking relations, property, etc. In fact, before we are able to do this forsaking and any good work, the instant faith is kindled in the heart, life eternal is already made ours, and that altogether out of pure grace for Christ's sake alone. The analogy of all Scripture is solid on this vital subject. Although both Mark and Luke refer to taking life eternal in the eon to come, at the end of the world, this changes nothing in regard to the way in which it first becomes ours. The entrance into the heavenly life is mentioned in order to impress upon the disciples what an infinite blessing awaits those who are called upon to forsake this or that temporality. What is any loss when we look at our heavenly gain?

The Fourth Part

When Jesus Actually Entered Jerusalem

Chapter 18:31 to 21:38

The fact that Luke intends to indicate a division in his Gospel at this point is generally recognized in spite of the chapter division, which should be made here and not at v. 43. The actual Passion history begins with chapter 22.

31) **Now having taken the Twelve aside, he said to them: Lo, we are going up to Jerusalem, and there shall be accomplished all the things that have been written through the prophets for the Son of man. For he shall be given over to the Gentiles and shall be mocked and shall be outraged and shall be spit upon, and, having scourged him, they will kill him. And on the third day he shall rise again.**

The long, leisurely journey down through Perea east of the Jordan is finished. Jericho is at hand and the comparatively short stretch of road to Jerusalem. So Mark 10:32 states that Jesus and the disciples were now on the way to Jerusalem, he was leading them forward. It was thus that at some spot along the road he took the Twelve aside ($παρά$ in the verb), away from even the other disciples who followed, and made the announcement and told them once more about all that should take place at the end of the journey. He had made this announcement before, in 9:22, 40; in Matt. 16:21; 17:22, 23. But all is now fully detailed and complete. Jesus sees it all and not merely through the eyes of the prophets but in direct vision so that the one commentary on his own prophetic announcement is the history of these events as soon as they occurred.

"Lo!" he exclaims, for all this is astonishing, indeed. "We are going up to Jerusalem," are now directly on our way with Jerusalem as our next objective. "We" in the verb means the Twelve and Jesus, for they are to be the direct witnesses of all that shall take place. Jesus himself wants them there. He must die at Jerusalem. There the prophets had died, 13:33, and there the greatest of them all must needs die. This was the heart of the nation, the seat of its authority, and no less a power would reject and kill him. Jesus would be put to death, not by some mob in a frenzy, on the spur of the moment, but by the great representatives of the nation in their very capital after going through deliberate legal forms.

"There shall be accomplished," finished and brought to an end (τέλος in the verb), all that had been written. It is the same verb that Jesus used on the cross when he cried, "It has been finished!" John 19:30 (also 28), τελέω. The perfect participle, "all that has been written," etc., means that all still stands thus recorded. Those who, like R., W. P., think that the dative τῷ υἱῷ τοῦ ἀνθρώπου might be construed with the main verb, overlook the fact that "all the things that have been written" needs a limitation. Not absolutely all were completed at Jerusalem but only those that had been written "for the Son of man," regarding him and the completion he should accomplish. So we construe this dative of personal interest with the participle and follow the natural order of the words.

Here we again have that significant διά with reference to the holy writers which is so constantly used in the New Testament. Trace it from Matt. 1:22 onward and note it in Luke 1:70. Robertson's translation "by the prophets" may be misleading. This "by" (ὑπό) belongs only to God (Matt. 1:22) and is never used with reference to the prophets. "By God through the prophets" is the Bible definition of inspiration. Διά introduces the medium; the prophets were God's media or instruments. God was the speaker and author; the prophets were his media for transmission. That is the whole of inspiration, of verbal inspiration, than which there is no other. "Son of man" (see 5:24), he who is man and more than man, is the proper title here.

32) We should compare 9:22 and 44, and then we shall see that all is new and thus an addition in this announcement save the killing and the rising on the third day. Even his being given over or delivered "into the hands of men" (9:44) is no longer indefinite but now specified (not referring to the act of Judas) : "to the Gentiles," who can be only Pilate and his men, and the ones who will hand him over can be only the Sanhedrin which is mentioned by its full title in 9:22. The prophets did not reveal the fact that the Gentiles would execute Jesus. This act, which was so horrible to the mind of any godly Jew, the deliverance of their Messiah into the hands of the Gentiles, is followed by three prophetic future passives which foretell what these Gentiles would do with Jesus. The sufferings at the hands of the Sanhedrin are recorded in 9:22; Jesus now adds: "he shall be mocked, he shall be outraged (insulted is too weak after mocked), he shall be spit upon"—by these Gentiles.

33) And then the final acts: "and having scourged, they will kill him," the Gentiles doing this in their way by crucifying him as Matt. 20:19 reports this announcement. Only here and in Matt. 26:2 did Jesus use the word "crucify," it is not found in the prophets. This is the climax, not only the horrible but the most abominable death which was inflicted on slaves and the worst type of criminals by pagans. Jesus calmly detailed it all—into this he was going, this was to be finished, this the disciples were to witness.

Then, with the same calmness, he again (9:22) declares: "and on the third day he shall rise again," ἀναστήσεται, the future middle which is used in the active sense. Note the wording: four passives regarding things that are done to Jesus; then one plural active, "they shall kill" (not another passive, "he shall be killed"), which points to the murderers; then one singular middle-active, which points to the resurrection of Jesus as being effected by himself. We first go down, down to the most terrible death, then at one tremendous stroke into the resurrection of glory. Compare the further remarks on this clause as found in 9:22.

34) And they grasped not one of these things, and this utterance had been hidden from them, and they were not realizing the things being said.

Compare 9:45 on the same inability to understand. We have little to add to the comment we have offered on that passage. Three verbs are again piled up to tell us of this ignorance of the disciples. The first is an aorist to express the fact: "they did not grasp," and the object is added, "not one of these things," not even a single item in the list. We then have either a periphrastic pluperfect: the utterance (ῥῆμα, the thing uttered) had been and thus continued to be hidden from them by something in their minds, namely their wrong preconceptions of the Messiah; or ἦν as an imperfect with a predicative perfect participle as a complement: the thing "was" to them "as something that has been and thus is still hidden" from them. Finally we have an imperfect: "and they were not realizing" all the things being said to them (present participle).

Yet this announcement, like those that precede, was by no means useless. Jesus was thinking of the future when all would have occurred just as he was now telling it in advance; compare 24:44-48. So to this day many a word of Scripture does not mean much to the reader until later in life when its meaning comes out with force to instruct and to comfort him. The Twelve probably tried to find strange figures in these terrible verbs and simply could and would not understand them in their literal sense.

35) **And it came to pass while he was drawing near to Jericho, a blind man was sitting by the side of the road begging. Now, when he heard a crowd passing through, he began inquiring what this was. And they reported to him that Jesus the Nazarene was passing by. And he shouted, saying, Jesus, Son of David, have mercy on me! And those leading began rebuking him, that he be silent. He, however, kept yelling much more, Son of David, have mercy on me!**

See 1:8 for ἐγένετο plus a finite verb and for ἐν τῷ with the infinitive. Jesus had crossed the Jordan and was following the usual route through Jericho, near the river, up to Jerusalem.

At first glance there seems to be a decided discrepancy between Luke and both Matthew and Mark. Luke has the miracle performed as Jesus draws near the city, Matthew and Mark as he leaves the city. Strange solutions are offered, even to postulating as many as three different healings. Yet the matter is simple, and all shadow of contradiction fades away when we have *all* the facts. Jesus passed through Jericho (19:1), and yet, although it was late in the day, no one in the whole town invited him to be his guest. On the other side of the town, out along the highway, Zacchaeus was waiting to see Jesus pass by. Jesus calls him down from the tree, invites himself to this publican's house, retraces his steps into Jericho, and spends the night with Zacchaeus. It was on this return to the city that the blind men were healed. Luke separates the events because he wants to tell the story of Zacchaeus in one piece, without inserting into it the story of the blind men. So Matt. 21:18-22 tells the story of the blasted fig tree in one piece, whereas Mark 11:12-14; 20-23 relate the two events separately.

Mark preserved the beggar's name, Bartimæus, and Matthew, who himself saw the miracle, informs us that the blind beggar had a blind companion. There is no contradiction between the evangelists as to the number of the blind men. It is easy to see how Bartimæus got even his name into one record. He was evidently the leader, kept up his frantic clamor against all opposition, and thus obtained the healing. The beggars are shown as sitting alongside the road. They had trailed the crowd out from Jericho with their guide but stopped at the edge of the city. Then, when the crowd surged back to the city, their golden opportunity came.

36) Being blind, this beggar, of whom alone Luke speaks, depended on his hearing, which told him that the crowd was already returning. He could not understand that, and so he went on to inquire, "what this was," the optative εἴη for ἐστί, R. 1044.

37) "They reported to him" means some of those in the returning crowd. They call the Lord by his ordinary personal name "Jesus," to which they add "the Nazarene" to distinguish him from others of the same name. "The Nazarene" is not derogatory although it is also not a term of honor. So this was the reason for the commotion on the road—for some reason Jesus was retracing his steps to re-enter the city. The present tense "is passing by" is not changed to the optative as is done in v. 36. It is a matter of the writer's choice.

38) The beggar never stopped to inquire why Jesus was coming back, or where he was at the moment; it was enough for him that Jesus was passing by somewhere in the crowd that was extending along the road. He at once shouted, not, "Jesus the Nazarene," but "Jesus, David's Son, mercy me!" the verb being transitive in the Greek.

We now see why all three synoptists record this miracle at this point in their story of Jesus. It is not for the sake of the miracle, for Jesus had healed many blind persons, but because of this address, "Son of David," the standard title for the Messiah among the Jews. Note that each evangelist reports the title twice and thus makes it prominent in the record. Now that Jesus is going to his death at Jerusalem he accepts the Messianic title openly before the multitude, accepts it with all its implication of royalty (1:32, 33). He had hitherto avoided it as much as possible because of the wrong political and worldly ideas the Jews connected with the Messiah-King they were expecting. Only in Samaria, to a lone woman, Jesus declared himself to be the Messiah. In Matt. 9:27, where the blind men address him as the Son of David, they are told to tell no man about their healing; and in Matt. 15:22, etc., Jesus is far away from the crowds, where no danger attended the use of the title. But now the time has come for all Judaism to know that Jesus is David's royal Son and Heir, the true Messiah, who is about to die as such. Politics and nationalism present no dangers now. The aorist imperative expresses great fervor in prayers; but here the petition is also for one great act of mercy from Jesus; hence ἐλέησόν με, "mercy me," extend an act of mercy to me. What the act is to be need not be stated.

39) We know only the fact that those in the van of the crowd tried to silence the beggar and not the reason for this attempt. Different reasons are advanced, but none commends itself; it is useless to discuss them. As it was in v. 41, ἵνα is elliptical and imperative, R. 994. The attempt to silence the beggar causes him only to keep yelling the more, Luke now uses ἔκραζεν, "he continued yelling." His one chance of healing shall not slip by. All three synoptists repeat the cry with the significant "David's Son."

40) **Now, having halted, Jesus ordered him to be brought to him; and he drawing near, he inquired of him, What dost thou want that I shall do? And he said, Lord, that I receive sight! And Jesus said to him, Receive sight! Thy faith has saved thee. And immediately he received sight, and he began follow-**

ing him, glorifying God. And all the people, on seeing it, gave praise to God.

Read Mark 10:49, 50 for what Luke tells far less vividly. It is the beggar's frantic cry that causes Jesus to halt. He cannot pass by with that cry ringing even faintly in his ears. Willing hands, that now cheer the beggar whereas they had tried to hush him before, bring him to Jesus.

41) In the question of Jesus θέλεις is followed directly by the deliberative subjunctive without ἵνα but has quite the same sense, R. 924. In the beggar's answer Luke writes Κύριε instead of Mark's Rabboni. The latter means more than rabbi and in Latin codices is translated *magister et domine*, two using *domine* alone. Zahn has "Rabbun"='Adon and states that it was used extensively in Jewish literature for God in connections like "Lord of the world" or "of the worlds." So the beggar's address in his petition harmonizes well with the Messianic "David's Son." On the imperatival use of ἵνα see R. 933 and 994; we may translate "let me receive sight" or "see again." The aorist is proper, for receiving sight is instantaneous. Jesus elicits this answer so that the man who cannot see may know what Jesus is doing.

42) The synoptists exercise great independence in relating parts of this story. Matthew tells us that Jesus was moved with compassion and placed his hands on the man's eyes. Mark writes only that Jesus told him to be going, and that his faith has saved him. Luke, too, is brief but reports the word ἀνάβλεψον, "receive sight" or "see again." The word regarding the man's faith is identical with the one that is addressed to the healed Samaritan leper in 17:19 and is discussed there.

43) All the evangelists state that the man's sight was restored at once, likewise that he went on to follow Jesus, Luke using the ingressive imperfect. Mark adds "on the road," i. e., joining the disciples who constantly

kept near Jesus. Luke tells how he was glorifying God for what he had done for him through Jesus, and how all the people gave praise to God. Both were certainly right. All the deeds of Jesus were to glorify and praise the Father, for they were, indeed, the deeds for which the Father had sent him into the world as the Son of David.

CHAPTER XIX

1) The story of the blind beggar interlocks with that of Zacchaeus as is explained in connection with 18:35. **And having entered, he was passing on through Jericho.** It was Thursday before the Passion week. On entering it, Jesus did not stop in the city. He passed slowly through it with a group of his disciples and a great following of others that was augmented as he made his way through the city. The reason is plain: the man with whom he intended to stop was not at home, he had gone out to get a glimpse of Jesus. Jesus knew where to find him, out on the other side of the city along the highway, perched in a tree. So he simply crosses the city until he finds the tree and his host for the night.

Jericho is now a degraded village which is probably not even located on the site where the city stood in Jesus' time. At that time Jericho was a city that was rich and prosperous indeed, was watered by the Fountain of Elisha and other springs, the whole oasis being green and flowery, rich in balsams, myrobalanum, honey, etc.—the city of fragrance, the city of roses, "paradise of God." It was the place to make a halt before the final ascent from a location 1,000 feet below sea level to 2,400 above, to the heights on which Jerusalem rested. A colony of priests lived here, and one might have expected that one of these descendants of Aaron would receive into his home the great Son of David (18:38, 39) on his only visit to Jericho, but the only man who was ready to receive him was of a totally different type.

2) **And lo, a man called by name Zacchaeus! And he was head publican, and he a rich man. And he was trying to see Jesus, who he was, and was not able due to the multitude because he was small in**

stature. And having run forward to the front, he climbed up a fig mulberry in order that he might see him because he was about to be passing through that way.

Instead of using the ordinary "there was a man called Zacchaeus," Luke introduces the man with an exclamation: "Lo, a man called by name Zacchaeus!" This is done because of the highly exceptional things he is about to write about this man. Yet only two pen strokes picture him in advance: his work and his wealth. He was "head publican," was employed, as is usually assumed, by a Roman principal who had bought up the taxes in that territory from the state and was collecting them. The "head publican" had a force of ordinary publicans under him and managed their business. Zacchaeus was rich, which must mean that he had considerable wealth. His business was lucrative so that, in spite of the odium that was attached to it among the Jews generally (see 3:12), some Jews were always ready to undertake this work. If not his work then his wealth made him a man of importance in Jericho.

He is the only chief publican of whom we read in the New Testament, and we are not surprised to find him located in Jericho with its heavy trade in balsam which was taxed at a high rate. The palm groves and the balsam gardens (now gone) were so valuable that Antony gave them to Cleopatra as a source of revenue, and Herod the Great redeemed them for his own benefit. The two αὐτός instead of a relative are in full accord with the Greek genius, R. 723.

3) The two imperfects "he was trying and was not able" to see Jesus due to the crowd and because of his short stature allow us to fill in his various efforts as Jesus made his way slowly through the city. He left his office and his work, but even when he got near Jesus, too many were between him and Jesus in order to see him. "To see Jesus who he was"="to see who

Jesus was," R. 488. All that follows shows that his desire was far more than the curiosity of the crowds who merely run to gaze on some famous man. His was a far more serious desire which impelled him also to go far beyond what curiosity alone is able to produce.

4) He ran forward to the front, some distance ahead of the great mass of people that was moving along with Jesus, and there climbed up a fig mulberry or sycamore fig, which grows to the size of our walnut trees, has heart-shaped leaves which are downy underneath and fragrant, and grows fruit in clusters on little sprigs. This tree stood along the road on leaving Jericho, where Jesus was about to be passing through; the genitive ἐκείνης (ὁδοῦ) is due, it seems, to διά in the verb (but see R. 494). Here, from his vantage point, Zacchaeus was sure to see Jesus. On occasions like this the natural excitement of all concerned allows more freedom than is usual. But even so, for this little man, who was wealthy and widely known, to neglect his dignity and to adopt the tactics of a boy and to perch up in a tree meant much indeed.

5) **And when he came to the place, on looking up, Jesus said to him, Zacchaeus, with hastening climb down, for today in thy house I must abide! And with hastening he climbed down and received him rejoicing.**

Jesus, of course, came to the place since this was the road he took. Do not say that that was accidental. Since the crowds surrounded him, a thousand things should have directed his eyes elsewhere. It is unwarranted to think that he looked up into this one tree accidentally, or that he always looked up into the trees along the road as he traveled. And other men very likely also climbed trees, that of Zacchaeus may have had several of them. What Luke states is that Jesus came to just this place, then looked up and invited himself to Zacchaeus' house. He knew that his host was in this tree, knew his name, knew his very heart. His program has been set. Zacchaeus is to hurry down and to do his part in it. Whatever Jesus needed to know in his work and his office, including his contact and his intercourse with men, that he knew; and this knowing was the use he made of his divine attribute of omniscience for his saving purposes. John 1:42-50; 2:24, 25. Only a rationalist like Paulus could suppose that somebody told Jesus who the little man in the tree was.

The action of Jesus surprised everybody; all gazed up at the little man in the tree and wondered who he could be that Jesus called to him. The most astonished individual was Zacchaeus himself. Content just to get a good glimpse at Jesus in order to impress that wonderful image on his heart, Jesus stops for him, for him personally, calls him by name, bids him come down so that he may take him to his house, that he may lodge him for the night. A tumult of thoughts and feelings must have surged through the little man's heart—this great and wonderful person was coming to be his guest! At that moment Zacchaeus knew that Jesus had read his whole heart even as Nathanael knew it and confessed it when Jesus uttered that one word to him about being under the fig tree. But in the case of Zacchaeus all had a special meaning, for he was not a mere publican as Matthew had been but one who had many a sin on his conscience and was aware of these sins. Yet Jesus was inviting himself to his house!

6) Note the correspondence: "with hastening climb down," and: "with hastening he climbed down," the minor point of the hastening being stated by a participle in the Greek, which is aorist and expresses action that is simultaneous with that of the main verb. The heart of Zacchaeus began responding to the heart of Jesus as when an organ key is struck, and the pipe for that key sounds and vibrates with its tone.

"He received him rejoicing." It was not a question of being thus honored by Jesus above all the people of Jericho. Far more vital considerations lay back of that joyful reception. This coming of Jesus to the publican's house recalled in the little man's heart the condescension of Jesus to publicans and open sinners (15:1, 2), all his willingness to help those whom others cast out, perhaps what he had said to them about the forgiveness of sins—and Zacchaeus with his troubled conscience longed for this forgiveness.

We cannot conceive the scene as some do who imagine that the house of Zacchaeus stood on the road toward Jerusalem and place the reception of Jesus at the door of the house and that the murmuring of the crowd occurred only when Jesus entered the house. The reception with rejoicing began right under the tree. There is a great probability that because of his wealth and his work as the head of a tax department Zacchaeus had his residence in the city, in one of its finest quarters. Nor were the people in ignorance regarding the intention of Jesus until they saw Zacchaeus ushering him in his door. Jesus declared his intention publicly under the tree—all that were near the tree heard it, and they were many. The whole procession halted while Zacchaeus climbed down from the tree. Jesus and his disciples started back to the city with Zacchaeus. All soon learned why. The crowd, too, went back with them.

7) **And, on seeing it, all began murmuring, saying, With an openly sinful man he went to lodge!**

This seeing and the consequent murmuring started right at the place where the tree stood. All that the aorist participle does is to state that the seeing preceded the murmuring, and the imperfect has this murmuring go on indefinitely. And this grumbling dissatisfaction was general—"all" objected. The emphasis is first on the phrase "with an openly sinful man" and next on the infinitive "to lodge," καταλύω, literally, "to loose," i. e., unhitch animals and make a halt for the night. To think that Jesus should *lodge* with *such* a man! The aorist "he went" is only the Greek for our perfect "he has gone" and applies the moment Jesus and Zacchaeus started to leave the tree and by no means only after Jesus entered the house of Zacchaeus.

This murmuring reflects very clearly the general opinion about publicans. They were classed as ἁμαρτωλοί, open sinners, not only because they aided the government which oppressed the Jewish nation but also because they themselves were notorious in practicing oppression by collecting excessive amounts and unlawfully enriching themselves. Whatever estimate Jesus placed on the first point—he never ordered the publicans to drop their business, and he did tell the people to pay their taxes—he certainly objected to any form of overcharging (3:12, 13).

Zacchaeus was a real sinner in the eyes of Jesus. By going to his house he did not even for a moment countenance this man's sin or let him remain undisturbed in it. The populace overlooked this fact and thus blamed Jesus as the Pharisees had blamed him. The people were right in one respect: it would not have been proper for Jesus to lodge with this publican if the latter were to remain as he was. Jesus never countenanced sinners who intended to remain the sinners they were. But he acted with his unerring knowledge in this whereas in our dealing with open sinners we are compelled to use ordinary prudence and caution lest our very goodness of heart subject us to deception and make us injure the cause we seek to aid.

8) **Now, having taken a stand, Zacchaeus said to the Lord, Lo, the half of my possessions, Lord, I give to the poor; and if I extorted anything of anyone I duly give back fourfold.**

Luke leaves much untold at this point. We cannot agree that Zacchaeus spoke as he did at the door of his house when the complaints rose and met his ears. Or that the mere impression of Jesus brought forth his words after entering his house. Jesus wrought on men's hearts by his Word, and that is what we assume here.

As he had done in Bethany (10:39) and wherever he was entertained, he turned host and dispensed the Word after entering the house of this publican.

Nor was this done in quiet converse with Zacchaeus, "which only the angels heard who rejoice over the sinner that repents," for the angels also hear the words that are spoken to sinners in public. In v. 9 Jesus speaks to Zacchaeus, but in such a manner that all the others also heard what he said. He speaks of Zacchaeus in the third person and mentions his "house," his household or family. It was in response to what Jesus said after entering the house, after the *cohortationes et monitiones* which Jesus brought to this entire household, that Zacchaeus replied as he did. All that were present saw fully why Jesus had invited himself to this man's home and agreed that the invitation was justified, no matter what the people outside might think or say. Zacchaeus, too, was a Jew who knew the Old Testament with its law and its gospel promises. Jesus used and advanced this knowledge. The Pharisees simply rejected men like this publican, Jesus helped to restore them.

Before the δεῖπνον or evening meal could be prepared, Jesus, the Twelve, Zacchaeus, and whoever else was present sat in Oriental fashion while Jesus spoke. When he ceased speaking, Zacchaeus stood up. Great things were taking place in his soul, and he acts with grave formality by rising from the rug or the divan on which he had been sitting. Jesus had made his house a church of God, and now Zacchaeus stands as though he were in the presence of God and makes his response to Jesus. He is making a weighty statement, hence we have the exclamation "lo." First he utters a vow or promise of thanksgiving: "the half of my possessions I give to the poor." This is the man's thankoffering for the pardon, the comfort of conscience and the peace of soul he has just received from Jesus. A priceless gift has been given to him, and he acknowledges the gift.

Thanks such as this presuppose faith. The act is wholly voluntary. Jesus made no demand upon him to give any of his wealth away. No special call was extended to Zacchaeus to leave his home to preach the gospel. He was not even told to drop his business as a publican. He might have done so voluntarily because of the temptations that were connected with the tax collecting of that day; if he continued in business he conducted his work in a clean way. Why he gave half and not a different fraction is hard to say. Love has and will always have its own generous measure as those know best who have been prompted by love.

Beside the confession of faith with thanksgiving Zacchaeus places a confession of sin that is coupled with restitution: "And if I extorted anything of anyone I duly give back fourfold." This "if" does not express doubt, for it is a condition of reality, and whereas all conditions are assumptions in the speaker's (writer's) mind, Zacchaeus would not have used this condition unless what he assumed was, indeed, real. The verb (as in 3:14) means to press money out of someone by false assertions. That was the sin of these publicans. To what extent Zacchaeus was guilty cannot be determined. He cannot have oppressed right and left, for he could then not have made fourfold restitution after giving away half of his wealth.

Ἀποδίδωμι = to give what is due. The law required that in cases such as this only a fifth more than the sum that had been illegally gained should be returned, Lev. 6:5; Num. 5:6, etc. But Zacchaeus voluntarily offers to treat any peculations of his as plain and simple theft, for which the law stipulated fourfold or fivefold restitution, Exod. 22:1; I Sam. 12:3; Exod. 33:15. Zacchaeus makes amends for his wrongs in the fullest possible measure. The idea is not that amends wipe out guilt. Proper amends are the evidence of a changed heart, and the amends which Zacchaeus intended to make should be regarded as such evidence. "When the

Lord enters a house, unrighteousness moves out." Besser.

9) And Jesus said to him: This day salvation came to this house according as he, too, is Abraham's son. For the Son of man came to seek and to save which has been lost.

In this way Jesus pronounced the absolution on Zacchaeus. Jesus spoke to him by making a statement *about* him in the hearing of all that were present. We cannot entertain the supposition that this was done before the house, in the presence of the multitude, however much the words of Jesus constitute a refutation of the murmuring. The emphasis is on "today" because Jesus this day brought the salvation to this house, and those dwelling there received it by faith. This "salvation" is rescue, deliverance, plus the state of safety that is thus produced. It is freedom from sin and guilt through the pardon of Jesus and the restoration of the soul to the favor of God as his child and heir. "This house" surely cannot mean only the building as though there now dwelt under its roof a man who was saved. While nothing specific is said about the family of the publican, "this house" speaks of it as also believing and thus being saved. The aorist ἐγένετο, "occurred" or "came," states the great fact.

This is "according as" (καθότι), in harmony with its cause, which is that "he, too, is Abraham's son." Jew though Zacchaeus was, a true son of Abraham he did not become until "today"; for Abraham is the father of believers, and faith alone makes us sons of his, Gal. 3:7; Rom. 4:11, 12, 16. Thus here, too, Jesus points to faith as being the subjective means of salvation, the faith he himself works in us.

10) With γάρ Jesus adds the mighty substantiation for this verdict pronounced on the publican and his family. Their faith and their salvation would be utterly impossible except for what "the Son of man" (see 5:24) came to do and was actually doing. Behind

the salvation of Zacchaeus is all the saving work of Jesus. The emphasis is on "came" which is placed forward for this reason, which tells of his coming in its entirety; it is a Messianic term, for Jesus is the One coming and as such was now present.

His great purpose in having come is "to seek and to save which has been lost." The aorists are important—actually to effect this seeking and this saving. Zacchaeus, like others, was evidence that the great purpose was vastly more than an intention. In Matt. 18:11 we have only the one verb "to save," here "to seek" is added, but in such a way that both form a unit. The seeking reaches out by the gospel and thus saves. The seeking and saving power in this gospel is the atonement which Jesus wrought, which was effective through the promises of the old covenant and through the fulfillment in the new. The neuter participle "what has been lost," just because it is neuter, states the object in the widest way, compare John 3:6 and similar neuters. The perfect tense has its present connotation: "has been and consequently is still lost," and this in the intensive sense: that which has perished and is now in that condition—a true description of the wreck that sin has made of us. Far from God, in night and darkness, shattered, broken, yea, dead and without a spark of spiritual vitality—this is to be "lost." It helps us to understand what seeking and saving had to do to reach and to restore the lost. According to the task so is the glory of its accomplishment, and so is the blessedness it brings.

11) Little need be said regarding the difference between the parable of the Talents and that of the Pounds. The former deals only with Christ's followers, the latter also with his enemies and was spoken before the company in Zacchaeus' house. The former speaks of talents which are unequally bestowed, the latter of pounds which are distributed equally. The two are decidedly distinct.

Now, they hearing these things, he furthermore spoke a parable because he was near to Jerusalem, and they were thinking that the kingdom of God was about to make its appearance at once.

Some are doubtful as to what "these things" mean. Others think of v. 8, Zacchaeus' disposing of so much property. "These things" refer to the seeking and the saving for which the Son of man came, of which the deliverance of Zacchaeus was a sample. Even the disciples were looking for other things since Jesus was near Jerusalem, only six hours' travel away. Here at the capital, after a little while, they thought the kingdom would make its appearance, be made manifest in great glory and earthly splendor. The sons of Zebedee had asked for the two most exalted places in this glory kingdom of their expectation. All that had occurred in the house of Zacchaeus was a minor matter to the disciples; they were keyed up for grander things. Προσθείς is used like an adverb: "he spoke futhermore," literally, "by adding." Μέλλει with the present infinitive speaks of the immediate future, and the present tense is unchanged from the thought in its direct form: "It is about to be manifested."

12) Jesus had to shatter and correct these false hopes. **Accordingly he said: A man well-born went into a distant country to take for himself a kingdom and to return. Moreover, having called his own ten slaves, he gave them ten minas and said to them, Do business while I am coming! But his citizens continued to hate him and sent an embassage after him, saying, We are not willing that this one become king over us!**

The figure of this "man well-born" who goes to take a kingdom, leaves rebellious citizens behind, and eventually returns is certainly transparent (τίς=our indefinite article). Jesus is picturing himself, royal and most highly well-born, David's son (18:38, 39) legally through Joseph (Matt. 1:16), actually through

Mary (see 3:23), to say nothing of the deity of his person. His character as it is displayed in the parable is likewise nobility itself.

The parable at once corrects the false ideas of the disciples. This nobleman leaves for a distant country and there, not here among his slaves, not here among his hostile citizens, he takes for himself a kingdom. This far country is heaven. After humbling himself on the cross Jesus ascended to heaven. And the kingdom with which he was invested was the rule and government of the world. That the kingdom of glory is not referred to appears from the fact that the citizens refuse to be ruled by this nobleman; and the fact that the church is excluded is shown by the placing of these rebels beside the slaves. Hence we have no article but only "a kingdom."

It is enough for the purpose of the parable to say that this nobleman "takes for himself" a kingdom and to leave out the Father who gives to him all power in heaven and in earth, Matt. 28:18. He, indeed, takes it in his own divine right. "To take" means at once on Christ's ascent into heaven and not at the end of the world. This nobleman remains away. How long is not stated except that it was long enough for his slaves to do much business; but he has gone eventually "to return." This is Christ's return to judgment at the last day, Matt. 25:31; 24:27. This is what Jesus bids his disciples to expect: he will leave them and will return after a long delay. No glory kingdom at once.

13) This royal prince has slaves who are significantly called "his own," i. e., of his own household. Their number, "ten," is symbolical just as we read about *ten* virgins in another parable, and just as God's commandments are *ten* in number, compare Dan. 7:24; Gen. 31:7. Baehr writes that, since ten closes the fundamental numbers and contains them all, it indicates completeness and also implies oneness. "Ten slaves"=all of them, none being omitted, and all as

one body. This symbolical number conveys nothing concerning the actual number of those who are Christ's own, not even that they are few. Nor is the conclusion sound that, since "ten" appears again at the end, Christ meant that he would return during the lifetime of the apostles. That would mean that "ten" is symbolical only in the case of the apostles, and that the parable has nothing to say about later generations of disciples; also that Christ was sadly mistaken about the time of his return—a false prophet. Yet notable men have held this view.

On leaving the prince gave the ten slaves "ten minas," meaning to each of the ten one mina which amounted to $560 in Hebrew gold, or $32 in Hebrew silver, or $17 in Greek silver. It is best to assume that Hebrew money is referred to. This sum is remarkable even if it is reckoned in gold as being more befitting a royal prince when it is compared with the talents mentioned in the other parable. A Hebrew talent is reckoned as being between $1,550 and $2,000, and one slave received five of these, another two, and the lowest, one. The talents picture our varying gifts, which men love to regard as being exceedingly valuable; but the mina signifies the Word of God as the means of grace, and too many value this treasure as being comparatively small. "Ten minas" is again completeness and unity. The prince left all his wealth in the hands of his slaves as one sum. Christ left all his spiritual wealth in the hands of his disciples.

Some misunderstand the mina and offer various opinions. Two points in the parable determine the interpretation: the mina is a capital for trading or doing business, and it is an equal sum for each slave. This fits only the Word which as a means of grace is to be used for the Lord by every disciple, and which every disciple has entrusted to him like every other disciple. In the entire work of the church it is the Word with its power that brings the increase. When Hutten and the knights offered Luther their swords, he waved them aside and said that *he* would protect *them* with the Word.

The command of the prince to his slaves is: "Do business while I am coming!" They are to trade with this capital and to increase it as much as possible. This word does not mean "to speculate," which would attribute to the prince the very thing that is charged against him by the wicked slave: taking what did not belong to him. The readings vary between the aorist imperative and the aorist infinitive, the former being the direct, the latter the indirect discourse. In either case the aorist denotes a complete job of trading.

We know of only the Word as a means of grace which is propagated by faithful preaching and teaching. The Word is not intended for mere private possession and individual enjoyment; it is a capital that is designed for doing spiritual business in the world. Warneck describes it as being both wholesale and retail business which is conducted by church organizations and by individuals.

The readings again vary: ἐν ᾧ (or ἕως) ἔρχομαι; but the former does not mean "till I come," nor does the latter, for both mean "while I am coming" and speak of the whole period of the prince's absence as being one in which he is coming since he is to be expected at any time. The era between Christ's ascension and his Parousia is the great mission era. When the gospel shall be preached in all the world as a witness for all nations, then shall the end come, Matt. 24:24. So the slaves took the entrusted capital in order to go about executing that trust.

14) The parable broadens and takes in "his citizens" (note that we now do not have the reflexive "his own" as in the case of the slaves). Those who take this to mean "his fellow citizens" forget that this man was "well-born" and entitled to take a kingdom. "His citizens" were the Jews as distinct from the disciples and

in a wider sense, as time moved on, the world generally as distinct from the church. These citizens "continued to hate him," the imperfect to indicate the continuance. No cause is assigned, for none existed: "They hated me without a cause," John 15:25. Though he was born as a man of their own nation and its royal line, the Jews hated Jesus; though he was divine in his nature and the noblest their nation could possibly possess, they hated him. And this is true regarding the divine Son of man in the whole world. All those who ought to bow before him and acclaim him as their heaven-sent king hated him, still hate him.

They did this to the extent that they sent an embassage after him which declared, "We are not willing that this one become king over us!" Note the wicked will, where the seat of this hatred is; also the derogatory demonstrative "this one" which does not deign to pronounce his name even as throughout the Acts the Jews used this word and avoided the use of "Jesus." His very name is still distasteful. Trench has interpreted the "embassage" they sent after him well: every martyr they slew beginning with Stephen, this line of martyrs running through the centuries, the last not as yet having been sent on this embassage. We may add every act of hostility to Christ and his Word and his church, for all these acts send the same notification "after him." Note the force of the punctiliar aorist: "to become king," to be set over us as king.

15) After describing what this prince left behind when he went for his indefinite stay in the far country, we are told of his return. **And it came to pass when he, after taking the kingdom, came back again, he said that those slaves to whom he had given the silver be called in order that he might know what they did gain by doing business.**

On καὶ ἐγένετο καί see 5:12; and on ἐν τῷ with the aorist infinitive 2:27 and 3:21. "And it came to pass" always introduces matters of importance. We are most carefully reminded that this nobleman is "he that took the kingdom" even as he went away for this very purpose (v. 12). The fact that he took it was a matter of course; the matter is mentioned to show that he returned as the reigning king. All power belonged to the human nature of Christ from its conception onward, but not until this nature was exalted to the right hand of God did it use this power in unrestricted majesty. The prince did not return at once after assuming his kingdom in the far country; the participle says only that he returned as a king. In the verb "he came back again" ἐπί describes this as coming back again "upon" his slaves and his citizens. So Jesus will come back, suddenly upon his church and upon the wicked world.

Then the accounting on the part of the slaves began. A hint is conveyed regarding the majesty of this noble prince who is now a king when he says that those slaves "be called" to whom he gave the silver. Who was to do the calling? We ask the same question in v. 24: "Who is to take away the mina?" and in v. 27: "Who is to bring and to slay the rebel citizens?" Ps. 103:20 answers: "His angels, that excel in strength, that do his commandments, hearkening to do the voice of his word." Jesus ascended alone, but he returns in the midst of the angel host of heaven. This is the prince who now comes as the king.

The purpose of summoning his slaves is a blessed one, "that he might know what they gained by doing business," the compound verb *erhandeln*, "trade in," over against the simple verb used in v. 13, "to trade," *handeln*. The subjunctive γνοῖ which is found in some texts is only a later form of γνῷ. The purpose of this summons is to reward all these slaves. The idea is that all these slaves will have faithfully done business, will rejoice to come and to make report as to how they have increased what "he had given" them (the past perfect without an augment). The fact that any slave should have been "slothful in business" (Rom. 12:11)—such an unnatural and outrageous thing is in no way contemplated by this friendly summons.

16) Now the first came along, saying, Lord, thy mina did make ten minas more. And he said to him: Well, good slave! Because thou didst prove faithful in a very little, be thou as having authority over ten cities! And the second came, saying, Thy mina, Lord, made five minas. And he said also to this one, Be thou, too, over five cities!

These two are representative of all the Lord's faithful disciples. "Thy mina" gets all the credit; the slave takes none for himself. This is characteristic of all Christ's believers. Paul writes: "Not I, but the grace of God." The psalmist: "Not unto us, O Lord, not unto us, but unto thy name give glory for thy mercy and for thy truth's sake" (115:1). Luther testifies: "I have done nothing, but the Word has done it all." These words are both sincere and correspond with the fact of the case—all the power is in the Word, not in those who preach, teach, and apply it. Would that all realized that fact and trusted the Word fully! We are only channels for the Word, and the only question regarding us is whether any obstructions in us as channels prevent the full flow of the Word. The very greatness of true success in trading with the Word humbles the heart and makes it exclaim: "Behold, what the Lord hath wrought!"

The preposition in the verb means "more" or "in addition to" the one mina. According to the symbolism of ten the gain of "ten minas" denotes the completest gain possible. The fact that Jesus enables a slave to make such a gain is astonishing indeed, full of the greatest encouragement for us all. What joy and glory for us sinners that such astounding gain is possible in our poor hands!

17) This nobleman now manifests all his nobility; this king acts in truly kingly fashion. We have first the exclamatory verdict: "Well!" Just the one word

and no more, but Oh the blessedness of that one word! And then the reward of pure grace; this elevating this slave over ten cities. The superlative "in a very little" is not absolute as though the Word were but a very little thing but compared with the ten cities that are now entrusted to this slave. The number is again "ten," which symbolizes the highest possible reward for this slave. The reward corresponds with the gain, but only because of the noble generosity of this prince who is now king. For this is a "slave" who belongs to his royal master with all his time, labor, and gain. He has no claim on his master, and that master owes him nothing. When that master rewards him, this reward is absolutely gratuitous. Unless that is held fast, the point of the parable is missed. Christ's disciples are to know that not at this time and in Jerusalem but when their Lord returns at the end of the world he, the King of kings, will elevate all his disciples to kingship to reign with him, II Tim. 2:12. This is what that crown means, of which the Scriptures speak so often as in II Tim. 4:8 and in Rev. 2:10; 3:11.

What are these "ten cities," and what does it mean to be over them? All we are able to say is that this pictures the highest degree of glory for the faithful in heaven. Beyond that we must wait until that great day comes. Even Jesus could speak of these supernal realities only in figures, for no human language is able to express the realities.

18) The second slave declares that the king's mina produced five and again places all the credit where it truly belongs. The difference in the verbs, his not saying "made five *more*," is without import, for these five were as much "more" as were the other's ten. The only point is the gain of five compared with the other's ten. Moreover, this man who brought less than ten represents all those who come with less than the full number. Five is the half of ten, and so other gains are fractions of the perfect number.

This is often taken to mean that the slave who can show less than a full gain is therefore less faithful in proportion. But we have come to doubt this. When Paul and Luther are pointed to as having gained tenfold with the Word, it should be noted that not all men were situated as these two were. Many a disciple is placed in lowly circumstances and could not possibly equal these two mighty servants of the Lord in the gain they made with the Word. Are the former, therefore, necessarily less faithful? The parable of the Talents and passages like 12:48 apply here. Many who have been intensely faithful will be able to bring only five minas, many even only one.

19) The wording of this slave's reward is briefer than that of the other. To argue that he did not do "well," or that he was not faithful in what had been entrusted to him, is contradicted by the great reward given him. The point does not lie in these features at all, for which reason the wording is briefer. The point lies in the proportional reward, and this proportion is equal. This is the slave who gives us most comfort since he pictures how all of us who are able to bring only a smaller return from our use of the Word will receive our great reward of grace—in the same heavenly proportion.

20) **And the other came, saying, Lord, lo, thy mina, which I had lying away in a sweatcloth! For I feared thee because thou art a man austere. Thou takest away what thou didst not put down, and thou reapest what thou didst not sow.**

Alas, that there should be this other! This is a parable, and in parables men are allowed to speak their inmost thoughts even as God sees and knows them. He, too, says "Lord" and "thy mina," but in what a different tone! What had he done with this capital that had been entrusted to him for trading? He had done nothing. "There is your money," he says to his lord. He never had and now has no use for it. He despised this lord and was sorry for himself because he was the slave of such a lord. The parable has him say that all this while he had had this mina lying wrapped in a sweatcloth (handkerchief) in some hidden place. Since this mina is the Word which is to be preached, taught, and applied, this is the worst that can be done with it by any professed disciple of Christ. If the slave were to make away with the mina, that would make him—in the figure of the parable—a rebel citizen. If a professed disciple rejects the Word openly, that would place him among scoffers and skeptics. Jesus is not picturing these by means of this slave but the sham disciples who take the Word but do nothing with it for themselves or for others. That sweatcloth is significant. It should be wet with the sweat of faithful work with the mina; without sweat it enfolds the mina itself, dead capital that might as well not exist.

21) This slave exposes his real attitude toward his royal lord. He professes that he lived in constant fear of him (the imperfect tense) as being an austere or severe man. If, instead of the manufactured, hypocritical fear, he had only had some genuine fear of his mighty lord! He did not fear to disobey him, to be faithless to the trust entrusted to him.

We are shown how this fellow regarded the prince's order to his slaves to do business for him: as a lowdown, grasping scheme to get what did not rightfully belong to him, taking up what he did not lay down, sowing what he did not reap, making his slaves slave for him in order to enrich himself with their profits. Not for one moment did he feel the honor that he, a slave and nothing but a slave, should be entrusted with his great lord's wealth, to handle it as if he were the lord himself. Not for one moment did he feel the nobleness of his lord in making him a trustee of his wealth and the still greater nobleness of his lord's intention by this means to raise these slaves to royal participation in his own reign.

This slave's falseness and selfishness are a true picture of all those in Christ's household who think that the Lord requires too much, that *he* will gain if *they* work for him, that they will lose if they sacrifice their ease and their pleasure. What does all such work bring them? And they are right in a way, it brings them nothing—there is nothing of worldly gain in spending and being spent for the Lord. Paul remained poor, lay long in prison, suffered a thousand hardships, died as a martyr, all in working for the Lord with the Word. Yes, it was a hard Lord who took all this from Paul!

22) He says to him: Out of thine own mouth do I judge thee, wicked slave! Wast thou aware that I on my part am a man austere, taking away what I did not put down, and reaping what I did not sow — and for what reason didst thou not deposit my silver at a bank, and I myself, on coming, would have exacted it with interest?

This prince is noble and kingly even in pronouncing judgment; he brings no other law to bear upon this slave than the one the latter has invoked: "Out of thine own mouth," etc. The editors accent either κρίνω, present, "do I judge," or κρινῶ, future, "will I judge." The sense is practically the same, for the verdict follows directly. In fact, it lies already in the address, "wicked slave," this adjective always meaning actively, viciously wicked, and thus being distinguished from κακός, which means merely "good-for-nothing."

From the slave's own characterization of his royal lord as being "a man austere," etc., it by no means follows that the slave was justified in laying away the capital that had been entrusted to him. No austere, greedy man could possibly be satisfied with such treatment of money that he wanted to have invested as capital. That is the trouble with these selfish people in the church—the very logic on which they act is a rank **fallacy,** by which they damn themselves with their own mouth. All from ᾔδεις to the end of v. 23 is one question, was uttered in one breath.

23) The deduction which the slave should have made is stated with a consecutive καί, in interrogative form; and διατί (as distinct from ἱνατί) asks for the reason this correct deduction was not acted on. If this slave knew his master as a severe man as he claimed, and if he did not himself want to do business with the money that had been entrusted to him as capital, the one logical thing for him to do was at least to regard this money as capital and to deposit it in a bank where it might draw some interest for this severe master. The expression means literally, "why didst thou not give upon a table?" The Greek "table" is our "bank" (derived from "bench") and refers to a banker's table where the loan "was given" to the banker.

Another consecutive καί states what would have followed: "and I myself (without asking anything further from thee), on coming, would have exacted it (legally demanded it—this technical sense of the verb is found in 3:13) with interest" ("usury" A. V., the old English word for "interest"). The condition (apodosis) is one of past unreality, the protasis being implied in the preceding. So the money would at least have remained capital by drawing interest. But not even this would the wicked slave do—so little he feared the man whom he said he feared so greatly.

The mina=the Word that is entrusted to us as capital with which to do spiritual business for the Lord. The least we can do with that Word is to secure the aid of other capable and expert disciples in getting some spiritual return from it, delegating and helping to assist them so that they may preach, teach, and apply it for us. That would show some concern for the Lord and his Word. But he who will not even pray in faith and support the Word that others preach with his money, he is, indeed, a wicked slave. To the condemnation that was thus pronounced the slave could give no answer, against it he had no defense.

24) And to those standing by he said, Take from him the mina and give to him who has the ten minas! And they said to him, Lord, he has ten minas. I say to you, that to everyone who has it shall be given; but from him who has not even what he has shall be taken away from him.

"Those standing by" are the same persons that were ordered to call the slaves in v. 15, the angels, who always serve as the servants to execute the Lord's will at the judgment. The fact that this wicked slave has the mina taken from him is only just—he never really possessed it. Rightly considered, this is enough. To be deprived of the Word, the fountain of life and salvation, is to sink into darkness and death forever. The talents that were distributed in the other parable are not the Word but the varying personal gifts of the disciples, hence Matt. 25:30 was needed in that parable.

25) It still surprises us to read that this mina is bestowed on the slave who already has a gain of ten minas. We should have given it to the one of the ten slaves who had achieved the least gain. But this is due to the fact that our minds have not yet been fully brought into harmony with Christ's.

26) The law in the kingdom of Christ is that everyone who has (by using the Word of God aright and by its getting gain for the Lord), to him shall be given (more and more gain by the Lord himself); but he who has not (by refusing to use the Word), by that very non-having he shall lose even what he has (the very Word itself which was originally given to him as it was to the others). "It shall be taken away" out of these wicked hands by God himself. Justice and mercy are thus combined, and if the king in the parable had followed a different course he would have exhibited neither grace nor justice, nor could he be the king.

Note that the mina is added to the ten that were gained, not to the one through which the gain was made. It is another gain and is rightly so classed, one that was bestowed purely as a gift as the rule of the ten cities was bestowed by grace and gift. This law works even in this imperfect world—what one lets slip falls to another who is more fit to have it. "I tell you" is the voice of authority, an authority that is gracious and just at the same time. This is said to us all through the parable ere it is too late. At the end of life it will, indeed, be too late to profit by this law. Now is the time to have that it may be given to us. Compare 8:18; Matt. 25:18.

27) **But these my enemies who did not want me to become king over them bring here and slaughter them before me.**

Πλήν is always adversative, R. 1187. The aorist infinitive is ingressive: "come to be king," "come to reign as king." The ἐχθροί are personal enemies. As rebels they had every inducement to drop their rebellion against this their lawful king. The command is again issued to the king's host (the angels) which accompanies him on his return.

Yes, this is Oriental imagery, exterminating the king's enemies in his very presence. But this drastic imagery fits the terrible reality. Let no one say that Jesus could not have uttered these words, or that they were only a part of the outer scheme of the parable, and that they are not to be interpreted as pointing to a reality. The destruction of Jerusalem with its streams of Jewish blood is the preliminary reality that is back of these words. It foreshadows the final reality, the last day, when judgment without mercy shall forever end all rebellion against Christ, the King.

28) **And having said these things,** to correct the false ideas of his own disciples, **he went on before them, going to Jerusalem.** The thought is that Jesus

answered his disciples and let it rest at that. In the morning, when they all left the house of Zacchaeus, he walked ahead of the little band and headed for Jerusalem.

29) Luke follows this statement with a brief account of Jesus' entry into the city. The fuller story is that on Friday Jesus went from Jericho to Bethany, rested there over the Sabbath, was given a banquet by his Bethany friends on Saturday evening when the Sabbath had ended at sunset, and made his entry into Jerusalem on Sunday.

And it came to pass (see 1:8) **when he drew near to Bethphage and Bethany at the mount called Olive-place, he sent two of his disciples, saying: Go into the village before you, in which, on going in, you shall find a colt that has been tied, on which no one of men ever sat. Having loosed him, bring him. And if anyone inquires of you, For what reason are you loosing him? thus you shall say, The Lord has need of him.**

We are transferred from Jericho (v. 1) to the Mount of Olives to witness the entry into Jerusalem. From John we learn that it was a Sunday. He makes clear that there were two multitudes of festival pilgrims, one which accompanied Jesus as he headed for the city, and another that, on getting the news of his coming, streamed out of the city to meet and to greet him and lead him into the city. John tells us also that the raising of Lazarus caused the great enthusiasm of the pilgrim crowds.

Judging from the way in which Mark and Luke combine Bethphage and Bethany, the two villages were situated close together, the former lying toward Jerusalem, off to the side of the main road. All trace of Bethphage has disappeared, but Bethany is still known. It lies this side of the ridge as one comes up from Jericho. Because Luke has said nothing about the visit in Bethany from Friday until Sunday he combines the two villages and says that Jesus was near them. He had started out from Bethany, and Bethphage lay a little to the side, and facing him (πρός) was the ridge (τὸ ὄρος) beyond which lay Jerusalem. This entire height was called 'Ελαιῶν (R. 154 on the accent), nominative: "Olive-place," "Olive-grove," or "Olivet," B.-P. 385. Jesus halted here. This time Jesus did not intend to walk but to ride into Jerusalem. No one knows which two of the disciples he commissioned to bring the colt to him.

30) They receive explicit orders. The little cluster of houses is right before them. All they need to do is to go right in and they will without effort find the colt that Jesus wants, the perfect participle stating that it is still tied as if awaiting them to get it. They are to untie it and to bring it to Jesus. Luke speaks only of this colt, a male according to the pronouns, and does not mention the dam since Jesus intended to ride only the colt. The dam was also brought but merely in order to accompany the colt since neither would be content to be alone.

The animal was nothing but the common ass of the Orient, regarding which it has been well said: The ass, the camel, and the woman are the burden bearers. All efforts which regard the ass on which Jesus rode as being a very superior beast (Smith, *Bible Dictionary*, and others), one that has nothing to do with the meekness of Jesus, are ill-advised. Since the days of Solomon no king bestrode an ass. Whatever asses of superior type and breeding existed in the Orient, the tiny village of Bethphage would be the last place to look for such stock. Nor is the ass more peaceful than the horse, it is only far inferior to it. The idea of peace is, however, in place, because asses were employed in the humble tasks that go with times of peace, horses when wartimes arrived. So meekness and peace combine in Jesus' selection of an ass for his entry into **Jerusalem**. To call the colt "untamed" and thus to see in its use by Jesus a symbol of his power over nature, is a fancy. The colt was naturally gentle enough. When Jesus states that no one had ever ridden it he indicates that it was fitting for him on this great occasion to ride, not an old animal on which others had ridden, but one that was entirely new.

31) The disciples are told just what to reply in case anyone says anything to them in regard to their taking the animals. One statement will be enough: "The Lord has need of him." We draw the obvious conclusion that the owners were very good friends of Jesus and his disciples and only too glad to render him this service.

32) **Now, on having gone, those that were commissioned found even as he said to them. And as they were loosing the colt, his owners said to them, Why are you loosing the colt? And they said, The Lord has need of him.**

Luke goes to some pains to tell us that things happened just as Jesus had told the two disciples they would occur. This is another plain instance in which Jesus used his supernatural knowledge for the purpose of his work and to the extent that was required by that work. It is plainly supernatural and as plainly limited by one purpose and aim.

33, 34) It, too, happened that the disciples were asked why they were untying the colt; and when they answered as Jesus had directed them they were allowed to take the colt. It was all so simple and easy, but behind it all we see Jesus as the divine Lord.

35) **And they brought him to Jesus. And having cast their robes on the colt, they mounted Jesus. Now, as he was proceeding, they kept spreading under him their robes on the road. And as he was drawing near to the descent of the Mount of Olives, the whole host of the disciples rejoicing began to praise God with a great voice concerning all the**

power works which they saw, saying: Blessed the King coming in the name of the Lord! Peace in heaven and glory in the highest places!

As soon as the colt is brought, all the acts that follow become spontaneous. Not on its bare back will the disciples let Jesus ride, they saddle and caparison the colt with their long, loose outer robes and walk in only their tunics. Two or three are thrown over the colt's back, and they then mount Jesus (the verb is causative: "cause him to gó up on").

36) This act suggests the next. Presently, as Jesus rides along, others also strip off their robes and spread them under (the preposition in the verb) on the road, making a carpet of their own clothes for Jesus to ride over. This was a spontaneous act of submission which was combined with the highest honor. The imperfect tense states that this was kept up. The robes were picked up in the rear and laid down again in front. The subject of the verbs used in v. 35, 36 is left indefinite, but v. 37 shows us a whole host of disciples, a large number of them helping to provide this carpet for Jesus; and he accepted this sign of devotion. Luke is brief and omits mention of the waving of the branches that were cut from the palm trees.

37) So Jesus came to the top of the ridge where it dips down to the valley of the Kidron, a little creek which is dry in summer, just beyond which there rose the walls and the towers of the Holy City. As they reached the top of the ridge, a magnificent view of Jerusalem across the valley burst upon their sight. There stood the Temple, its golden roof flashing in the sun. Back of it rose Zion hill, and the whole city in all its magnificence was spread before their eyes. So the writer saw the present city with the Mohammedan Dome of the Rock in the old Temple's place. The late afternoon sun shone on the old-gold dome, and imagination brought back the scene of Palm Sunday.

It was here that the holy enthusiasm of the whole crowd of the disciples (regarding as such all who jubilantly greeted him this day) began to reach its height. The memory of all the power works they had seen Jesus do in the past (the Greek is content with the simple aorist εἶδον whereas we should say "had seen"), δυνάμεις, to indicate deeds that show divine power, made them praise God, one shouting to the other that Jesus had done this, another that he had done that. This crowd came from all parts of the country, a large number also from Galilee; they were pilgrims on their way to the great Passover festival. They had seen many miracles; add also the one mentioned in 18:35, etc., and especially, as John 12:17, 18 states, the one that had been wrought upon Lazarus. Luke has the neat idiom which draws the antecedent into the relative clause and makes it and its relative keep their case after περί.

38) All the evangelists give us quotations from this shouting, each selects such words as he deemed it best to preserve. All four, however, report the shouting: "Blessed the King coming in the name of the Lord!" and vary only as to the word "King." All four show that Jesus was being brought into Jerusalem as the great and long-expected Messiah-King. Jesus accepted this acclaim, he was this King and now came as such, and all the world should know this. But the whole manner of his coming shut out all political and nationalistic ideas as he had ever shut them out—riding on an ass, acclaimed because of his miracles, and no wrong note to feed false hopes.

The perfect participle εὐλογημένος, "has been and is now blessed," makes God the one who rests his blessing upon Jesus. We should note that ἐρχόμενος is specifically Messianic, for the title of the promised Messiah was "the One coming"; this participle means that Jesus is this person. And he is "King" in this Messianic sense even as some added "son of David"

(Matthew) and "the kingdom of our father David" (Mark); note 1:32; 18:38, 39. The blessing of "the Lord" (meaning *Yahweh*, for which Κύριος is the translation, 1:9 and repeatedly in the first chapters) is not a mere verbal benediction but the bestowal of all the gifts and treasures of Jehovah that are implied in his benedictory words; and the acclaim means that Jesus is bringing this blessing with him to dispense its riches here in the nation's sacred capital. "In *Yahweh's* name," which is quite generally understood to mean "by the Lord's authority," means, "in connection with the Lord's own great revelation," i. e., his promises; see 9:48.

Luke alone reports the shout: "Peace in heaven and glory in the highest places!" which recalls the angles' song recorded in 2:14, the sense being practically the same. On "peace," which is here the condition of peace, see 7:50. "Peace in heaven" means that God is at peace, at peace with men as is evidenced by this Messiah-King who is blessed and sent by him and is now entering Jerusalem. The neuter plural ἐν ὑψίστοις refers to places and is a phrase that denotes heaven. Regarding this peace glory shouts and songs are to resound throughout the exalted places of God's abode, the angels glorify him for making peace through the Messiah.

How much of all that they were saying did this "host" (πλῆθος, the same word is used with reference to the angels in 2:13) of the disciples or friends of Jesus really understand? John 12:16 tells us that the Twelve did not at this time realize that they were fulfilling Zech. 9:9. Further than that we say only this, that whatever wrong, earthly expectations still clouded the minds of all the disciples, this much is certain, a holy enthusiasm swept their hearts on this Sunday, a wave of true spiritual feeling and joy, which was the direct product of the power works of Jesus and caused them to use this holy language in praise of God.

Jesus, too, therefore, accepted this welcome by his every act and lent himself to this enthusiasm by riding into the city as the King of Israel that he was.

39) And some of the Pharisees from the crowd said to him, Teacher, rebuke thy disciples! And answering he said, I say to you, that if these shall be silent, the stones will yell.

These Pharisees had come along with the multitude that went out from Jerusalem to meet Jesus (John 12:18). They had never before witnessed such a demonstration. It seemed to them that all the world was running after him (John 12:19). They saw no way to stop what was blasphemous praise of Jesus to their ears except by an appeal to Jesus himself that he rebuke this enthusiasm. So they worked their way up to him, perhaps halted him, and made their demand. "Teacher" is only the ordinary "rabbi" which Luke never employs as a title of Jesus.

40) They certainly got their answer. With the authoritative "I say to you" Jesus tells them that if these friends of his should be silent, the stones will yell. This is usually understood as being proverbial language which says that Jesus must be welcomed this day. The reference to Hab. 2:11 corroborates neither idea. Jesus speaks prophetically of a time when "these" shall, indeed, cease their acclaim, and when the lifeless stones shall, indeed, "yell" with piercing shrieks when not one stone is left upon another in Jerusalem itself. That yelling will be the voice of judgment for rejecting the Messiah-King. By wanting the disciples to be silent these Pharisees were asking that this yelling of the stones begin now. This is a clear instance of the future indicative after ἐάν, R. 1010, which makes this a condition of reality, R., W. P.

41) And when he got near, on seeing the city, he sobbed over it, saying: If thou hadst realized in

this day, even thou, the things for peace—! But now they were hid from thy eyes!

In v. 37 Jesus was approaching the top of the ridge when the acclaim began; he now reached the ridge and had the panorama of the city before him. In v. 37 we thus have the present participle: "he drawing near," and now the aorist tense of the verb: "he got near." At sight of the city, as he was riding amid the shouting, jubilant crowds, Jesus "burst into sobs" (ingressive aorist). His own words show why he let his feelings break forth.

42) He saw the true condition of the city, which was the very opposite of the joy of this pilgrim host that had gathered from afar for the Passover. He saw also the judgment that was descending upon the wicked city just as clearly as he saw and foretold in detail what was awaiting him in the city on the following Friday (18:32, 33). Cause, indeed, for tears and sobs from a heart like his (v. 10). The first sentence is left unfinished, only the protasis of past unreality is stated without the apodosis. It is thus a case of aposeopesis that is highly effective for expressing Jesus' deep feeling (R. 1203). "If thou hadst realized" is quite sufficient and implies that Jerusalem had not realized even "in this day," i. e., the time of Jesus and not merely this Sunday. Jerusalem had all along not realized. R. 834 prefers the aorist ingressive: "if thou hadst come to realize."

"Even thou" brings out the full pathos of this cry that comes from Jesus' heart. What Jerusalem never realized were "the things for or toward peace" that Jesus had all along made such efforts to bring to her, those of the heavenly gospel of peace and salvation through faith in him as her Messianic King. If Jerusalem had realized these things, her Sanhedrin and all her inhabitants would be welcoming Jesus as were these pilgrims from afar, who had come only for the days of the festival and were not inhabitants of the city. But this apodosis is omitted. We see no warrant for regarding this unfinished sentence as an unfulfilled wish.

"But now they were hid from thy eyes!" Here, too, the aorist expresses merely the past fact, and all that we can say is that we should in English say "have been hid"; "are hid" found in the A. V. is not correct, nor is the aorist effective in the sense that the end of the action is stressed (R. 835), an act of hiding that at last hid completely. "Were hid" does not refer to the *goettliches Verhaengnis* but to the wicked perversity of Jerusalem herself. The subsequent, judicial will of God, that those who obdurately will not see shall not see, is not expressed in these words of Jesus but in the next two verses. Compare 13:34, 35, where the second of these verses states God's judicial will.

43) **For days will come upon thee, and thine enemies will throw a rampart around thee and will encircle thee and will hem thee in on every side and will dash to the ground thee and thy children in thee and will not leave stone upon stone in thee in return for that thou didst not realize the season of thy visitation.**

Ὅτι introduces the future destruction as evidence of the fact that Jerusalem did not know and that the things for peace were hid from her. Καί piles one thing of the same kind upon another, and here the mass rises higher and higher. In order to increase these "and" in their cumulative effect we have the first one where "when" would otherwise be used: "the days and" (when). Because these terse sentences describe so vividly just what happened in connection with the siege of Jerusalem, those who deny predictive prophecy even to Jesus ascribe these verses to Luke and declare that he wrote them *ex eventu,* after the fall of the city, and put into Jesus' mouth what he never said and what it is claimed he could not have said. One must then suppose that Isaiah did the same thing when he foretold the same details regarding the fall of Jerusalem (under the name "Ariel") in 29:1-4. Luke wrote 18:32, 33, and all the prophets and the evangelists the prophetic parts of their books in this way. The χάραξ is a palisaded wall or rampart. The Greek says: "hem thee in from every side," the action being viewed as coming from the enemy.

44) The city and her children or inhabitants were to be dashed to the ground, the latter to be slain; and this destruction was to be so radical as not to leave one stone on another—an absolute and utter ruin. 'Ανθ' ὧν="in return for that which" and is usually translated less precisely "because." Jesus reverts to the guilt of Jerusalem in that she did not realize "the season of her visitation," ἐπισκοπή, which is used regarding both a gracious and a punitive visit. The verb is used in 1:68, 78; 7:16, "to look in upon someone." God's looking in upon us with his grace continues until a certain time; then those that refuse that grace shall receive a far different visitation from him whom they have spurned.

45) And having gone into the Temple, he began to throw out those selling, saying, It has been written, And my House shall be a House of Prayer; but you, you made it a robbers' den.

This occurred on Monday, and Luke records it chiefly for the sake of the words which Jesus uttered. The ἱερόν is the entire Temple complex, its courts as well as its buildings. Jesus threw out both buyers and sellers, Luke mentions only the latter and omits the details that are found in Matt. 21:12, 13; Mark 11:15-18.

46) Jesus brands this desecration of God's Temple with one mighty statement of Scripture. "It has been written" implies: "and stands so to this day." Jesus quotes Isa. 56:7, but interpretatively by using "my

House shall be" for "shall be called." House "of Prayer" uses this word in the wider sense, "of Worship." But what did the authorities do with this holy House? Jesus tells them by using Jer. 7:10: "You, you made it a robbers' den." This does not mean that they robbed God's House, for robbers do not rob their own den, they make it their refuge. So even when they desecrated the Temple these Jews imagined that their running to the Temple would shield them from penalty. The Temple will not protect the wicked who seek to make it their refuge. The church is no refuge for sinners who come there to be safe with their sin. Jer. 7:12-15 declare what God would do with this Temple —he would destroy it even as he destroyed Shiloh for the same cause.

47) **And he was teaching day by day in the Temple. But the high priests and the scribes were seeking to destroy him, also the foremost of the people; but they did not find what they should do, for all the people were hanging to him by hearing.**

From Sunday onward Jesus kept teaching in the Temple until he left it for good toward evening on Tuesday. He spent his nights at Bethany or elsewhere outside of the city in order to prevent an arrest before his time. Luke informs us that only the Sanhedrin (see 9:22) "was seeking to destroy him." The resolution to do that had been passed previous to this occurrence. Their intention was some kind of judicial murder. "The high priests and the scribes" is a standard title for the Sanhedrin although, as is the case in 20:1, "the elders" were at times added as constituting the third group. But Luke adds at the very end "and the foremost of the people." This does not read like a designation for "the elders," especially since Luke adds "the elders" in 20:1. These foremost people were not members of the Sanhedrin but those who were prominent generally, who were in full accord with the great official body.

48) Despite all their seeking and scheming they were not able to find what they might do. Pleonastic τό before the indirect question merely marks this as being the object clause; the subjunctive is deliberative. They asked themselves often: "What shall we do?" The difficulty lay in "the people," which means the great mass of pilgrims from all parts of the country and not the inhabitants of Jerusalem who seconded the hostility of the authorities. Luke does not say that the Sanhedrin feared the people, but he says as much when he writes that the people all "hung to him by hearing" his teaching. The verb is very strong: they could not tear themselves away from him. The spelling of this imperfect form ἐξεκρέματο, which governs the genitive αὐτοῦ, varies; this form is derived from ἐκκρέμαμαι. This love of the pilgrims for Jesus held the Sanhedrists in check.

CHAPTER XX

1) **And it came to pass on one of the days, he teaching the people in the Temple and proclaiming the gospel, there came upon him the high priests and the scribes with the elders and spoke, saying to him, Tell us, by what authority art thou doing these things, or who is he that gave thee this authority?**

Luke is seldom specific as to the time and the place and even here writes only "on one of the days," yet we infer from Matthew that this occurred on Tuesday morning soon after Jesus began teaching and "gospeling." The verb that is used regarding the Sanhedrists means that they suddenly stood over Jesus. The matter had been arranged on the day before, hence this body of Sanhedrists is present, not, indeed, the entire seventy members of the court, but most of them, for the three terms that are used designate the official body. They did not crowd through the closely packed pilgrim hearers or interrupt Jesus in his teaching; from Mark we learn that they waited until Jesus walked to another place and then confronted him.

It was rather late to ask about the authority on which Jesus acted, for this was the third day of his last week. Nor do the Sanhedrists come prepared to arrest Jesus, should his authority be deficient. When Jesus refused even to name his authority, they did not even forbid him to teach further, they withdrew in defeat. This shows how the presence of the pilgrim hosts affected the murderous intention of the Sanhedrin.

2) Also the form of the challenge is mild, it is couched only in a question. Its two parts constitute but one question, for *what* the authority is appears

when *who* its giver is gets to be known. The ἐξουσία is both the right and the power that goes with that right. "These things" must refer to more than the teaching, for any rabbi had the right to teach in the Temple or elsewhere. "These things" include the royal entry of Jesus, the cleansing of the Temple, his whole bearing, and also his miracles. Since it comes from the Sanhedrin, the body that had been entrusted with the care of the whole nation, this demand is in place. Jesus must show his authority, and this must be legitimate and adequate in every respect. And he would certainly be glad to show it, provided he actually had such authority; if he even hesitated, this would raise the suspicion that he had no authority at all, or that he was afraid to show such authority as he had since it was inadequate. It is on these considerations that the Sanhedrin acts and maneuvers under a show of right.

But the Sanhedrists had thought farther. They had always known that Jesus claimed authority from God, his Father. These men expected Jesus to assert once more that such is, indeed, his authority, and they intend then to demand of Jesus the fullest proof for his having God's authority, being prepared on their part to deny the validity of any proof Jesus might venture to offer. They had everything planned as to just what Jesus would have to say and just how they would nullify his claim. But when we compare John 2:18, where three years before this time the same Sanhedrists made the same demand of Jesus, we see that they have not advanced a single step beyond their first challenge. Unbelief is negative and thus unprogressive in its very nature.

3) **And answering, Jesus said to them: I will request you also myself for a statement, and do you tell me, The baptism of John—was it from heaven, or from men?**

The Sanhedrists knew the authority by which Jesus acted; their one purpose was to deny him this authority and to do this so as to impress the people; for to admit this authority was to accept Jesus as the divine Messiah, against which acceptance everything in them rebelled most violently. By his counterquestion Jesus is not at all refusing to declare unto these Sanhedrists what he had already long ago both declared and proved to them. His counterquestion is the opposite of an evasion. Jesus merely returns the question to the questioners and substitutes John for himself and puts in the two alternatives that alone apply and thus makes the question almost self-answering, and so he asks them to state the answer themselves. Note that the Greek abuts ὑμᾶς κἀγώ, which makes the pronouns clash with emphasis.

4) "The baptism of John—was it from heaven, or from men?" The two ἐκ denote origin but plainly involve authority. For if John's baptism was "out of heaven," had its origin in God's will and command, its authority was divine; but if "out of men," out of some man's ideas, then the authority was just nothing. Jesus centers the question on the baptism of John since this was the heart and core of John's work which involved all that he was and did. He is therefore also called "the Baptist." Jesus also states the two alternatives: "from heaven" or "from men"—*tertium non datur*. A third possibility could not be assumed even for the sake of argument. If not divine, then human; if no divine authority, then no authority at all.

The Sanhedrists face two horns of a dilemma, from which no escape is possible, and on one of which they must impale themselves. Jesus centers the question on John because his own authority is identical with John's. Their work was one. The correct answer regarding John was the correct answer regarding Jesus. All that Jesus needed to do was to hand that answer back to the Sanhedrists. A subtile irony is involved: these men ask Jesus what they ought already to know from their acquaintance with John. Hence he uses the dignified verb ἐρωτᾶν—Jesus proceeds "to inquire." Just one little "statement" is all that Jesus asks.

5) **Now they reasoned with themselves, saying: If we say, From heaven! he will say, For what reason did you not believe him? But if we say, From men! all the people will stone us, for they are persuaded that John is a prophet. And they answered that they did not know whence.**

It was the unbelief of the Sanhedrists that caught them in this deadly dilemma, unbelief and the type of immorality that goes with its defense. They were not in the least concerned about the truth regarding John; what persuaded them were the consequences of the two possible answers they could give. They thus found themselves impaled by giving either answer. They *will* not say, "From heaven," for Jesus will then demand the reason (διατί) why they did not believe John, and there is no reason except their ungodly will.

6) They *dare* not say, "From men," when this crowd of pilgrims is packed around them, all of whom are still persuaded (the periphrastic perfect with its strong present force) that John was a prophet, no matter how flagrantly the leaders had been untrue to him and to his baptism. To assert that John's authority was not divine, to deny his being a prophet might precipitate a riot. These fanatical pilgrims might rush in to stone their own authorities with the stones that were close at hand by reason of the new structures which Herod was erecting at this time.

7) So there was only one course left to them: pitiful and disgraceful surrender. They dodge the issue which no decent Jew dared to dodge. They claim that they did not know whence John's baptism was. As Sanhedrists it was their supreme duty to know, and they confess that they were derelict in this very duty. No; they had not expected to have their well-planned move against Jesus end so swiftly and so calamitously for themselves.

8) **And Jesus said to them, Neither do I on my part** (emphatic ἐγώ) **tell you by what authority I am doing these things.**

The reply of Jesus implies that these Sanhedrists have refused to answer his question, deliberately refused as arrant cowards. Since the correct answer to Jesus' question is the correct answer also to the question of the Sanhedrists, by refusing to give the one they refuse to receive the other. So Jesus is compelled to refuse to offer it to them.

9) Jesus continued with the parable of the Two Unequal Sons (Matt. 21:28-32) and, when the Sanhedrists tried to leave, detained them to hear another parable, one that more plainly revealed their murderous temper. **Moreover, he began to speak to the people this parable.** "To the people," to the mass of pilgrims who were packed solidly around the Sanhedrists. Jesus is through with these men; he is holding them so that they may hear what he has to tell all these pilgrims about them, their wicked leaders. We should not lose sight of the tense, dramatic nature of this scene (v. 19).

A man planted a vineyard and leased it to vinegrowers and went abroad for considerable time.

A few, simple strokes of the brush and the entire picture is before us in vivid, plastic form. It matches the striking parable found in Isa. 5:1, etc., but the action is entirely different. Isaiah makes Israel as such guilty, Jesus the rulers of Israel. Luke abbreviates by stating only that the vineyard was planted; Matthew and Mark add the details that this great vineyard was fenced and equipped in every way. "The vineyard of the Lord of hosts is the house of Israel, and the men of Judah his pleasant plant," Isa. 5:7. So the great owner of this wonderful vineyard leased it to vinegrowers, "gave it out," ἐξέδοτο (R. 308). The rental was to be a part of the harvest as the following shows, not cash as some suppose.

He did this because "he went abroad," literally, "went far from home," and did this for quite a stretch of time—a feature that is noted also in other parables, 19:12; Matt. 25:14, 15; Mark 13:34. This going abroad pictures the great trust that is imposed on the leaders of Israel: the precious vineyard of God's people was completely in their care. Yes, God brought Israel from Egypt into Canaan, planted, fenced it, equipped it there, and placed it under these spiritual rulers whose office was continuous. The prophets appear elsewhere in the picture, they were sent at special times for a special purpose.

10) **And in due season he sent to the vinegrowers a slave in order that they should give to him part of the fruit of the vineyard. But the vinegrowers, after hiding him, sent him out empty.**

A vineyard is naturally planted for the sake of the fruit it will yield. But this parable does not center our attention on the productivity or unproductivity of the vineyard or of its vines as does the parable recorded in Isa. 5 but on the vicious actions of these vine-growers, to whom the vineyard had been leased, and who were now to meet the terms of the lease. The point to be noted is not the condition in which the vineyard was under their management. We are to see the outrageous vine-growers when the owner now sends for his share of the harvest (partitive ἀπό).

The slaves who were sent on this mission are the prophets, and Mark and Luke indicate the intervals at which God sent them to the leaders of Israel. When God sent them he expected fruit, contrition, faith, true obedience. It is unwarranted to think only of the law, of law works, of "the need of redemption" that is produced by the law. Vineyard is law and gospel, the full riches of divine grace, and fruits according, the chief being faith.

The first slave who is sent by the owner these wicked vine-growers "hide," literally, "flay" or beat bloody, and then send away empty. This is plainly atrocious; there is not a single mitigating circumstance. We have a plain case of the future indicative after ἵνα, which is a construction found only in the Koine.

11) **He added to send another slave; but him also, after hiding and insulting, they sent out empty. And he added to send a third; but this one, too, after wounding, they threw out.**

The imagery is astounding. No man ever did what the owner of this vineyard did. After his first messenger had received such treatment and came back bloody and empty-handed, any other owner would forthwith have called in the police, ousted those vicious vine-growers, and brought them to justice. The hearers might well exclaim: "Why, we never heard of such an owner who would send slave after slave to have these atrocities repeated, and finally send his own son to be killed!" They had, of course, never heard of anything like this. But that is the very point Jesus wants to make. It takes unheard-of imagery to picture the unheard-of wickedness of these Jewish leaders, who murdered not only the prophets whom God sent them but were now about to murder also God's own Son. It is disappointing to observe that the commentators fail to note these features of the parable and other similar features in other parables. Read Matt. 23:34; Acts 7:52; Heb. 11:37, 38. According to tradition Jeremiah was stoned in exile in Egypt, and Isaiah was sawed asunder by King Manasseh.

Another feature should not be overlooked: as Jesus recites these points in the parable he is looking these very vine-growers squarely in the eye, and they know that Jesus has them in mind. The situation is dramatic in the extreme. The fact that no human lessor of a vineyard ever did a thing such as that which is depicted here brings out the full enormity of the reality of which these Sanhedrists were guilty. The patience of God toward Israel's rulers is without parallel in all human history—an illustration must be invented to picture it, and that illustration must be unreal.

The second slave is treated worse than the first; insults are added to the blows.

12) The third is treated still worse. He is thrown out, covered with bleeding wounds. "He added to send" is a Hebraism (R. 1078) which uses the verb instead of an adverb: "he sent again." Luke mentions only three slaves, Matthew and Mark speak of many and record stoning and actual killing. The way in which Jesus spoke the parable included all these features, the evangelists abbreviated, and each did so in his own way.

13) **And the lord of the vineyard said: What shall I do? I will send my son, the beloved. Perhaps this one they will respect.**

The unheard-of action reaches its climax: the owner actually resolves to send his own son to these vicious vine-growers. With a touch of pathos and with a second article which makes the verbal prominent Jesus adds, "the beloved" and recalls this very word that was used in 3:22 and in 9:35 and thus points to himself as being this "son." The parable becomes prophetic by telling what the Sanhedrin would do with God's beloved Son in three days. Where is the earthly father who would send his beloved son as God did actually send his? But the parable had to say this about the owner's son. The son, too, is sent. God's Son resembles the prophets in this respect, and yet they were only δοῦλοι, "slaves," he is and remains "my Son, the beloved." The prophets were God's "slave-servants" as a result of being sent; Jesus is sent as a result of being the Son. In the one case the mission makes the man, in the other the man makes the mission.

The second future passive of ἐντρέπω, "to turn at" with the idea of turning with respect at the approach of someone, is used without the passive idea (R. 819), it is like the transitive aorist. "Perhaps" in the parable is no mere part of this humanly impossible imagery but is inserted to show how far God was willing to go with the leaders of the Jews, i. e., send his Son on a mere "perhaps." The problem of the foreknowledge of God does not belong here. This imagery goes far deeper as regards God. On the one hand we have the incomprehensible love and patience of God that are exhibited in all these sendings; on the other hand we have the justice of God which lets the Jewish leaders fill the measure of their guilt to the very brim, yea, to overflowing, by the killing of even God's son. To bring in the foreknowledge and to puzzle about that only breaks up the parable by trying to have it say what its imagery does not include.

14) **But, on seeing him, the vine-growers began reasoning with each other, saying: This is the heir. Let us kill him in order that the inheritance may become ours! And having thrown him out outside the vineyard, they killed him.**

The climax has been reached. Jesus tells his murderers exactly what they are on the point of doing. They are keeping it under cover. Jesus tells them openly to their faces before the assembled pilgrim crowds. The lessons in killing that were taught these Jewish leaders by all former persecutors of the prophets they are putting into final practice for the killing of God's own Son.

The parable is exceedingly exact at this point. This reasoning with each other does not picture only the secret thoughts of the Sanhedrists; John 11:47-53 states that this is exactly how they did reason. They killed Jesus because they feared to lose their position and their power over the nation. Their blind unbelief hid the spiritual nature of the kingdom from them; and thus the fact that they could never retain the outward rule when its inwardness was foreign to them remained hidden from them. "Let us kill him" is the hortative subjunctive. The murder of Jesus was deliberately planned as Jesus tells the very men who planned it. After Jesus was out of the way, who was there to dispute the religious rule of the nation with the Sanhedrists? After he was dead, the inheritance was theirs.

15) Jesus does not say merely that the vine-growers killed the heir; no, they first threw him out outside the vineyard. This agrees too closely with the place where Jesus was put to death, John 19:17; Heb. 13:12, 13, "without the gate," "without the camp," to be a meaningless feature of the parable, compare I Kings 2:13; Acts 7:58. Jesus died on Calvary, outside of Jerusalem, "cut off in the intention of those who put him to death from the people of God and from all share in their blessings." Trench.

What, therefore, will the lord of the vineyard do to them? He will come and will destroy these vine-growers and will give the vineyard to others.

It does not need to be said that these vine-growers will not be able to escape justice and retain the vineyard as their own. Justice must strike them at last. There is still the lord of the vineyard to deal with. He will come, but not as the slaves and as the son came. He will not seek fruit, he will come to do something with these vine-growers.

16) Jesus asked this question with the intent that the pilgrims are to answer it, he was letting them complete the parable (Matthew). Mark and Luke simply state the answer as being one that is self-evident. Just judgment shall descend upon these murderers and shall destroy them, and the lord of the vineyard will give his vineyard into other hands. The future tenses are volitive: the lord "will do" all this. **But when they heard it they said, God forbid!** literally, "May it not be!" an optative of wish, one of the few optatives that are still used in the Koine.

Some regard this statement as an exclamation on the part of the Sanhedrists. They, indeed, saw the meaning of the parable, but it only enraged them. The answer of the pilgrims, which completed the parable, came involuntarily from the lips of some one of their number. In the next instant, when it flashed into their minds what this answer really meant, the exclamation rose from others: "God forbid!" But this did not mean that God should not punish these wicked vine-growers, that he should leave the vineyard in their possession in spite of the murder of the heir. The cry meant that these pilgrims hoped to God that it would not come to such a terrible end as the killing of the heir and the judgment on the vine-growers. The fact that all who heard the parable understood its real drift should not be doubted. Matt. 21:45 makes this plain as regards the Sanhedrists. The interpretation is, therefore, unwarranted that even these pilgrims were so steeped in self-righteousness that they thought that the control of the vineyard could never be taken from the Jewish leaders. Likewise the opinion that the pilgrims thought that Jesus had in mind the substitution of complete Roman and pagan control of the Jewish Temple and religion.

17) **But he, having given them a look, said: What, then, is this that has been written:**

**A stone which those building rejected,
This became corner head?**

Everyone fallen on that stone shall be crushed together; but on whom it falls, it shall pulverize him.

The parable is dropped, its possibilities have been exhausted since its imagery could not picture the resurrection of Jesus. The Sanhedrists have heard their verdict in the language of the parable. They are now to hear that this verdict has been recorded in their own Scriptures. Jesus quotes Ps. 118:22, 23, the very psalm from which the Hosanna shouts were taken on Palm Sunday; and after quoting it Jesus restates in his own words what this quotation means for his present hearers.

There is a pause. Jesus looks at all the people who are packed closely before him, all intent on every word that comes from his lips. The pause and the look add to the tension. "What, then, is this that has been written" in your own Scriptures and stands thus written to this day? The psalm, which was known to all, was, most likely, composed in order to express the joy of the people after the return from the Babylonian captivity, at the time of the laying of the cornerstone of their new Temple or at the time of the dedication of the completed structure. It contained the prophetic lines which Jesus quotes. More will happen than the rejection of the Sanhedrists and their replacement through better leaders. An entirely new structure will be raised. The old covenant will yield to a new covenant, of which Jesus, who was rejected by the Jews, will be the mighty cornerstone.

The climax of the parable, the death of the son himself, is repeated in the first line of the psalm: "A stone which those building rejected," the nominative λίθος being attracted into the accusative by its relative, R. 718. The killing=the rejection, the verb signifies to discard after testing. Those who are building are the Jewish leaders, the Sanhedrin, the vine-growers of the parable. But what happened? That very stone "became corner head" (the absence of the articles stresses the quality of each noun). Jesus is the "son" that was killed, the "stone" that was rejected as being unfit to be used anywhere in the building. But his death and rejection did not eliminate him. On the contrary, this made him what the new structure needed: "corner head," cornerstone (εἰς is predicative like the German *zum Eckstein*). The dead Jesus rose from the grave.

The idea in cornerstone is not that of "bearer and support" of the building. This would be the whole foundation. Jesus may, indeed, be called the foundation

($\theta\epsilon\mu\epsilon\lambda\iota os$) as he is in I Cor. 3:11; but in Eph. 2:20 he is distinguished from the foundation, he is the cornerstone. As such he is set at the chief corner and thus governs every angle in the foundation and in the building itself. Jesus does this in the great spiritual temple of God, the new covenant. Luke abbreviates and omits the direct, literal statement that is found in Matt. 21:43.

18) This is contained in the general statement about this stone which the Jews rejected save that the figure of the stone is now used in an entirely new and independent way. Jesus presents two possibilities: one may fall on this stone by opposing Christ; or the stone may fall on such an opponent, Christ may strike him with his judgment. The singulars speak of the individual persons, for the guilt of unbelief and hostility is always personal. In Isa. 8:14 and in Luke 2:34 Christ is presented as a stone of stumbling and a rock of offense. The fall on this stone never hurts the stone in the least but only damages the one who falls (the aorist participle to designate the one act of falling); "he shall be crushed together" keeps the figure. This may not be fatal, recovery may be possible. But when this stone itself falls on the unbeliever "it shall pulverize him" like winnowing the dust out of grain, the verb recalls Ps. 1:4 and Matt. 3:12. The chaff shall fly in all directions like dust. Judgment can be pictured with no greater severity.

19) **And the scribes and the high priests sought to lay hands on him in that very hour; and they feared the people, for they knew that he spoke the parable against them.**

Two terms suffice to designate the Sanhedrin which had been indicated by three in v. 1. The aorist "they sought" and the phrase "in that very hour" convey the thought that the rage of the Sanhedrin was aroused to the pitch of arresting Jesus right then and there (Tuesday morning). They realized that the parable was directed against them but did not realize that by their rage they were justifying that parable in its severest part. Despite all their power and the entire body of Temple police at their command they lacked the courage to satisfy their rage at once.

20) **And having watched their chance, they commissioned spies hypocritically representing themselves to be righteous in order to lay hold of him by a word, so as to deliver him to the jurisdiction and the authority of the governor.**

In v. 1 and in v. 19 the Sanhedrin as such operates, a goodly number of the seventy appear together. They now act separately, first the Pharisees, then the Sadducees (v. 27) make their attempts against Jesus. The fact that the present move was made by the former Luke indicates only by saying that their spies pretended to be "righteous," strict observers of the Pharisaic regulations. We translate the participle: "having watched their chance," not: "having watched him." That chance came soon, when a lull in the teaching occurred.

These spies were disciples of the Pharisees plus a few Herodians (Matthew and Mark), *Spitzel* as Zahn aptly calls them. They were new men whom Jesus had not met before and in regard to whom he might easily be deceived. The idea is not that the disciples of the Pharisees are to pretend that they were having a dispute with these Herodians about paying the tax, and that both parties now come to Jesus to settle the dispute. No; these disciples of the Pharisees are to pretend to conscientious scruples about the tax as though wondering whether they as righteous men ought to pay it; and the Herodians are sent along as witnesses whose word would go much farther with Pilate than would that of any disciples of the Pharisees.

We meet "Herodians" in the Gospels only incidentally. They were a minor political, nonreligious party among the Jews, supporters of the alien Herodian dynasty which ruled under Cæsar and was far preferable to the Jewish nation than Cæsar's direct rule through Roman procurators would have been. The Herodians thus favored the Roman tax because of the dependence of the house of Herod on Rome. In all such matters the Pharisees opposed them and ever demanded complete independence from Rome and autonomy for the Jews. In their estimation any Roman tax was "unlawful" in the sight of God. Yet as the Pharisees joined hands with their opponents, the Sadducees, in their attack on Jesus, so they here ally themselves with their other opponents, the Herodians, in their attempt to destroy Jesus. After three days Herod and Pilate became friends in a similar fashion.

The purpose ($ἵνα$) for which these spies are sent is to lay hold of Jesus, of some statement of his. Verbs of taking hold are followed by the genitive, and we here have two: "of him" and "of a statement" (R. 508), and we should not combine "of his word or statement." The scheme is to get Jesus to say something that can be construed as being treasonable. The intended result ($ὥστε$ with the infinitive) is that, with the Herodians as witnesses, they may hand Jesus over "to the jurisdiction ($ἀρχή$) and the authority of the governor" (Pilate), and may so get rid of Jesus. It is a misconception to think of the death penalty which Pilate alone could decree. The cunning scheme was to make Jesus guilty of an infringement upon Roman law so that Pilate would arrest and try Jesus and relieve the Sanhedrin entirely. Whether the penalty would be death or less mattered little. It was a damnable trap, and the Pharisees confidently expected to catch their victim.

21) **And they inquired of him, saying: Teacher, we know that thou speakest and teachest rightly and dost not accept a face but teachest the way of God in truth. Is it lawful that we pay tribute to Caesar or not?**

The delegation comes with an astounding acknowledgment of the teaching and the character of Jesus, it is almost as if they themselves were about to become Jesus' most ardent disciples. Their great *captatio benevolentiae* is to throw Jesus off his guard. Their masters have coached them well, for they have put into the mouth of these their disciples an acknowledgment of Jesus which every Jew should have made most sincerely. In their lying fashion they ape truth quite perfectly. Jesus did speak and teach "rightly," correctly, in an orthodox way. He did not accept a face (Hebraistic expression), say to a friend what he would not say to an opponent. He was never swayed by fear or by favor. He taught "the way" that had been marked out by God for every Israelite to follow "in truth," literally, "on the basis of truth," without a single deviation.

This elaborate preamble will certainly induce Jesus to live up to the estimate thus made of him: he will consider no man, not even Cæsar in Rome, when he gives his answer. He will speak without the least reserve to men who think of him so highly. And he is thus assured in advance that, whatever men like the Sanhedrists would do, the men who are now speaking to Jesus will prize his answer and will thank him for it with all their hearts. The scheme was certainly beautifully devilish.

Jesus lived up to this estimate of him, His answer was far beyond anything these fools thought possible. The way in which they tried to lure him into their snare was silly. Even a lesser mind than that of Jesus could have detected the false tone in their flattering words.

22) And now the question: "Is it lawful that we pay tribute to Cæsar or not?"—"we" who above all want to walk in "the way of God"? The answer is almost laid on the tongue of Jesus. He whom no man's fear or favor could possibly sway would not even stop

to think but would say outright, "It is certainly not lawful!" Luke uses φόρος, the wider word for "tribute" as it is paid by one nation to another; Matthew and Mark use the more specific κῆνσος or poll tax that is levied upon every individual for his own person and is thus especially galling as a mark of servitude to the Roman power. The poll tax was, of course, tribute in the fullest sense of the word.

23, 24) Now having perceived their craftiness, he said to them: Show me a denarius! Whose image and superscription has it? And they said, Caesar's. And he said to them, Well then, duly give the things of Caesar to Caesar and the things of God to God!

John 2:24, 25 explains this instant perception on the part of Jesus. He always knows whatever he ought to know in his work, and no man ever deceived him for a moment. Luke calls it "craftiness" (literally, the ability to do anything but to be understood here in an evil sense), Matthew labels it wickedness, Mark, hypocrisy. Jesus charged them with tempting him (not, however, according to the text of Luke) and addressed them as "hypocrites." These liars had no defense. Yes, Jesus told them the truth and told it without fear or favor!

25) And yet, unworthy of any answer as they are, Jesus gives them an answer and does it in a way that has gone ringing down the centuries. He demands to be shown a denarius, the coin with which the poll tax was always paid, which was in purchasing value equal to the price of a day's labor, the wage of a Roman soldier, 17 cents today but irrespective of our money values in labor and in trade. The Roman senate had the right to mint only copper coins; the right to mint gold and silver coins was reserved for the emperor. The denarius was a small silver coin that was usually stamped with the emperor's head (occasionally with that of a member of his household) and invariably with the name and the title of the reigning emperor.

The coin is produced promptly. "Jesus begins in a childish and foolish way as though he did not know the image and the inscription and could not read, so that they quickly thought, surely, here we have him, he is afraid and intends to dissimulate about the emperor and dares not speak against him. But he takes the word right out of their mouth and makes them surrender with their confession. They dare not be silent, for just as they bade him answer, so he now bids them answer. If they were silent, he would say, 'If you will not give answer to my question, neither will I answer your question.'" (v. 8). Luther. Besides, the question seems so innocent and harmless that they see no reason to pause and thus reply, "Cæsar's." While digging a pit for Jesus, they have tumbled into it themselves. All that Jesus does is to point this out to them.

Trench, *Synonyms*, I, 78, points out the exact meaning of εἰκών, "image," which always implies a prototype, which it does not merely resemble but from which it is drawn. It is the German *Abbild* which presupposes a *Vorbild*. The emperor's face is depicted on the coin; so the sun shines in the water, the statue presents the man, the child is the image of its parent. But ὁμοίωμα or ὁμοίωσις, "likeness," means only resemblance and does not itself include derivation: two men may look alike; one egg resembles another.

In ἀπόδοτε the preposition gives the verb the meaning "to give what is due," what our obligation requires us to give (not "give back," R., *Tr.*). The perfection of Jesus' answer was recognized fully by his hostile questioners the moment they heard it, and few have ever found fault with it although some have failed to see all that these brief words convey. The perfection of the answer is its completeness. The Jews looked at the poll tax by itself; the only way in which to look at it was to place it among all "the things of Cæsar" and then to look at these in connection with (καί) all "the things of God." Then all difficulties, those regarding the tax and a thousand others, disappear at once. The trouble with so many casual (case) questions is that we look only at the one question and fail to rise to the comprehensive view which takes in the whole domain of which the one question is only a trivial part. Jesus always saw the whole, and Paul rises to the same height, notably in solving the intricate problems in Corinth. The wisdom that does this is from above.

Jesus asked for an actual coin, one that was to be taken out of the wallet of one of his questioners. All of them carried such money. He makes them say that this is the emperor's coinage. They have accepted it, are using it, and it is their money, the money that is accepted by their entire nation. This means that their nation belongs to the empire. This coinage was one of the advantages they enjoyed under the emperor's rule, a sample of other like advantages. The emperor was their ruler; this coin with his image, which was taken from their pocket, was the incontestable evidence of that fact. In the providence of God the Jews were this emperor's subjects. That suffices.

And that settled all their obligations toward the emperor, the matter of paying him the poll tax that was now in force and rendering all other duties toward him. Τοίνυν, "well then," makes this plain. "Duly give to Cæsar the things of Cæsar" includes *all* their obligations to "the higher powers ordained of God," Rom. 13:1-7. "The things of Cæsar" include, not only tribute, but also fear and honor. It makes no difference whether any government makes this easy or hard for us. Our part is plain—let the rulers look well to theirs as being answerable to God, who likewise rules over them.

But this is only part of the answer. The question: "Is it lawful or not?" referred to God: "Is the payment of this tax in harmony or in dissonance with our obligation to him?" Therefore Jesus adds: "and the things of God to God." This "and" places the two obligations side by side. There is no clash between them, quite the contrary. Neither obligation interferes with the other. "The things of God" are all that our relation to him involves: contrition, faith, love, worship, obedience, submission to his providential guidance, even to his correction and chiding.

But we misunderstand Jesus when we understand him to say that the obligation to God has nothing to do with the obligation to our government. Even the Pharisees and their disciples were not so shallow as their question shows. The "and" of Jesus intends to cancel the "or" of his questioners (v. 22). These are not alternatives, they harmonize, yea, more: when we are giving to God what is God's we will for his sake give to the ruler what is his. For our obligation to God includes everything in our life, its citizenship as well as our religion. This "and" connects a small field with the whole field. And only by seeing both in their true relation do we see either aright. From Cæsar Jesus rises to God—no man would suppose that he merely parallels them.

The emperor's image was on the coins that were in the pockets of the Jews, and Jesus pointed to that image when he said, "Duly give to Cæsar," etc. He connected the obligation with the image. When he now adds in identical words: "and the things of God," etc., who can help but think of a corresponding connection of this obligation with an image, namely the image of God in which he created us and which his Son restores in us? To say the least, the thought is captivating. And in fact, only as we truly attain in us God's image will we truly render to him what is his due from us.

Jesus acknowledges the state as a divine institution that is willed by God. His own conduct before Pilate exemplifies this fact, in particular his word recorded in John 19:11. His word about Cæsar regards the state and our relation to it as a separate domain, and the doctrine of the separation of church and state is thus the only legitimate conclusion that can be drawn from what he says. Yet church and state are not mere parallels and equals. Our obligations to God are the whole life, those to the state one part of this whole. Whereas church and state are separate in the way indicated, there is no gulf between them. They are not like two watertight compartments. The church will always put conscience, namely as it is governed by God, into our relations to the state (Rom. 13:5). The church constantly contributes this to the state. Rom. 13:3, 4 makes plain what the state normally contributes and always ought to contribute to the church. Thus each aids the other, but the church aids in the higher way. When either seeks to control the other, usurps the functions of the other, havoc results for both as history bears witness.

26) And they were not able to lay hold of the utterance before the people; and after marvelling at his answer they were silent.

The vicious intent was completely frustrated. "Before the people" means that all these were pilgrims standing about as witnesses, ready to testify to just what Jesus had said and to prevent any twisting of his words. On Friday the leaders tried to make out that Jesus had said the very opposite about Cæsar, but these pilgrims could then not expose the lie. So even these wicked fellows had to marvel; and when they bethought themselves that this was giving Jesus credit they became silent and left (Matthew).

27) Now some of the Sadducees, who claim there is no resurrection, having come forward, inquired of him saying: Teacher, Moses wrote for us, if one's brother dies having a wife, and he be childless, that his brother shall take his wife and raise up seed for his brother.

Matthew tells us that this took place on the same day (Tuesday). This time a group of Sadducees (freethinkers, loose livers) confronts Jesus. We read of no prominent personages being among them and may thus think of ordinary Sadducees who, in keeping with the opposition of their entire party to Jesus, had conceived of a way to trip Jesus and at the same time to maintain their skeptic views against the orthodox Pharisees. "Who claim there is no resurrection" summarizes their position on the point at issue; εἶναι is the tense of the direct discourse (ἐστίν) just as we still use the present tense in general and doctrinal propositions. "They inquired" implies that they acted respectfully; and "teacher" is the Greek for "rabbi," which Luke translates thus.

28) These Sadducees, however, use no flattery as did the disciples of the Pharisees (v. 21). Feeling their lofty superiority as Sadducees, they were naturally disinclined to exalt Jesus even by hypocrisy. Josephus comments on their coarse manners, a sample of which appears in John 11:49. Although they address Jesus formally as "teacher" they really intend to show what a wretched teacher he actually is. They briefly summarize the Mosaic law regarding levirate marriage (Deut. 25:5, etc.). The purpose of the law was not to let the dead, childless brother's line die out; the first son of the new marriage (not any of the other children) would be regarded as the dead man's child.

29) All this is a preamble. Now there comes the real question. **There were, accordingly, seven brothers; and the first, having taken a wife, died childless; and the second and the third took her. Moreover, also the seven left behind no children and died. Finally also the woman died. In the resurrection, therefore, of which of them will she be wife? For the seven had her as wife.**

The logic presented in this case is intended to be a *reductio ad absurdum* for the defenders of the resurrection. This is done by means of a supposed dilemma, either horn of which offers an impossible, untenable, really ludicrous situation. The fallacy of the logic lies in the falsity of the assumption that in this Sadducaic dilemma *tertium non datur*. These men thought that they were wielding a two-edged sword, either edge of which would prove fatal to Jesus, and never dreamed that he would strike the flat side of their blade and snap it off at the very handle.

These deniers of the resurrection still have many followers. The theological view that Judaism acquired the doctrine of the resurrection at a late day (say at Solomon's time), and that it was little known even after that period is not tenable. Abraham believed that God could raise his son from the dead (Heb. 11:19). Only the skeptic Sadducees disbelieved the resurrection, and their objection shows only how extensively and intensively the doctrine was held. The Scripture evidence is abundant between these terminals, and even Abraham speaks of the resurrection as something that was long and fully known. And always, as in the case of these Sadducees, this is the resurrection of the body. This must be said for the sake of the modernists who speak of a spirit-resurrection—as though the spirit is buried like the body.

The Sadducees cite the case of the seven brothers as being a real case, and Jesus does not contradict them regarding its reality. It is wrong to call even Sadducees liars without proper evidence. Whereas they use this case, which runs up to seven brothers, because they had it, two brothers would suffice for the sake of the argument, and such cases were certainly numerous among the Jews.

30) The second and the third brothers are mentioned briefly.

31) Then in summary all seven are referred to. None leaves issue of any kind, all die in succession. If even a girl had been born to one of the brothers, a claim might have been set up for him.

32) The death of the woman is necessary for the argument in order to transfer all the persons concerned into the other world and thus to show by actuality and not merely hypothetically how absurd the resurrection appears when it is considered in the light of Deut. 25:5, etc. The old trick of playing one word of Scripture (one that seems to suit our error) against some great doctrine of Scripture, which is buttressed by a number of Scripture statements, was practiced already in the days of the Sadducees.

33) So the conundrum is propounded to Jesus. Supposing for the sake of argument that there is a resurrection, and that these dead bodies of ours rise again from their graves—what about this woman? All seven brothers were equally her husband—in the resurrection will all seven together be her husband? The very idea is monstrous already in this life and how much more in the life to come! Or which one of the seven will be her husband, and why the one, and why not some other one of the seven, she having had a child by none? When seven hold equal rights, why set aside six? Again an impossible situation. The Sadducees are thus certain that there is no resurrection, and that Moses himself proves it in Deuteronomy, and that no man can overthrow this solid proof. We may well suppose that they had tried this proof against many a Pharisee and had made a laughingstock of every opponent. Jesus was to be their next victim.

34) **And Jesus said to them: The sons of this eon marry and are given in marriage; but those deemed worthy to attain that eon and the resurrection from the dead neither marry nor are married, for they are not able to die anymore, for they are angel-like and are sons of God as being sons of the resurrection.**

The bubble that has been blown by the folly of the Sadducees is punctured. Luke omits the preliminary words that are preserved by Matthew and Mark and at once goes to the essentials. The Sadducees run in a false premise on this question of the resurrection, one that is absolutely foreign to Moses and the Scriptures, namely, that in the other world the same conditions prevail that are found in this world. Where does the Old Testament teach anything of the kind? Thus as to marriage and the entire marital relation, this is intended only for men as being "sons of this eon," of this world age.

35) "Those deemed worthy (by God) to attain that eon (the heavenly and eternal one) and the resurrection from the dead" are past marrying (used with reference to men) and of being married (the simple passive used with reference to women). Jesus is speaking only of the blessed dead, for the question of the Sadducees relates only to these. The fact that these attain "the resurrection from the dead" must be added, for the question about marriage involves the body, not disembodied souls in heaven prior to the resurrection of the last day. On the phrase ἐκ νεκρῶν see 9:7; it is made emphatic by means of the second article (R. 776); on αἰών see 16:8.

36) Jesus explains how this is to be understood by means of two γάρ clauses, the second resting on the first. The entire arrangement of sex, marriage, reproduction, childbirth, and any laws pertaining to these, is valid for this eon only, for the earthly life, and not for that heavenly eon and the life there, for men no longer die there. "Where there is no dying, there is also no succession of children," Augustine. No replenishment is necessary in heaven. As the number of the angels was complete and fixed from the time of creation onward, so will that of the blessed in the resurrection and from that day onward be. In that respect the blessed will then be ἰσάγγελοι, "angel-like" ("as the angels," Matthew and Mark), which is better than "equal to the angels" (our versions). Jesus does not

say that the blessed shall be angels but angel-like as regards sex and marriage. The blessed shall have their bodies "in the resurrection of the dead" and differ therein from the angels.

The view that the angels, too, possess corporeity is wholly without Scripture support. This theosophical, speculative idea assumes an ethereal, firelike body for the angels; and when it is consistently held, a body of some indefinable form also for God. But the Scriptures know angels only as πνεύματα, "spirits," and use this term in many connections as being the opposite of all that is bodily or corporeal. See the fuller discussion in Philippi, *Glaubenslehre,* II, 296, etc. When angels appear to men on earth they are given a form in order to be visible just as Jehovah assumed a form in the theophanies.

We may add, however, that in the resurrection our bodies will be lifted above the narrow limitations of earthly matter as we know it at present; they will be made perfect instruments of the spirit so as to accord in all things with the glorious conditions of the eon to come.

Luke has preserved the addition to "angel-like" which defines further what Jesus means: "and are sons of God as being sons of the resurrection." Their resurrection is not used as evidence or as proof that they are God's sons by faith; the evidence for this kind of sonship lies in the works of faith. Their resurrection is proof or evidence for their sonship in the new and glorified nature which even their bodies shall have by virtue of the resurrection. Faith brings ethical sonship, a new relation to God; the resurrection a metaphysical sonship in which the entire nature is filled with God's glory. Why this sonship should not be angel-like according to the title "sons of God" which is applied to the angels in Job 1:6; 2:1; 38:7 is hard to see in spite of strong assertions to that effect.

37) This pertinent instruction concerning the condition of the blessed in heaven eliminates the entire argument of the Sadducees which rests on the false assumption that our bodily conditions in heaven will be like the conditions that obtain here on earth. But the Sadducees had appealed to the Scriptures (like Satan in 4:10, 11) falsely; Jesus now crushes this appeal by himself appealing to the Scriptures (as he did in 4:12) truly. The Scriptures *are* the true court of appeal. Jesus unmasks one of the hidden batteries of Scripture and delivers a volley that is the more annihilating since it comes from an entirely unexpected quarter.

But that the dead do arise even Moses disclosed at the bush when he speaks of the Lord as the God of Abraham and the God of Isaac and the God of Jacob. Now he is not God of dead men but of living men, for all are living for him.

"But that the dead do arise" has the present tense which occurs in doctrinal declarations. The verb is emphatic since it is placed before the subject and is thus contrasted with the assertion that the dead do *not* arise. This opening clause states the point at issue, and "the dead" as well as "they do arise" make it plain that the bodily resurrection is referred to. The Sadducees referred to Moses, Jesus points to that same Moses.

The question is asked why he used Exod. 3:6 or its parallels and not obvious passages like Dan. 12:2. The answer that this was done because the Sadducees rejected all but the Pentateuch is hardly convincing. To set the right Moses against a falsified Moses seems entirely proper. Another point is probable. The Sadducees drew a deduction from a passage in Moses, drew it falsely; Jesus also uses a passage from which he draws a deduction, draws it truly—one that clearly lies in the Scripture words themselves and goes not an inch beyond these. He thus shows how deductions are to be drawn.

Jesus says, "Even Moses disclosed at the bush" and means what Moses wrote in Exodus regarding this theophany. It was, however, the Lord *(Yahweh)* himself who used this covenant name concerning himself there at the bush. Moses disclosed it when he wrote Exodus—another example of how Jesus makes Moses the author of the Pentateuch. Κύριον (the translation of *Yahweh*) is the object of λέγει, the present tense to indicate the fact that Moses speaks so to this day; and τὸν Θεόν κτλ is predicative to the object. This is the great covenant name of God in which all the Jews gloried. What an innocent thing to announce what every Jew knew: that Moses had recorded this name in Exodus! But now, like a blinding flash for these self-confident Sadducees, there comes the revealing word: "He is not a God of dead men but of living men!" And the terse explanation: "for all are alive to him." Θεός is the predicate, and οὐκ ἔστι contains the subject: "he is not." The emphasis is on the contrasted genitives: "of dead men"—"of living men," which is reenforced by the fact that they all live as far as God is concerned.

38) "Dead men" are men whose *bodies* are lifeless, who are lying in the graves as such. If there is no resurrection, then the bodies of the great patriarchs Abraham, Isaac, and Jacob, with whom God made his great covenant, would lie dead forever, and that would make God "God of dead men"—an impossible thought. That would mean that death was not conquered; that death, which was holding its prey, was stronger than God; that redemption had failed and had left death still triumphant. But no; the resurrection proves that God is "God of living men." Death has suffered its deathblow. Redemption has not failed. It has turned the death of God's saints into a mere sleep. The proof is the resurrection by which God wakes these dead bodies from their slumber. The dust of God's saints may, indeed, look to our eyes as other dust, dead dust;

in reality God, Christ, heavenly power are over and in that dust—it is *living* dust, we shall see it live in glory forever. "For they all live to him" whatever men may think or say. Thus the very name and title which God gave himself in the Old Testament as early as Exodus proves the resurrection. So closely is the resurrection connected with the covenant God.

The interpretation is offered by some that the souls of the patriarchs were in *sheol,* the "realm of the dead," and that Christ intended to release their souls from *sheol,* and that this would be their resurrection and prove God to be the God of the living. But this interpretation turns Jesus' refutation of the Sadducees into a farce. They denied the resurrection of *the dead bodies,* and to substitute no matter what statement regarding *only the souls* would be a piece of deception, which, if detected, would destroy not only the pretended proof but even the entire character of Jesus. The same is true when *sheol* is disregarded, when God is made the God of the living only because the souls continue to live after leaving their bodies. It is juggling words to say that the patriarchs were "not absolute dead men, non-existent men" but "living" because enjoying eternal life in heaven. Then the Sadducees (ancient and modernistic) would be right in asserting that no resurrection of *the dead bodies* will take place. Jesus himself would be a Sadducee. He would only pretend to say "that the dead do arise" when he in fact says nothing like that at all.

39) And answering, some of the scribes said, Teacher, excellently didst thou speak! For no longer dared they inquire a thing of him.

Matthew tells us that the multitude was astonished, Luke that even the hostile scribes who stood by felt compelled to commend Jesus for his answer. This means much more than is ordinarily supposed. To win commendation from such hostile men was a great triumph. These scribes were, of course, Pharisees and as such were firm believers in the resurrection (Acts 23:6-9). But not because Jesus agreed with them regarding this doctrine did these scribes commend him; their praise was intended for the way in which Jesus proved the doctrine. In their contention with the Sadducees the scribes had never been able to wield such effective weapons. This was what inspired the praise.

40) The Sadducees were silenced for good and all. Mark 12:28 tells about one of the scribes who asked another question but not with evil intent. Luke's statement is not in contradiction to Mark's, for it refers to the Sadducees.

41) Jesus has been questioned repeatedly; he now in turn propounds a question. It is addressed to the Pharisees (Matthew), and Luke has only the briefest record of it. **Now he said to them: How do they declare the Christ to be David's son? For David himself says in the Psalms Book, The Lord said to my Lord, Sit at my right till I place thine enemies as a footstool of thy feet! David, therefore, calls him Lord, and how is he his son?** Luke omits the dialog and centers on the main point that the Jews, in particular the scribes, all declare the Messiah to be David's son.

42) But now the main question: "How can David in Ps. 110 say that the Lord *(Yahweh)* said to his Lord *(Adonai)* to sit on his *(Yahweh's)* right," etc.? The Hebrew is very expressive: $n^{e}um$ *Yahweh*, "communication of Jehovah," *Eingerauntes*, something secretly whispered into the ear, the communication of a mystery. The right (plural in the Greek) is the power and the majesty of *Yahweh*. The Hebrew imperative *sheb limini* has itself become a title of the Messiah: "Sheblimini." The Greek views the direction "from or out of" the right as it appears to the beholder. In this psalm David sees his *Adon* invited by *Yahweh* to exercise all the divine majesty and power.

43) And he is to do this until *Yahweh* puts all this *Adon's* enemies as a footstool of his feet. He shall reign supreme in the universe. Jesus was facing some of these enemies at this very time. The psalm continues in the same strain and makes this *Adon* of David divine in every way.

44) Now the question which is so deadly for these Pharisees yet so illuminating for all believers—David calls this person *Adon,* divine Lord and Master, in the psalm: "how is he his (David's) son?" In other words, how can the Messiah be at the same time David's divine Lord and David's son? The terrible error of the Pharisees and their scribes is exposed. They saw the Messiah only as David's son, great and mighty, indeed, but only human. His deity, which is so plainly disclosed in the psalm, they never saw. They dared not say that he was *not* to be David's son—they knew that he would be. On the other hand, they dared not deny David's inspired word that the Messiah would be David's Lord and thus very God. When they were confronted with the psalm they had no answer whatever but simply refused to admit the Messiah's deity. They were like our modernists who, however, go still farther and deny even his Davidic descent.

45) Luke reports only a few sentences from the discourse which fills Matt. 23, the warning against the Pharisees and scribes and the terrible woes pronounced upon them on this Tuesday. **Now, with all the people hearing, he said to his disciples,** etc. The people are the pilgrims who are present for the Passover celebration; the disciples, the large number that was attached to Jesus. From Matt. 23:13, etc., we see that the Pharisees and scribes are addressed in the second person. They, too, are still present. In their very presence, with all the pilgrims listening, Jesus warns his disciples against them and their ugly sins

and then turns upon them with his devastating woes. This is dramatic in the extreme.

46) **Beware of the scribes who desire to walk in festal robes and love salutations in the market places and the first seats in the synagogues and the first reclining places at the dinners—who devour the houses of the widows and in pretense go on praying long. These shall take more abundant judgment.**

With προσέχετε we supply τὸν νοῦν: "hold your mind to it to avoid the scribes," etc., in all their ungodly and utterly selfish pride. They like nothing better than to parade about in the long, white, rich robes that are worn only by dignitaries on great occasions. They aim to be recognized and treated as such dignitaries by all who see them coming in their grandeur. They purposely visit the crowded market places, there to be effusively saluted right and left by all who witness their parading. And, of course, in the synagogues they must have the most prominent seats in front with the elders, for as scribes they expect to be requested to impart their wisdom to the audience. Likewise at any δεῖπνον, the main meal of the day that is eaten at evening, they expect the chief places on the couches. Each couch accommodated several people, and the place toward the left end was the chief. These were concrete samples of their unholy pride, all rested on their claim to special sanctity after the Pharisaic type.

47) Now Jesus turns the page and in a flash shows the selfish greed of these scribes. Because of their holiness appointed to administer the property of widows, they used their position of trust "to devour" even the homes of these helpless widows. They boldly disregarded all that the Old Testament said about the widows and the fatherless, both in admonition and in warning, and little by little, with a show of right, worked this property into their own hand. And "in

pretense," in rank hypocrisy, to cover up their robbery, "they go on praying long," making long prayers —the longer, the more impressively holy in the eyes of unthinking men.

Now Jesus turns another leaf, and on it is written: "These—and all like them—shall take (as their due portion) more abundant judgment" when the day of reckoning comes. The noun is neutral and does not itself intimate the verdict, which can, however, be only condemnation. "More abundant" refers to the rank hypocrisy which is added to the ugly greed. In the judgment their guilt shall be piled up, and the verdict shall be doubly, trebly heavy. Yes, Jesus was right in warning his disciples as he did, and the pilgrims who heard it might also well take this warning as being intended for themselves.

CHAPTER XXI

1) Jesus is still in the Temple courts on Tuesday. Mark 12:41 describes him as sitting where he could see the people depositing their offerings. He is not teaching, and the disciples stand about until Jesus calls them to tell them what the widow had done. Both in Mark and in Luke this narrative is set alongside the warning against the greed of the scribes who devour widows' houses. Here there was one of those widows offering the last she had to the Lord. **Now on looking up he saw those throwing their gifts into the treasury, who were rich.**

Stier utters an exclamation of surprise that, immediately after delivering the most scathing woes against the scribes, Jesus is able to sit down calmly and to express his appreciation of the gift of a widow. Thirteen trumpet-shaped, metal receptacles *(shapharoth)*, each marked with a Hebrew letter, stood in the court of the women to receive the gifts of the worshippers for the benefit of the Temple and for the Temple tax. The singular τὸ γαζοφυλάκιον, "the treasury," may refer to all of them. On looking up, Jesus beheld those throwing their gifts into them, and the adjective used is predicative: "rich," i. e., "who were rich." Mark says that the multitude did this and then refers to the rich who threw in much. Luke is briefer and remarks only that Jesus noted the rich.

The Jews gave freely for the support of the Temple and its worship in addition to the tithe. It is said that the city was in a flourishing condition at this time. The sons of Jacob have always known how to increase their substance. Mark adds the detail that the rich threw in much. We may say that most of them did this ostentatiously so that men might see and exclaim because of their liberality. Jesus silently watched them making offerings.

2) **Moreover, he saw a penniless widow throwing in there two lepta. And he said: Truly I tell you that this penniless widow threw in more than all. For all these out of what abounds to them threw in for gifts, but she out of her want threw in all the living which she had.**

Jesus "saw" and noted this widow and the amount of her insignificant gift. Mark uses the word "poor" which means "beggarly," Luke the one which means "poor" in the sense of "penniless" or "destitute." Her appearance betrayed that fact. But Jesus sees more, namely that she was a widow, and that these two lepta were "all the living which she had." This was not a guess but an exercise of that supernatural knowledge which Jesus always employed wherever he needed it for his work. Let us remember, too, that God always has a special eye on widows and on orphans, and so Jesus does here also.

No name is inserted in the record, but this widow has had "a good name" in the church of all ages. Every man's gifts stamp him with a name, and when the gift is small like that of this widow, the giver's name is not always in the same class as hers. The indefinite pronoun used with "widow" is only our indefinite article and is used often by Luke.

This widow "threw in there two *lepta*," which were called so from their smallness, each was an eighth of an *assarion*, the two making a *quadrans*, about the fourth of a cent in value. Bengel remarks that she might have retained one of the two *lepta*. She has been judged by worldly wisdom which declares that she should have kept the money for her support, and that, as far as the Temple was concerned, her gift amounted to nothing. Why was it that Judas objected to the richer offering of Mary in Bethany? Worldly wisdom always makes a fool of itself. In the case of the widow it sees neither the faith and trust that filled the woman's heart nor the true act of worship she performed. All these are more precious in Jesus' eyes than were the largest gifts that were bestowed by the Jews in the Temple that day. Hypocrites attempt to imitate this widow's gift and think that, if they give all their living, God will have to provide for them. But God cannot be thus bought or tempted. Poverty may be made a great curse as well as a great blessing. It becomes a curse when it fills the heart with anxious care and worry. It becomes a blessing when it impels the poor man to cast himself upon God who has promised to care for his children.

3) Mark tells that Jesus called his disciples to him and made his pronouncement upon the widow's gift as *de magna re* (Bengel). Here was something for them to learn concerning the principle on which gifts are to be valued in the church. Did the widow hear what Jesus said about her? This is usually answered in the negative, but it is not as unlikely as some think when we consider that Jesus often spoke commendation in the hearing of those whom he praised. "Truly" stresses the fact that his judgment was a true one; and "I say to you" indicates the authority on which this judgment rests. Jesus does not compare the widow's gift with that of any one rich giver but with all the gifts of all the rich who gave that day. In the estimation of Jesus the widow's two *lepta* amounted to more than the combined sum of all these wealthy givers. It is the quality that makes a gift more or less in Jesus' eyes.

4) The disciples may well have looked at Jesus with questioning eyes and wondered what made him rate the widow's gift so highly. He explains at once ($\gamma\acute{\alpha}\rho$). "All these" might have taken in many more rich givers than those who came to the Temple that day, for despite all their quantity they could never have equalled the quality of the widow's gift. For all these

gave "out of what abounds to them," out of what they have above their needs. But the widow gave "out of her want," out of what was wholly insufficient to provide even the barest necessities.

Right here a tremendous difference appears even as the two ἐκ phrases are intended as opposites. Jesus touches only this one point and not any display on the part of the rich. Gifts that are given out of our superfluous income and gifts that are given out of want and necessity are not on the same level. To give the latter requires much more in our hearts than to give the former.

Jesus adds far more regarding the widow's gift: she gave "all the living which she had," the last two *lepta* that she had wherewith to buy food. Tissot paints this scene with the woman carrying a child on her arm. That child helps to bring out the thought expressed by Jesus. "Oh," one said, "if that was all she had, two *lepta*, she might as well have thrown that in—it would not have helped her anyway!" So spoke one who was too blind to see what this widow's gift involved. A fourth of a cent could, of course, help her very little; but that is true of a million dollars as well. No man lives by the bread he is able to buy; millionaires die as did Dives with his tables loaded—not only beggars like Lazarus. We live only by the word that goes forth out of God's mouth, by his will that is expressed in that word.

When this widow gave all the living she had she gave herself completely into the hands of God. Her last act with the final bit of her living was an act of worship in true faith that now looked only unto God who cares for the destitute who trust in him. What makes so many gifts so small? The fear that the givers will not have enough for themselves. They depend on what they have, not on God who gave them even that and can give them much more.

Did the widow starve? I do not think so. But let us not overdraw the picture. She has been pictured as going home with a heart singing with joy. Let us rather say that she was ready to starve if that were God's will. She was ready to accept that from the God she trusted. And if God did not let her starve, she took what he sent her as being sent only by him. To live thus and to give thus with such a faith means to earn the highest commendation of Jesus.

5) **And with some saying concerning the Temple that it had been adorned with beautiful stones and votive offerings, he said, These things which you view, there shall come days in which there shall not be left stone upon stone here, which shall not be thrown down.**

Matt. 24:1 and Mark 13:1 tell us that Jesus and the Twelve are in the act of leaving the Temple on this momentous day. All that we are able to gather from the synoptists is that this occurred at the close of Tuesday, and that Jesus never again entered the Temple courts. Because that leaves Wednesday without a recorded event or word, harmonists are inclined to assign something to Jesus that he did on Wednesday, but the synoptists' records include only Tuesday. Jesus must have spent Wednesday quietly in Bethany and on Thursday made arrangements for the Passover celebration in the city.

Mark has one of the Twelve draw the attention of Jesus to the beauty of the Temple. Matt. 23:38 explains how this took place. The disciples thought: "Are all these grand structures actually to be left desolate?" Some of the beautiful marble columns were forty feet high. Fifty years had already been spent in rebuilding the Temple (John 2:20). In addition to the beautiful stones there were the "votive offerings" that had been donated and dedicated by rich individuals, which were exceedingly costly, such as the golden vine at the entrance portal which had branches as tall as a man, (Josephus, *Ant.* 15, 2, 3; II Macc. 3:2, 3). Ἀνάθεμα with the short vowel means a curse, devoted to God for destruction; but ἀνάθημα with a long vowel is a gift that has been set aside for God, *ein Weihgeschenk*, R. 187.

6) Jesus repeated the prophecy that he had uttered in 19:44, that the place would not only be left desolate, but that not one stone would remain upon another—all would be absolute ruin. "These things which you view" may be regarded as an absolute nominative, *nominativus pendens* (R. 459), or as an adverbial accusative (R., *Tr.*): "as for the things," etc. That was all Jesus said on the way out of the Temple courts.

7) **But they inquired of him, saying: Teacher, when, then, will these things be; and what the sign when these things are about to occur?**

Matthew and Mark add the detail that this inquiry was made when Jesus reached the Mount of Olives and sat down there for awhile, Mark supplies the information that Peter, James, John, and Andrew came to Jesus with the double question. The writer stood on the slope of Olivet toward evening and looked across to the Temple hill where the Mohammedan Dome of the Rock (sometimes called the Mosque of Omar) now stands, its dome of dull gold magnificently lit up by the slanting rays of the sun, the city on Zion hill rising behind to a higher elevation. So Jesus sat with Herod's magnificent Temple and the brilliant Sanctuary (Holy and Holy of Holies) sparkling in the dying sun with their golden roofs. It was thus that he spoke this discourse about the destruction of Jerusalem and the end of the world.

The question introduced with "when" asks for no date, and Jesus never gives a date (Acts 1:7; Matt. 24:36; Mark 13:32). This "when" belongs together with "the sign" which shall indicate the nearness of

Jesus' return to judgment and of the winding up of the world age. It is useless to speculate regarding as to just what these four disciples meant with their double question; the synoptists record it only for our understanding as to how Jesus came to deliver this important discourse.

8) **And he said: See to it that you be not deceived! For many will come on my name, saying, I myself am he! and, The season has come near! Do not go after them! Moreover, when you shall hear of wars and tumults, be not terrified; for it is necessary that these things occur first; but not at once the end.**

The way in which Jesus begins shows that his heart is full of concern for his disciples. The introduction to the great discourse is a strong warning. They are to "see to it," to keep their eyes open, "that they may not be deceived" ($\pi\lambda\alpha\nu\tilde{\alpha}\nu$, to trick one to believe what is not true). There is only too good a reason for this warning. "Many will come on my name" (see this phrase in 9:48), will use my own revelation as the basis for their lying, deceiving claims, and even say boldly, "I myself am he!" (emphatic $\dot{\epsilon}\gamma\dot{\omega}$), namely the Christ whose return is promised (Matthew and Mark). Others may be less brazen, but on the basis of his name (revelation) they will figure out the date of Christ's coming and proclaim that the season for it "has come near," is thus actually at hand.

The procession of such deceivers from Simon Magus and Barcochba onward to the great Antichrist and the little antichrists goes on to the end of time. Some are petty and have some little sect of fanatics following them, some sit on thrones like the popes in their long succession; some are out for the hard cash; some are viciously lascivious. The sad thing is that they succeed in their deceptions, for all men have an affinity for religious error, and many yield to it with avidity and develop the strongest fanaticism. They find no limit in perverting to their own ends what the Scriptures say about the kingdom. "Do not go after them!" means: "Do not become their followers."

9) The structure of the discourse is plain. After the opening warning (v. 8) Jesus tells of the signs that run through the course of time (v. 9-11); he then tells the disciples what awaits them in the near future (v. 12-19); he next describes the destruction of Jerusalem and the end of the Jewish nation (v. 20-24); upon this there follows the description of the Parousia (v. 25-33). The discourse closes with admonitions that apply to the entire time until the end (v. 34-36).

The disciples would soon hear of wars and tumults, especially as these ushered in the destruction of Jerusalem and the nation, although Jesus is speaking generally of any and of all wars, rebellions, and turmoils that occur in the course of time. "Be not terrified!" Jesus says. He explains that these things occur of necessity; δεῖ is used to express any type of necessity, here one that is due to the condition of the world and to God's judgment in dealing with that condition. Such wars and tumults, one may say, are only natural in a world that is full of wickedness. Hence the disciples must not be terrified but must take them as a matter of course.

Note the emphasis on the adverb: they must occur "first," and then the plain addition: "but not at once the end," i. e., of the world. Wars, etc., are only general signs, constant reminders, but do not signify that the end will follow closely upon any one of them. This word: "not at once the end," refers to the plural "wars," etc., and shows that Jesus saw the years stretching on and on and answers the claim that he expected the world to end during the lifetime of his disciples.

10) **Then he went on to say** (see 3:7 on the imperfect) **to them: There shall rise nation against nation and kingdom against kingdom. Both great**

earthquakes and famines and pestilences from place to place shall there be; both terrors and great signs from heaven shall there be.

"Then he went on to say" marks a break but only to show that Jesus now presents the whole matter at length and in detail. The fact that nation rises against nation, kingdom against kingdom, is not intended to explain how wars, etc., result, for they, of course, result in this way. This statement reveals the abnormal and the desperate condition of the world when nations and kingdoms cannot dwell peaceably side by side. We may regard ἐγερθήσεται as a passive: "shall be raised up," or as a middle: "shall raise itself up" and thus "shall rise." The passions that cause these uprisings need not be mentioned.

11) The two τε ... καί present two further groups of disturbances, and each has two members. In v. 10 the abnormal condition obtaining among the nations is referred to; Jesus next mentions the abnormal condition that prevails on the earth, and coupled with this the abnormalities that occur in the heavens. All of them proclaim in a succession of mighty voices that are great enough for all the world to hear that conditions are abnormal and are hurrying the world to its end. The earth itself shall rock with mighty earthquakes; the very earth on which we live is unstable. Every quake gives warning of the approaching end. The same is true also on the earth: "famine and pestilence from place to place," these two form the second member of the first "both and" group. Instead of bringing man its fruits for his bodily life the earth deals him pestilential death, now here, now there (distributive κατά). Since earthquakes precede, famines and pestilences are to be understood in the general sense and not merely as being the results of wars.

"Both terrors and great signs from heaven" include all the manifestations in the skies and the heavenly bodies, both as being terrifying to men and as signs that the disturbances and the dislocations here on earth affect the whole universe and thus foretell its end. Comets, eclipses, meteors, and rarer siderial phenomena are referred to, finally also those that are specified in v. 25, 26.

12) **But before all these things they will lay their hands on you and will persecute, delivering you to the synagogues and prisons, being led before kings and governors for the sake of my name.**

"Before all these things" is very clear as also the following specifications show which deal with the early days of the church, and which reflect the later persecutions only in a general way. The story of the Acts is the earliest commentary on what is stated here. The plural verbs are indefinite, "they" in these verbs refers to the enemies of the gospel. To lay hands on=to place under arrest; to deliver to the synagogues=to place on trial before the Jewish synagogue courts; the addition "and prisons"=to lodge in prison as condemned criminals.

Instead of proceeding with a finite verb: "they shall lead you before kings," etc.; or with an active participle: "they leading you," both of which would imply the same Jewish enemies as the agents, Luke simply adds the passive participle in the accusative which modifies ὑμᾶς understood: "you being led before kings," etc., since Jews would not do this but Gentile enemies of the gospel would. These are pagan kings and governors (Felix, Festus, the Roman emperor in the Acts; likewise in the ten great persecutions of the early church). The final phrase, "for the sake of my name," of the revelation connected with me, should be construed with the entire sentence as explaining why all these vicious acts will be perpetrated upon Christ's disciples. On this prospect of the most violent persecution Jesus ever spoke in plainest words to his followers. And all this would strike them because of one thing only, because of him.

13) It will turn out for you for testimony.

That will be the great and glorious outcome of all this suffering of yours for my name's sake: it will be your highest and most effective testimony for me before your and my enemies. We have an instance in Acts 4:11, etc. The idea is not: testimony of your loyalty to me or testimony that exonerates you before the tribunals. All this suffering for Jesus' sake is testimony for him, the very testimony he wants us to bear. Acts 9:15, 16.

14) Fix, therefore, in your hearts not to meditate beforehand to make defense for yourselves, for I myself will give you a mouth and wisdom which all your opponents shall not be able to stand against or to speak against.

Compare Mark 13:11. Once for all, during all these persecutions the disciples are to place this in their hearts (aorist imperative), not to think ahead as to how they will defend themselves (passive deponent, R. 334), aorist to express the whole act of defense. The same thought is found in 12:11, 12. In those trying hours, while they are lying in frightful dungeons, are perhaps beaten, are physically unfit, mentally upset, their natural worry would be about what they should say at their trial by conning over ($προμελετᾶν$) their answers to the judge now in one, now in another way. Jesus tells his disciples to dismiss this entirely from their minds.

15) "I myself" (emphatic $ἐγώ$), he says, will take care of you. Since this is to turn out as your witness for me (v. 13), "I will give you mouth and wisdom" at your trial, against which all your opponents ("those lying opposite you") will be unable to stand, unable even to speak. Note "mouth and wisdom," word and thought combined into one.

Jesus promises the disciples inspiration, verbal inspiration in the critical hour of their need. And its product will be so wonderful as to astonish the disciples themselves when they see that their opponents are defeated and silenced as they so often saw them defeated before Jesus. But this means only that the testimony of the disciples which will be placed on their tongue by Jesus will be so strong and not that the disciples will in every case be acquitted and set free. Despite all his good testimony Jesus himself was crucified. The argument is unanswerable: if Jesus is able and ready to grant verbal inspiration to the disciples for their proper defense at court, will he do less for the testimony of his written Word to all men and all ages? In all these passages: Matt. 10:19, 20; Luke 12:11, 12; Mark 13:11; and the present one it is verbal inspiration that is promised and not some inspiration in general.

16) **Moreover, you will be betrayed even by parents and brothers and relatives and friends. And they shall put some of you to death. And you will be hated by all because of my name. And a hair of your head shall in no way perish. In your patience you will gain your souls.**

Compare Matt. 10:21, 22. Something different is added by δέ; it is the fact that even those who are nearest to us by blood and friendship will use this very nearness and knowledge of our discipleship to denounce us with the result that some (partitive ἐκ) shall be put to death by the authorities—just as Jesus was betrayed unto death. Blood ties are strong, and so is friendship, but hatred of Christ and the gospel destroys them utterly and turns them into the very opposite.

17) The periphrastic future is used to bring out the durative nature of this hate; it is always thus that the world hates Christ's true disciples. Jesus explains in John 15:18-21 why this is the case, and why we must never expect anything else. Jesus uses διά and states that his name causes this hatred, name again signifies his revelation, that which fully reveals him,

who and what he is. Men who reject this name hate those who love it and, when the time comes, will show that hate and even let it go to the extreme.

18) Just as Jesus comforts and makes a great promise to those who are arrested and put on trial, so he again comforts and cheers with promises those who in any way suffer the world's hate and must perhaps yield up their lives. Καί adds coordinately the adversative thought that not a hair of their head shall perish. Although they are killed, not a hair of theirs shall perish. The word about "a hair out of your head" recalls Matt. 10:30 which speaks of the care of providence that extends as far as every numbered hair on our heads. The sense must be the same here. When a disciple suffers persecution, even death through wicked men, let him not think that God has forgotten him—he is in God's care and keeping to the last hair of his head. Nothing, absolutely nothing occurs to us without God's own will.

We do not need the allegorical interpretation, "hair perishing"=losing the very least of the Messianic salvation; or the generalizing references to John 10:20 or Phil. 1:21. Nor does this passage mean that the bodies of the disciples shall in the resurrection not be minus a single hair which they had in life or at the moment of death; or, broadly generalizing, that the bodies of the martyrs are to have full participation in the *Lebensrettung*, which is true of all who die in faith and not of martyrs only.

19) Compare Matt. 24:13 and Mark 13:13. In v. 18 Jesus makes a great, comforting promise, in v. 19 he adds to that, provided we have the future tense; important texts have the aorist imperative κτήσασθε which makes the paragraph end with an admonition—the promise seems far more natural. But even then the verb cannot mean "possess," which would require the future perfect tense since only the perfect tenses of this verb mean "to possess" (Abbott-Smith, *A Manual*

Greek Lexicon), all the other tenses mean "to gain," "to acquire." The word ὑπομονή is likewise used regarding patience or brave holding out under adverse things, inflictions, etc., and is never used with reference to God because it would not apply to him (Trench, *Synonyms*).

Another point to be noted is that ψυχή is used as it is in Mark 8:35, 36 and in John 12:25, as referring to the immaterial part of man which animates his body, which is as such called "the life." To suffer for Christ, to die for him, seem like losing the life (soul in this sense); but if we hold out bravely, instead of losing anything of life or life itself we shall do nothing but gain these very lives (souls). What is lost is transient and lost to the soul anyway in the end. They who strive for nothing more will have no gain of any kind at the end but an irreparable and eternal loss; but they who suffer for Christ, even die for him with brave, true hearts, achieve everything, gain their own "souls" in this pregnant sense of the term.

20) **Now when you see Jerusalem being encircled by soldier camps, then realize that her desolation has drawn near. Then they in Judea, let them begin fleeing to the mountains, and those in her midst, begin to get out; and those in the country places, let them not be coming in to her; because days of vengeance these are that all the things that have been written be fulfilled.**

Jesus is answering the question asked in v. 7, but in the fullest and the completest manner. He first states the general signs of the end (v. 8-10); then the persecutions that shall start immediately after Pentecost (v. 11-19); and now in a most masterly way the destruction of Jerusalem and its dreadful fate which last on to the Parousia of the Son of man. Here the mistaken view of the critics is plain when they assert that Luke recorded the prophecy concerning Jerusalem from his knowledge after the event (v. 20-24)—how about all the rest of it which takes us on to the end of the world? Is this, too, written after the event?

The fact that Jerusalem is presently to be encircled by soldier camps that will be setting siege to the city is not stated as something that is new but as something that has already been foretold (19:43); it is, therefore, put into a subsidiary clause. The present participle speaks of this encircling as being in progress, and the Greek word "soldier camps" of the army of the Romans as settling down permanently in camps for the siege. Then, before the encircling is completed, before it is too late, let the disciples know what is impending: Jerusalem's complete desolation has come near, is now at her very doors. This desolation is her complete destruction.

21) The following imperatives give the disciples specific orders as to what to do. Those who are living in Judea, the war area, are to start fleeing to the mountains, namely those outside of Judea, beyond the Jordan in Perea, where alone they will be safe. This injunction is put first because it includes all the other commands. Those who are in the city are to hasten and to get out and are not to dream that the great walls and the towers will afford them protection. Those who are outside, in the country sections around the city, are by no means to run to the city. All of them are to get away posthaste.

The Jews generally did the very opposite. Everybody rushed into the city so that it was filled with people when the Romans closed it in, and then, because of the mass that was filling the city, the most horrible sufferings began and increased to an extent that stands out with horror in all history. The Christians followed the bidding of Jesus. Eusebius 3, 5 reports that the congregation in Jerusalem followed a revelation that had been received by reliable men before the war and migrated to Pella in Perea. As far as one can judge, this must have occurred at the very time when bloody factions in the city were making an abomination of the Temple.

22) Why this precipitate flight? Jesus has already said that Jerusalem's desolation is at hand. He now adds more, namely that these are "days of vengeance" (compare the verb and the noun in 18:3, 5, 7). The word is neutral: "the handing out of justice," which may be in vindication of the right or in retribution for the wrong, here it is the latter. Jerusalem shall receive the punishment for all her unbelief and her crimes against the gospel, and this will not be some incidental punishment but her complete and final rejection by God: "that all the things that have been written be fulfilled"—all of them, completely fulfilled (aorist), in a final reckoning. We may look at the postexilic prophets, Zech. 14:2; 11:4-14; Mal. 3:1, etc., and the prophets before the exile whose words were fulfilled already in earlier devastations of Jerusalem but were now attaining a renewed and final fulfillment.

23) **Woe to those with child and to them suckling in those days, for there shall be great anguish on the land and wrath for this people. And they shall fall by the sword's mouth and shall be led captive into all the Gentiles. And Jerusalem shall be trampled by Gentiles until Gentile seasons shall be fulfilled.**

Jesus' heart melts at the thought of the hardships that will come upon pregnant and upon suckling women in those days, the former being burdened with unborn babes, the latter with babes in arms. This pity of Jesus is intended also for such Christian women who are caught amid all the hurry and the dangers of the flight.

"For" explains. "Great anguish" is subjective and "wrath" objective, the divine wrath which must descend when the cup of wickedness is full and overflows. "On the land" and "for this people" are synonymous. The fate of Jerusalem involved the entire Jewish land, for this land is but a small area and is more than almost any other land tied up with the fate of its capital.

24) The two statements about those who shall be devoured by the mouth (Greek idiom) of the Roman short sword that was used by the Roman legionaries and about those who shall be carried away as captive slaves into all the Gentile nations of the Roman Empire are striking prophecies that were most literally fulfilled. Josephus, *Wars*, 6, 9, 3, states that 1,100,000 Jews were slain and 97,000 carried away as captive slaves. The figures have been considered too high whereas, if anything, they are too low. The city was closed in during the Passover season, and the number who attended this festival in A. D. 65 Josephus, *Wars*, 2, 14, 3 reports with accuracy, namely over 3,000,000, counting only 10 to a paschal lamb. The significance of this slaughter and this exile into slavery is the destruction of the Jewish nation as a nation. Deprived of Palestine, the Jews were scattered among all the Gentiles of the Roman Empire. They have never again obtained their land, small as it is. The Zionist movement is the latest attempt of the Jews to repossess their land, and it has thus far failed.

The periphrastic future is used because the idea to be expressed is durative: "Jerusalem shall continue to be trampled by Gentiles." We know that this has continued to the present day, three-fourths of the population of Palestine and Jerusalem are the worst type of Gentiles, fanatic Mohammedans who fiercely oppose the Jews. But Jesus states how long this subjection to Gentiles will last: "until Gentile seasons shall be fulfilled." Note the absence of the articles, which stresses the two nouns; also the plural "seasons," more than one. The seasons referred to continue from the destruction of Jerusalem to the time of the Parousia. The plural "seasons" is justified because of the length of the time involved, and because of the different Gentile nations that have in turn occupied Jerusalem.

The opinion that the plural intends to reach back to the earlier conquests of Jerusalem is not indicated. This thought is carried still farther when "Gentiles" is taken to mean "pagan kingdoms," and when we are told that such kingdoms have always and will always rule the world and shall end with the Parousia. No; up to the final dispersion of the Jews and the disruption of their nation the seasons were those of the Jews; this was the chief nation in the world to God, with it he had made his covenant. Then God's wrath rejected this nation, it fell from the covenant, and the gospel and its new covenant passed to the Gentiles, the non-Jewish nations of the world. It did this to such an extent that all Jews who become Christians are lost to their race even physically and become absorbed among us who are still called Gentiles by the Jews. And so "Gentile seasons" are those that date from the rejection of the Jews.

These "seasons" do not, however, mean "gospel seasons" as such but seasons in which God seeks his people and builds his church among Gentiles or non-Jews with only a remnant now being drawn from the Jews. The expression has nothing to do with world kingdoms, whether they existed before or after the fall of Jerusalem. There is no fulfilling of such kingdoms and empires. God has set no climax or consummation for them. God has, however, set a consummation and fulfillment for his church and has appointed these seasons for his work among the Gentiles. He is done with the Jews as a nation, his work is now confined to non-Jews. Chiliasts understand "until" to mean "until the millennium" when the Jews as a nation—they have never been a nation since the fall of Jerusalem!—shall be converted, shall become the head of the Christian Church, etc. Neither in this discourse of Jesus or in any other Scripture is such a reinstatement of the Jews foretold.

25) **And there shall be signs in sun and moon and stars and on earth distress of nations in perplexity at the sound of sea and billow, men expiring from fear and expectation of the things coming upon the inhabited earth, for the power of the heavens shall be shaken.**

The connection is certainly not with v. 11 and with the signs mentioned there, for they shall run through all time, but the ones that are now foretold are the winding up of the world. The connection is with the preceding "until" clause. The "Gentile seasons" shall last until the final cataclysm comes. The millennialists insert their thousand years between v. 24 and 25, which is certainly an unwarranted eisegesis. What the signs that occur in the heavenly bodies shall be is stated in Matt. 24:29, the sun and the moon shall be extinguished, stars shall fall from their courses. Who can imagine the consternation that is thus caused on earth? Jesus describes it graphically: "distress of nations," their hearts are held as in a vise, "in perplexity" or utter loss of what to do "at the sound of sea and billow" roaring and raging in the dislocation of the entire world.

26) "Men fainting" is too weak, "expiring" is better, "from fright and expectation (apprehension) of the things coming on the inhabited earth," $τῇ\ οἰκουμένῃ$ ($γῇ$). "For the powers of the heavens" by which God held the universe of the skies plus the earth in place "will be shaken," will rock and totter, everything being dislocated in ruin when God's omnipotent hand reaches down to wind up the affairs of the earth and of man. What these two verses describe is not a succession of events but a simultaneous disruption.

27) **And then they shall see the Son of man coming in a cloud with power and great glory.** But

when these things are beginning to occur, lift yourselves up and raise your heads because your redemption is drawing near.

All these disintegrations are the heralds that usher in the Son of man at his Parousia (see 5:24 on the title). "They shall see" means all men who are then living on the earth. If the curious question is asked as to how men who reside on all sides of the globe shall simultaneously see the Son of man at the last day, the answer is that the whole universe and the earth will be completely changed beyond anything that we are able to comprehend with our present notions of time and space. Where will all the countless millions stand at the judgment, and how long will it take to have each one called and judged? The skeptic may be assured that he will have a place reserved for him, and his name will be reached in what we might now call the first minute.

"Coming" is that significant participle which is used so often regarding Christ's first coming that it became one of his Messianic names: "The Coming One." That name is still his in view of his second coming. But it will then occur "in a cloud in company with power and great glory"—he who was once spit upon, scourged bloody, mocked, and crucified. Regarding the clouds read Dan. 7:13; Acts 1:9, 11. They are God's chariot, Ps. 104:3; Isa. 19:1, a symbol of his heavenly majesty. This "power" is Christ's omnipotence which is manifested already in the cosmic upheaval; and his "great glory" is the sum of all his attributes that shine forth in splendor (Tit. 2:13; I Cor. 1:4; II Thess. 1:7; I Pet. 1:7; 4:13).

28) Some restrict "these things" to the ones that are mentioned in v. 25, 26; but "beginning to occur" seems to take in more than the catastrophic events that are recorded in these two verses require. Besides, Jesus is telling the Twelve what to do at the beginning of these things. We must go back at least to v. 20 and

may go back still farther. At every sign and indication of the end of the world the Twelve are to straighten up and to raise their heads like men who are in joyful expectation of a blessed event. We may apply these words to ourselves, seeing that the signs mentioned in v. 8-11 still continue; but we must leave the original sense of the peremptory aorist imperatives as being addressed to the Twelve. Others may lament and become frightened, not they; for their ἀπολύτρωσις is drawing near, the word is used in the wider sense, not as release by payment of a ransom, but simply as release or liberation from suffering, tribulation, and the like (Rom. 8:23; Eph. 1:14). They should feel as the captive does when he hears men coming to unlock his cell and to give him the liberty for which he longs.

29) **And he spake a parable to them. See the fig tree and all the trees. When now they shoot forth, seeing it, you realize of yourselves that now the summer is near. Thus also you, when you see these things occurring, realize that the kingdom of God is near.**

The fig tree helps only to individualize and is thus placed beside the others. But this fig tree has been allegorized. It is referred to the Jews and the other trees to the Gentiles. This is regarded as a reference to the fig tree which Jesus cursed (Matt. 21:19, etc.). So the Jews were cursed but shall be restored at the time of their final conversion. The dead fig tree will thus grow and again bear fruit. This is a sample of what millennialists find in simple Scripture words.

30) What Jesus says is that the trees that are budding and showing tender green inform all who see them that summer is near. They realize it themselves, need no one to teach them. Cold and discomfort are disappearing, lovely days are coming soon.

31) So all the signs of which Jesus speaks proclaim that "the kingdom of God" is near. A beautiful

parable, indeed! To the children of this world, who scorn this kingdom, every sign that this world, in which all their treasure rests, is breaking up must bring dismay. But the treasure of the disciples is in the kingdom, and every sign that proclaims its consummation must fill them with joy. Here is the winter of our discontent, there is the heavenly summer of our hopes and longings. "The kingdom of God" signifies Christ's rule of glory which follows his present rule of grace.

32) Amen, I say to you that this generation shall in no wise pass away until all things occur. The heaven and the earth shall pass away, but my words shall in no wise pass away.

With great solemnity and using his well-known seal for verity and authority (see 4:24), Jesus declares that "this generation" shall in no wise (οὐ μή, the strong negation for the future) pass away until all that he has predicted shall occur. The view that γενεά, especially "this generation," refers to the contemporary generation, those who were living at the time when Jesus spoke, is not tenable. A look at the use of *dor* in the Old Testament and at its regular translation by γενεά in the LXX, when the sense is evil, reveals at once that *a kind* of men is referred to, the evil kind that reproduces and succeeds itself in many physical generations. Ps. 12:7: "Thou shalt preserve them from this generation *forever;* 78:8, the fathers (many physical generations of them); 14:5, "the generation of the righteous"; 24:6; 73:15; 112:2; Deut. 32:5, 20; Prov. 30:11-14; Isaiah often; Jer. 7:29; etc. In addition to the Gospels note Acts 2:4; Phil. 2:15; Heb. 3:10. The evil in the men referred to is sometimes indicated by modifiers as is done in Matt. 16:4; 17:17; Mark 8:38; etc., but the context often does this. In the present connection the meaning of "this generation" is more than plain, for the Parousia is described in v. 27. "This generation" and πάντα extend that far.

Nor is "this generation" the human race or the Christians. But those who are on the right track and think of a class of moral men that continue to the end nevertheless are mistaken when they include all the wicked in "this generation." Why such a solemn assurance with "amen, I say to you," for a thing that is so obvious as that a race of wicked unbelievers and persecutors shall persist through the ages? "This generation" consists of *the type of Jews* that Jesus contended with during this Tuesday (19:45—20:47). He foretells the destruction of their nation (v. 20-24); and one might easily conclude that this would surely end the generation of Jews who were like the Pharisees and the Sadducees. But no; we are solemnly assured (and for this the assurance is in place) that this type of Jews will continue to the very Parousia. It has continued to this day. The voice of Jewish rejection of Christ is as loud and as vicious as ever: he is not the Messiah, not the Son of God! Here is Jesus' answer to those who expect a final national conversion of the Jews either with or without the millennium.

33) The statement about "my words" is general and should be left so. Jesus does not restrict it by saying "these my words," namely the ones that were just spoken in prophecy regarding the things that will occur between then and the end. Such a restriction would imply that other words of his would, indeed, pass away, i. e., as having no reality back of them and thus being soon forgotten. Because all the words of Jesus do not pass away, therefore also these about the end will stand unshaken as being utter verity and truth. This is made very striking by reference to the heaven and the earth, of whose passing away Jesus had just spoken. Sky and earth have stood so long, but even these will at last pass away completely. But not so the words of Jesus which stand forever; οὐ μή is again the strong negation of the future.

This mighty assurance follows hard upon what Jesus has just said about "this generation," and however much it includes, most certainly applies to the word about the endurance of this generation. This ought to make it plain that "this generation" cannot refer only to the generation that is then living, and that Jerusalem would be destroyed before it would be dead. Why such an assurance for an event that is so near at hand by a comparison with the heaven and the earth's passing away at the end of the world? Untenable also is the view that Jesus thought that the end of the world was to follow hard upon the fall of Jerusalem, and that "this generation" would see it. This makes Jesus a false prophet; all that he said about the end would thus have been proven false by many a century. This view forgets the "seasons of Gentiles" and Matt. 24:14.

Jesus says positively that the physical heaven and the earth "shall pass away." But this has been thought to mean: as little as heaven and earth shall pass away, so little, too, shall Jesus' words pass away. The one impossibility would be more possible than the other. This needs no refutation.

Another idea is that Jesus meant that heaven and earth will pass away, but not before all the words of Jesus are fulfilled. But this, too, is incorrect. Jesus says that his words will never pass away, they will stand eternally. And this means that every word of his will be fulfilled to the uttermost and thus stand forever because of this fulfillment. The fulfillment, once accomplished, cannot be wiped out or even altered. Thus Jesus' words stand forever.

Does the passing away of the heaven and the earth refer to their annihilation, sinking back into nothingness; or does it refer to a transformation into a different form of existence? We cannot obtain the answer from the verb παρελεύσονται which some think refers to annihilation. We consider together all the passages which deal with this subject; we dare not stop with one or two of them. The most decisive is Rom. 8:19-23 together with I Cor. 7:31 (only the σχῆμα, fashion of the world, shall pass away) and Rev. 21:1-5 (the divine heaven and the earth are to be united into one). So the physical heaven and the earth will be changed completely; when they are changed at the Parousia, we shall not recognize them. But the words of Jesus will never undergo even the slightest change in either meaning or form; every word of his is sealed with its absolute fulfillment.

34) **But take heed to yourselves lest perhaps your hearts be weighted down in drunken nausea and drunkenness and anxieties of life, and that day come upon you suddenly as a snare. For it shall come upon all those sitting on the face of all the earth. But be watching in every season, begging that you prevail to escape out of all these things about to occur and to stand before the Son of man.**

The admonition that the disciples need in view of what Jesus has revealed is now uttered in the plainest words. They are to take heed to themselves "lest perhaps," etc.; the admonition is stated in negative form. This is made positive in v. 36. They are not to be weighted down but are to be wide awake in watching and praying (v. 36). It is not the dulling effect that is stressed but the load and the weight upon the hearts which prevent them from attending to watching and to prayer.

Κραιπάλη is just the common term for *Katzenjammer*, the nausea and the headache that are caused by heavy drinking and nothing specifically medical (*contra* Zahn, Harnack, and Moffatt). Let us remember that the medics still use many common words in their common meanings just as they did in Luke's day. This *crapula* (Latin) goes together with "drunkenness" but brings out the vile effects that drag the drunkard down. In all the turmoils and the convulsions of the world, as already in all common distress, men resort to drink to drown their troubles. Others love debauchery of all kinds for its own sake. With these loads Jesus couples the "anxieties of life," distracting worries about the life we live here (the Greek has a handy adjective derived from βίος, which we cannot duplicate). Even disciples are liable to make their earthly affairs supreme, especially when the world becomes disturbed.

The weights that Jesus mentions are like samples of the things that drag the hearts down; they lead us to think of all else that might hurt us in the same way. For hearts that are weighted down thus that day is bound to come suddenly as a snare. The Greek uses the adjective αἰφνίδιος and makes it predicative to ἡμέρα whereas we use the adverb "suddenly." The A. V. connects "as a snare" with the next verse, but this would place γάρ too far back. Besides, "suddenly" is not strong enough to indicate the coming of that day upon those who are weighted down as is described. It will come upon them (the verb itself being used regarding a sudden confrontation) with sudden, deadly effect as when a bird or an animal is caught in a noose or a net. So the flood came upon those who were living in Noah's day, and fire and brimstone upon the cities of Sodom and Gomorrah (Matt. 24:36-39). The warning applies to all because the coming of that day impends constantly.

35) To say that this day will come upon all men on earth, and to offer this in explanation (γάρ) of its sudden arrival like a deadly snare for certain people, would be pointless; for who would think that this day comes only for some men on a part of the earth? It is this thought that has drawn "as a snare" to v. 35 (A. V.) and caused the R. V. to insert "so." Coupled with these constructions is the misunderstanding regarding

καθημένους which is translated "all them that dwell on the face of the earth" when "dwell" is another verb, and this verb means "to sit." The point lies in this sitting, resting content here on the face of the earth, caring nothing for anything higher. On all these over all the face of the earth that day shall come. And sitting thus, sunk in the things of earth, explains (γάρ) how all these shall be caught in a fatal snare.

36) We now hear the positive part of the admonition: constant wakefulness in the sense of alert watching (durative present imperative), and this "in every season," no matter how some of them may appear. All this watching is to be coupled with "begging," the ἵνα clause stating the substance of this supplicating. The A. V. translates the reading καταξιωθῆτε, "that ye may be accounted worthy" (it has the clause denote purpose), but the attested reading is κατισχύσητε, "that you prevail." No inner reasons militate against this reading, on the contrary, the inner reasons support this reading. We are to be strong enough to down (κατά) every temptation to grow slack in our watching and to give way to the worldly ways that are depicted in v. 34, strong enough with spiritual strength "to escape out of all these things about to occur," not to be caught suddenly in them as in a snare. They will occur, indeed, and affect also the disciples but not so as to overwhelm them because they are unprepared.

The second part of our prayer must be positive: "to stand before the Son of man" (v. 7), see 5:24. He who is man and more than man will come on that day, and to stand before him means to stand unharmed in his judgment, the Hebrew *qum* in the sense of *bestehen* over against falling under his adverse judgment. The form is passive: "be made to stand" and thus "to stand" by his grace. In Eph. 6:13 we have the active with reference to a victorious standing. Note that both "to escape" and "to stand" are aorists to indicate effective acts, actual escape and standing on that day.

All others will be caught as in a snare; those who watch and pray will have their prayers heard, will escape and stand with joy before the divine judge, the glorious Son of man.

37) Now the days he was engaged in teaching in the Temple; but the nights, going out, he kept lodging in the mount called Olive-place. And all the people rose early for him to hear him in the Temple.

Luke closes his account of the public ministry of Jesus with these summary statements. From Palm Sunday onward Jesus spent "the days" (accusative of extent of time) teaching in the Temple courts. That this included Wednesday is doubtful. The Gospels seem to stop their records on Tuesday after the great discourse concerning the fall of Jerusalem and the end of the world. One cannot, however, be certain on this point; we state only the impression the records make. When Luke speaks of "the nights" (the same accusative) as being spent on Olivet, this does not exclude Bethany which lay just over the ridge; Mark 11:11 and Matt. 21:17 state that Jesus went to Bethany at least on Sunday night. It seems probable that Jesus spent some nights in Gethsemane, but that is all we can say. We regard Ἐλαιῶν as a nominative as it is in 19:29, "Olive-place"; see R. 267.

38) All the pilgrim crowds kept rising early for him in order to get to the Temple courts at once and to miss nothing of his teaching there. Luke alone reports this interesting fact.

CHAPTER XXII

The Fifth Part

The Consummation, Chapters 22 to 24

1) **Now there was drawing near the Festival of the Unleavened Bread, called Passover. And the high priests and the scribes were seeking how to make away with him, for they were fearing the people.**

The festival was called τὰ ἄζυμα, "The Unleavened" (things), or as here, "The Festival of the Unleavened" (neuter plural, "bread" is added in the English only to round out the thought) because of the removal of all leaven from the homes for the seven days from the 14th to the 21st of Nisan, the 14th that year being a Thursday. Luke adds the other Jewish name "Passover," πάσχα, Hebrew *pesach*, which is derived from Jehovah's passing over Israel to shield it from the death angel. The tenses are descriptive imperfects and picture the time and the situation. Whether Luke is reckoning the nearness of the festival from Tuesday evening when Jesus spoke the great discourse recorded in 21:8-36 or has in mind an earlier time cannot be determined. He can scarcely have thought of Wednesday.

2) The common designation for the Sanhedrin names "the high priests and the scribes" (see 9:22). The supposition that the elders were not involved is untenable (Matt. 26:3 names the elders). The question they considered was not whether to make away with Jesus—they had long ago decided to do that—but *how* to make away with him; the article before the indirect question only makes plain that this question is the object of the verb. To make away with someone, ἀναιρέω,

means to murder him. In the present case judicial murder was planned and not assassination. The explanation with γάρ tells us why this "how" perplexed the Sanhedrin and made ways and means a problem. Because the pilgrim crowds constantly surrounded Jesus it was anything but safe to try to arrest him in public. Matt. 26:4, 5 tells us to what decision the Sanhedrin came, namely to use subtlety but to wait until the festival was over and the pilgrims had dispersed.

3) **Now Satan entered into Judas, called Iscariot, being of the number of the Twelve. And having gone, he spoke with the high priests and commanders how to betray him to them. And they rejoiced and made a bargain to give him money. And he agreed and began to seek a good opportunity to betray him to them away from a crowd.**

"Satan" would be a proper noun even without the article. This word designates the head of the infernal kingdom and not merely some demon as Zahn supposes. Luke's statement tallies with John 13:2. We see that this is not a case of common demoniacal possession. Satan himself makes Judas his tool by filling his mind with traitorous thoughts and moving his will to act on them. This is mental possession, giving Satan control of mind, heart, and will. "Satan entered into Judas" by no compulsion but as a welcome master who is received by a willing slave. This entrance was made gradually or by stages. Luke speaks of it in a summary way, but John 13:2, 27 reveal its stages. The devilishness of the betrayal of Jesus by Judas has always been recognized.

The introduction of the traitor is aways tragic: "being of the number of the Twelve," one of this sacred number, one who was raised so high by Christ, one who was destined for one of the apostolic thrones in heaven—and now one who not only lost all this grace and glory but reversed it to the absolute opposite: a tool of Satan, sold for thirty pieces of silver to the whole world's execration as one traitor beyond whom none in the whole world can go. See 6:16 on "Iscariot."

4) No one can say just when Judas offered himself for the damnable deed. It may have been as early as Saturday night after the Supper at Bethany, see the interpretation of Matt. 26:14. Whenever the time was, Judas conferred with no less personages than the high priests themselves, Caiaphas and some of his relatives in the Sanhedrin. These, it seems, had the executive control. Luke adds the στρατηγοί, the commanders of the Levitical Temple police. The probability is that Judas found that he could obtain an audience with the high priests only by first going to some officer of this police force who was on duty in the Temple. This officer took the traitor to the chief *strategos*, and such Temple officers were thus present when the deal was made. The proposition was in some way "to betray Jesus to them," τό before the indirect question as in v. 2. Judas proposed to do the betraying (aorist subjunctive), the manner of the act was as yet left undetermined.

5) It is Luke who tells us that these deadly foes of Jesus "rejoiced." Whereas they feared that the whole nation was being carried away by Jesus (John 11:48; 12:19), one of his own intimate followers is willing to sell him for a price (Matt. 26:15). It was almost too good to believe, a turn no one would have dared to predict. Luke passes over the dealing about the price. The bargain was, in fact, struck promptly. The aorist συνέθεντο means that the silver was paid then and there. Matt. 26:15 says that the money was weighed out to Judas (see the comment on the passage); Matthew also records the amount, 30 shekels or 60 denarii, about $10 (Zech. 11:12, 13). Judas would do nothing until he had the money paid down. He intended to run no risks in regard to getting his money later on. The priests were shrewd enough to bind the man by paying him at once; he might otherwise fail them. They ran

no risk whatsoever, for they had the power to arrest this man at any time. Judas returned to Jesus with the blood money in his bag.

6) Luke writes that "he agreed." He was fully satisfied and closed the bargain. All that was left was to find the favorable moment to consummate the betrayal. The infinitive is complementary to the noun (R. 1076), and τοῦ may or may not be added. "Away from a crowd" was, no doubt, a stipulation of the bargain which was absolutely necessary to the success of the plot.

7) **Now there came the day of the Unleavened Bread, in which it was necessary that the passover be slaughtered.**

This was the first day of the festival, compare v. 1 on "the unleavened" (things). This was Thursday, the 14th of Nisan, which was counted in with the other seven days and thus made eight. "The passover" signifies the lamb, it was named so from the festival (v. 1). The imperfect ἔδει refers to a past obligation that continues into the present, here one that is met, R. 887. The verb θύω, here the passive, is used to designate the slaughtering of this lamb in the Temple court of the priests on this Thursday afternoon.

8) **And he commissioned Peter and John, saying, Having gone, make ready for us the passover in order that we may eat.**

The point of this narrative in all the synoptists is the way in which Jesus directed the two disciples. All the disciples were, of course, concerned about celebrating the Passover. Mark 14:12 brings out that fact; yet this Passover was intended for Jesus in a special way, note "for thee" in Matt. 26:17. The question as to where their celebration was to be held was raised by the disciples, who, however, have no place to suggest. Jesus gives the necessary directions. He and the Twelve are, apparently, in Bethany, and it is early on

Thursday morning. Matthew does not need to tell his readers, as Mark does, that Jesus commissioned only two, for every reader of Jewish descent knew that only two men were allowed to bring the lamb into the Temple court. Luke alone tells us who they were. They receive the general order to get "the passover" ready so that all might eat it. In v. 1 this word denotes the festival, in v. 7 the lamb, and now the lamb and all else that was needed for this sacred feast.

9) **But they said to him, Where dost thou want that we prepare? And he said to them: Lo, you having entered into the city, there will meet you a man carrying a jar of water. Follow him into the house into which he goes, and you will say to the master of the house, The Teacher says to thee, Where is the guestroom, where I may eat the passover in company with my disciples? And he will show you a large upper room that has been tiled. There make ready. Now having gone, they found just as he had said to them; and they made ready the passover.**

The chief point in the entire transaction is "where" Jesus intends to celebrate this his final Passover. The subjunctive is deliberative in an indirect question and is left unchanged from the direct.

10) All the synoptists indicate that Jesus withheld the direct answer to this question. He told Peter and John that they would meet a man whom they could readily identify by the fact that he was carrying a jar of water, most likely on his head. This was a woman's task and was exceptional in the case of a man. The apostles were not to accost this man but were simply to follow him into whatever house he entered.

11) To "the house lord of that house" (pleonastic genitive) Jesus directs them to say that the Teacher is asking him through them where the κατάλυμα or guestroom is where he may eat the passover with his disciples. All they will need to say is "the Teacher." The

houseowner will know that this is Jesus; will know the two disciples and who the rest in the party are, in fact, will understand also what Jesus further directs his messengers to say about his time (season) being at hand (Matt. 26:18). This man is one of the friends of Jesus who is so ready to do him a service that all that Jesus needs to do is to send him word.

12) Jesus adds that this houseowner will show them a large, fine upper room, one that has a tiled floor and is unusual in this respect. The perfect participle has its present connotation. Mark 14:15 has a second participle, "in a state of readiness," which is added without a connective. This participle refers to the equipment of the room, tables, couches, etc. Our versions insert "and" in Mark, which is due to their misunderstanding of the first participle, the one that Luke, too, has, which does not mean "furnished" with rugs on the floor or with furniture as some think. The verb means "to spread" (note "to spread under" in 19:36) and here refers to the beauty of the floor which was covered with tile (so Luther, *gepflastert*, and Zahn, B.-P. 1237). The remarkable fact is that the room was still available. For we should remember that the host of pilgrims was so great that every available room that seated from ten to twenty persons would be taken for this Thursday when all must eat the passover, and room would be at a premium.

It goes without saying that we here have a duplicate of the incident recorded in 19:29, etc., the same use of the supernatural knowledge of Jesus in things that are necessary for his mission, and the same purpose to inspire faith and confidence in the disciples. But more must certainly be said. Judas was watching for a favorable opportunity to betray Jesus, and what better opportunity could he find than this Passover meal when Jesus would be alone with his disciples in the evening, and all the pilgrims who were eating their passover would be scattered in little groups? To prevent any move on the part of Judas, Jesus withholds all information that the latter might attempt to use, withholds it from all the disciples. Even Peter and John would not know until they reached the house, and they would be busy with the preparations that had been delegated to them and would not return to Jesus. When the time came, he would take the ten to the house, and not until then would Judas know the place—too late for him to do anything. Jesus thus made certain that he would celebrate this last and so important passover in perfect peace and security. And thus, too, he indicated to Judas that his plans for betrayal were blocked for the time being.

Some think that Jesus had talked over matters with this unnamed man in Jerusalem; the word that Jesus sends him shuts out that idea rather decisively. And also the surmise that Jesus quietly told Peter and John the man's name, and that the Twelve easily guessed who the man was without being told. Some think that the name was withheld only in the records in order to shield the man from Jewish molestation as late as the time when the Gospels were written. But Jesus must then have proceeded as he did for a reason that lay far beyond the moment; and this would be no reason at all, for the Twelve learned the man's name that very night, and many others must soon likewise have known it.

We cannot agree that Jesus and the Twelve had been in this man's house often, and that Jesus thus knew all about that large, tiled upper room. If that were true, Judas would have at once guessed the place, and all the precautions of Jesus would have been in vain. No; the tiling is mentioned as being something exceptional and entirely new to the Twelve. They saw that room for the first time that night. Zahn states that this was the house of Mark's father, who was still living; the house was later known as that of Mark's mother Mary and was used by the disciples during those years. The man with the jar on his head is supposed to be the youth Mark himself. Quite a combination is thus built up, but it does not rest on the facts that are stated in the narrative.

13) Peter and John found exactly what Jesus had foretold and made everything ready for the celebration.

14) **And when the hour came, he reclined at table and the apostles with him.**

This occurred at evening (Matthew and Mark) on Thursday; but with the appearance of the first star in the sky the Jewish Friday began. Luke at once puts us into the beautiful, secluded upper room and shows us the thirteen persons who were reclining at table for the Passover meal.

15) **And he said to them: With desire did I desire to eat this passover with you before I suffer. For I say to you that I will in no wise eat it till it shall be fulfilled in the kingdom of God.**

Luke reports only a few things that transpired in the upper room. Moreover, as he has so often disregarded the sequence of time in his preceding chapters and has neglected to mention either the time or the place, so he continues to do in his account of the Passover meal. We rely on the other evangelists for our sequences. The first thing that happened is what John 13:1-17 records; but v. 2, "supper being ended" (A. V.), should be corrected. At the beginning of the actual Passover meal Jesus told his disciples how strongly he had desired to eat this his final passover with them. "With desire did I desire" is regarded as a Hebraism (infinitive absolute) although the Greek, too, uses the cognate noun or participle for intensifying the verb (R. 531): "with great desire." The idea is untenable, however, that Jesus had not been certain that he would be able to eat this passover with the Twelve, that he had feared that his arrest, if not also his death, would be effected before this passover could be eaten. The statement that he greatly desired to eat it hints at no doubt whatever; the aorist shuts out that view.

The last phrase, "before I suffer," explains this strong desire. The thought is the same as it was in 12:50b; John 12:24, 27. The nearer the hour of suffering and death came for Jesus, the more he longed for it to come in order that the great work might be done and redemption be actually wrought. The two aorist infinitives are effective, not "to be eating" and "to be suffering" (present tenses), but "to accomplish the eating" and "the suffering."

16) In most instances γάρ does not state a reason but adds only some explanatory statement that aids in understanding what has just been said. So the solemn "I say to you" explains that the next passover that Jesus will eat with his disciples will be the heavenly one. It will occur when this earthly Passover "shall be fulfilled in the kingdom of God," when all that it prefigured about the Lamb of God that was slain for our sins and about our participation, through faith, in this sacrifice for our sins will reach its ultimate fulfillment in the kingdom of glory in heaven. So the passover that Jesus is now eating with his disciples is the last; the next will be celebrated in glory. Although we reject οὐκέτι before the two negative particles on textual grounds: "any more" (A. V.), "henceforth" (R. V.), it expresses what is meant: Jesus will eat this passover but no other until he eats the heavenly one. We have the usual strong double negative with the futuristic aorist subjunctive φάγω.

17) **And having received a cup, after having given thanks, he said: Take this and divide it unto yourselves, for I say to you that I will in no wise drink from now on from the fruit of the vine until the kingdom of God comes.**

We dismiss all the difficulty that has been raised regarding these verses, even to making radical alterations of the text when they were viewed as being part of the institution of the Lord's Supper. Matt. 26:29 should have barred out these ideas. The similarity of the "until" clause found in v. 19 to the one that is used in v. 16 should have done the same. Luke is combining statements that contain the same general thought, that this is the last Passover on earth for Jesus until he partakes of the fulfillment of it in heaven (v. 15, 16), and that this is the last wine that he will drink until he drinks it new in heaven (v. 17, 18). The fact that Jesus did not utter both statements successively makes no difference to Luke. From Matt. 26:29 and Mark 14:25 we see that the second was uttered at the end of the meal, after the institution of the Lord's Supper.

Compare our comments on Matt. 26:21 for an account of the ten formal stages of the Passover meal. In the tenth stage the second part of the *hallel* was sung, the fourth cup was passed, sometimes a fifth, which was followed by the conclusion of the *hallel*. It was this fourth or fifth cup to which Luke refers. Someone handed it to Jesus, and he received it and pronounced a benediction over it. It is not necessary to assume that a servant was present, and we need no assurance that it was not Mark or Mark's father (see v. 12). Jesus and the Twelve were entirely alone. One of the disciples replenished the cup each time this became necessary. The same was true with regard to the lamb, the bread, and the *chassoreth,* which were placed on the table by the disciples themselves as they were needed. If a servant or the head of the house had been present he would have attended to the washing of the feet after Jesus and the ten had walked from Bethany. The owner of the house, a son of his, the servants would themselves be eating their passover in groups that were large enough to consume a lamb.

The blessing spoken by Jesus must have been the one that was customarily used in connection with the last cup. The question is asked as to whether

Jesus himself partook of this final cup (some think that it was the very first) before he told the disciples to divide it among themselves. This needed not to be mentioned, for the person who acted as the housefather at the Passover always drank first. Jesus certainly partook of the entire Passover in the way that was customary among the Jews at this time, which included drinking of the ceremonial cups each time they were passed. The claim that Jesus drank no wine at all at this Passover because it was not required in the original Mosaic ritual is untenable. How could he do this and not only tell his disciples to drink, as he surely does here, but even use some of this Passover wine in the Lord's Supper?

18) Again, as in v. 16, we have the solemn assurance that he will in no wise drink again of wine until the kingdom of glory at the end of the world has come (ἔλθῃ, aorist, punctiliar). He will die this very day (Friday). If this was sad, the "until" clause points to the glorious drinking at the consummation of the kingdom. Πίω is the futuristic aorist subjunctive like φάγω in v. 16. The argument, that is starting already in connection with v. 16, as to whether this glorious eating and drinking will be a sublimated actual Passover, whether it will be identical with the feasting that is mentioned in v. 30; 13:29, with the marriage supper of the Lamb, Rev. 19:9, is useless because all the heavenly joys are described in figurative language in the Scriptures.

The efforts that are put forth to read wine out of this account are unavailing. Because οἶνος, the word for "wine," does not occur, the presence of wine is at least gravely questioned, which means practically denied. Luke's "the fruit of the vine," *pheri hagiphen*, the lovely liturgical term for the wine that was used in the Passover ritual, which Matthew makes even more specific by writing "*this* fruit of the vine," the one that was regularly used in the Passover and was used at this

Passover by Jesus, is misunderstood by these commentators, for they assert that grape juice fits this phrase better than does wine—although such a thing as grape juice was an impossibility in April in the Holy Land of Christ's time. It could be had only when grapes were freshly pressed out, before the juice started to ferment in an hour or two.

Vastly more important is the thought that Jesus will not only die today, but that by his dying all the Jewish Passovers have served their purpose and are really at an end. For which reason Jesus also this night instituted the Sacrament of the New Testament which is to be used until the time when the kingdom of God comes. The two references to the kingdom that occur in these verses have been used to argue for chiliasm, and "the fruit of the vine" also affords an opportunity to insert the chiliastic dream of Papias concerning the miraculous vine that grows endlessly and produces enormous clusters of grapes.

19) And having taken bread, having given thanks, he broke it and gave it to them, saying: This is my body, that in the act of being given for you. This keep doing for my own remembrance. And the cup likewise after dining, saying, This cup the new covenant in my blood, that in the act of being poured out for you.

A glance at the textual authority for the words found in v. 19: "that in the act," etc., and in v. 20: "that in the act," etc., makes one wonder why the R. V. added its marginal note. But one is surprised at Zahn who uses this textual omission as a peg on which to hang arguments about Theophilus' still not being in the church, the esoteric nature of the Sacrament, and the pagan slanders regarding this Sacrament, as if such arguments were sufficient to remove from Luke's text, not only these two participial modifiers, but also the remainder of v. 19 and the whole of v. 20, and to claim that Luke never pretended to give an account of the Sacrament. Were it not because of the name of the man who revises the text thus, the matter would be unworthy of notice.

From Matthew and from Mark we note that the Supper was instituted at the close of that part of the Passover when all were freely eating the Passover food. No one was to be stinted. So at the time when the housefather would have gone on to the next ceremonial act, the eating of the last morsel of the lamb, and thereby stopped all further eating, Jesus proceeded to do something that was entirely new. The new act is also an eating and a drinking, but only of the bread and the wine, and only by the disciples; it also has its thanksgivings, but these and the added words refer directly to Christ's sacrificial body and blood and their saving effect. The disciples understood from the first word onward.

Jesus first "took bread," the participle indicating that this is only a preliminary act. Note that this participle is an aorist, and that all the participles (save, of course, the two λέγων) and the main verbs that refer to the acts of Jesus are aorists, all being historical and stating so many facts. The entire account is so simple and so lucid in its wording that even a grammar the size of Robertson's has hardly anything to note. In its margin the R. V. translates ἄρτος "loaf." But no loaves in our sense of the word could be baked of unleavened dough. This *artos* was a thin sheet of unleavened bread, pieces of which were broken off for the purpose of eating. The author saw these thin sheets of bread baked on a hot plate in Syria; the woman stacked them up and gave us one that was still hot, which we broke and divided among our party in the ancient way—how else could we have eaten it properly?

The second act is still preliminary, hence an aorist participle is again used, εὐχαριστήσας, "having given thanks." Matthew and Mark have εὐλογήσας, "having blessed," but they use the other word regarding the wine, which shows that the two words denote the same thing. None of the four accounts of the Supper has preserved the words of thanksgiving that Jesus spoke over the bread and the wine. We shall not go astray when we say that these words referred to the bread (and the wine) that was in Jesus' hands and to the heavenly gift that the respective element was to convey. This blessing thus enlightened the disciples and prepared them for the proper reception of the bread and of what it conveyed (of the wine likewise), for they were to receive both intelligently and were not to wonder what Jesus was trying to convey to them. All we can say about these words is that, after they were once spoken by Jesus, they remain efficacious for all time wherever the Sacrament is celebrated. Because of their very nature they could not be efficaciously repeated, and that seems to be the reason the power that guided the holy writers had them omit these words from their records.

The acts of breaking and giving go together in the sense of distributing. No symbolism attaches to the breaking, for "a bone of him shall not be broken," John 19:36. The bread was broken merely for the purpose of being eaten. "Bread is an inanimate thing: how can breaking it be like the putting of a human being to death? Breaking bread is the very symbol of quietness and peace, who would dream of it as an appropriate symbol of the most cruel and ignominious death? Bread is the representative food, and, used in metaphor, is the symbol of spiritual and supernatural food. The breaking of bread is the means of giving it as food, and as a symbol, the symbol of giving and taking a higher food. No one would dream of the breaking of bread as the symbol of killing a human body; and if so extraordinary a symbolic use of it were made, it would require the most explicit statement on the part of the person so using it, that such was his intent; and when he had made it, the world would be amazed at so lame a figure." Krauth, *Conservative Reformation*, 723. In regard to the wine we have no counterpart to the breaking of the bread, which shows that the breaking was only incidental for the purpose of distribution.

No man is able to say just how Jesus "gave to them." Nor is the point vital, just so that each received. When we now adopt a mode of distributing we cannot say that *any* mode will do, for various modes that are used at present indicate wrong views of the very nature of the Sacrament and in regard to those who are entitled to receive it. Our mode must harmonize with the essentials of the Sacrament in every way and also with the spirit of its original institution. Luke leaves out "Take, eat," as being included in the act of giving the bread.

And Jesus now states what he is really giving them: Τοῦτό ἐστι τὸ σῶμά μου, "This is my body." Matthew and Mark report no more, for these few words, indeed, contain the essential fact. But Luke has the addition with a separate article like an apposition and a climax (R. 776): "that in the act of being given for you;" the present participle which is a description of what body Jesus had in mind, namely his own actual body that was about to be sacrificed on the cross. Paul adds to body "which is for you," i. e., in sacrifice. We should note that τοῦτο is neuter and hence cannot grammatically or in thought refer to ἄρτος, which is masculine. The English "this" and "bread" hide this distinction in gender, yet no real student will ignore it. "This" means "this bread which I have now consecrated by blessing and thanksgiving"; or more tersely: "this that I now give to you"; *hoc quod vos sumere jubeo.* "It is no longer mere bread of the oven but bread of flesh, or bread of body, that is, bread which is sacramentally one with Christ's body." Luther.

Much has been written about ἐστί, which is merely the copula that connects the subject and the predicate. Jesus spoke in Aramaic and used no copula in that language, for he needed none; but this does not remove or alter in the least the inspired ἐστί in the Greek records. It is impossible to have it mean "represents" as the efforts of Zwingli have conclusively shown.

"My body" means exactly what these words say: "in truth and reality my body." Luke's and Paul's modifiers say this a second time. The ὑπὲρ ὑμῶν διδόμενον cannot refer to anything but the true body, for no symbol of the body, no bread, nothing that was figurative in any sense was this day being given for our redemption upon the cross. The participle is exact, the act of giving had begun, Jesus was already betrayed.

In a large number of instances the preposition ὑπέρ, "in behalf of," "for" or "for the benefit of," conveys the idea of substitution, "instead of." See Robertson, *The Minister and his Greek New Testament*, the entire chapter on the use of ὑπέρ in the papyri. Mark uses this preposition regarding the blood. It is only the rationalizing question as to *how* the Lord could give his disciples his true and real body by means of bread when that body stood right before their eyes that has caused the trouble in regard to these exceedingly simple words. Some answer this "how" by assuming a transubstantiation of the bread into the body so that Jesus does not give bread at all but only his body. Others answer this "how" by declaring it impossible for Jesus to give his body, he gives only bread, this as a symbol of his body.

We refuse to answer the question as to the *how* because the Lord has completely withheld the answer. We could probably not understand the answer because the giving of Christ's body in the Sacrament is a divine act of omnipotence and grace that goes beyond all mortal comprehension. The Lord declares *the fact*: "This is my body," and we take him at his word. He knows the mystery of this giving; we do not. Any rationalizing objection that this involves a gross, carnal, Capernaitic eating of the raw flesh is unconvincing; the first disciples, who had the body of Christ's humiliation before their very eyes when Christ's bodily hand gave them the gift of his sacrificial body, never dreamed of such an eating. "My body" does not mean "a piece of my body."

Luke and Paul preserved the words which ordered the disciples to repeat this sacrament: "this be doing for my own remembrance." It would be unfair to play Matthew and Mark against Luke and Paul on this point; or to call what Luke and Paul have added beyond Matthew and Mark later liturgical additions by the church. This view breaks down when it comes to the blood. It would leave only the commands "this be doing," etc., which are not liturgical. The four records are four historical testimonies, and any point in any record that is not found in the rest is only so much valuable addition. In the case of Matthew and Mark the permanency lies in the very nature of the sacrament, for not the Twelve alone but all disciples of all time were to be partakers of Christ's body and blood for the assurance of their salvation. They were right in this because Jesus ordered the repetition and by it established the institution of the sacrament.

"This" be doing refers to what they saw and heard from Jesus. In so sacred a rite the church has kept close to what the inspired records present. As by his thanksgiving and his blessing Jesus separated the bread and the wine that are used in the sacrament from all other bread and wine, so we, too, do by the act of consecrating the elements that are to be used. We cannot repeat the thanksgiving that was pronounced by Jesus, which is withheld from us because, after it was once pronounced by him, it is efficacious for all time. So we use the words of the sacred records themselves since they, more and better than any other words we could invent, convey our intent regarding the bread and the wine we intend to set aside for the holy use. To the words of the institution the church adds the Lord's Prayer as also coming from Jesus' own lips and as aiding in consecrating and setting aside for the sacramental use the specific bread and wine to be used. To omit the consecration would leave the bread and the wine and its eating and drinking an ordinary act. The mere intention of the pastor and the people cannot suffice, for if the intention is truly present it would express itself in the consecration, the more so since the sacrament is a public act. Nothing can be left in doubt in so sacred an act that is intended for the church as a whole, and nothing of a doubtful nature can be allowed.

First the consecration, then the distribution so that all may eat and drink. Matthew and Mark have the word "all." But this includes only all who are entitled to the sacrament, which means those who believe and confess (by word and by act) that they are true disciples of Jesus and truly believe all that Jesus says and gives in the sacrament, the worthy, I Cor. 11:28, 29. In the phrase "for my own remembrance" the strong possessive pronoun is used in an objective sense (R. 685). The purpose ($εἰς$) of the remembering is to recall Jesus, but not only in a general way: he is to be recalled by all that this sacrament includes for every communicant.

20) Matthew and Mark report the consecration of the cup exactly as they do the consecration of the bread. Luke, like Paul, summarizes with "likewise." He also uses the article: "the cup." Whether a different cup was used for each of the four or five drinkings during the Passover, or whether only one cup was refilled as it was needed, is uncertain and of no moment. The point is that Jesus instituted the sacrament with a common cup that was used for all the disciples. Any change in what Jesus did, which has back of it the idea that he would not do the same thing today for sanitary or for esthetic reasons, casts a reflection on Jesus which is too grave to be allowed when he is giv-

ing us his sacrificial blood to drink. "Cup" may mean the empty vessel, the filled vessel, or only the contents of the vessel; in each case the context decides which sense is to be preferred. The contents are here referred to, and τοῦτο refers to the consecrated contents alone.

Much has been made of the phrase μετὰ τὸ δειπνῆσαι, "after the dining." The sacrament has even been divided into two distinct acts. The body was given first, then there followed further Passover eating, finally, at the end, the blood was given. The phrase intends simply to state that this sacramental cup has nothing to do with the cup and the drinking of the Passover ceremonial. This was an entirely different cup, one that was passed after the Passover dining had been concluded. A similar statement did not need to be made regarding the bread, for this was never passed around during the Passover in a ceremonial way.

The cup contained wine that was mixed with water. No comment was needed on this subject until the advocates of prohibition sought to eliminate wine from the sacrament and from its original institution. Matthew's specific expression *"this* fruit of the vine," the one that was regularly used in the Jewish Passover, shuts out anything but actual wine and blocks all attempts to introduce grape juice, raisin tea, or diluted grape syrup. The matter is of utmost importance and is beyond our powers to alter. To alter a testament is to invalidate the document. Hence the use of any other liquid than actual wine renders the sacrament invalid so that it ceases to be the sacrament; and any declaration that it *is* the sacrament nonetheless is unconvincing.

Moreover, wine means grape wine and not wine that is made from berries or anything else; it must be "this fruit of the vine." On all these questions, in so grave a matter as that of Christ's body and blood and the most intimate communion of the whole adult membership of the church with Christ, anything and everything that would cause even a doubt as to the genuineness of the sacrament must be kept out. Christ's testament stands as he made it; when men alter it today, neither they nor anybody else is able to assure us that it is still the original testament.

The sense is the same when Matthew and Mark write: "This is my blood, that of the new covenant, etc., and Luke: "This cup (contents) is the new covenant in my blood," etc. What has been said regarding the body applies equally to the blood. But they are given separately, first one, then the other, for the blood flows out and separates from the body in the sacrifice, the blood is shed. Note the article in the two predicates: "the blood of mine," and "the new covenant," which makes these predicates identical and interchangeable with the subjects, R. 768, a point that is not to be overlooked.

Monographs have been written on the term $\delta\iota\alpha\theta\acute{\eta}\kappa\eta$ in connection with the Hebrew $b^e rith$. We note that the translators of our versions waver, the A. V. has "testament" in our passage, the R. V. "covenant" with "testament" in the margin. Compare the full treatment in C.-K. 1062. We offer the sum of the matter. The Old Testament dealt with the promises God had given to his chosen people. God placed himself in "covenant" relation to Israel. The heart of this revelation, like the promises and the gifts of God to Israel, is wholly one-sided. It is always God's covenant, not Israel's; and it is never a mutual agreement. This covenant, indeed, obligates Israel, and Israel assumes these obligations, but the covenant itself emanates entirely from God. The LXX translates $b^e rith$, "covenant," with $\delta\iota\alpha\theta\acute{\eta}\kappa\eta$, "testament," since this term has the strongest one-sided connotation. A will or testament emanates only from the testator. Christ brought the fulfillment of the Old Testament promises. The result of this was that God's people now have the inheritance and are God's heirs, joint-heirs of Christ, Rom. 8:17. It is thus that in the New Testament $b^e rith$ becomes διαθήκη, "will and testament" by which God bequeathes to us the blessings Christ has brought.

Both the old $b^e rith$ or covenant and the testament of Christ's fulfillment were connected with blood. The former could be sealed with the blood of animal sacrifice: "Behold the blood of the covenant, which the Lord hath made with you concerning all these words," Exod. 24:4-8. This blood typified and promised the blood of Christ by which we inherit, through Christ's death, all that his blood has purchased and won for us. The old covenant could be written in animal blood because it consisted of promise; the new testament could be written only in the blood of the Son of God because it conveys the complete fulfillment of the promise, the actual purchase of our redemption.

The word "blood" is a reference not merely to "death" since a specific death, namely a sacrificial death, is here involved. No other type of death could establish the testament. Hence we have the crowning modification: "that in the act of being poured out for you." The present participle has the same sense as the one used in v. 19. Jesus means that this pouring out of his sacrificial blood has now begun. And he has, indeed, truly entered upon his sacrifice. So body and blood appear separately in the sacrament, yet they appear together, side by side. There is no sacrificial body without sacrificial blood and vice versa. The Scriptures never speak of the *glorified* body or the *glorified* blood. The miracle of the sacrament is not that Christ makes us partakers of his *glorified* body and blood but of the body *given* and of the blood *shed* for us on the cross. The sacrament draws on Calvary and not on heaven. We have it as it was instituted the night in which Jesus was betrayed and not on Easter Day.

21) **Nevertheless, lo, the hand of him betraying me with me on the table! Because the Son of man**

goes according to what has been determined. Nevertheless, woe to that man through whom he is being betrayed! And they began to search with themselves which then of them was he about to perpetrate this thing.

Matt. 26:21-25; Mark 14:18-21; John 13:18-30 make it certain that Jesus exposed the traitor *before* he instituted the Holy Supper, and John states that Judas left at once. Luke speaks of the traitor *after* the Supper and uses statements that are taken from the account of his exposure as this is found in the other evangelists. But that is all he does, he does not narrate the exposure. Another point to be observed is that Luke cannot mean that v. 21 was spoken immediately after the institution of the Supper. The opinion cannot, therefore, be held that Judas, too, received the Supper; nor the other opinion that Luke intends to correct Matthew and Mark as to the time of the exposure of Judas, or that Luke did not know when the exposure took place. We have seen that Luke disregards the connection of time in a number of narratives and arranges his material according to the contents of the sections involved. We have seen this in v. 15, 16 where he refers to the opening of the Passover which is at once followed by v. 17, 18, its close, and there is nothing to indicate the great interval between the events. We now have the same thing with regard to these excerpts from the exposure of Judas. We shall see the same thing in v. 24, etc., which also precedes the Supper.

Some would begin a paragraph with v. 21 because they think that the exposure of the traitor brought on the strife on the part of the rest about who of them was the greatest. Such a connection is, however, not at all obvious. Luke adds the words about the traitor to those of the Supper because they show how Jesus will be brought to his sacrificial death. Jesus' body will be given, his blood shed in death. When Jesus said this, as his exposure of the traitor had already shown, he knew that it would be accomplished through the foul deed of Judas.

Πλήν always contrasts (R. 1187); it does so here. Since Luke has told us only about the bargain made by Judas (v. 3-6) and has now written the words of Jesus about his body and his blood being given and shed he conveys to us the full knowledge with which Jesus spoke as he did. When he reclined for the Passover Jesus knew that the traitor's hand was on the table with him. The words are an exclamation (we supply no "is"). The present participle describes Judas as being now engaged in the betrayal, which was true ever since the deal he made in v. 3-6.

Jesus characterizes Judas as a second Ahitophel, the man who turned traitor to David and ended by hanging himself. He is the full prototype of Judas; and it ought to be noted that this is all we have in the Old Testament regarding Judas—we lack even a single prophecy. II Sam. 16:15-17, 23; Ps. 41:9 (John 13:18); Ps. 55:12-14. This was the Passover of Jesus, the Twelve were here at his invitation, not he at theirs. Jesus shows how despicable, how utterly base the action of Judas was in which he was now engaged. The word that was spoken before the whole company had to strike the conscience of Judas with fearful force. He who could resist impacts such as this one was beyond hope.

22) Μέν and the following πλήν contrast, but the former is not "truly" (A. V.) and can hardly be rendered into English. Why is it that the awful thing, that as Ahitophel sat at David's table while he was betraying the hand that fed him, should now happen to David's antitype Jesus? "Because the Son of man goes according to what has been determined." Acts 2:23. This thing did not happen merely by chance; nor was Jesus the prey of Judas who was helpless in the hands of the traitor. He who is man and yet more than man (see 5:24) goes (to his death) according to

God's own determination. The idea is not that God determined the betrayal by Judas—that was the traitor's own act; God determined that his Son should not deliver himself from that betrayal (Matt. 26:54) because God desired our salvation through the sacrifice of his Son.

"Nevertheless," although Jesus was to die thus, "woe to that man through whom he is being betrayed!" Luke does not add that it were better if he had never been born, Matt. 26:24. Judas is fully responsible for what he is doing. He is willingly letting Satan rule his heart (v. 3). Not only this, by all his efforts to reach the heart of Judas Jesus is trying to save him from his terrible deed. His resistance to these efforts raises his guilt to the highest degree. Jesus could have been delivered into the hands of the Sanhedrin without the intervention of Judas. Why must he, one of the sacred Twelve, make himself the devil's tool? Διά expresses the medium or tool, not the agent, who was Satan. The "woe" is full of pain and deepest grief but points to Judas' guilt.

23) All that Luke adds is the disturbance that occurred among the eleven who could not believe their ears, each being afraid of himself and so searching which one of them "then" (since Jesus spoke so plainly and positively) was about to commit this thing; πράσσειν is used in an evil sense, "to perpetrate," and the optative is due to the indirect discourse.

24) Moreover, there occurred also a strife among them as to which of them was accounted to be greater.

Luke alone has preserved this incident. The same question had arisen before, in 9:46, etc., compare Matt. 18:1-5; Mark 9:34-37. There is some dispute as to where to place this incident in the history of the evening, and as to what caused this question regarding rank to be raised. Knowing that Luke so often disregards the sequence of time, we shall not follow those who think that because Luke places this incident after the account of the Lord's Supper it must have occurred after the Supper.

The difficulty is to find anything that resembles a reasonable place for such a strife at the end of the stay in the upper room. But we do find a place for it at the beginning. It occurred when Jesus arrived in the upper room. Someone had to volunteer to wash the feet of the company before the Passover meal began. Custom required that service for all who entered a house, especially to dine, and certainly to dine as this company now proposed to dine; compare 7:44. There was, however, no servant for the task and no house lord to perform it in place of the servant. These persons were themselves engaged in celebrating the Passover elsewhere in other groups. Who, then, of the disciples was ready to volunteer? Water, a basin, and towels were there in readiness, having been provided by the owner of the house (John 13:4, 5). No one volunteered. It was then that the dispute arose. Each disciple thought himself too good, too great, to stoop beneath all the rest. Jesus stepped in and washed their feet and also his own and shamed them all, John 13:4.

This is better than to assume that the strife arose because of the placing of the disciples at table, because John and not Peter reclined next to Jesus, because John had been invited to this place by Jesus and was thus honored above the rest, and because all of them, like the Pharisees, sought the foremost places. They had dined together so often before this time that we may well assume that they had their fixed order of places and adhered to it now, that, as always, John was next to Jesus. Then, too, after they had reclined, the Passover itself began and left no room for this strife. They started it before they reclined, before their feet were washed. The article before the indirect question is like that found in v. 4 and 23 (R. 739). The idea in δοκεῖ is that of general estimate, not "which one appears to be greater," but "which one ranks as being greater," i. e., greater than the rest. The Greek uses the comparative whereas we should prefer the superlative.

25) But he said to them: The kings of the Gentiles lord it over them, and those exercising authority over them are called benefactors. But you not so! On the contrary, the greater among you let him be as the younger; and the one leading as the one ministering. For who is greater, the one reclining or the one ministering? Is it not the one reclining? But I myself in your midst am as the one ministering!

Jesus practically repeats what he had said on this point a few days previously (Matt. 20:25-28). He simply had to repeat it when he saw how slow the disciples were to learn. Yet the repetition is now re-enforced in a peculiar and a most effective way. The kings of the pagan nations find their greatness in lording it over their people, acting as supreme lords with all the people being beneath them. And when they exercise their authority over them as kings they also assume great titles such as εὐεργέτης or σωτήρ in proof of their boasted greatness. "They are called" does not mean that their people voluntarily and out of gratitude add such titles to the names of their kings, but that these kings are called thus because they want to appear to be and to be regarded as being so great.

26) That is the pagan way. Jesus puts a quietus on it as far as his disciples are concerned: "But you not so!" We insert no verb; why weaken the prohibition? Their principle of greatness is the absolute reverse: "on the contrary," ἀλλά after a negative. "The greater let him be as the younger," who, because of his youth, feels that he must stand back. Jesus means that any disciple who is truly spiritually great will always show his greatness, not by putting himself above others in lordly fashion, but by putting himself

below others like an undistinguished young man. This is certainly not to be done in a hypocritical fashion but in all sincerity and humility.

Jesus repeats this in other words and makes the matter clearer: "the one leading (let him be) as the one ministering." The one who is really chief in the sense that the others gladly follow him and regard him as their leader is in all his leading to act as one who is rendering free, voluntary, glad service and ministration to others. He is to lead as a *diakonos*, one who offers and performs a voluntary task; he will then be chief indeed. Jesus used the same word in Matt. 20:26, but in v. 27 he advanced even to *doulos* or slave. Alas, men have often followed the pagan way of greatness in the church! They thus lost the very thing they sought. For the reverse of these statements of Jesus is also true.

27) Jesus takes an illustration from the very situation that obtained at the Passover when every disciple feared that he might lower himself if he acted as a servant for the others in washing their feet and cleansing their sandals. This is frequently the force of γάρ, "for example." Certainly, the person who is reclining at table is regarded as being greater than the one who waits upon him, attends to his feet, waits at table, etc. That is the worldly estimate regarding the two. But see: "I myself among you am he that is serving," I, whom you rightly call your divine Lord and Master, I have washed your feet as your humblest servant, John 13:14, 15. In this there lay the very greatness of Jesus. Nor was this such a great humiliation for Jesus, who would in a few hours stoop beneath the shame of the cross and the most ignominious death, Phil. 2:8. If it is objected that all this that is recorded in Luke could not be understood because he did not narrate the foot washing, it should be remembered that Luke often indicates that he has a knowledge of things which he himself does not record. Moreover, after noting

12:37 any observant reader would fully understand these comparisons of Jesus.

28) **But you are they that have remained through with me in my temptations. And I on my part am assigning to you, even as my Father did assign to me, a kingdom, that you may eat and drink at my table in my kingdom and may sit on thrones judging the twelve tribes of Israel.**

Here greatness in humiliation and self-abasement; there greatness in exaltation and glory. Jesus acknowledges the faithfulness of his disciples. We already know the exception he made (v. 21-25; John 13:10, 11). They have continued on through (διά in the verb) with Jesus in all his temptations, i. e., the tests that were brought upon him by opposition and hatred of all kinds. "You," emphatic, in contrast with others who turned away, John 6:66-69.

29) The emphatic ἐγώ, "I on my part," places Jesus over against the emphatic "you" occurring in v. 28: *You* held out, and *I* now appoint. The verb is used with reference to testamentary appointment, but not so here where it is used with the disciples as well as with Jesus as the object; "appoint" is enough. Jesus is entering his passion but here, on its very threshold, performs an act of divine majesty which is exactly like the one the Father had performed for him when he appointed Jesus the everlasting King (1:32, 33). "A kingdom" is to be construed with both of the preceding verbs. The word always means "royal rule" and then secondarily also the domain in which it is exercised. The stress is sometimes on the former as is the case here; but in v. 30 "in my kingdom" includes also the domain.

30) What this appointment includes, namely the highest exaltation, is added by the subfinal, appositional ἵνα clause. The disciples shall dine at Jesus' royal table (v. 16 and 18); note all the passages which describe heaven as a magnificent feast. As kings who

have been appointed such by him they shall dine together with the King. We need not hesitate a moment about making the future καθίσεσθε (some texts have the subjunctive) depend on ἵνα as continuing this appositional clause. We need not begin a separate sentence. Dining as kings with the King, the apostles shall then also rule with him as kings as has already been promised in Matt. 19:28.

Jesus does not say on "twelve" thrones because of Judas—significant omission; but he does say "the twelve tribes of Israel" because the place of Judas is to be filled by another—significant retention. But have ten tribes not been lost and been absorbed among the Gentiles after having been carried away by the Assyrians? The only Jews we now know are the descendants of Judah and of Benjamin. All is plain when we do not restrict the apostolic judging to the Jews. They shall judge the present Jews and the lost ten tribes who were absorbed among the Gentiles by judging all the Gentiles. And this supreme royal judging shall be accomplished by their inspired Word. The apostles are now in heavenly blessedness (Matt. 8:11) with Abraham, etc.; and the Word of Christ himself will judge all men at the last day, John 12:48b. All judging will be ended after the judgment at the last day.

31) The Western class of manuscripts, which the A. V. follows, make a break here and insert: "Now the Lord said." We should no longer question the fact that Jesus warned Peter twice, once in the upper room as John 13:36-38 fully establishes, and again on the way out to Gethsemane as Matt. 26:30-36 and Mark 14:26-32 also fully establish. Luke records a part of the warning that was given in the upper room. By comparing Luke with John we see that Peter's assurance and Jesus' word about the cock belong together, but that John does not indicate how his words fit in with those of Luke; he expects us to know what Luke has written.

Simon, Simon, lo, Satan did ask to have you to sift as the wheat, but I myself begged concerning thee lest thy faith eclipse. And thou, once having turned, make thy brethren firm.

The doubling of the address expresses deep solicitude; it is like the doubling in "Martha, Martha," "Jerusalem, Jerusalem," and in David's heartbroken cry: "O Absalom, my son, my son!" The emotion differs in each case but is deep in all of them. Whereas "Simon" was the name that was commonly used to designate him, in the present instance it is the proper term, not "Peter, Peter!" which would apply to the rocklike nature of the apostle, which was so lacking in him this night. Jesus addresses only Simon although what he says applies to ὑμᾶς, "you," to all the eleven. We see why Jesus does this. In the first place, the others are present and hear that they are all involved; in the second place, περὶ σοῦ, "concerning thee," follows and shows that Simon was involved in a special way —we know that this was due to his denial of Jesus, regarding which Jesus also warns him in v. 34 before them all.

"Satan did ask to have you," etc., draws back the curtain and in a startling way reveals who was back of the ordeal through which the eleven would pass this night. The verb means *ausbitten* but in the sinister sense of *ausgeliefert verlangen* and intends to allude to Job 1, Satan's request to try out Job. Satan is not free to assail us at will and with what power he pleases. Satan may try us out only by God's permission and to the extent of that permission—a mighty comfort for us all. God is faithful in all our temptations and ever makes a way of escape, I Cor. 10:13. The exposure which Jesus makes of Satan's intent is to aid Simon and the eleven as all the warnings of Jesus do. Although they will be struck down by Satan's assault, their escape and recovery are already planned, and Jesus is taking the first steps in that plan.

The infinitive with τοῦ states the object of Satan's asking: "to sift (you) as the wheat." Satan did not, of course, use this figure; his request was made with the thought that the disciples would not be wheat but only strawy stuff that would remain in the sieve to be burned. This figure belongs to Jesus who uses it to illustrate what the coming ordeal is to be for the disciples. Wheat must be sifted, wheat cannot escape sifting. It must be cleaned because of its value.

Yet this simple simile of Jesus should not be made an allegory with a number of points of comparison. There is really only one *tertium comparationis* or point of comparison, namely the violent and continuous shaking of the sieve to cause all the sound, solid wheat to fall through on the pile of wheat below while all the shaking leaves the strawy and chaffy stuff in the sieve. So the disciples were with God's own permission to be put through the severest trials to see whether they, indeed, had faith or not. When Jesus returned to this subject on the way out to Gethsemane, he used another figure, that of smiting the shepherd and scattering the sheep, which pictures the same painful experience, Matt. 26:31.

32) It was Simon, impetuous and headstrong Simon, who would get into the greatest danger by his own fault. That is why Jesus addresses him and lets the others only hear. And that is why Jesus begged in supplication for him personally lest his faith totally eclipse (active aorist subjunctive), utterly fail and go out. If the question is asked as to why Jesus did not pray equally for the rest, we see in John 17 that he did pray for them, but the story of Peter's denial shows that he was far worse than the others. Why did Peter need the warning given in v. 34, he and not the rest? For the same reason that he needed the personal and individual intercession which the rest did not need equally with him. The aorist "I did beg" implies that Jesus' supplication was not in vain. It was God's will

that Simon, too, be sifted like the rest, but it was not his will that Simon should disobey Jesus' warning. It was this sin of Simon's which caused the great Advocate to intercede for him.

But we should not get the idea that Jesus' prayer was heard by God in an absolute or arbitrary way. God and Jesus used the means that proved effective in Simon's case. The warning about the cock's crowing after the threefold denial was such a means. A point is usually brought out by reference to Judas. Would he not have repented as Simon did if Jesus had interceded for him in the same way? The answer is that Jesus applied even stronger means, mightier warnings to the traitor, applied them all in vain. And while he was applying these means he certainly also prayed for Judas, and yet Judas went to perdition. The prayers and intercessions of Jesus are not absolute. Man's wicked will is able to damn him nonetheless. The grace, the means, even the greatest, and the intercessions can all be nullified in their effect. Christ's omniscience knows the outcome in advance.

It is this foreknowledge which already now tells Peter that his faith will not perish utterly. This telling is a part of the means for saving him. So also is Jesus' order to him, that, after he has once turned, he should make his brethren firm, namely when they, too, passed through the sifting attacks of Satan. Why did Jesus not give such a command to the other disciples? The answer is not that of the Romanists: because Peter was to be the first pope; and not that of many others: because he was the foremost of the apostles and their leader. The answer is almost the opposite. Because he fell so deeply, fell as none of the rest fell, therefore, when he recovered, he was the one who could help the others by means of his own sad experience, could make the wavering faith of the others firm again so that it would not give way as his own faith had given way almost completely. His brethren are the other ten. The fact that Simon would aid his brethren in the wider sense in a similar way throughout his ministry is only a deduction. Jesus deals only with the ordeal of the apostles. We see that he is thus preparing the means for their recovery, in the case of each one the means which he needs and that will be most effective, special means for Simon's special case and his recovery as an effective means to help them all to recover. Even his present command to Peter, which is based on his foreknowledge, is to help them all.

The participle ἐπιστρέψας is intransitive and speaks of Simon's having turned back from his fall in repentance. This is not conversion in the absolute sense as though every spark of Simon's faith had gone out, but in the relative sense as when a disciple turns back from a course that has almost destroyed his faith. "Once" on having turned, Jesus says, because he is not specifying when the turn will take place. We cannot agree that this participle is transitive: "once having turned thy brethren, make them firm." So little does the adverb "once" support this sense that it actually forbids it since "once" intends to leave unsaid just when Simon will turn and recover, and that this turning of his alone will enable him to do anything for his fellow apostles. We catch a glimpse of Simon's aid to them in 24:34 where the others are jubilant in reporting that Jesus had appeared to Simon.

33) **But he said to him, Lord, together with thee I am ready to go into prison and into death! But he said, I tell thee, Peter, a cock will not crow today till thrice thou didst deny to know me!**

It is thus that Simon answers the warning of his Lord. How can Satan harm Simon when he is so strong, so valiant? Why, if it should come to such a test, even prison and even death have no terrors for him. He does not say: "By thy help," or "By God's help." Simon's reaction to Jesus' warning and intercession for him is that Jesus can count on him and need never worry about a man who is as brave as he is. Poor, proud Simon!

34) Over against Peter's contradicting words Jesus places his authoritative "I tell thee!" Jesus overrides Peter's self-confidence and trust in his own powers. Straws are they in the hurricane that is about to descend. Why did Jesus now change from "Simon" to "Peter"? It is too weak an answer to say, "In order to remind him that he was not acting and speaking like Peter, the Rock." He was trying to do that very thing, and Jesus practically says to him: "So thou art already Peter—thou, who this very night, before the cock crows, wilt have already denied me no less than three times!" Peter will give his own words the lie. He will be so frightened at prison and death that he will openly deny once, twice, three times, in fact, that he even knows Jesus. The verb means "to say no" and thus "to deny," and the aorist expresses the fact.

This crowing of a cock is not some casual crowing of an individual cock. Two crowings were distinguished, one that occurred near midnight, the other just before dawn. They helped to divide the night into the midnight or silent period, the period before dawn, and the period after dawn. Pliny calls the fourth watch *secundum gallicinium*. Mark 14:30, in the second warning to Peter, refers to both crowings: "before the cock crows twice," i. e., before the day dawns. Luke and John refer only to the crowing before dawn. The phrase is not a mere expression of time but refers to other actual crowings of the cocks that night.

The word is also spoken with a special purpose. It does more than merely to foretell how soon Peter will fall, it already prepares the help to raise Peter from his fall. Peter will actually hear the crowing when it begins; that will bring Jesus' word to his mind; and this together with a look from Jesus' eyes (v. 61) will cause the tears of repentance to flow. The effort to discredit the evangelists by advancing the contention that no chickens were kept in a city like Jerusalem, and that no cocks crowed within range of Peter's ears, has long ago been met by ample evidence to the contrary.

35) **And he said to them, When I sent you without purse and wallet and sandals, you certainly did not lack anything, did you? And they said, Nothing. And he said to them: But now he having a purse, let him take it up, likewise a wallet. And he not having a short sword let him sell his robe and buy one. For I say to you that this that has been written must be accomplished in me, And he was reckoned together with lawless ones. For also this concerning me has an end. But they said, Lord, lo, two short swords here! And he said to them, It is enough!**

Luke alone has this section. It connects most naturally with what precedes. Jesus puts a question, and the interrogative particle μή confidently expects the negative answer which the apostles also give. No; they never lacked a thing when Jesus sent them out on a missionary tour through all Galilee. At that time he told them to go entirely empty-handed, to take not even a purse, for they were to carry no money whatever, not even a wallet, for they were to carry no eatables and no clothing that require a wallet, and not even a pair of extra sandals to replace those they would soon wear out by constant travelling. Always and always they found friends who provided them with what they needed on hearing their message and the name of Jesus. They learned the great lesson of absolute trust in their Sender. He did provide for them through the name and the fame with which he had filled all Galilee. Never once had he failed them. See 9:3 on πήρα. It was not a beggar's bag, for Jesus and his apostles never went as beggars (*contra* Deissmann).

36) But now, when Jesus sends out his apostles into all the world after his resurrection, the situation will be completely changed. Jesus, their Sender, will, indeed, still take care of them, but not in the former

way. They will have use for a purse (money) and a wallet (to carry food, clothes, etc.). Friends will, indeed, provide for them, but they will not at once and in every place find friends, and so they will need money, etc., as they go along. Let them take a purse and a travelling bag.

They will need even protection and at times so badly that a sword will be worth more to them than their outer robe, the latter being a great necessity, especially as a covering at night when they were camping out in the open. So Jesus tells the apostles to buy a Roman short sword, if necessary, even at the price of their outer robe. It is better to freeze at night than to be killed. After "he not having" we supply μάχαιραν as the object; not, as some do, "purse and wallet" from the preceding sentence. The latter would lead to the idea that the apostles were to demand food and lodging at the point of the sword when it was otherwise not forthcoming.

This matter of having a sword even at the price of a cloak becomes plain when we look at the map and at II Cor. 11:26, 27. Paul, for instance, travelled extensively, the other apostles did likewise. We find Peter in Rome, and tradition reports to what far countries some of the others went. On foot, over mountain roads and passes, through uninhabited, desert regions their way would take them. Paul experienced hunger, thirst, fasting, nakedness (not enough cover), freezing. And worse than this: robbers, brigands, some of his own countrymen (Jews), some heathen. Yes, a sword would be needed for protection.

This injunction means that the apostles are to use ordinary prudence in their labors. The language is not figurative. Purse, wallet, sword are not to be allegorized into something spiritual as the ancient fathers thought they must be. The injunctions are concrete and simply use specific examples to indicate a complete course of conduct. Jesus will, indeed, be with his apostles, but he will be with them amid many hardships and dangers, amid the care and the prudence which he himself bids them exercise.

37) The sentence introduced by γάρ is not a statement of proof; γάρ offers an explanation as it does in hundreds of cases. With authority Jesus explains his previous directions about using ordinary prudence in their apostolic travels (for purse, etc., refer to travel). Due to God's redemptive plan, this written prophecy must of necessity be accomplished in Jesus: "and he was reckoned together with lawless ones," Isa. 53:12. Καί is not due merely to the exactness of the quotation but implies that in addition to other inflictions this, too, will be added, that in his death he will be reckoned as belonging in the same class with lawbreakers, will be crucified between two criminals as if he were also a criminal. Who reckons Jesus thus is not stated, need not be, since Jesus has told plainly enough into whose hands he would be delivered. The addition of τό merely makes a substantive of the quotation.

This explanation of Jesus' is far stronger than the idea that the apostles cannot expect to fare better than their Lord did. Because he was crucified between criminals Jesus will be execrable to all Jews and an object of utter scorn to the Gentiles when they are told that such a person is their Savior. When the apostles come as the messengers of One who hung between criminals they will be greeted and treated accordingly. So it will be well to take a purse, etc.

"For also this concerning me has an end" adds a further explanation. The reckoning of Jesus among lawbreakers is one of the last things of those which concern him in his earthly life; but a little while and "what concerns him" will be at an end. This means that nothing further will happen in his life to alter the impression that is left by his being reckoned among transgressors. After he has once been reckoned so by the world, the world will find nothing in him that would lead it to reckon him as belonging in another class of men.

It is strange to note how commentators labor with these few words by having τὸ περὶ ἐμοῦ mean "the being about me"; or "that written about me" (forgetting that this includes everything until the final judgment); or "with me there is an end" (when the opposite was the case); or "my relation to you apostles," or "my official career."

38) The apostles answer by pointing to the two swords they had with them. So this word about the sword was what impressed them chiefly. It was indeed pitiful. They failed to grasp even the fact that Jesus spoke about their future needs and travels and thought only of the present. But this literalism on the part of the apostles should not cause us to go to the opposite extreme and to say that Jesus did not mean "sword" at all. He, indeed, meant sword and not something allegorical.

But there now comes the puzzle regarding these two swords in the upper room. How came they there? We are told that they were not swords at all but butcher knives, and they are specified—one for cutting the lamb's throat, the other for carving the roasted lamb at table. And one asks involuntarily why one good knife was not enough for both operations. But "sword" in v. 36 and "swords" in this verse are the same word and cannot be given two meanings as has been proposed. The view that the apostles carried swords as they followed Jesus, or even that on this night of the Passover celebration any two of them had come armed with swords, is untenable. The fact of Peter's having a sword in v. 49 cannot be explained in this way. We may accept the view that many Jewish men carried swords, in particular the Galileans; but this is of little help. We can think of only one explanation: "Lo, two swords *here!*" means that they hung right there in the upper room and belonged to the owner of the house. Peter took one of them on leaving. We need not assume that another apostle took the second—Peter was the bold and brave man. Nor need we think that Peter did not ask for permission to take the sword. When the company left the house, those who were gathered there with the owner of the house and his family for their Passover must have seen Jesus and his disciples and have spoken to them.

The reply of Jesus: "It is enough!" intends simply to end the matter, for it was rather hopeless for Jesus to say any more after he was pointed to the two swords that were hanging on the wall. Why assume that he spoke in irony when sad resignation is enough? Nor does Jesus mean that these two swords will suffice for tonight; nor ambiguously that they will do, or that this ends the matter. The view that by taking only two swords they could not be charged with armed resistance is untenable; Peter's one sword would have brought on calamity if it had not been for the prompt repudiation and interference on the part of Jesus. And the view that two swords were enough to prevent rowdies from attacking Jesus on the way out from the city is also unconvincing. The whole city was busy and quiet, which enabled Jesus and his little company to come into the city and now to leave it without even attracting special attention.

39) **And having gone out, he went according to his custom to the Mount of Olives; moreover, his disciples followed him.**

Luke uses only general terms when he mentions the locality to which Jesus went on leaving the house that had the upper room; but he adds the important phrase "according to his custom," which John 18:2 expands by explaining that Judas knew the place and came there to seek Jesus. We may take it that Jesus returned to Bethany only on the night of Palm Sunday (Matt. 21:17), on the following nights he remained in Gethsemane and perhaps slept in the open in this retired and sheltered place. It goes without saying that Jesus used this grove with the friendly permission of its owner just as he had the use of the upper room in the city for the Passover and the ass for his triumphal entry on Palm Sunday. Jesus knew that Judas would seek him here, therefore he again went to this place. By that choice he was already delivering himself into the hands of his enemies. How easily he could have frustrated the traitor's plans by going to some entirely strange place this night!

40) **And having come to the place, he said to them, Be praying not to enter into temptation!**

"To the place" refers to the one where Jesus usually stayed, which Matthew and Mark call Gethsemane. And all that Luke reports is this injunction to all the disciples to continue praying, to ask God not to let them enter into temptation. This word is used here in its full sense as it is in the Lord's Prayer. The disciples must go through the ordeal of this night, and their prayer was to be, not that they might escape that, but that it might not become a temptation to them to fall from their faith in Jesus as Peter so nearly did. Ordeals become temptations when we listen to the devilish suggestion that God has abandoned us, and that it is useless to cling to Jesus as our Lord.

41) **And he tore himself away from them about a stone's throw and, having knelt down, continued praying, saying, Father, if thou art willing, take this cup away from me; nevertheless, let not my will but thine go on being done.**

Luke gives only a summary account in these verses. The verb is passive but middle in sense: "he tore himself away from them," B.-P. 154. We see what it cost him to leave the disciples because of the great battle that his soul was now fighting. But he must fight it alone, they could not help him. Luke speaks only of the disciples and says nothing about the three whom Jesus kept near him. His withdrawal for a distance that one can throw a stone (accusative of extent) refers to the disciples whom he had left near the entrance whereas the μικρόν used by Matthew and by Mark refers to the few paces he had withdrawn from Peter, James, and John. This is sometimes overlooked. Yet it explains how these three saw and heard all that the synoptists report about the agony of Jesus. Heb. 5:7 adds the detail that Jesus prayed, not merely aloud, but with "strong crying (κραυγῆς ἰσχυρᾶς) and tears." Luke states that Jesus knelt while praying, the others that he fell on his face. Both are true, he knelt and then sank prostrate; he may also have raised his body now and again. Luke has the imperfect "he continued praying" without distinguishing the three separate acts of prayer.

42) On Golgotha "my God, my God," was wrung from Jesus' lips, here he still says, "Father." It is the voice of the Son in his intimate relation to this Father. Yet the pain and the distress of this cry "Father" are those of the Son in his humiliation. From the first word onward the Son's praying was the most perfect submission to his Father's will. Even a mere hint that he could not or in some way would not submit is absent. It is the Son in his humanity who prays thus; his Passion was suffered by way of his human nature. The word "cup," which is used figuratively, does not refer merely to its contents but to its bitter, burning, deadly contents. The verb means "bear it by me" so that I will not need to drink it.

"If thou wilt" includes "if it is possible" as is recorded by Matthew and thus means: "if it is possible for thee to will" that I be spared drinking this cup. It would, however, be unwarranted to think of abstract possibility in this connection, of the possibility of leaving the world unredeemed. No; that possibility is shut out; only the other is voiced, that of accomplishing redemption without Jesus' enduring the full penalty for the world's sin. And even this thought is wrung from the human lips of Jesus only now when the last decisive step is to be taken that brings the horror of all the world's guilt and curse upon him.

The agony of Gethsemane will always remain full of mystery for us because of the mystery of the union of Christ's two natures. For one thing, we have no conception of what sin, curse, wrath, death meant for the holy human nature of Jesus. Since he was sinless he should not die; and yet, because he was sinless and holy he willed to die for our sin. The death of Jesus was far different from that of the courageous martyrs. They died after Jesus' death had removed their sin and guilt; the sting of their death was removed through Christ's death. But Jesus died, being made sin for us, being made a curse for us, the sting of death penetrated him with all its damnable power. The world's sin had, indeed, been assumed by Jesus during his whole life, but here in Gethsemane the supreme moment of that assumption had come. With the coming of Judas and his band Jesus actually stepped into the death that was to atone for the world's sin. All that is horrible, unspeakable, hellish, and damnable in our guilt rose up to meet him, and his whole nature shrank from the contact.

Πλήν is adversative: "nevertheless," whatever the Father determines, this stands fast for Jesus: "let not my will but thine be going on to be done," the imperative being durative to express a course of action and not merely one single act. Let it all come, not as Jesus may will, but as the Father wills. That is absolute submission, for the words mean that Jesus puts away any will of his own and makes the Father's will his own instead. That was the supreme act of Jesus' will. Never for an instant would Jesus will anything but the Father's will.

43) Luke alone reports the incidents of the angel and the bloody sweat. The textual question involved may be dismissed very briefly. Verses 43, 44 were can-

celled from the text, not for textual, but for dogmatical reasons, as being derogatory to the deity of Christ, and because they were used by the Arians when they denied his deity. Present objections rest on the claim that these verses contain only legendary elaborations and not historical facts.

Moreover, there appeared to him an angel from heaven strengthening him. And being in agony, he went on praying more intensely. Moreover, his sweat became as clots of blood going down on the ground.

The questions are raised as to whether the angel appeared only to Jesus, whether his appearance was visible to him, and, if it was, whether the disciples saw the angel or only concluded that an angel had visited Jesus when he finally returned to them calmly and courageously. "There appeared to him" is one of the regular expressions that is used to indicate the visible appearance of angels, glorified beings, and of heavenly visions (1:11; Acts 7:35). To be sure, this angel's appearance was granted for the sake of Jesus, whom he was to strengthen; but since the three disciples were chosen as special witnesses of the agony they undoubtedly were to witness also its supreme part and thus saw the angel come to Jesus.

Some of the ancients objected to the idea that the Son of God should need an angel to give him strength. They overlooked the fact that this strength was intended for the human nature of Jesus during this ordeal; also, that the strength came from the Father, and that the angel was only the Father's medium. It was the Father's answer to Jesus' prayers, a visible, tangible, miraculous answer that came directly from heaven at the moment when it was most needed. Do not ask why the Son's own deity did not strengthen his poor human nature; be satisfied that the Father gave the strength. Why argue about the persons when the facts as to what they did are plainly before us?

There is a tendency to make this strengthening spiritual and not physical. But this is unwarranted. Bengel is right, it was *non per cohortationem sed per corroborationem*, not stimulating the spirit of Jesus by exhortation but strengthening his exhausted body by means of new vitality. The body of Jesus was about to give way and expire in death under the terrific strain; the prayers reveal the mighty power of Jesus' spirit. This angel, we may say, performed the same service as did those mentioned in Matt. 4:11. The angel's coming for this purpose was the Father's answer that he, indeed, willed that Jesus drink the cup, that he accepted the submission of Jesus' own will in this regard, and that his strengthening would fully enable also Jesus' body and human nature to do their hard part. This is the basis of Heb. 2:9, Jesus' being made lower than the angels, namely by his agonizing human nature; but only in this respect, for the angel gave Jesus strength, not from angelic sources, but from the Father.

44) The aorist participle γενόμενος is punctiliar: Jesus reached the point where he was "in agony." But "agony" should not be extended to mean "death agony" (*dass er mit dem Tode rang*, Luther), for Hobart shows that even the medics used ἀγωνία only with reference to severe mental distress. The fact that the entire struggle carried the body of Jesus close to dissolution is apparent from the start. We here have the reverse. The new strength that was imparted by the angel brought the agony of the struggle to its highest pitch. The mind and the body that were sinking lower and lower beneath the strain rallied powerfully to face the full horror of the curse and the wrath that were impending. That is why Jesus went on to pray more intensively in this supreme moment (the adjective does not mean "more" or *mehrfach*).

The intensity of the struggle produced such physical reaction that the sweat of Jesus became bloody.

Severe mental distress and strain drive out sweat from the body, a fact that is constantly observed. The fact that this may reach the point where the tiny blood vessels of the skin are ruptured and permit blood to mingle with the sweat is attested medically. Aristotle speaks of bloody sweat as does Theophrastus, and in 1805 Gruner compiled medical data on the subject (R., W. P., and Nebe, *Leidensgeschichte*).

"As clots," θρόμβοι, means that the blood mingled with the sweat and thickened the globules so that they fell to the ground in little clots and did not merely stain the skin. "How did the witnesses see this?" it is asked. It is enough to say that they saw it when Jesus returned to them. Why did Mark not record this when he had Peter as his authority, who was one of the three? That is a question one might ask about a hundred things regarding each of the Gospel writers. We cannot state with definiteness just why each writer included this and not that.

45) **And having risen from the prayer, on having come to the disciples** (these minor actions are expressed by means of Greek participles), **he found them fallen asleep from sorrow; and he said to them: Why are you slumbering? Having arisen, keep praying lest you enter into temptation!**

The agony is ended. Jesus is no longer agitated by the prospect of taking the step into the depth of the sin and the curse that were awaiting him; he now proceeds to take that step. He takes it with absolute firmness, with a courage that is utterly beyond us, with the sureness of victory and triumph. So he comes to the disciples and finds them asleep. Luke speaks only of their final sleeping and condenses his account. It has been claimed that this sleeping was a psychological impossibility under the circumstances of that night. But it is well known that great and continued heaviness of soul brings on an inner dullness of mind and thus the physical reaction of sleep; the soul yields to its burden and no longer rallies against it as Jesus so strongly urged when he bade the disciples to watch and pray.

46) "Why are you slumbering?" is full of reproof. Luke indicates this much and records no more. The same is true with regard to the bidding that the disciples keep praying lest they enter into temptation as is explained in v. 40. In his own great ordeal Jesus is solicitous about these dull disciples lest the coming test become a fatal temptation for them. While he is bearing his own burden he helps them also to bear theirs. He received no support whatever from them; they needed all his support, and he did not stint in giving it to them.

47) **He still speaking, lo, a multitude! And he, called Judas, one of the Twelve, was going before them.**

The report about the arrest is also severely abbreviated. Jesus said more than the few words that are here recorded, and it was while he was saying these last things to them that a great host of men suddenly appeared. Luke exclaims: "Lo, a multitude!" The grove was most likely walled in with stone, stone being ready to hand almost anywhere. This army was noted through the entrance which was a little distance away. Luke says nothing about its composition save the intimation "with short swords and clubs" in v. 52. The former were the weapons of the Roman legionaries, the latter the weapons of the Levitical Temple police. John adds the torches and the lanterns and gives further details about the detachment that was sent with Judas. The Levitical police were under their στρατηγός or "general." It was made up of the Roman cohort, not the entire 600 that were stationed at Antonia but about 200 under their chiliarch or chief commander.

The Sanhedrin had sent this entire force. Their own men had failed them on a previous occasion (John 7:45, etc.), and so they now took no chances. Because of the danger (Jerusalem being full of pilgrims) the

Sanhedrists seem to have had no trouble in persuading the chiliarch to accompany the short expedition and to take a force of legionaries that would be sufficiently able to cope with any eventualities that might arise on bringing Jesus to the city as a prisoner. Yet we nowhere have the least intimation that Pilate's cooperation was sought. The intimations point the other way, see the author on John 18:1, etc.

All four evangelists make Judas the guide of this multitude, and the synoptists call him "one of the Twelve" in this connection. The fact that this statement intends to match v. 3 is obvious. Nor are we able to find a canon in literature which forbids a writer to express his horror more than once. If "out of the number of the Twelve" is tragic in v. 3 it is even more so in v. 47, for the traitor is now actually carrying out his act.

And he drew near to Jesus to kiss him. But Jesus said to him, Judas, with a kiss dost thou betray the Son of man?

Luke's account is exceedingly brief and states only the main facts. About 200 Roman soldiers and certainly no less a number of Temple police and besides that a nondescript rabble that ran along to see the excitement block the entrance to Gethsemane. Jesus steps out to meet this throng, his disciples are ranged behind him. He is perfect master of the situation, and all that occurs does so only with his consent. Things certainly seem to be playing into the traitor's hands. Here is Jesus, and he cannot escape. Luke omits the prearrangement of the sign of the kiss and states only that Judas promptly carried out the scheme: "He drew near to kiss him." There is no evidence for the statement that Luke does not say that Judas did kiss Jesus. He writes two aorists, and these imply that he both got near and did kiss Jesus.

Nor was this just one kiss. Matthew and Mark use the compound verb which means to shower with kisses, *abkuessen.* Judas prolonged the act as if to tell the captors: "See, this is the man you want!" Judas at the same time acts the black hypocrite as if his heart is breaking because of what is now to happen to Jesus. He still thinks that he is deceiving Jesus. Some add that he wanted to close the mouth of Jesus as long as possible, to disarm him, lest he even now use his strange power to frustrate his arrest.

48) Jesus does not hurl the traitor from him nor use his omnipotent power to blast him then and there. He submits to his traitorous kissing—it is his Father's and his own will to accept all the indignities, shame, suffering, agonies which men will heap upon him even unto death. But Jesus is not silent. Not himself does he shield, not in his own interest does he speak; but for the last time he strikes a terrific blow at the traitor's conscience. The synoptists agree that he spoke just one, brief, penetrating word. The conscience of Judas was seared—no repentance followed.

"With a kiss dost thou betray the Son of man?" Judas is asked to realize what he is doing in order to be terrified at his own act. The emphasis is on the first and the last Greek word: "with a kiss—dost thou betray?" The kiss, the great and universal sign of friendship and love, is used here for the basest and most damnable act, the betrayal of no less a one than "the Son of man," he who is man and yet more than man (see 5:24). Judas performs his vicious act in the most vicious and atrocious way. John 18:4-9 brings out the truth that the kissing and the betrayal of Judas amounted to just nothing, for Jesus points himself out to his captors, prevents any molestation of the eleven, and delivers himself up. It was thus and not upon Judas' kiss that the chiliarch and possibly also the Jewish commander ordered men to step forward to take Jesus a prisoner.

49) **But those around him, on seeing what will be, said, Lord, shall we smite with a sword? And**

a certain one of them did smite the slave of the high priest and took off his ear, the right. But answering, Jesus said, Permit this far! And having touched the ear, he healed him.

What makes the eleven so brave that, when they see "what will be" (the substantivized future participle), they are ready to fight a whole mob with their one little sword? This certainly calls for some explanation, for even such a rash man as Peter would not expect to conquer several hundred armed men with one sword. John 18:4-9 makes the situation plain. The whole multitude had gone down, had tumbled over each other, at one question that was directed to them by Jesus who stood masterfully before them. Add the excitement of the moment and the secret conviction of the disciples that their Lord could not fall into the hands of his enemies, and we see that the disciples expected to sweep everything before them. The direct question with εἰ is usually considered Hebraistic and also elliptical, R. 1024; but εἰ may be a mere interrogative particle and nothing more, B.-D. 400 treats it under interrogative particles.

50) Before Jesus is able to answer a blow is already struck by Peter. It is rather remarkable that all the synoptists do not mention Peter's name in this affair. It is suggested that even as late as the time when they wrote they desired to shield him because the Sanhedrin was still in power; the fact is that we really do not know the reason. Peter slashed at the first man before him, the slave of the high priest, and intended to split his head open; but the man evidently dodged, and the sword sheared off his right ear, being stopped by the heavy armor on the servant's shoulder.

The article "*the* slave" puts this man in a class by himself. He is not one of the Temple police; he belongs to the high priest himself. He thus appears to be a trusted and important member of the high priest's own household who had been sent with this expedition as the high priest's personal representative. That explains why he is out in front under Peter's sword. And that, too, is why John, who was so well acquainted with the high priest's family, states his name (Malchus) and even refers to his relative.

51) "Answering" does not refer to the question that is asked in v. 49; this Greek participle is frequently used in a wider sense with reference to any response to a situation or an action. So Jesus here responds to the crucial situation that had been so suddenly created by Peter. The other three evangelists record Jesus' rebuke to Peter, Luke omits that and tells how Jesus stepped in, saying, "Permit this far!" and healed the man's ear.

The translation and the sense of this brief word are in dispute. Some hold that because of the participle "answering" it is addressed to the disciples, but it is certainly no answer to their question. Then, too, the words are separated: "Let be, no farther!" and tell the disciples to go no farther. As καί indicates, the word evidently accompanies the healing act. Jesus' captors were about to lay hands on him, and after Peter's striking the blow a rush of the captors might be made upon the disciples. Jesus steps forward, says to the captors, "Let be up to this!" namely, "Permit this much!" that is, that he be allowed to touch and to heal the ear, and at once suits the action to the word.

This is a remarkable miracle, the last that Jesus wrought, and it is performed in the interest of one of his captors. It has been called his only surgical healing. "Having touched the ear" leads some to think that the ear was not severed, that only a slight cut had been made that caused bleeding so that Jesus only stopped the bleeding. But it is hard to believe that the blow had done no more serious damage. The better view is that the ear was slashed off and hung by a shred of skin so that a mere touch of Jesus restored it perfectly.

What impression did this miracle make? We hear of none. But up to his dying day Malchus bore in that healed ear the mark of Christ's omnipotence and grace. This is one of the plain miracles which ought to settle the contention that faith is necessary in the person to be healed—or did Malchus have faith? With his prompt act Jesus stopped any bad consequences of Peter's act for the disciples whom he was shielding.

52) **Moreover, Jesus said to the high priests and commanders of the Temple and elders who had come against him: As against a robber did you come out with short swords and clubs? Day by day being with you in the Temple, you did not stretch out your hands against me. But this is your hour and the authority of the darkness!**

All the synoptists record the protest of Jesus against his arrest and against the manner in which it was made. Mark writes that he spoke to his "captors," Matthew to them "in that hour," then and not later. Luke alone states just who the persons addressed were, "the high priests, Temple captains (we see that there were several, which shows how numerous the Temple police present were), and elders who had come out against him."

The presence of high priests and elders has been questioned as being very improbable. This view forgets that everything that occurred in Gethsemane was "improbable." The Temple captains, of course, went with the men whom they commanded. But is it asking too much to think that some of the Sanhedrists, who had ordered this expedition, could not restrain themselves sufficiently to remain in the city but followed the armed force to see whether the move would be successful? They had now caught up with it and were in front in order to see everything. Jesus says nothing to the Romans, he speaks only to these Sanhedrists and to their captains. His words are uttered after his hands have been bound with a rope and he stands there apparently helpless, just before the commands are given to face about for a return to the city. The words are calm, measured, without trace of excitement; but they are keen, cutting to the quick for these leaders who now gloat over their capture.

Jesus asks them to consider just what they have done. As against a robber, from whom the most violent resistance had to be expected, they went out with a great expedition, all were armed "with short swords and clubs" as if expecting a regular battle—all this to arrest one lone, unarmed man! The whole thing is actually ridiculous.

53) Why, "day by day" (distributive κατά) he was with them in the Temple, in their very midst, where they had the fullest authority and the easiest opportunity, and they never stretched out their hands against him or made one move to place him under arrest. If there were any cause for arresting him, why had they raised no hand day after day? Jesus had not hidden from them—he had no cause to hide. He had none now, nor had he hidden; on the contrary, when they said that they wanted him, he had told them who he was. And now all at once, in the middle of the night, this army of legionaries and Levite police for an arrest, and for such an arrest! To protest to these men is, of course, useless; and yet no proper protest is useless although men disregard it, for it registers the truth, and truth stands forever.

Nor are these Sanhedrists and these captains to think for one moment that they have really effected this capture of Jesus with their superior cunning in hiring a traitor and with their crush of arms. Not a bit of it. They could and would have captured nothing. Other forces are operating here. "This is *your* hour," and the emphasis is on the pronoun, the one that God (according to the Scriptures of the prophets, Matthew) appointed for you to execute your devilish deed; "and the authority or power of the darkness" which operates in and through you. Note how the two possessives are linked together: "your"—"of the darkness." They are the tools and the agents of this darkness.

Let us also note the article: *"the* darkness," and the fact that this article always appears with this noun and denotes not only this specific darkness but almost personifies it as possessing a power and an authority. Jesus speaks of it at various times as though it were a monster of evil, of hell itself. God is letting "the darkness" exercise its power this night. That and that alone is why this mob is scoring such a huge victory against a single humble man! Let these Sanhedrists think with what power they are tied up as tools. The interpretation that "hour" and "the darkness" refer only to the night as though Jesus were saying: "You had to choose a dark hour of the night, you did not dare to select a daylight hour!" is so trivial that one wonders how anyone could seriously propose it.

54) **Now, having seized him, they led him away and led him into the house of the high priest.**

Luke combines the seizure and the leading, but from Matthew and from Mark we see that the seizure took place before v. 51-53 were spoken. "To the house of the high priest" means to that of Caiaphas (Matthew) and indicates that Luke knew all about the night trial of Jesus before the Sanhedrin as this is narrated by Matthew and by Mark although he himself makes no record of this trial. None of the synoptists refers to the preliminary examination that was conducted by Annas in order to fill in the time. In v. 61 Jesus is led from the trial before the Sanhedrin to some place of safekeeping until the morning session of the Sanhedrin confirms the death sentence that had been passed at the night session.

But Peter was following from afar.

Luke tells the entire story of Peter's fall in one paragraph. His account is extremely brief and says nothing about the other ten disciples, nor even that

Peter managed to get into the courtyard with the Temple police. We gather the latter only from Peter's being there. The chiliarch and the legionaries departed after delivering the prisoner. Pilate had no hand in the matter, or they would have delivered the prisoner to him. A detachment of the Temple police was retained in the courtyard to await any further orders. John informs us that he was the one who helped Peter to enter this courtyard.

55) Now, they having lit a fire in the middle of the courtyard and having sat down together, Peter was sitting in their midst.

The night was cold (John), hence there was a fire in the open court, which fire was made of charcoal and made no smoke. The men sat around it warming themselves. Peter tried to act as though he were one of them and sat down in their midst. He had no business there, Jesus had told him not to follow. He made the excuse to himself that he wanted to see the end (Matthew). We always invent good reasons for doing what we ought not to do.

56) But a maid, having seen him sitting before the light and having gazed intently on him, said, This fellow also was with him! But he denied it, saying, I do not know him, woman!

Peter imagined that he could carry it off, and that no one would pay any attention to him. But he had not reckoned with this maid. From John we learn that she was the very maid who had let Peter in upon John's request to her. She and another functioned as doorkeepers at the passageway that led from the street into the open inner court. It was a common thing to employ women in this capacity. She left her post at the entry when she saw him sitting facing (πρός) the fire, fixed her eyes intently upon him for a little in order not only to make sure but also to draw the attention of the men, and then made her startling assertion. This must have occurred some time after she had let Peter in, long enough after to get the fire going and the men settled around it.

What made this woman go after Peter as she did? Was she afraid that she had let the wrong man in, and did she take this means of making herself safe? If so, then what about John whom she knew much better? The καί in the assertion shows that this maid had arrived at the conclusion that Peter must be a disciple of Jesus from the way in which John intervened to persuade her to let Peter in. Yet she makes no issue of John. Was she merely teasing Peter with perverse feminine delight, trying to make him uncomfortable when she saw him hiding his identity? Her words do not sound like banter. She most likely wanted to make herself important. She wanted these men to know that she knew something that they did not know. They were talking about Jesus and what had just taken place and yet did not know that right in their own midst there sat one of Jesus' own disciples. All, no doubt, cocked their ears when she made her assertion.

57) The suddenness of the exposure, its publicity before the crowd about the fire, the feeling that he was in mortal danger at once upset Peter and filled him with panic. He saw no way out except to lie out. The devil loves to pounce upon the foolhardy and to sweep boasters off their feet. The evangelists agree in making the denial a complete disowning of Jesus.

It took only a menial maid to fell the chief of the Twelve. Gone were all his high and heroic protestations to Jesus, gone all the spurious courage from his heart and from the hand that had snatched out the sword in Gethsemane. Here stands the arrant coward who is unable to confess his heavenly Lord and cringes in lying denial. Some think that Peter was scared without real cause, that he misjudged the situation and could have confessed without real danger to himself. But whether there was a cause or not, fright operates in either case. Peter was surely in danger. We may take it that he would have been arrested forthwith, taken before Annas, and held at least for a time; and if his slashing off Malchus' ear should have become known, serious punishment might have been the result.

58) And after a little another man, on seeing him, said, Thou, too, art one of them! But Peter said, Man, I am not.

Peter waited only long enough to have attention safely withdrawn from him and then quietly made for the πυλών, the long entryway that led out from the courtyard to the street through the front side of the building. He wants to get out, to leave the place. But this precipitates the second and severer denial. Matthew says that "another" (feminine, hence "maid") saw him. Mark says "the maid, having seen him, began again to say," etc., which must be the one who exposed Peter in the first place. Luke writes ἕτερος, masculine, "another man." This looks like a contradiction but is in perfect agreement when we note the situation. Peter had been exposed, and the matter was being talked about. On a night like this more than one maid would be on duty at the entry. Peter runs into two maids and a man, all three of whom are certain that he is a disciple of Jesus, "one of them." Others are standing in the entrance since there was a crowd. So Peter is again recognized, and by three persons, and his case seems more desperate than before.

Mark states that the cock now crowed. This was the first crowing even as Mark notes that there would be two (14:30). Peter never heard it in his excitement. And this time he added an oath to his denial in order to secure credence when he thought that his word was not enough. He acted even as though he did not know Jesus' name. And yet these very lips of his had uttered Matt. 16:16 and John 6:68, 69!

59) And about one hour having intervened, another man began to affirm positively, saying, Of a truth this fellow, too, was with him, for also he is a

Galilean. But Peter said, Man, I know not what thou art saying! And immediately, he yet speaking, there crowed a cock.

Peter promptly gave up trying to get out through the entryway. Twice he had been positively challenged, and we can imagine the uneasiness and the fear with which he now tried to efface himself in the crowded courtyard. Luke knows that this continued for a full hour. But just when this delay begins to give Peter a feeling of security, the most decisive effort is made to identify him as a disciple of Jesus. Matthew and Mark say only that some of the men standing by, who had evidently been discussing Peter, came over and confronted him. Luke makes one of them the spokesman, and John supplies the detail that this was a relative of the Malchus whose ear Peter had cut off. Here was danger, indeed.

With great positiveness: "of a truth," i. e., in spite of thy previous denials, Peter is charged with having been "with him," namely in Gethsemane where this relative of Malchus' was almost sure he had seen Peter. So Peter had not succeeded in allaying suspicion about himself, he had only directed it into new and more effective channels. "Also" adds the undeniable fact that Peter was a Galilean to this man's other assurance. This is corroborative evidence ($\gamma\acute{\alpha}\rho$), for all of the disciples of Jesus hailed from Galilee with the sole exception of Judas, and all Galileans were recognized as such by their peculiar Aramaic brogue. John adds the detail that Peter's challenger asked directly whether he had not seen Peter in Gethsemane. This time the net seemed to be closing completely around Peter.

60) Luke is kind when he records only Peter's denial which states that he does not know what his challenger is talking about. It was much worse than that: he cursed himself and called on God with oaths as he stated that he did not know. We see that Peter

is ready to resort to anything in order to save his hide. He has lost even his ordinary manhood and is now a groveling coward, too pitiful to look upon. Even now Peter was not arrested on suspicion and held for judicial investigation. But right then and there, while he was still shouting his protestations, "there crowed a cock"—the subject and the verb are reversed, each is thus made emphatic—who started his crowing just before the dawn begins to lighten the sky (see v. 34).

61) Nobody paid any attention to this crowing —save one man. **And, on turning, the Lord looked at Peter. And Peter was reminded of the utterance of the Lord, how he said to him, Before a cock crows today, thou wilt deny me thrice. And having gone outside, he sobbed bitterly.**

It is debated as to how Jesus could be close enough to look upon Peter at this moment. The best answer is that the Temple police were just then leading him from the hall of trial through the open courtyard to some place of detention until he should be wanted again. With his face contused, black and blue from the blows he had received, with spittle still defiling his countenance, Jesus looked upon poor Peter. No wonder that look went home. Luke alone reports this great fact. In the midst of his own awful passion Jesus' Savior heart thinks of Peter and with a look at the man on whose lips the fearful denials are still trembling reaches into that man's soul in order to save him.

It is best to keep the passive: Peter "was reminded" instead of understanding it in the middle sense: "remembered." For it was this look of Jesus that awoke the memory of Peter. The cock's crowing and the Lord's passage through the court and his look at Peter were so timed by divine providence as to effect the saving result in Peter's soul. Jesus had spoken that word about the cock (v. 34) because he foresaw Peter's situation at this moment and intended that Peter should recall that word to his great benefit. So the tension of his fear was released at last, the warning of his Lord's love came back in his soul, the way to genuine repentance was opened.

62) It seems that Peter had no difficulty in getting out of the courtyard. Some jump to the conclusion that he would have had no difficulty at any time. But the maids kept the door locked, and Peter did not risk it to demand an exit. It was the transfer of Jesus that changed the situation. The crowd of the Temple police, that had been kept waiting in the courtyard until this time, were now ordered out, and Peter could thus leave without difficulty.

Matthew and Luke state his repentance with two words: ἔκλαυσε πικρῶς, the verb denotes loud, audible weeping: "he sobbed bitterly." The adverb refers, not to the physical sobbing, but to the bitterness of the contrition that is back of it. Contrition includes the realization that we have sinned and the consequent genuine sorrow for our sin.

The story of Peter has two important sides: first, Jesus prophesies, and the fulfillment, which is frantically denied, follows to the letter; second, the foremost of the apostles falls most terribly and is yet restored when he repents. For all time this calls sinners to the pardon that Jesus brought for them.

63) **And the men having Jesus in charge went on to mock him by beating. And having blindfolded him, they went on inquiring of him, Prophesy! Who is he that struck thee? And many other things, blaspheming, they went on to say against him.**

It is plain that Luke reports the same mockery that is recorded in Matt. 26:67, 68 and in Mark 14:65; and no confusion of the two sessions of the Sanhedrin, one of which was held at night and the other after daylight, which turns both into one in Luke's record can hope to find credence and lead us to place the mockery that is recorded in Luke anywhere but where, according to Matthew and Mark, it occurred, at the end of the night session, after the Sanhedrin had condemned Jesus to death. We also see how Luke wrote: he tells about the denial of Peter, adds the mockery of the Sanhedrin, then the final official condemnation, all forming a climax. It is thus that he omits the story of the night trial and takes from it only the mockery with which it ended.

We should not think only of the guards that held Jesus as being the men that mocked him. A few guards of the Temple police stand beside Jesus at his night trial by the Sanhedrin, and after vain efforts Caiaphas succeeds in having this legal body vote the death penalty for Jesus on account of blasphemy. The moment this is attained a beastly, brutal, almost incredible outrage follows. "The men having Jesus in charge" are the Sanhedrists themselves, the few Temple police are only their minions. These Sanhedrists rise from their judicial seats and stage the mockery. These supreme judges of the nation, in whom all the dignity and the grandness of the nation should be vested, show their real nature as being rowdies of the lowest type. The proud Sadducees, the aristocrats of the Sanhedrin and the nation, reveal what they actually are: common, coarse rabble. After they have shouted their illegal verdict, which definitely repudiates any reverence for God and his laws, they lose even the commonest human decency. As they surround the lone, bound prisoner these judges show what is in their hearts and in the judgment which they have pronounced.

Luke restrains himself when he writes only: "they went on to mock him by beating," the participle denoting blows that bruise and break the skin. Mark and Luke speak of blows with the first, and both add the vilest of insults, spitting into Jesus' face. In their cowardly brutality they cannot act viciously enough against this bound and defenseless victim and hurt him as much as possible just as savages might do.

64) Mark and Luke report the special mockery of Jesus' prophetic powers. Someone conceived the idea of throwing something over Jesus' head to blindfold him while slap after slap rained upon his face, blows of the fist, too, according to Mark, and then with ribald laughter his tormentors shouted to Jesus to "prophesy" and to tell them which one had struck him.

65) This is offered only as a sample, for "other things" and "many" of them these Sanhedrists said against Jesus as they blasphemously reviled him. The imperfects are descriptive and picture how this mockery went on and on. Having become tired of their mockery at last, the Sanhedrists order the police guard to take Jesus out. Mark reports that the guards received him with fisticuffs and followed the noble pattern given them by their illustrious superiors. The condition of Jesus at the end of this ordeal is easier to imagine than to describe. There were literally fulfilled Isa. 50:6 and Jesus' own prophecy spoken in 18:32 and Mark 10:34.

66) **And when it became day, there was gathered together the eldership of the people, both high priests and scribes; and they brought him back into their Sanhedrin, saying, If thou art the Christ, tell us!**

This is the early morning session of the Sanhedrin, of which Matt. 27:1 and Mark 15:1 make report; but our versions do not understand the situation when they translate that the Sanhedrin took counsel and held a consultation on how to put Jesus to death; what was done was to pass the final resolution which confirmed the death sentence that had been passed at the night session. In capital cases the Jewish law required a second session of the Sanhedrin, and that after an interval of at least a day; moreover, the law prohibited night sessions. The Sanhedrin, once having Jesus in its power, was determined to rush him to death because it feared the uprising of the pilgrim hosts that were then in the city. So the illegality of the night trial was simply disregarded. But the formality of holding a second session was found feasible even though it was illegal since a day had not passed and since the finding of the illegal night session was to be confirmed. Yet the holding of a second session lent at least a show of legality.

Mark makes it plain that this early morning session was one of the full court, and Luke does the same. In the LXX and in Acts 22:5 "the eldership of the people" designates the entire Sanhedrin, and the apposition "both high priests and scribes" adds another regular designation for this legal body. Luke does the same as Mark did, he makes doubly plain that this decisive session was one of the entire Sanhedrin as a Sanhedrin and not one of only some executive part of the body. At this session the death sentence could have been held up, altered, or set aside entirely; but in full assembly the Sanhedrin confirmed that sentence and proceeded to have it executed forthwith. So "they brought him back into their Sanhedrin" to face his judges once more. The case is to be reviewed and the evidence examined once more. And we note that Luke now writes even "Sanhedrin," a third name for the high court. It was composed of seventy or seventy-one judges, but all of them did not need to be present; the absence of a few was immaterial at any session.

67) The question is put to Jesus as to whether he is "the Christ." This is part of the question that was put to him by Caiaphas at the night session (Matt. 26:63). He had given an affirmative reply to the question, and upon that affirmation his death had been decreed. But the matter is entirely changed when the question is now divided and Jesus is asked only whether he is "the Christ" or Messiah. To affirm or to negate this question is not by any means to repeat or to retract the answer that Jesus gave at the night session. The question is asked in order that the Sanhedrin may

now once more hear the answer and may thus know whether or not to confirm its former verdict. But by asking this question, which is only a part of the original one, the Sanhedrists make it impossible for Jesus to repeat his yea.

But he said to them: If I shall tell you, in no wise will you believe. Moreover, if I shall inquire, in no wise will you answer. But from now on the Son of man will be sitting at the right of the power of God.

In order to understand this reply we should remember that in the thought of the Sanhedrin "the Christ" or Messiah had a nationalistic, highly political, purely earthly meaning. Jesus could never affirm that he was "the Christ" when his hearers were thinking of such a Christ. On the other hand, he could not say no, that he was not "the Christ," for this would be understood as though he were in no sense the Christ whereas he was the Christ in the true sense of the word. The question itself had, first of all, to be cleared up. Hence Jesus answered: "If I shall tell you," namely in what sense I am the Christ, "in no wise will you believe" what I say about myself. For the thought that was farthest from these Sanhedrists was to believe that Jesus was the Christ that he actually was.

68) Jesus adds: "Moreover, if I shall inquire, in no wise will you answer." This goes closely together with what precedes. Jesus means inquire as he inquired in 20:41-44 when he also received no answer. This is not an inquiry about reasons for his arrest, reasons why they did not think he was the Christ, and the like. No. To tell them whether he was the Messiah he would have to explain that he was the Messiah in the Scriptural sense; and if he took them into the Scriptures and from these showed them the Messiah he was and asked them if this were not so, they simply would not answer just as they had refused to answer before this time. Jesus thus briefly and clearly gave

the only reply he could give to this question about his being "the Christ."

69) Jesus might have stopped with this. But he will not leave this court without clear testimony as to who he really is, and in what exalted sense he is the Messiah. A plain yea or nay would have misled; hence Jesus repeats, with slight abbreviation, the declaration he had given at the night trial, Matt. 26:64: "But from now on," etc. The idea that he is referring to his Parousia is obviated by the phrase "from now on," which refers to a definite time. This phrase refers to Jesus' death, to effect which the Sanhedrin is now assembled. That death will place Jesus at the right of the power of God—that is the Christ he really is. He so testifies once more:

He calls himself "the Son of man" (see 5:24) because his glorious enthronement refers to his human nature, this as joined to the divine. And this is also his self-chosen Messianic title, which he used regularly instead of "Messiah" or "Christ" in order to avoid the Jewish political conceptions and entanglements. "The right of the power" names the power instead of the omnipotent God himself; yet the genitive is not possessive: "the right that belongs to the power," but appositional, "the right that is the power." To sit at this right is to exercise this power; and this invariably refers to the human nature of Jesus. This is the nature that is about to be glorified at the resurrection, about to ascend visibly to heaven, about to join in the divine reign. That nature appeared before the Sanhedrin in deepest humiliation, and these men could not conceive that all his lowliness would in a little while give way to divine glory. Without indicating it Jesus is once more using Ps. 110 as he did at the night trial, the very psalm with which he had silenced the Pharisees on Tuesday as recorded in 20:41-44. The humble Jesus had given some displays of divine power in his ministry; but these would be as nothing compared with the everlasting operation of his power by his human nature in glory.

Jesus repeats enough of his former testimony to recall also the rest that he had said; he lets that suffice. The Greek uses the idiomatic plural for "the right," without the article; and ἐκ, "from" God's right, the direction that is opposite from that of our "at."

70) And they all said, Thou, then, art thou the Son of God? And he said to them, You yourselves are saying that I am. But they said, Why have we yet need of witness? for we ourselves heard from his own mouth.

Luke uses the plural throughout this account and says nothing about Caiaphas' doing the questioning. To conclude from this fact that Caiaphas was not present is unwarranted, for he was the head of the opposition against Jesus and led the procession that took Jesus to Pilate. To conclude that Caiaphas let the meeting proceed as it would without direction is also unwarranted. He was president, and he presided. He may have asked the question about the Christ. The point to be noted is that this is only a corroboration session, the sole purpose of which was to verify and on verifying to confirm the verdict that had already been rendered. It was thus that any of the judges or a group of them together might ask this or that question to satisfy themselves. Not until all were satisfied would the votes be recorded by the scribes, and that would make the verdict final.

So now not merely Caiaphas, one or the other, or a few, but literally all shouted the question: "Thou, then, art thou the Son of God?" That was the other half of the original question (Matt. 26:63) for the affirmation of which they had condemned Jesus to death. That was one reason why it was again asked, in fact, had to be asked. More than this, Jesus had just made a statement that plainly involved his deity. Did he claim deity for himself? This, too, compelled the asking of the question. Finally, they saw what Jesus had pointed out, namely the inadequacy of their first question as to his claim to be the Christ. It is thus that everything became focused on this second question. There were excitement and eager tenseness, which Luke lets us feel by saying that the question came from all.

One worded it thus, another in another way, but it passed through the whole court, and all demanded to know whether Jesus claimed deity for himself. Οὖν bases the question on what Jesus had just said about his elevation to God's right hand. "Thou" is decidedly emphatic and lets us feel how incredible it seemed to this court that Jesus could possibly be God's Son, and how outrageous that he could possibly make such a claim. "The Son of God" is understood in the full sense of deity. Modernism has this term mean something less by stating that God was immanent in the man Jesus who was an actual, bodily son of Joseph; or that "the Son of God" meant only "Messiah."

"*The Son*," the Sanhedrists say, not "a son" among many. They do not for a moment affirm that God has no such Son, that God is not three persons but only one person. The Jews are now Unitarians, but in Jesus' time the Jews were not Unitarians. The issue between them and Jesus is never the claim that no Son and no Spirit exist, that Jesus believes fables when he speaks of the Father, the Son, the Spirit. The issue is always as it is so decisively worded here at this supreme moment: "*Thou*, art *thou* this Son?" That this man Jesus, this bruised, beaten, captive, helpless man who is now in their power, that *he* should be this Son, very God in human form, is to these Jews a thing that is at once incredible and blasphemous in the highest degree. It was because of this claim of Jesus regarding himself that they had passed the death sentence upon him at the night session. Now everything trembles in **the** balance as the question is once more reached at this morning session for purposes of legal verification.

Jesus forthwith, without if, and, or but, affirms that all-decisive question exactly as he had done under oath at the night session. He does it in the common idiom of the day, the one he had used before: "You yourselves are saying that I am," which means: "I am the Son of God exactly as you are saying it in your question." This idiom could use either the present tense as it does here: "you are saying," or the aorist as it does in Matt. 26:64: "thou didst say," i. e., just now; for the Greek uses the aorist to designate things that have just happened (R. 842, etc.) whereas we prefer the perfect: "thou hast (just) said." If any proof that this answer is an unqualified affirmation is needed for those who do not know the Greek, they have it here in the court which heard that answer of Jesus and heard it as his decided affirmation and, therefore, at once confirmed its verdict of death.

What Matthew and Mark bring out so plainly in recording the main facts of the night trial, what John brings out in the trial before Pilate (John 19:7), that Luke, too, brings out by recording the main facts of the morning session of the Sanhedrin: Jesus was condemned to death by the Jews, not because of this or that lying charge that was preferred against him, not on false testimony but because of his being what he in very truth was: "the Son of God." It is Jesus himself who here places us at the parting of the ways: we either join these Jews in their verdict that he lied and perjured himself when he declared to them that he was the Son of God; or we join Jesus, "who is the faithful Witness" (Rev. 1:5), "the faithful and true Witness" (Rev. 3:14), and worship him as "the Son of God" in the verity of that name.

71) The result of this affirmation was that the Sanhedrin declared that it could dispense with anything like further testimony. What was the use of fol-

lowing the regular procedure and calling in witnesses to establish the original verdict? They themselves had just heard (the aorist to express what has just happened) more than enough "from his own mouth."

"Witness"—why, they had none, had had none at the night session. They knew it, yet they speak of witness as if they had a twinge of conscience on this point. It was easy to dispense with witness when they knew not whom to get to testify to this affirmation. Time was crowding them; they must get to Pilate before the city woke up to what they were doing with Jesus. So they close the case in short order. Nobody dared to call a halt in any way. The fact that Jesus might be "the Son of God," that his miracles, his teaching, his personality, the Scriptures themselves, God's own voice from heaven on three occasions, even the Baptist (John 1:34) had attested the fact of Jesus' Sonship counted as nothing with this court. This witness—they had no need of it. It is still barred out by all who agree with the Sanhedrin.

Luke does not report the formality that the death penalty was confirmed; he did not need to report this, for he at once relates that the Sanhedrin proceeded to have that penalty executed.

CHAPTER XXIII

1) And the whole crowd of them, having arisen, led him to Pilate. And they began to accuse him, saying, This fellow we found perverting our nation and hindering to pay taxes to Caesar and claiming himself to be a Christ-king.

It is Luke who brings out the fact that no less than "the whole crowd of them" led Jesus to Pilate. This means the entire Sanhedrin plus a considerable detachment of the Levitical Temple police. A sufficient force must have been taken along because Jesus was to be led through the streets of the city and was to be under guard before the Praetorium of Pilate until Pilate took him in charge. Any attempt to rescue Jesus that might be undertaken by the pilgrims who were still in the city had to be blocked in advance. Pilate was to be impressed; the size of the Temple guard and the whole body of the Sanhedrin were to show him the dangerous character of the prisoner that was thus brought to him. It was early morning, but Roman courts were always available early in the day. The Praetorium, which is called thus as being the seat of the praetor or commander of the soldiery, must have been the fortress Antonia at this time. Pilate's tribunal was in front of the building, the Romans dispensed justice in the open.

2) We must insert John 18:28-32 at this point (on which see the author's exposition) because it is so necessary in order to get the full story. After they had arrived at the Praetorium, Pilate comes out, seats himself as the judge, but learns that all that the Sanhedrin wants of him is to execute the prisoner on the basis of the verdict it had already rendered. The Sanhedrists lose out in this first skirmish. Pilate refuses to be a mere tool of theirs, they are compelled to take the role

of accusers, and Pilate is the judge in the case. It is thus that "they began to accuse him" before Pilate.

But they are not consenting to a new trial by the governor. Not at all; they offer him only a statement of what they as a court have already "found," the finding on which they have decreed the prisoner's death. Τοῦτον is highly derogatory, "this fellow"; and "we found" is a legal term which states the finding of their trial. This implies that they went into the case in due legal form and established everything through witnesses. They state this because they are not ready to have Pilate do all this over again as though this amounted to nothing in his court.

They name the crimes on the basis of which they have passed the verdict of death on Jesus. We are dumbfounded to hear them, for not one of these crimes was even breathed at their two court sessions. The great Sanhedrin faces the Roman governor with the rankest lies. Nor was there one man who dissented, one man who opened his mouth to tell the truth about what they had "found." Caiaphas and a few leaders do the speaking, but all the rest lend their assent. This need not surprise us. They who plotted judicial murder are capable of carrying it out by means of bold lying.

Three capital crimes are charged against Jesus. "Perverting our nation," turning it this way and that way from its peaceful course, working it up in dangerous agitation, is the first crime. The emperor wanted peace; other rebellions had been started and had to be put down; Jesus was another agitator. The present participles that are used in stating the crimes signify that Jesus was now engaged in these nefarious acts. They say "our nation" and use ἔθνος which the Jews seldom used because it put them into the same class with the other "nations"; they loved the term λαός which was used in the sense of the covenant "people" that was exalted above all the ἔθνη or nations. They prefer the secular word in this instance in order not to ruffle Pilate. They count on his having heard of the fame of Jesus in Galilee, among the Jews generally, and here in Jerusalem, where his royal entry had occurred last Sunday, and all the thousands of pilgrims had enthused about him. So this was it: they wanted Pilate to think of a dangerous agitation by this fellow, and that the Sanhedrin has stepped in and squelched it and brought the leader of it to book. What more need Pilate say except to order the fellow's execution forthwith?

The other charges are added with two "and," which means coordination but also that all three are of the same kind. "Hindering to pay taxes to Caesar" has the plural of φόρος, the same word that was used in 20:22, which is used to designate tribute received from a subject nation, the Greek verb being "to give." The Sanhedrists had tried to trick Jesus into a declaration that such taxes that were paid to Caesar were unlawful for godly Jews, but his declaration had been the very opposite. This is a bold lie indeed! But how can Pilate get at the truth? They were wholly safe in even this lie. But when Pilate hears even an intimation of this kind, it must arouse his suspicion. Rebellion against Roman taxation had already caused trouble enough, and Pilate was fully aware of the fact that the Jews chafed under this tax and would respond to any agitation to throw off this galling yoke.

The climax is the third crime: "declaring himself to be a Christ-king." We think that the two words should be regarded as one concept and not, as is generally done, as two: "Christ, a king." The view that "Christ" meant nothing to Pilate and that "king" was therefore added, shows only that "Christ" should then have been left out and "king" alone used. If "king" is only an apposition, we should then have "*the* Christ." No; "a Christ-king" these Sanhedrists say, namely one who capitalizes the Christ-hopes of the Jews and is therefore vastly more dangerous than any ordinary pretender to the throne of Israel would be, like Herod the Great and men who had only political interests. Pilate and anyone who was slightly acquainted with the Jews knew of this Christ-hope of theirs. This charge is made the last, the climax, and throws light on the other two.

3) Did the enumeration of these crimes impress Pilate? Very little. But since they are finally stated, he proposes to proceed as the judge to try the case, but not by any means immediately to underwrite the verdict that the Sanhedrin wants executed. And, in fact, if these were the crimes of which Jesus was guilty, it would be easy also for Pilate to determine that fact.

But Pilate inquired of him, saying, Thou, art thou the king of the Jews? And he answering said to him, Thou sayest it.

Read the exposition of John 19:33-38. Pilate rose from his judgment seat and entered the Praetorium and gave the order to bring Jesus inside it for examination. He takes the most direct manner for investigating the charges; he will begin by examining the prisoner. He could do this outside of the Praetorium, but that would leave the prisoner in the hands of the Jewish police. By his going inside the building the Jews are compelled automatically to hand this prisoner over to the Roman soldier guards of Pilate. He did not examine Jesus in secret. The Romans were wholly averse to secrecy. Any Jews who cared to hear the examination could come into the Praetorium—Pilate certainly would not cater to their unpleasant scruples about ceremonial defilement by examining Jesus on the outside. The Roman guards heard the examination, and also other persons may have been there.

As the governor Pilate had kept a watchful eye on every movement in the land under his jurisdiction. He had undoubtedly heard about Jesus but never of any royal pretensions on his part, of any force of men he was gathering, of any political disturbance whatever. The emphasis is on σύ: "Thou, art thou?" etc. Pilate's question is tinged strongly with incredulity. He cannot bring himself to think that this man, beaten, bruised, arrested, alone, was pretending to be a king that was hostile to Rome.

There is also mockery in the question. The dignity of Jesus had not as yet had a chance to impress the governor. Pilate despised the Jews and at first regarded Jesus as being only another Jew. "The king of the Jews"—did this Jew think himself to be "a Christ-king," "the Jews' king"? Grand king he would be for the Jews! Pilate had quite a different picture in his mind of what earthly kings looked like.

Pilate takes up only the charge about being some kind of a king, for the other two charges were contained in this one. The synoptists report with exceeding briefness so that John felt the need of supplementing their brevity. Jesus did, indeed, affirm that he was a king, John states that he explained fully what kind of a king he was. The synoptists let us infer this from the way in which Pilate spoke and acted after the examination into this kingship. "Thou sayest it" is like the affirmation recorded in 22:70 and in the parallel passages, also in John 19:37, and the quibbling about its not being a definite affirmation ought to cease.

4) **And Pilate said to the high priests and the multitudes, I find no crime in this man.**

Pilate came out again and took his seat on the judge's throne facing the Sanhedrists, their police force, and the other crowds of spectators who had gathered by this time. Some think that he left Jesus inside the building and had him brought out later; but it was ever the Roman custom to confront prisoners with their accusers. Jesus was led out of the Praetorium behind Pilate. The governor delivers his judicial finding. He acquits Jesus. Whatever the Sanhedrin claims to have found, Pilate asserts that he has found the opposite. The neuter adjective αἴτιον in the sense of crime or criminal charge is used as a noun. Pilate is not, however, true to himself or to his verdict. He stops short with his bare announcement; he does not forthwith order the prisoner discharged and give him the necessary protection; he does not order the crowds of Jews to disperse and to leave the premises and, if necessary, drive them off by ordering out the cohort. This is the first fatal flaw in the action of the Roman judge.

5) **But they kept insisting, declaring, He is exciting the people by teaching through the whole of Judea, also starting from Galilee till here.**

Mark adds the detail that they brought on more accusations, Matthew and Mark that Pilate asked Jesus why he answered nothing to all this, and that he marvelled at Jesus' silence. But Pilate had rendered his verdict. Did he intend to turn the defense of that verdict over to Jesus? Was it not his business to examine into any new charges if he deemed them worthy of attention? Jesus disdains to answer these trumped-up charges. Pilate shows that he, too, scorns them because he does not take them up.

The silence of Jesus leaves the responsibility where it belongs, on Pilate, the judge. Luke records only the charge of exciting (shaking to and fro) the people (λαός this time). "Also starting from Galilee till here" in the very capital of Judaism reminds Pilate that seditions usually start in turbulent Galilee. Pilate lets the Sanhedrists offer this indignity to his high court after pronouncing the verdict. He sits there, looks at Jesus, asks him to answer, and takes no measures to clear out the Jews. Since when must the judge's verdict please the plaintiff when it acquits the defendant? Since when may the plaintiff assail the verdict before the judge himself?

6) **Now, on hearing it, Pilate inquired whether the man was a Galilean. And on learning that he was**

from the jurisdiction of Herod, he sent him up to Herod, he, too, being in Jerusalem in these days.

After Pilate acted as though he must obtain the consent of the Sanhedrin to his verdict of innocence, all he could do was merely to delay the fatal outcome. The mention of Galilee caught his ear, and a new thought flashed into his mind: he would get rid of this entire affair by turning it over to the ruler of Galilee. So he asked whether the prisoner was from Galilee. A criminal might be tried before three courts, the *forum originis, domicilii,* or *delicti,* at the court of his birthplace, of his domicile, or of the place of the commission of his crime. Jesus had lived and worked in Galilee for so long a time that he might well be remanded to the jurisdiction of Herod. There is no need of discussing Bethlehem as being the actual place of Jesus' birth.

7) Yes, Pilate was told that Jesus, whose home was at Capernaum and who grew up to manhood in Nazareth, was "from the jurisdiction of Herod" (the Greek retains "is" in the indirect discourse after a past tense). Pilate forthwith sent Jesus to Herod. "Send up" is a legal term for remanding one to trial. "Sent up to Herod" means that Pilate turned the case over to Herod. Strange, indeed! It was too late to do such a thing, for Pilate had rendered his verdict. By doing it nevertheless, more decisively than by listening to new charges he disregarded not only his verdict but even the fact that he had rendered one. The whole case is thrown wide open, and legal procedure and legal safeguards are thrown to the wind. The trial has ended, what follows is no longer a trial but only a miserable jockeying and haggling; the outcome could not be in doubt after this sort of thing was begun.

"Herod" is the only name that is used in the New Testament, but this is Herod Antipas, one of the sons of Herod the Great. He had inherited and was by Rome granted only a portion of his father's dominion and ruled as tetrarch over Galilee and Perea. When

Mark calls him "king," this was a title that was used by the people. He did plan to become king and to regain Judea and his father's entire territory. When, at the instigation of Herodias, he made the attempt at the time when Caligula became emperor, his brother Herod Agrippa accused him before the new emperor, who sent him into exile for the rest of his life. This was the Herod who had taken his brother Philip's wife Herodias, who had beheaded John the Baptist, who feared that Jesus was the Baptist returned from the dead, whom Jesus called "that fox." Desiring to be the king of the Jews in the full sense of the word, he who was only a nominal Jew was giving himself the appearance of Jewish zeal at this time and also attending the Passover festival at Jerusalem.

8) **Now Herod, on seeing Jesus, was exceedingly glad, for he was wanting to see him for a long time on account of hearing concerning him, and he was hoping to see some sign being done by him.**

Pilate hit it right as far as Herod was concerned by sending Jesus to him. Herod was pleased with the friendly gesture on the part of Pilate in turning the Galilean prisoner over to him right here in the procurator's own domain, and he was actually delighted to have his long desire finally granted actually to see Jesus of whom he had heard so much for so long a time. The periphrastic imperfect ἦν θέλων is strongly durative: "was wanting"; the English would use the past perfect "had been wanting." In temporal phrases the Greek idiom ἐκ indicates the point of departure (R. 597), reckons from the far point to the present; the Greek likewise employs plurals in certain cases, here "considerable times." Διά states the reason for this constant desire, and the present infinitive denotes that he kept hearing about Jesus all the time.

This might have been a desire like that of Zacchaeus, which was due to the way in which Jesus treated poor sinners who were distressed and uneasy about their sin and guilt—and Herod certainly had awful sins on his soul. Luke dispels all such thought. What Herod hoped for from Jesus was that with his own eyes he might see the performance of some sign or miracle by Jesus. He regarded the miracles of Jesus as nothing but exhibitions that put on a novel and an astounding show. Kings often entertained their courts and themselves by calling in some expert and having him perform his feats for their delectation. That is what Herod hoped to secure from Jesus at some time. And when he now had Jesus before him he thought that the hour had come to have his craving satisfied.

The man was utterly shallow; as far as Jesus was concerned, he entertained not even a serious thought or wish regarding him, to say nothing of anything spiritual. Jesus had filled his land with the gospel and divine works of grace and mercy. It was all lost on Herod who looked only for diverting entertainment from him. "To see some sign occurring by him" (present participle) means a view of such a sign as actually taking place before the eyes.

9) **And he continued to inquire of him in many words; but he answered him not a thing.**

Jesus was most likely brought before Herod by a detachment of Pilate's soldiers who, on delivering their prisoner, return to the Praetorium. Having taken over the prisoner from the Sanhedrin, Pilate would hardly return him to its custody. We imagine that Herod's court assembled quickly, and that quite a scene was staged. Pilate had sent Jesus to Herod, which means that Herod was to conduct the trial and determine the prisoner's fate. But he does nothing of the kind. His long desire is now to be gratified, and so he proceeds with that and only that end in view. All his extensive questioning of Jesus is not judicial in any way. Herod does not sit in the judge's seat or function as a judge. Various opinions are naturally held as to the questions with which he plied Jesus. "In many words" means "at length," with many questions. They most likely turned on what filled his mind, the signs. How did Jesus do them? Were they real? How about this sign and that of which Herod had heard? And especially whether he would do one for Herod right now. Herod's "many words" reveal his light mentality. He rattled on, and it took a while for him to understand the situation.

Jesus met this flow of questions with absolute silence. Over against Herod's volubility he placed this calm, dignified, impressive, and most significant silence. The reason lies on the surface. We may be assured that, if Herod had proceeded as a judge and in the proper judicial way, Jesus would have given the necessary answers. The supposition that Jesus disallowed the jurisdiction of Herod is untenable. Herod was staging a show, and that made Jesus silent. This silence was a rebuke to Herod. It showed the scorn of Jesus for "this fox" and his antics.

10) But the high priests and the scribes were standing strenuously accusing him.

"The high priests and the scribes" designates the Sanhedrin in the current manner. They had followed in a body with their force of Levitical police. They were ready to accept a trial by Herod and were determined to have Jesus remanded to death. But a trial was far from Herod's mind. The descriptive imperfect used in v. 9 is continued by εἱστήκεισαν, this past perfect being used as an imperfect and the perfect as a present. As soon as the Sanhedrists could do so they voiced their most strenuous accusations against Jesus and reiterated them at every opportunity. This was to be a trial, and they were trying to do their part.

Moreover, they may well have feared that, if Jesus amused Herod by working some miracle before him, Herod might be so pleased as to try to retain Jesus in his court to show him off on occasion. So they used all their vigor. But that is all. Herod did not seem to hear. He was too shrewd to take over this trial from Pilate. For one thing, he was under no obligation to the Sanhedrin, saw no special advantage in taking up this trial, and, more important still, saw the great advantage of returning Pilate's compliment by restoring the prisoner to him. So the Sanhedrists barked in vain.

11) Having, however, set him at nought and mocked him, Herod with his following, after throwing around him a shining garment, sent him up to Pilate.

This is the answer of Herod to the Sanhedrin regarding Jesus, a sort of verdict in answer to their accusations, which repeated in a way those that had been made before Pilate in v. 2. He refuses to take Jesus seriously, he makes light of the whole affair, he finds Jesus harmless, and he does not care to determine any crimes of his. He is satisfied to get a laugh out of this unexpected encounter and to let it go at that. Fear of the pilgrims who were attending the festival does not actuate him, and all superstitious fears of Jesus as being the Baptist returned to life have been dispelled this long time. Nor had Jesus ever directly assailed Herod in his preaching as had the Baptist. He had received his two hundred talents regularly from his provinces and had paid Rome in due order without any disturbances about the taxes. The personality of Jesus in no way registers anything in this tetrarch's mind. So he has his fun with Jesus and duly sends him back to Pilate's court.

Three aorist participles state the subsidiary actions that preceded the return of the prisoner to Pilate. The silence with which Jesus answered Herod's questions led Herod to "set him at nought," to treat him as nothing. This was intended to be tit for tat. Did Jesus treat Herod as nothing by refusing to answer the gracious questions of so high a ruler as this tetrarch? Very well, let Jesus understand that this was pure condescension on the part of the ruler, and that, as far as he is concerned who pretends to be king of the Jews, he is just nothing to Herod.

The phrase σὺν τοῖς στρατεύμασιν does not mean "with his men of war" (A. V.), "with his soldiers" (R. V.), "with his forces" (M.-M. 593) **for** the simple reason that the tetrarch would **certainly not** enter the domain of the Roman procurator with anything like a body of troops, especially at the Passover. Luther is correct: *Hofgesinde;* as are the German commentators: *Gefolge,* "his following" or retinue. Herod certainly made a grand display at Jerusalem, but never with a military force. The second participle about the mockery seems to be added in explanation of the first: by mocking Herod set Jesus at nought, his whole court followed its illustrious chief's lead. The details are left to our imagination.

Only one item is specified. Before the order was given that Jesus be led away Herod threw a shining garment around Jesus and dismissed him. The color of the garment is debated, and some assert that almost any color could be "shining" if the robe had a brilliant sheen. Although this is true enough, this word λαμπρός is so often used (also regarding angels) in the sense of brilliant white as to make this meaning very probable here. Priests wore white, but no reference to anything priestly appears in the narrative. White was worn frequently by the great and illustrious, and Herod therefore chose such a robe for Jesus. He or one who had been commanded to do so threw it around Jesus over his other clothing. Herod intended that, when Pilate saw Jesus, he could see at a glance what Herod thought of the man. "Sent up" is the same court term that was used in v. 7.

Herod and Pilate have been compared with each other. Both men find Jesus harmless, not in the least dangerous, at most a fanatic. But Herod laughs at

Jesus and makes a great joke of him; Pilate is impressed more and more by Jesus, goes to great lengths to set him free, and labors to rid himself of the bloodguilt of his death.

12) Moreover, both Herod and Pilate became friends with one another on that day, for they were in enmity with each other.

This states the result of Pilate's sending Jesus to Herod. As far as Jesus was concerned, the action was of no moment for him except to prolong his Passion and to let this minor Jewish ruler add his mite to the Jewish rejection of the Savior. No one knows why Herod and Pilate had been enemies until this time. Whether the event that is related in 13:1 contributed to the cause is problematic. Pilate had nothing to do with depriving Herod of Judea as a part of his domain, and that had been done before he was appointed governor. The fact that they were neighbors, ruled adjacent territory may have furnished friction enough. Yet this turned into friendship when each offered the other the compliment that is here recorded. For when Herod returned Jesus to Pilate's court he said in effect that he would approve any disposition of the case that Pilate might make. The Sanhedrin brought Jesus to Pilate because it was forced to do so; after being asked to take the trial Herod freely placed it into Pilate's hand. Although Pilate again had the troublesome case on his hands he felt the honor that had been accorded him by Herod, the more so since they had been at enmity.

The participle with the imperfect of ὑπάρχω resembles a periphrastic tense form, the participle repeating the durative idea, and πρό in the verb bringing out the idea of a previous condition. This friendship of Herod and Pilate is really not a case where enemies join hands against Jesus, for both men regard Jesus as really being harmless. This is a case where men subject the highest interests, those that center in Christ and in religion, to their own cheap personal ends. And the latter is just as bad as the former.

13) Now Pilate, having called together the high priests and the rulers and the people, said to them: You brought this man to me as turning away the people. And lo, I myself, having made examination before you, found no crime in this man as to the things you are charging against him. No, nor Herod, for he sent him up to us, and lo, nothing worthy of death has been done by him. Therefore, after chastising, I will release him.

As Pilate sent a message to Herod with the prisoner, so Herod likewise sent a message on returning the prisoner. A Roman guard transferred Jesus to Herod; how he was returned to the custody of Pilate is not clear, save that Pilate again has him in the hands of his guards, and Jesus is not in the hands of the Jewish police. Luke places us at the point where the governor has once more ascended his elevated seat as the judge. The Sanhedrists and the people generally were scattered about before the Praetorium. When Pilate takes his place, and Jesus is standing under guard near by, he has everybody summoned. "The high priests and the rulers" are the Sanhedrin, but "the people" are also included, of whom there must have been a great number. Why "the people"? Because Pilate felt sure that many of these were friendly toward Jesus, the mass of them certainly were not, like the Sanhedrin, set on doing him to death. He counted on them to support his effort to save Jesus.

14) Pilate thus speaks to this entire assembly as the judge. His tone and his language are judicial. He sums up the case. All sounds well until the last statement. There the fatal weakness of this judge again appears, for he ends by making a proposition and by implication asks that it be accepted. No real judge dare speak in this way. He states first that they have brought this man to him "as turning away the people"

and uses "as" to designate the alleged crime (R. 966). He includes in the one clause all that was charged in v. 2; but διά in the participle that is used in v. 2 means only agitation whereas the ἀπό in Pilate's participle means removal from the right course.

One would suppose that such a charge would have some ground, but "lo" ushers in a statement to the contrary. "I myself," says Pilate, "after making due examination before you, found no crime in this man as to the things you are charging against him." The pronoun ἐγώ is emphatic, and ἀνακρίνας is the legal term for making a judicial examination of a prisoner who is under indictment (note Paul's use of this term in I Cor. 9:3). "Before you" means in open court. We see that Pilate's questioning of Jesus was not secret (John 18:33) but according to due legal procedure, those who cared to hear were present.

Αἴτιον is used again as it was in v. 4; Pilate states once more that no crime or basis for a criminal charge "was found." He adds the relative clause: "of what things you are charging against him," i. e., keeping on with your accusations. Pilate speaks of all the charges that were made in v. 2. Is the genitive ὧν due to the genitive τούτων which is involved in it, thus being an attraction from the accusative ἅ: "of those things which" you are charging; or is this genitive due to the verb itself in the clause? R. 511 is undecided; the latter seems better although the former is generally held.

15) Pilate has the strongest corroboration for his finding as a judge: "No, nor Herod." The strong adversative ἀλλά: "but neither Herod," is well rendered by "no." The evidence for this is the fact that Herod "sent him up to us," the majestic plural indicates Pilate's court. "Sent up," the legal term for remanding to trial, is the same as it was in v. 7 and 11. The surprise of this brings another "lo." Herod, in whose domain Jesus had wrought so long and publicly, who was in the best position to know about any criminality,

knew of nothing at all on which even to start a trial by probing in a judicial investigation such as Pilate had instituted. Jesus has perpetrated (πράσσω) nothing that is worthy of death. "Not guilty!" is the verdict of the two courts. The periphrastic perfect is intensive (R. 903) and reaches from the past to the present.

16) What ought to conclude this speech? "Therefore, I herewith release him! The court is dismissed." Pilate could even now correct his mistakes for not having made this declaration at the end of v. 4 and for sending Jesus to Herod. But no; he says, "Therefore, after chastising, I will release him." He offered a proposal, a compromise. He virtually asks that the Sanhedrin accept this in lieu of the demand for the death penalty.

Pilate alone has mentioned death; but this is done only because the original demand made of Pilate was to execute Jesus on the verdict of the Sanhedrin, and because the crimes that are charged in v. 2 were capital crimes. Pilate acquits Jesus of these crimes, acquits him completely: "nothing worthy of death." But why, then, chastise the prisoner? Has Pilate or Herod found a lesser crime? No. No lesser crimes were even charged, and the prisoner has certainly not incriminated himself in some degree. This chastisement is a morsel that is offered these insistent accusers. Pilate is asking whether they cannot be satisfied if he orders this. They will then not lose face by being turned down completely. They will have accomplished much, if not all. Pilate was again hopeful, but every play he made only made his defeat surer.

To yield an inch from his first verdict (v. 4) overthrew the entire verdict. That is why the Sanhedrists hung on. All they had to do was to hang on, and they did. He who yielded so much would yield also the rest. It was just as unjust to chastise Jesus for no crime that merited chastisement as to put him to death without proving a crime that was worthy of death. Pilate's proposal is a self-indictment of criminal injustice. He shrank from the bloodguilt of executing Jesus; he did not shrink from chastising him. The fearful inconsistencies of worldly logic in moral matters are astounding. To hope to escape the devil by paying him a half-price is the folly of making him certain that you will pay also the other half.

What does "chastise" mean? The consensus of opinion is to scourge, and all those who argue to the contrary have yet to specify what else it could or did mean. Luke does not narrate the scourging but abbreviates that part of the narrative. It meant to stretch the bent body over a low stone pillar and to lash the back with whips of three lashes which had pieces of bone or lead fastened to the tips. This cut and slashed the skin and the flesh, the loaded tips tore deep holes. The vitals were sometimes bared at the sides of the abdomen, and men at times died during the ordeal. This is what Pilate proposed.

Some texts add v. 17: "Now he must needs release unto them at the festival one"; but this sentence is an insertion from Mark 15:6 and Matt. 27:15. It supplies what the following account needs.

18, 19) We receive help from Mark 15:6-8 at this point. The crowds of people who had gathered before the Sanhedrin were constantly increasing. Among them, we may suppose, were many friends of Jesus, and some of them shouted to Pilate to follow the custom of releasing unto them a Jewish prisoner at the Passover festival. Pilate took this up at once. John 18:39 states how he did it by acknowledging the custom and proceeding to follow it right here and now. The custom seems to date as far back as the era of the Maccabees and was probably intended to symbolize the release of ancient Israel from its Egyptian bondage.

We may suppose that the usual method was followed: the governor nominated two candidates, the people by acclamation chose one (Matt. 27:17); no one knows whether more than two were ever offered for choice. Pilate not only made the nomination but also indicated the choice he wanted made. For this reason he nominated Jesus and the worst criminal who was at this time lying in his prison. A pause occurred which enabled the people to determine on their choice —Pilate was certain that, no matter how the Sanhedrists voted, the people would demand Jesus. So he again took his seat as the judge and demanded to know the choice. This is where Luke places us.

Now they raised the yell altogether, saying, Make away with this fellow but release to us Barabbas! who because of a riot made in the city and because of murder was one that had been thrown into the prison.

Matthew explains this unanimity of the crowds; the Sanhedrists and their Levites among the police got busy on the instant, circulated among the crowds, and stirred them up with inflammatory words to vote as they did. Ἀνέκραξαν=sie schrien auf, "they raised the yell."

The name Barabbas is recorded by the evangelists only for the purpose of fully identifying the man whom the Jews preferred to Jesus. They do not play on the composition "son of Abba" and say that "Abba" denotes some prominent rabbi, and that this formed a kind of parallel to Jesus' title "Son of God." The textual evidence that this man was called "Jesus Barabbas" is so inferior as not to need discussion. Yet, in spite of the textual evidence, some would retain "Jesus" on the plea that no scribe would have inserted "Jesus" in any text and that it must, therefore, be original. But the very reverse seems to be true. Those who love to allegorize and play with names and words seem to have inserted Jesus in order to obtain: "Jesus, the Son of God," and "Jesus Barabbas (the son of Abba)."

We discard these fancies and the poor ground on which they rest.

This degenerate son of a respectable father lay "in the prison," the prison of Pilate in Jerusalem, and was at this time charged with participating in a riot or insurrection and with committing murder. The impression is left that he was caught red-handed, and that he would beyond question be condemned to the cross. Luke's ὅστις instead of the simple relative states that he was "such a one as," etc. R. 860 calls ἦν βληθείς a periphrastic aorist verb, ἦν itself being aoristic. B.-D. 365 calls this construction "entirely incredible" since it is never found except rarely in the poets; but the failing of B.-D. is his willingness to change the readings of exceptional cases. The matter is cleared up grammatically by making the participle the predicate to ἦν which states what Barabbas "was," namely, "one lodged in the prison." The participle needs no article when it occurs in the predicate.

Pilate set Jesus and Barabbas up as the candidates. He aimed to secure the strongest possible contrast: here one who was alleged to be royal, "a Christ-king" (see v. 2), there the lowest and most vicious criminal. But Pilate's intentions turn out unfortunately. By putting up these two he put Jesus into the same class with Barabbas—certainly not Barabbas into the same class with Jesus. This Jewish custom dealt with the pardoning of some criminal by the governor at the Passover. Jesus is thus really classified as a criminal together with this other criminal. Did Pilate not see this? He never sees far enough. The injustice that is done Jesus is outrageous. The worse this criminal Barabbas is, the more terrible is the injustice that is done Jesus. The Sanhedrists saw what this proposition of Pilate's really meant as far as Jesus was concerned and used it to the utmost. Although he wanted to save Jesus, by devious, not by straight and courageous means in honest Roman justice Pilate himself helps to destroy

Jesus. This thing of using questionable and wrong means to accomplish good ends has wrecked more men than Pilate.

The whole crowd does far more than to vote for Barabbas; and Pilate has his great share of guilt in what they do. They do not raise the yell: "Release Barabbas for us!" but first of all yell: "Make away with this fellow!" i. e., Jesus who is standing right there. Αἶρε="make away with him," i. e., put him to death; on this evident meaning compare John 19:15; Acts 21:36; 22:22. That was the very alternative Pilate had placed before the Jews by proposing Jesus as a candidate beside Barabbas. The choice was two-edged; it was not merely that one of the criminals should go free, but equally that the other should go to his death.

Pilate reckoned on two things: first, that nobody would want a criminal like Barabbas to live, and second, that the people would not want a man like Jesus to die. But natural justice is not so certain a motive among men in critical hours; one may appeal to it with safety only in calm days. The Sanhedrists had cunning arguments to defeat this sense of justice in the people at this critical moment. All saw that Pilate, the hated representative of Roman power and oppression, was trying to shield Jesus. Pilate had indicated that he wanted Jesus chosen; Pilate had put up this wretch Barabbas to attain this very end. Were the people going to let Pilate dictate thus? Did they want a Messiah of Pilate's choice? Did they think that a Messiah who would be under the thumb of Pilate was the true one? Nay, nay, never; make away with him!

20) **But again Pilate called to them, wanting to release Jesus. They, however, continued calling at him, saying, Crucify, crucify him!**

Luke does not state what Pilate said when he called to the people after the choice was made. Matt. 27:22, Mark 15:12 tell us: Pilate asked what he was to do with Jesus if they wanted Barabbas released. The pitiableness of Pilate is now evident. He had taken his chance on the choice and had lost out completely. And to haggle about it made the people's insistence violent. Luke says that he called out because he wanted to release Jesus. Did he hope that the crowd would tell him that it wanted Jesus too? Pilate had maneuvered himself into the complete defeat of his desire to release Jesus. He had brought his case to the point where such a thing was no longer possible—except by the strong measure of calling to his commanders and ordering out the Roman troops.

21) The crowd promptly calls back to Pilate and keeps it up in a mighty chorus and tells him what to do since it seems he must depend on them: "Crucify, crucify him!" That was how they wanted Pilate to make away with him. Some of the Sanhedrists probably first raised this shout, the rest of the crowd then took it up. Pilate had conducted the case in such a manner that not he but this crowd and the accusers, their leaders, were acting as the judge, rendering the verdict, and pronouncing sentence.

The question is asked as to how these Jews, whose death penalty was stoning, came to demand crucifixion for Jesus. The fact that Barabbas was to have been crucified, and that Jesus was now in a way taking his place seems a doubtful answer. The Jews had turned Jesus completely over to Pilate; they had washed their hands of Jesus. Deprived of the right of inflicting the death penalty themselves, they hold Pilate to its infliction, and that meant crucifixion for Jesus. Stoning would have had to be done by their own hands; let this pagan do the bloody work for them. Nor would Pilate have beheaded Jesus, the common Jew; only Roman citizens (Paul was one) received that mode of death.

22) **He, however, for the third time said to them: Why, what base thing did this man do? No capital crime did I find in him. I will, therefore,**

after chastising, release him. But they went on insisting with great voices, asking as their due that he be crucified. And their voices began to prevail.

Luke's record is the clearest in regard to this third appeal of Pilate's, compare Matt. 27:23; Mark 15:14. It has come to this point that Pilate has entirely forgotten that he is the judge, even the governor and highest judicial authority in the land. He actually pleads with this crowd and the implacable Sanhedrists. In questions γάρ is little more than an intensive particle, R. 1149; it is like the *denn* in a question, B.-D. 452, 1 And κακόν is no longer a capital crime but any "base thing." "Show me even that much," Pilate pleads.

As far as "a crime of death" (qualitative genitive), a capital crime, is concerned, he repeats vainly that he found nothing like this in Jesus. But it is no longer the judge that pronounces this verdict from his judge's seat; the judicial tone and bearing are completely gone. So he reverts to his former compromise (v. 16), to chastise Jesus and to let it go at that. But his very tone must have betrayed the fact that he had no hope of its acceptance. This verse is highly illuminating for an understanding of the character of Pilate. The Jews had taken his measure.

23) **They merely continue their insistence and shout the louder** at the sight of his complete weakening. And they are right—one more shove, and over he goes. The verb means "to lie upon" and thus to insist. It is used figuratively only with regard to tempests and the press of wind, which cannot be brought in here as R., W. P., desires, as if the shouting were a tempest. The middle of αἰτέω is used to express business demands, "to ask what is due," what one has a right to ask, R. 805. It was thus that Pilate was now asked to crucify Jesus. The crowd is not begging a favor but demanding its rights. Rights on what grounds? Grounds—they needed none with regard to a judge like this.

Luke records that "the voices of them began to prevail," and good texts add: all of them "and of the high priests" (A. V.). The latter was probably stricken because it placed the high priests together with "them," namely the common people. But Luke's imperfect "began to prevail" intimates that the battle against Pilate was even now not entirely won. The aorist used in v. 24 reports that it was won when Pilate finally pronounced sentence. This did not, however, happen until John 19:1-15 had occurred, the scourging and the mockery plus the presentation with, "Behold the man!" All this is not the preparation for crucifixion but the final, desperate effort on the part of Pilate to save Jesus by making him so pitiable a figure that nobody could possibly any longer think of him as being a king.

24) All this, too, failed, more than failed, it brought on the climax. **And Pilate gave sentence that their demand be done. And he released him who because of riot and murder had been thrown into prison, whom they were asking as their due; but Jesus he delivered to their will.**

Luke is the only evangelist who states that Pilate passed sentence on Jesus in due form. But the sentence was not death because of some crime even though it was only an alleged crime; it was "that their demand occur," that the Jews get what they had asked as being rightly due them. The αἴτημα plainly continues the idea of αἰτούμενοι and carries it over to ἠτοῦντο, all speak of what the Jews demanded as their right. This is, indeed, a strange form of sentencing.

25) The execution of the sentence follows, and we now see that the sentence included two parts. The first was the release of Barabbas. "He released him" by an order to the commanding officer who passed the order on to a subaltern. The enormity of this act is brought to the reader's mind by a repetition of the contents of v. 19 concerning the man's criminality

and the addition that this was he "whom they were asking for all the time (durative, imperfect) as their rightful due." Not a pagan or a pagan mob asks thus but the great Sanhedrin of the Jewish nation, their supreme religious court, which is backed by a great crowd of their people. Think of it—this they asked! And they got what they asked—deserved to get their request.

The other part of the sentence was also executed. Note the chiasm: the two verbs outside, the two objects abutted between them. We have only the simple name "Jesus" in plain contrast to the full description of the other man. "He delivered to their will" does not mean that Jesus was turned over to the Jews; it is useless to argue for that idea, for this contradicts all that follows. Pilate's soldiers executed Jesus, and that was "their will," the will of the Jews. John 19:16.

26) Immediately after the sentence had been pronounced Jesus was led away to the place of execution. No law required a delay. No such law existed in the provinces. The imperial laws regarding this point applied only to Roman citizens, and these were not crucified.

And as they led him away, taking hold of Simon, a Cyrenian coming from the country, they placed on him the cross to carry it behind Jesus.

The synoptists only imply that Jesus bore his cross on the way to execution, John 19:17 tells us that he did so. The prisoner was generally led through the most populous streets; the place of execution would generally be near a highway where many people would congregate. The traditional *via dolorosa*, which is now shown in Jerusalem as being the street over which Jesus passed, is of late construction. The city was destroyed several times, and many of its levels were greatly changed. In places the declivities were filled with debris so that some streets are as high as 60 or 80 feet above their original levels.

All the evangelists only imply that after the procession had gone some distance for some reason a man had to be provided to carry the cross for Jesus. From Matthew we gather that this occurred after the procession passed out of the city gate. We are certainly correct in thinking that Jesus broke down under the load, broke down so completely that even his executioners saw that no blows and cursings of theirs could make him stagger on. The effect of all the abuse that had been heaped on Jesus since his arrest became apparent.

The cross was no light load. Much has been written about its form, whether it was an × or a T or had a crossbeam †, and whether the beams were fastened together from the start. All the evidence points to the form which the church everywhere accepts, but it is often pictured as being much too high. Jesus bore his cross and not merely the crosspiece or *patibulum*. By literally bearing his cross Jesus lends a powerful effect to his figurative words about our taking up our cross and bearing it after him.

The evangelists say little about Simon. He hailed from Cyrene but was now a resident of Jerusalem, one of the many Cyrenians who were dwelling there (Acts 2:10). Mark names his two sons, who, it is agreed, later held prominent positions in the church. From these data the general conclusion is drawn that Simon's strange contact with Jesus led to his conversion and thus to the prominence of his sons in the church.

Luke and Mark know that he had been out in the country that morning (ἀπ' ἀγροῦ, one of the many phrases that need no article) and was just coming in at this hour (shortly before 9 A. M.). No Jew would, of course, work out in a field on a festival day such as this, and to assume this in the case of Simon in order to build up other hypotheses regarding him is a proceeding that is quite futile. The executioners of Jesus simply took this Jew and forced him to carry Jesus' cross. They pounced on the first man that came along, perhaps caught Simon right at the city gate, where he could not escape. No Roman soldier would lower himself by carrying a cross for a criminal. So the soldiers caught a Jew and probably thought it a good joke on this unsuspecting Jew that had to carry another Jew's cross.

27) Now there was following him a great crowd of people, also of women who were beating their breasts and bewailing him.

As we have learned to know Luke, this incident may have preceded that which is mentioned in v. 26; but even then we have no reason to suppose that the account about the women is not true, that Jesus was too weak to utter the words that are attributed to him. The great crowd that was following Jesus was the one that had insisted on his death at the Praetorium, and was, no doubt, augmented as the procession passed through the narrow streets of the city.

"Also of women" means that there were many of these, and since Jesus turns and addresses them, they must have walked together and been able to get close to him. Beating themselves (their breasts) and bewailing him means that they were raising the Jewish death wail for him as being one who was as good as dead, compare 8:52 (Jairus' daughter). "To bewail" is used in this sense in 7:32; Matt. 11:17, and from θρηνεῖν we have ὁ θρῆνος, *Totenklage,* lament for the dead. One thing is certain, the temper of the crowd that helped to cry "crucify, crucify" is not the temper which all the inhabitants of Jerusalem harbored toward Jesus.

28) But having turned to them, Jesus said: Daughters of Jerusalem, stop sobbing over me, but be sobbing over your own selves and over your children. Because, lo, there are coming days in which they shall say, Blessed the barren and the wombs which did not bear and breasts which did not suckle!

Then shall they begin to say to the mountains, Fall on us! and to the hills, Cover us! Because if they do these things in the green wood, what will be in the dry?

It is not so certain, as some assume, that Jesus could not have turned while the cross was on his shoulders. These were women from the city, for "daughters of Jerusalem" cannot mean only "Jewish women" and thus also include women disciples of Jesus from Galilee. What Jesus says to them also fits only inhabitants of the doomed city. These women sobbed for Jesus as being one who was dead. They were moved by sentiment and gave rein to their emotions. Their lamenting is one of excessive pity for Jesus, and as a lament for the dead is filled with hopelessness. They see him helplessly carried to his death, unable to escape his doom.

Such tears for Jesus are utterly wasted, such sentimentality is wholly fruitless. Hence the bidding: "Stop weeping over me!" In negative commands the present imperative often means as it does here to stop an action already begun, R. 851, etc. These women were not weeping for the sins of their rulers in sending Jesus to the cross, for the sins of the crowd that did Jesus to death, for the sins of their nation which could reject David's son, for their own sins as daughters of this wicked Jerusalem. These women may have helped to acclaim Jesus, but they were not his disciples. "Not over me," says Jesus, for these women knew nothing of what he was doing this day: dying for their sins and for those of all sinners.

Πλήν, "nevertheless," tells them that others need their tears, need them very badly. They themselves and their children are these others. Jesus had already wept his tears over them (19:41). He has in mind heart-breaking tears over themselves and their children because of the doom of judgment that is awaiting them. These women are representative. Hence we have this record of their weeping. The sufferings of Jesus still arouse the emotions of especially the softhearted. But all sentimentality regarding Jesus is useless even when it brings tears to the eyes. Let sinners weep for themselves and for their sins, let them sob like Peter (22:62), their tears may then lead to something that is worth while.

29) What moves Jesus to utter these imperatives? Ὅτι tells these women, and "lo" brings out its astonishing nature. What they see and what they bemoan with fruitless sentiment are the beginnings of the calamites that will overwhelm them and their children. "There are coming days" such as they would not think possible—yet they are already on the way. The plural ἐροῦσι has an indefinite subject, it is like the German *man wird sagen*, anybody and everybody will say. They will call the barren blessed, an unheard-of thing among Jews, among whom children were esteemed to be the greatest of blessings, and childlessness, especially barrenness, a sign of God's displeasure and even a curse.

The sentence is misunderstood when it is thought to consist of three members. We have two, first the general statement: "Blessed the barren," and next the exposition: "and the wombs . . . and breasts." The fact that this expository clause is but one the absence of the article with "breasts" indicates even as wombs that give birth and breasts that give nourishment (this is the sense of the verbs) belong together. A glance at 19:43, 44 which tells of the calamities that are on the way for Jerusalem makes this abnormal beatitude plain. When those horrors arrive, blessed is the woman that has no children to multiply her agonies. Read Josephus, *Wars*, 6, 34, the most horrible thing in human history that has ever been set down in writing.

30) The distress will be so terrible that "they will begin to say (again the indefinite subject which refers to those who are in the distress of these days) to the mountains," etc. Jesus appropriates the prophecy

of Hos. 10:8 which was spoken against Samaria about her destruction by the Assyrians, but the two clauses are transposed. The sense is the same; what Hosea said of the Samaritans in their evil days the Jews will say equally in their evil days when Jerusalem is besieged. They will prefer a sudden, cataclysmic death by mountains falling upon them and by hills covering them to the daily, continued terrors and horrors of the siege. The word βουνός is a rare Cyrenaic term that is found also in 3:5 and means "hill."

31) Jesus explains with ὅτι why such cries will, indeed, be justified. The explanation is stated in the form of a self-answering question: "If they do this in the green wood, what will occur in the dry?" ἐν = in the case of, R. 587. Something far worse will surely occur in the dry wood. The green wood is Jesus in his sinlessness, the dry wood the Jews of Jerusalem in their sinfulness which had reached a state where it was ripe for judgment. The subject is again an indefinite plural: "if they do," which is shown to be such by the following "what shall be or occur." If Jesus must suffer as he does, sinless as he is and bearing only the sins of others, what will they have to suffer who sin until the judgment? On the green wood see Ps. 1:3; on the dry Jer. 5:14; Jude 12. The entire expression which is taken from Hosea is used again in Rev. 6:16 in connection with the final judgment. The subjunctive γένηται is deliberative, R. 934.

32) **Moreover, there were led also other two, malefactors, to be made away with together with him.**

Δέ adds this fact, and the imperfect describes the act. "Other two" or "two others" means in addition to Jesus. These were "malefactors" or criminals, "robbers," according to Matthew and Mark. The point of note is that they were to be made away with "together with him" and fulfill, as Mark notes, the prophecy that Jesus was reckoned among transgressors, Isa. 53:12, even as Jesus himself had foretold in 22:37. We do not know why these two condemned men had not been crucified before this time. The reason Pilate ordered them to be crucified with Jesus is plain. It was intended as a slap against the Jews and should be combined with the superscription that was placed over the head of Jesus. Pilate intended that everybody should see the kind of king the Jews had brought to him, one that belonged among criminals by their own demand. He takes his vengeance out on these Jews by stigmatizing their king, stigmatizing him by means of their own finding. Pilate disregarded what this did to Jesus himself. We note the same thing in his having Jesus scourged and mocked to show the Jews what a helpless, abject, pitiful figure they were calling a dangerous king. At that time it was his object to save Jesus; saving him is now past, and the weak, defeated Pilate can take only this vengeance on his successful opponents.

33) **And when they came to the place called Cranium, there they crucified him; also the malefactors, the one at the right, the other at the left.**

The place was called Golgotha, and Matthew translates this Aramaic term Κρανίου τόπος, "Cranium place"; Luke says simply that the place was called "Cranium." It bore this name because the hill was shaped like a cranium, the top of a skull. The name was merely "Cranium" or "Calvary" (from the Latin), not "The Skull" (R. V., no article accompanies the name), and certainly not "The Place of a Skull."

The site is in dispute, but it has been certain for many years that the site which is now shown in Jerusalem in the Church of the Holy Sepulcher is spurious *in toto*. Far more acceptable is the cranium-like hill outside the walls which is now occupied by a Mohammedan cemetery, a hill that rises above the recently discovered "Garden Tomb" (also called "Gorden's Tomb" after its discoverer). This place bears many marks of being the place of crucifixion, namely the peculiarly shaped hill, and of the entombment in the garden beneath and away from the hill.

Among the astounding things of Scripture are the records of the supreme events—one word to describe the crucifixion of God's Son, one word his resurrection. Events so tremendous, words so restrained! Who guided these writers to write in such an astonishing manner? This is one of the plain marks of divine inspiration in the very product itself. The intention is evidently, and that on the part of all the evangelists, *not* to describe the awful act of crucifixion. The fact, not the details, is to fill the reader's mind.

From the great mass of evidence that has been collected we gather that the cross was first of all planted firmly in the ground. Only under very exceptional circumstances were the crosses high. That of Jesus raised his feet no more than a yard above the ground, for the short stalk of hyssop which was 18 inches long was able to reach Jesus' mouth. A block or a heavy peg was fastened to the beam, and the victim sat on this. He either mounted it himself and was perhaps assisted by the executioners, or they lifted him up to the seat and then fastened his body, arms, and legs with ropes. Then the great nails, of which the ancient writers speak especially, were driven through the hands and the feet.

A hundred years ago about everybody was certain that the feet of Jesus were not nailed to the cross—in spite of 24:39: "Behold my hands and my feet!" Exhaustive investigation has convinced all who have seen the evidence that also the feet were nailed, and each foot with a separate nail. The central seat or peg kept the body from settling to one side after the ropes were removed. None of the old writers ever mentions a loincloth. The agony of crucifixion needs no description. We mention only the hot sun, the raging thirst, the slow approach of death which was sometimes delayed for four days. It was a great relief to the malefactor to learn that he was to die on the very day on which he was crucified.

"Also the malefactors" means that they were crucified in the same way that Jesus had been crucified. Painters follow their fancies when they depict the malefactors as being only tied to their crosses with ropes. All the evangelists state that Jesus was placed between the two malefactors, probably by order of Pilate, although the soldiers, too, would naturally have arranged the crosses in this manner, Jesus being the one important victim. The Greek writes ἐκ and measures out from Jesus to the right and to the left and uses the plural without the article.

34) **But Jesus went on to say, Father, dismiss it for them; for they do not know what they are doing! Moreover, in dividing his garments they threw lots.**

See 3:7 on the imperfect ἔλεγε; it describes the act of speaking and thus asks us to dwell on it. This is surely the first word that Jesus uttered while he was on the cross. The question of the text need not detain us; the attestation for its retention is strong, and the absence of this verse in some texts was most likely due to inability to grasp the meaning. A conflict with the word that was spoken to the daughters of Jerusalem is untenable; and demands to know how it could be known that Jesus spoke this word are easily answered. The view that Jesus spoke thus only in his heart contradicts the verb that he "said" this. Luke alone records this prayer. It was uttered while the crucifixion was in progress or immediately thereafter.

This simple prayer is astounding; all interpretation will leave much to be added. The climax of suffering is now being reached, but the heart of Jesus is not submerged by this rising tide—he thinks of his enemies and of all those who have brought this flood of suffering upon him. In this connection one should dwell on the whole Passion history and on the fact that it meant agony for Jesus. He might have prayed for justice and just retribution; but his love rises above his suffering, he prays for pardon for his enemies. Such love exceeds comprehension and yet reveals the source whence our redemption and our pardon flow. "Father," Jesus addressed God and even now spoke as the Son, as one who accepted filially all that his Father is permitting to come upon him. His Father is with him and hears his Son say, "Father," and what this Son now utters will meet a full response in the Father's heart, for he so loved the world that he sent his own Son to die for the world, and this dying is now at hand.

The verb ἀφίημι, of which we here have the second aorist imperative, belongs under the explanation of the noun ἄφεσις which is given in 1:77. "Forgive" is not expressive enough: "remit," "dismiss," "send away" render the true sense. The object is not stated but is plain from the added clause: dismiss "what they are doing." The αὐτοῖς, "to them," is also discussed. Who are these for whom Jesus is interceding? The answer is very readily given that the grammatical connection makes the Roman soldiers the antecedent of the pronoun. There is then discussion about the guilt of the soldiers, as to how much they knew, and to what degree they were responsible for the execution of their orders, also whether they had helped to mock Jesus in the Praetorium, and even whether they were abusive in nailing Jesus to the cross.

But such discussion is rather confusing. We have the antecedent in Jesus' own words: he is praying for those who do not know what they are doing in bringing him to his death. Acts 3:17 tells us that this included the people; Acts 13:27 adds those dwelling in Jerusalem and their rulers, and I Cor. 2:8 corroborates the inclusion of the latter. Were Caiaphas and Pilate included? We prefer not to pass judgment on individuals, for God alone knows the hearts and to what degree they sin against better knowledge. Nor do we bring in the distinction between vincible and invincible ignorance, such as can be and such as cannot be helped by the person concerned. To be sure, the former involves greater guilt, but who of us can say to another person: "This you could and should have known"?

Nor was this prayer absolute, i. e., that ignorance removed all guilt or made it so slight that the Father could dismiss it without further ado. No; the very first word "dismiss it" states that these are terrible sins, something grave and serious to dismiss. This is not a case of brushing away a few feathers. This is also true with regard to the ignorance. The sinning that is connected with the Passion of Jesus is so open, flagrant, deliberate, and so multiplied that everybody who was involved knew it. It is unwarranted to claim ignorance for these outrageous sins, or to think that Jesus supposed that ignorance was back of them. "What they are doing" is defined in I Cor. 2:8, namely this that they were crucifying the Lord of glory, or Acts 13:27, that they were fulfilling the prophets, or Acts 3:15-17, that they were killing the Prince of Life. It was *this* ignorance that Jesus referred to. All these men who did Jesus to death were an ungodly, unregenerate lot who were living in all kinds of sins besides those they perpetrated on Jesus. What good would it do them to have only the latter canceled? This prayer of Jesus involves the thought that these men may and will yet learn just what they have done, that it was God's own Son, the Prince of Life, the Lord of Glory, and not just a man, whom their ungodliness killed.

This shows us the fulfillment of this prayer which Jesus had in mind. By no means a pardon without repentance—that would run counter to all Scripture and to the very redemption Jesus was now effecting. But a pardon through repentance when the truth would be brought home to them as the Acts passages brought it home. The knowledge that was thus wrought, which consisted of the light that would operate upon them as law and as gospel, as revealing their horrible sin and also the redemption that Jesus effected when they killed him, that knowledge was the means Jesus had in mind for causing their repentance and thus their remission, and not of one sin only but of all their sins. In other words, Jesus prays that the Father may give these murderers of his time, grace, and the knowledge that may bring them the Father's pardon.

It is remarked that Jesus does not say: "I myself dismiss it for them; for," etc. Why not? Because he is the Intercessor with the Father. He is acting as our High Priest. But did he not pardon others, even the malefactor (v. 43)? Ah, but all these repented. His intercession cannot take the place of absolution. Intercession is made for those who are still impenitent, absolution is intended only for the repentant.

John 19:23, 24 describes the division of the garments in detail. Luke states only that it was made, and in this case by casting lots. A common way was to place lots in a helmet and to shake them until one flew out; another way was to reach in and to draw out lot by lot. If the former way was used, one man was designated, and the first lot that flew out was his, the lot being marked for a certain portion of the four that had been arranged; John tells us that there were four. In the case of the valuable tunic of Jesus three lots would be blank, the other would win. The clothes of the victim were the perquisites of the executioners, the victim being treated as one that was already dead. The soldiers were great gamblers. It was nothing exceptional for them to gamble for the clothes of Jesus. The clothes of the malefactors were probably divided in the same way.

35) **And the people were standing beholding. Moreover, also the rulers were turning up the nose,**

saying, Others he saved; let him save himself if this fellow is the Christ of God, the elect.

Recall the crowd of people and of women that followed the procession out to Calvary (v. 27). All that Luke says about the people is that they were standing while looking on. This spectacle fascinated them; the past perfect of this verb is always used as an imperfect. A great circle of spectators surrounded the central scene. Instead of saying that καί implies that the people, too, were turning up the nose like the rulers, the statement should be reversed: the rulers, too, were standing like the people. Others besides the rulers did, indeed, mock Jesus while he hung on the cross as Matthew and as Mark report, but their very language shows that these were men of the city who knew what had occurred at the night trial and threw this into Jesus' teeth. In addition we see "also the rulers," Matthew naming all three classes of the Sanhedrin, which is exceptional for him since the naming of two classes generally suffices. It is unwarranted, then, to think that only a few Sanhedrists persisted to the end, and that the rest were detained by duties at the Temple or elsewhere. No; so fascinated were they and so determined to see the end with their own eyes that they were out here on Calvary as a body.

Even here in public they throw their dignity to the winds, forget who they are, and, like the common herd, give way to their basest passions. What they are capable of we saw in 22:63-65. They cannot now spit on Jesus, but they certainly stab him as deeply as possible with their cowardly and vicious tongues. They go on turning up their noses at Jesus, a gesture of insulting disdain (Ps. 22:7), the imperfect tense is descriptive of what they did for some time. Luke records only their chief slanderous contribution. "Others he saved" is by no means an admission that he did save others but the very opposite. The denial that he really ever saved anybody is based on his inability to save himself.

For this is a sneer. It is plainer in Matthew where they go on: "King of Israel is he!" and mean that he is anything but that. All his miracles are derided—they must be spurious or he would help himself.

"Let him save himself," they taunt him, "if this fellow (οὗτος, derogatory) is the Christ of God, the elect," i. e., if he is really this as he claims. Compare 22:67, 70 in the second Jewish trial, and Matt. 26:63 the first. The Sanhedrists challenge Jesus to save himself by his Messiahship and thus to prove that he is God's veritable Messiah. Many texts read: if he is "the Christ, the elect of God"; but the sense is unchanged because the verbal ἐκλεκτός is passive and implies that God made Jesus his elect. Luke alone has this addition, which recalls 9:35, but certainly not as being the source of this sneer. It is a problem as to how the Sanhedrists came to add "the elect." Did they draw it from Isa. 42:1? The claim that it means the same as "only-begotten" in John 1:14 is only turning the other claim around that "only-begotten" means no more than beloved. All we are able to say is that "the elect" goes with "the Christ," God had appointed and chosen him for his office. The fact that Jesus was dying on the cross was plain evidence to these Jews that God had not elected but had rejected Jesus. Luke's "elect" seems to equal Matthew's (27:43) "if he will have him."

36, 37) And the soldiers also began to mock him by coming up, offering him sour wine, and saying, If thou art the king of the Jews, save thyself!

It is not probable that the soldiers would have joined in the mockery if the example of the noble Sanhedrists had not stirred them up to do so. Matthew and Mark report that the Sanhedrists mocked Jesus as being "the king of Israel." That certainly recalled to the soldiers their own mockery of Jesus in the Praetorium upon Pilate's own order when they fixed up Jesus as "the king of the Jews" with a crown, purple robe, scepter, and ribald obeisance, etc., as they picked up the idea from Pilate himself who kept calling Jesus king of the Jews, in fact, sent out an inscription with this title on it to be fastened to Jesus' cross. So these soldiers renew their mockery. But they pick up the new idea from these Sanhedrists to shout at this king of the Jews to save himself if he is this king.

But they put action into their mockery. They do their mocking by coming forward and by offering Jesus sour wine, ὄξος. All three participles denote mode and manner, all three modify "they were mocking" and show how this was done. It will not do to confine the mockery only to the words the soldiers spoke. This *oxos* was the common, cheap sour wine that was provided for the soldiers, with which they refreshed themselves during their long wait. It was their ordinary drink, and no other was available here. Coming up to the cross of Jesus, the soldiers offer him a drink, hold out their wine to him, and tell him just to step down and to reach out and to take it. It was a cruel way to mock the sufferer who had had nothing touch his lips since the night before.

This mockery on the part of the soldiers is recorded by Luke alone. It took place *before* the darkness fell at noon. It has nothing to do with Matt. 27:46-49; Mark 15:34-36; John 19:28-30, which occurred *after* the darkness, just before Jesus died. Yet some would weld Luke's brief account together with these other accounts —a task that is fruitless.

38) **Now there was also an inscription over him, The King of the Jews this.**

This is the parenthetical δέ which inserts a statement that is helpful for understanding what precedes. The mocking soldiers used only what Pilate had put into this inscription. John amplifies the synoptists' accounts on this subject by telling us that Pilate wrote and placed the inscription (by his agents, of course); that when the Jews saw it on Calvary they went and objected, but that Pilate would not change a word of it.

It is quite certain that the inscription was placed on the cross over the head of Jesus at the time of his crucifixion, and there is only a bare possibility that the inscription was an afterthought on the part of Pilate and was a bit later brought by a messenger to the centurion who was to have it put up. Inscriptions that stated why a man was crucified were common. These were also carried and displayed on the way out to the place of execution although they were not hung from the culprit's neck, for which view no evidence has been found. We read nothing about inscriptions in the case of the malefactors—the mind of Pilate seems to have been taken up chiefly with Jesus. Not, however, until Jesus was crucified did the inscription appear and were the Jews aware of it and of the writing it bore.

It was written in three languages, which fact explains the slight variation of the wording as this is recorded by the four evangelists. All four have "The King of the Jews." Read the accounts of the trial before Pilate and see that it started with the charge of Jesus' being the king of the Jews, and that Pilate constantly and to the very last kept repeating "king of the Jews." Forced to crucify Jesus by these vicious Jews, he will do so, but only as "the king of the Jews" as they have charged. This is Pilate's revenge. He writes their own charge over the head of Jesus. But was it a crime to be "the king of the Jews"? Strange crime that would be.

This title proclaims that Jesus is innocent of any crime. Pilate sets it down as a simple fact that Jesus is "the king of the Jews"; he had examined Jesus and found it even so and had also learned what kind of king Jesus was. So he writes it for all to read, and the title is a vindication of Jesus. But it galled the Jews— their king crucified as a malefactor! They tried vainly to change this accurate caption. God's hand was back of this; just as they could condemn Jesus only for being what he really was, God's Son, so they are able to bring him to the cross only as what he really was, "the King, the one and only King of the Jews." All their own and all the soldiers' mockery of Jesus as the king must take place under this silent title, which speaks so loudly to the ends of the world in three languages by proclaiming that he is, indeed, "the King of the Jews."

39) Moreover, one of the suspended malefactors began to blaspheme him, saying: Art thou not the Christ? Save thyself and us!

Both Matthew and Mark state positively that both robbers reviled Jesus. Any effort to change their testimony casts reflection on their veracity. To assume that they use a plural of the category and have only one malefactor in mind is unfair to their direct statement. After hearing the Jews shout about saving others these malefactors are carried away; they want to be saved from their excruciating pain and so join the chorus. Luke shows the sequence: Sanhedrists, soldiers, malefactors. But Luke speaks only of one and shows us the other as doing the very opposite. This is not a contradiction but only an addition, and a mighty important one, to the records of Matthew and Mark.

At first both malefactors reproached Jesus, but before very long one of them came to repentance, and it is this fact that Luke records. He grew silent, and then, when the other again broke out in reviling, he revealed the fact that he had changed. Is this so impossible? Both were hardened rascals when they were led out with Jesus. But they came to see and to hear mighty things regarding him from that moment onward. They were facing a slow death. The human judgment that had been visited upon them presaged the divine judgment that awaited them so shortly. It took until this time to produce a salutary effect in the one. The denial that it could take place is met by the fact that it did take place. The only difficult matter is to explain why the same effect was not accomplished also in the other, but the fact is again that it was not accomplished.

"Art thou not the Christ?" with its interrogative word οὐχί (the strong οὐ) which implies that the question must be strongly affirmed shows how this impenitent malefactor wanted Jesus to be the Christ, wanted it for his purpose. He will let this Christ save himself, but he must then certainly save also him and his companion. That is all he wants a mighty Christ for, to escape the cross and death, to go on living his wicked life, to cheat justice. There is no shadow of repentance, no trace of faith in Christ. The question and the demand sound like one more effort on the part of the man to prod Jesus, to make him act by taunting him with the statement that he is perhaps not the Christ after all and cannot save anybody as the Sanhedrists implied.

40) But answering, the other, rebuking him, said: Dost thou not even fear God, seeing thou art in the same judgment? And we for our part justly, for we are duly receiving things worthy of what we did. But this man did nothing out of place.

Why does this malefactor answer when the other had addressed Jesus and not him? Because the other had presumed to speak for both: "Save thyself and *us!*" He rightly and most emphatically disavows that presumption. Jesus is silent amid all the mockery and reviling; "as a sheep before her shearers is dumb, so he openeth not his mouth," Isa. 53:7. He simply endures it all. The answer was a rebuke, it was calm but straight and true. If we list the good works of this man that were done after his inward conversion, this is the first: a godly rebuke to a blatant mocker that recalls the fear of God to him and defends the Christ he mocks. This is a necessary work, one that Christians often shrink from performing for fear of men. And this malefactor speaks out before all these other mockers, retracts what he has previously uttered to the same effect, and takes his place beside Jesus. Already by rebuking the other he confesses his own true faith in Jesus.

We combine the negative with the verb: "dost thou not even fear," the present tense expresses the enduring fear; not with the pronoun: "not even thou," or with the object: "not even God," as has been done. At least the fear of God ought to have shut the other's mocking mouth. The fear had entered the speaker's heart. It is the dread of a holy and righteous God. Ὅτι is consecutive (R. 1001), "seeing that," etc., and points to the consideration which the fear should have followed, which is "that thou art in the same judgment." Note that κρίμα is a neutral term, "judgment," not "condemnation" (our versions and others). All three had received "the same judgment," one that remanded them to the cross and to a terrible death.

41) This malefactor at once states the great difference fully and clearly. Note the balance of μέν and δέ, which the English is unable to reproduce; also the emphatic contrast ἡμεῖς, "we for our part," and οὗτος, "this man" (purely deictic). "And we for our part justly" is an open acknowledgment that the judgment which had been pronounced upon the two malefactors was fully deserved. And γάρ proves it: "for we are duly (ἀπό in the verb) receiving things worthy of what we did," ὧν is the genitive after ἄξια and is attracted from ἅ, the accusative after the verb.

That is this malefactor's open confession of sin. How does he come to it at this late moment in his life? We have only one answer: it was wrought in him by his contact with Jesus. They know little about great sinners who reduce this man's sins, who regard him as a kind of patriot, one whose zeal was misdirected, or as a man who had already met Jesus in his wanderings and had been touched by him. He was "a robber" (Matthew and Mark), and the plainer a man's sins are, the more readily he may yield to the divine law in contrition for them. Many a black sinner has turned thus from his past life with unexpected suddenness.

Jesus was "in the same judgment" with them, was, like them, hanging on the cross; but, lo, the vast difference: "This man did nothing out of place." Ἄτοπον is by no means a mere euphemism for "criminal"; the words that were spoken to Jesus put that fact beyond question. Not even an unseemly, merely improper thing, this malefactor declares, has Jesus done. Yet where is there a man in all the world who has not done something "out of place"? We need not even know a man in order to be justified in charging him with the blanket charge of having done any number of things that are improper and even worse. Yet, after seeing Jesus only for an hour or two and under such frightful circumstances, this malefactor knows that he is stainless? Let us not forget that these very circumstances were media in revealing the real nature of Jesus' person. If never man spoke like this man (John 7:46), and the Sanhedrin's own police confessed it and were ready to take the severe consequences, neither did any man ever suffer like this man, and this malefactor confessed it. It is his first confession of faith. Do not ask to know all that transpired in his heart, do not dissect his knowledge and weigh it on your scales. Accept the testimony of his own confession as we accept yours.

42) **And he continued to say, Jesus, remember me when thou comest in connection with thy kingdom! And he said to him, Amen, I say to thee, today in company with me shalt thou be in the Paradise!**

The text which is here translated is so assured that any change that is based on textual grounds must be rejected. As far as σήμερον, "today," and the punctuation are concerned, see the text-critical survey in Zahn. We leave textual questions to expert text critics and discuss them only in necessary cases; here all is clear in that regard. See 3:7 on ἔλεγεν and note that it means: "he continued to say." However exceptional the lone word "Jesus" (here a vocative) may be as an address, it was used here. Since the malefactor now speaks to Jesus directly after speaking to the other malefactor, some form of address was needed. The change to "Lord" lacks support, and also the change to a dative: "he continued to say to Jesus."

The more one contemplates this malefactor's prayer, the more one is moved by it and grateful to Luke for its preservation. Jesus is dying on the cross, he is in a worse condition than either of the malefactors, is hounded to his death by all those about his cross, and yet this malefactor sees in him the One who will come in connection with his kingdom. This is the old Messianic verb "come," and Jesus is the One that comes. We leave ἐν as meaning "in" and do not turn it into εἰς, "into" (A. V.). Εἰς may, indeed, crowd out ἐν and follow a static verb or a verb of being, but ἐν never =εἰς. This fact is highly important here.

"When thou comest *into* thy kingdom," i. e., at thy death, is not what the malefactor either says or means. "When thou comest *in* thy kingdom," i. e., in connection with it, means at the end of the world. The ἐν is here used in its original sense, "in connection with." Jesus will come for the consummation of his kingdom and in that way "in connection with it." And it is then that this malefactor wants to be remembered, the aorist imperative to denote one act only. This man does not see only the divine Messianic King in this dying Jesus, he sees him "in connection with" his Messianic kingdom in the day when that kingdom is to be consummated fully.

We now see what lies in the humble petition "remember me." It is the opposite of being forgotten, which means excluded from that kingdom. "Remember me"=O heavenly King, include me, do not bar me out because of my sins and crimes! But why does he speak of that final day of the world and not of the fast-approaching hour of his death? Either includes the other. We think too much only of the latter, too little of the former.

The old conception of the Messiah placed him in connection with his glory-kingdom. In the case of the malefactor the fact deserves attention that he did not think of a political, earthly kingdom as the Jews did who debased and falsified the glory-kingdom. Jesus was indeed entering death, was not "saving himself" as his mockers cried who thought that his dying would prove that he was never the Messiah. The faith of this malefactor had risen above these vain Jewish dreams. Furthermore, this malefactor speaks of the great coming at the last day also because it is resurrection day. Why would there be a glorious coming at all, why should the great God stand at the latter day upon the earth, unless, as Job says in 19:25-27, "yet in my flesh shall I see God," with "mine eyes" (see the author's *Eisenach Old Testament Selections*, 1054, etc.)?

All this means that this malefactor was a Jew. Bengel tried to show the opposite; he argued that kingdom, Paradise (not the fathers, Abraham, etc.) pointed to a Gentile. But the Jews understood both terms, and the Gentiles had to learn the meanings that the Jews knew. So the view cannot be maintained that the impenitent malefactor represented impenitent Judaism and the penitent malefactor the believing Gentiles.

43) If the malefactor's word was an *exquisitissima oratio*, what shall we say of the reply of Jesus? It certainly exceeds the *oratio* of the malefactor. We once more meet the seal of verity, "amen," coupled with that of authority, "I say to thee" (compare 4:24). It should no longer be necessary to explain that "today" cannot be construed with "I say to thee." To be sure, Jesus is saying this today—when else would he be saying it? The adverb "today" is a necessary part of Jesus' promise to the malefactor. In fact, it has the emphasis. It would usually take three or four days until **a man**

would die on the cross, so lingering was death by crucifixion. But Jesus assures this malefactor that his sufferings will cease "today." This is plain prophecy and at the same time blessed news to this sufferer. But Jesus says vastly more: "Today in company with me shalt thou be in Paradise!" This is an absolution. By this word Jesus acquits this criminal of sin and guilt. He accepts him as one of his own. By this word he here and now unlocks heaven for him.

Jesus knows that he himself will die today. It is not yet noon. If we may hazard a guess, it is between ten and eleven o'clock, and Jesus died at three. He and the malefactor will be together in Paradise before night sets in, μετά states only that they will both be there. Paradise is heaven, the abode of God, of the angels, and of the blessed. The view that it must be distinguished from the Paradise that is mentioned in 12:4 and in Rev. 2:7 is untenable. How many Paradises are there? The LXX translate the *Gan-Eden* in Gen. 2:8, etc., with this Persian word "Paradise" and name heaven after the blessed Garden of Eden just as the Jews named it Abraham's bosom. Jesus himself made this certain when he commended his spirit into his Father's hands, v. 46. If there be a difference of opinion about the Father's hands, see Stephen as he tells Jesus to receive his spirit and practically repeats Jesus' words about his own spirit. The spirit of Jesus went to his Father in heaven, and the spirit of the malefactor together with it.

On what is the contention, which is so prevalent, based that the souls of Jesus and the malefactor went into the so-called intermediate place, the *Totenreich*, the realm of the dead, which is not heaven or hell but a place between the two, and is yet itself divided into an upper part and a lower, the upper being called "Paradise" while there is no special name for the lower? On the ground that Jesus is speaking "after the manner of the rabbis of his time." Since when does

Jesus adopt any belief of the rabbis of his time? And the proof that the rabbis taught thus has yet to be furnished.

The question is sometimes asked as to what the malefactor thought Paradise to mean. But Jesus, who knows the entire supernatural world, uttered this word and not the malefactor. So we are also told that Jesus did not enter heaven until the time of his ascension, and that his soul and the malefactor's went elsewhere at the time of death. But Jesus ascended to heaven in his human nature and bodily, an act that was totally different from his death and the repose of his soul in his father's hands. Jesus also did not say: "Today thou shalt be in purgatory!" Yet if a sinner ever deserved a long term in purgatory, this malefactor was such a one. His immediate transfer into heaven is proof that is fatal to the idea of a purgatory or of an intermediate place.

The malefactor had thought only of the far day of the Messiah's return and of blessedness that was awaiting him there. Jesus assures him that this blessedness will begin in a few hours. "Together with me" tells him that he will, indeed, be remembered. Where did the malefactor think his soul would be until that distant day? Why ask when he is dead? Whatever he thought, Jesus told him where it would be, told him, too, with authority and not as the scribes did, Matt. 7:29. Think how many sinners have echoed this malefactor's prayer! "Remember me!"—faith has always found that prayer enough. On the cross the Father hands his dying Son a trophy of victory in the repentance of this malefactor. This was refreshing to the soul of him who had come to seek and to save the lost.

44) Luke hastens with strong strides to report how Jesus died. **And it was already about the sixth hour, and darkness came over the whole earth until the ninth hour, the sun failing. Moreover, the curtain of the Sanctuary was rent in the middle. And crying**

with a great cry, Jesus said, Father, into thy hands I commit my spirit! And having said this, he expired.

The first great sign in connection with the crucifixion of Jesus is this strange darkness that occurred (ἐγένετο) from the sixth Jewish hour, our noon, until the ninth, our three o'clock. This darkness came when the sun was at its zenith and was shining with its strongest light and lasted for three hours into the afternoon. All astronomical learning excludes the explanation that this was due to a natural eclipse of the sun. This cannot take place when the moon is about full. Skirmishing through all the ancient records also produces no satisfactory results. There is only one conclusion: this darkness was wholly miraculous as were also the following signs. God darkened the sun's light by means of his own.

The fact that this darkness covered exactly what all the synoptists say it did, "the whole earth," ought not to be questioned. Yet many contend that ἐφ' ὅλην τὴν γῆν means only "over the whole Jewish land" or even over only Jerusalem and the vicinity. These understand γῆ in the sense of "land, region, country." But it then seems strange that "whole" should be added, and that the expression "that" land is not used. Those who translate "over the whole earth" sometimes spoil their correct view by saying that this is only "a popular way" of writing, and that, since the darkness extended over a good deal of territory, the evangelists simply wrote "over the whole earth" although they did not really mean that.

45) But Luke adds: τοῦ ἡλίου ἐκλείποντος, "the sun failing," and thus states that the cause of this strange phenomenon lay in the sun. When the sun itself "fails," the entire dayside of the earth is in darkness. Some think that the darkness set in gradually, grew intenser, and then receded. The evangelists offer no support for this supposition. We are not told why the darkness lasted just three hours.

Various explanations for this darkness are offered. One is that nature suffered together with Jesus; another, which is offered frequently, that the sun could not endure to look upon Jesus' sufferings—yet it looked upon the first three hours of those sufferings; and the sun cannot be personified in the way that is thus attempted. Closer to reality is the explanation that this darkening was a moral reaction against the killing of Jesus. It was more. This darkness signified judgment. It was not a mere reaction of the sun but a sign that was wrought in the sun by God. Darkness and judgment go together, Joel 2:31; 3:14, 15; Isa. 5:30; 13:9, etc., and other passages that deal with the judgment such as Matt. 24:29; Mark 13:24, etc.; Luke 21:25. But this judgment was not one that would occur at a distant day but one which took place during the darkness itself, on the cross itself, in the person of the dying Savior himself. For just before the darkness lifted at the ninth hour Jesus uttered his agonizing cry: "My God, my God," etc. At this climax of the darkness there occurred also the climax of the agony of Jesus who was under God's judgment for the world's sin. He endured it for the world, hence it was fitting that the whole earth should be darkened at this time. Most excellent texts read: "and the sun was darkened," in fact, this reading should be preferred.

Matthew and Mark record the death first and then the rending of the curtain in the Sanctuary; Luke does the reverse. This is not a discrepancy. Both acts occurred practically simultaneously, and in narrating them either could be placed first. Luke loves to combine similar things; so he follows the account of the darkness with that of the rent curtain. The καταπέτασμα τοῦ ναοῦ is the inner curtain or veil that hung between the Holy and the Holy of Holies. In the Herodian Sanctuary a second curtain hung in front of the Holy Place. This, too, was at times called *katapetasma*, and the plural is used to designate both curtains. But the regular term to designate the outer curtain is κάλυμμα, and the other term was used only occasionally. Yet this has led some to think that the evangelists referred to the outer curtain, but this is done without good reason.

The inner curtain is described in Exod. 26:31; 36:35; II Chron. 3:14. Josephus, *Wars*, 5, 5, 4 has the following: "This house, as it was divided into two parts, the inner part was lower than the appearance of the outer, and had golden doors of 55 cubits altitude, and 16 in breadth. But before these doors there was a veil of equal size as the doors. It was a Babylonian curtain; embroidered with blue, and fine linen, and scarlet, and purple, and of texture that was truly wonderful. Nor was this mixture of colors without its mystical interpretation. For by the scarlet there seemed to be enigmatically signified fire, by the fine flax the earth, by the blue the air, and by the purple the sea; two of them having their colors the foundation of this resemblance; but the fine flax and the purple have their own origin for that foundation, the earth producing the one, and the sea the other. This curtain had also embroidered upon it all that was mystical in the heavens, excepting that of the (twelve) signs (of the zodiac) representing living creatures." The thickness of the curtain corresponded with its great size, and its strength was according.

This mighty curtain was all at once rent or split in the middle, ἐσχίσθη μέσον, or we may translate μέσον (an accusative used as an adverb) down the middle. Matthew says "from above to below," he starts at the top. The two pieces fell apart and thus exposed the Holy of Holies. Consternation must have struck those who saw this sight. Jesus died at three o'clock, the curtain must thus have been rent at the time the priests were busy with the evening sacrifice. Many eyes saw what happened. Even the sound of the rending perhaps attracted general attention. We have not the least reason to think that only one or two priests, who were for the moment busy in the Holy, saw the curtain rent or found it rent.

This rending was miraculous as were the other signs. We have no intimation that it was caused by the earthquake, that the curtain was stretched so tightly that it split in two when the earth shook. It would then not have split from the top down to the very bottom but would have been torn in several directions. The idea that it was fastened to a great beam at the top, and that this beam broke in two and thus tore the curtain is only conjecture.

The significance of this torn curtain is easily understood. Only once a year the high priest alone dared to pass inside this curtain, on the great Day of Atonement, as he bore blood to sprinkle on the ark for the cleansing of the nation. In Herod's Sanctuary the Holy of Holies was empty, for the ark of the covenant that stood there in Solomon's Temple had been removed. When this curtain was rent, God proclaimed that the ministration of the Jewish high priest was at an end. What this high priest and his annual function typified was at an end because the divine high priest, Jesus, had come and had entered into the Holy of Holies of heaven itself with his own all-atoning blood. Heb. 9:3-15; Heb. 6:19, etc.; 10:19, etc. When chiliasts say that the Jewish Sanctuary and its services will be restored in the millennium they would restore what God abrogated with the rending of this curtain and thus place themselves in contradiction to God on this matter of the final atonement.

46) Luke alone reports what must be considered the last word that was spoken on the cross. All the synoptists speak of the mighty shout with which Jesus died. He rallied all his powers in order to speak his two words: "It is finished!" which are reported by John, and : "Father, into thy hands," etc. In his agony on the cross he could cry only: "My God, my God!" Now, as he did in his first word (v. 34), he is able once

more to say, "Father." Jesus returns to the Father as his Son after having executed the Father's saving will. It is the Son incarnate who had given his life into all this agony and death. Spent to the utmost, weary unto death, yet knowing that the mighty task was finished, finished forever, and that all its glorious fruits would follow—so this Son calls out "Father" and lays his human spirit into his Father's hands. See v. 43 and the view that "the Father's hands" must be placed in heaven. Those hands—the plural is most noteworthy because it is exceptional—are mighty indeed, omnipotent, and they are true. It is a terrible thing to fall into these hands (Heb. 10:31) but ever the height of blessedness to commend oneself into these hands.

The aorist participle expresses action that is simultaneous with that of the aorist verb. This last word was uttered with a mighty voice. Jesus did not sink slowly into death and grow weaker and weaker until he could do no more than whisper. Although he was dying of wounds and intense suffering he could within a brief period rally his final strength and die with a victorious shout. This has been denied, but in considering all that pertains to the human side of Jesus the only safe course to follow is to abide by the recorded facts and not to generalize from the experiences of men, because the body, mind, and soul of Jesus were unhurt by sin as ours are.

Why it should be denied that the loudness of voice was intended for men seems strange—for whom was it intended? To say that it expressed the intensity of the feeling of Jesus' soul is well enough, but even we do not shout when we are intense in our feeling toward God. But all the world was to know: "It is finished!" and all the world to know: "Father, into thy hands," etc. The intense satisfaction and joy in Jesus' soul were not to be a secret between him and the Father but were to be fully revealed. He had been mocked again and again: "Save thyself!" Here was the answer: after the Father's will had been done, the Son goes home!

Ps. 31:5 is referred to, and Jesus is said to utter his cry just as David uttered his. But the difference between David and Jesus is sometimes overlooked. First of all, this is the Son's "Father," which reduces David to a small type of the eternal Antitype. David, too, was not dying, hence the LXX translate "shall commit"; Jesus dies and says, "I commit." The difference is still greater when we note that David is beset by enemies, from whom God is to deliver him, and when this deliverance of David's is made to rest on the fact that God has redeemed him. All this is far removed from Jesus who is himself the Redeemer and whose enemies are removed. To argue that Jesus, like David, cries out in his distress, is to forget that all the distress is past, that Jesus has shouted in victory: "It is finished!" and that he now lays his spirit into his Father's hands in peace and joy.

The appropriation of David's words on the part of Jesus is thus to be understood only in a limited sense and should not be stressed beyond this narrow limitation. The force of the middle voice should be noted, παρατίθεμαι, "I deposit." We misunderstand this word when we think that it refers to complete submission, a placing in God's hands, so that he may do as he desires with the spirit of Jesus; no, this is a committing for the space of only three days. Jesus lays down his life and takes it up again, John 10:17, 18. Jesus makes this deposit for himself (middle), and the Father keeps his spirit in this way.

All the evangelists use choice words when they report Jesus' death. None is content to say that "he died." They all refer to the spirit or πνεῦμα, none only to the ψυχή although dying is also expressed by a use of the latter. As being a true man Jesus had both ψυχή and πνεῦμα; see 1:46 on the important distinction. Like

Mark, Luke writes ἐξέπνευσε, "he expired," breathed his last; but this follows hard upon the word about "my spirit" so that we may say that "he breathed out his spirit"; John says that "he gave up his spirit," and Matthew that "he let go the spirit."

While it is true that when he died the *psyche* of Jesus ceased to animate his body, which then hung lifeless on the cross, it was yet eminently proper for the evangelists to describe his dying by no reference to the *psyche* but by reference only to his *pneuma;* for never did the body of Jesus rule his person through his *psyche*, it was always his *pneuma* or "spirit" that exercised complete control. So it is true enough that when he died Jesus breathed out his *psyche,* and his body became inanimate; but much more is said when it is stated that his *pneuma* and all its exalted powers left his body.

Yet the exalted expressions that are used by the evangelists should not lead us to think that Jesus' death differed from our own. The separation of his soul and spirit from the body was the same as ours is. Nor was the Logos separated from the human nature of Jesus when he died. Body, soul, and spirit constitute the human nature of Jesus just as they do ours, but in him the ἐγώ or personality was the Logos. The death of Jesus affected in no way the union of the Logos with the human nature. This death affected only the human nature, for by it alone was the Son able to die. God's Son died in his human nature, and in that alone. Compare Delitzsch, *Biblische Psychologie,* 400, etc., on the whole subject.

The πνεῦμα of Jesus left his body, and thus he died. It is unwarranted to refer to John 10:17, 18 to prove that Jesus died, not from physical causes, but by a mere volition of his will. That passage deals with the entire action of Jesus in giving himself into death for us. He laid down his life when, as he said in advance, he voluntarily entered his Passion, the end of which would be death by crucifixion. It was the physical suffering that killed Jesus, the Scriptures assign no other cause. But we conceive of his death as being one of peace and joy, a triumphant return to his Father after the hard and bitter work of redeeming the world.

Certain older medical authorities have held that the actual death was induced by a rupture of the walls of his heart so that we might satisfy our sentimental feelings by saying that Jesus "died of a broken heart" although breaking one's heart is not physical at all, Acts 21:13. Our latest and best authorities inform us that a heart lesion could result only from a degeneration of the heart, and this occurs only in older persons upon whom disease has left its effects. This answers also the tentative suggestion that some artery perhaps burst and caused his death.

47) Now the centurion, on seeing what occurred, began to glorify God, saying, Certainly this man was righteous!

"What occurred" includes the earthquake and the rending of the rocks (Matthew). Mark states: "That he expired thus." We now learn that no less an officer than a centurion commanded the detail that crucified Jesus. We cannot say how many soldiers were ordered out for the execution; some think of only twelve, four for each person who was crucified, yet an additional guard for the sake of safety may well have been added. Matthew combines the centurion with his men and says that they were all affected alike. He adds that they were frightened, and the nature of this fright is religious.

When Matthew and Mark record the exclamation that Jesus was the Son of God whereas Luke writes that he was righteous, the two exclamations were combined. Both exclamations were uttered. Considering the centurion alone, of whom Luke writes, he had seen how Jesus was brought to the cross, had witnessed his conduct throughout the ordeal, had heard the mockery by which Jesus was reviled as claiming to be the Son of God. Then came his death with the cry "Father," the earthquake, and the rending of the rocks. Taking it all together, we see why the centurion exclaimed as he did.

"God's Son" was directed against the mocking taunts. "Righteous" is directed against the whole treatment that was accorded Jesus, the effort to make him a criminal and executing him as being one. Ὄντως, "actually," "certainly," sets this declaration over against all that the Jews might think and claim. The centurion agrees with the malefactor in regard to who and to what Jesus was. Why reduce these confessions to the lowest possible level? If they amounted to next to nothing, why were the inspired writers allowed to set them down for all time? The Christian view is to let these confessions stand in their full weight. Legend reports that this centurion, (his name being reported as Longinus) became a believer; evidence points also to the fact that the legionaries who were at this time stationed in Jerusalem were Gauls, i. e., Germans. The imperfect is ingressive: "began to glorify"; and since Jesus is dead, the centurion says that he "was" righteous, i. e., that there was nothing against him. So Jesus won other victories in his death.

48) **And all the multitudes that had come along together for this spectacle, after viewing the things that occurred, striking their breasts, began to return. But all those known to him continued standing far off, also women, those who together used to follow him from Galilee, looking on at these things.**

The plural "multitudes" is correct, for the city was filled, not with thousands, but with tens of thousands. Thus great crowds "came along together for the spectacle," θεωρία is found only here in the New Testament but is otherwise used to designate a theatrical show.

Yet when these crowds saw the show, viewed the spectacle of what occurred, even they were struck in their hearts. Luke says nothing about the earthquake, etc., but includes its occurrence in "the things that occurred." Now that it was all over, they began to stream back to the city, the imperfect pictures them as being on the way; but they were beating their breasts, and Luke names this involuntary gesture to indicate with what feelings they were leaving. They came to witness a show, they left with feelings of woe. God's sign language that crowned the six hours that Jesus was on the cross and the manner of his death made even these crowds realize that something terrible had been done when Jesus was sent to the cross. Oh, oh, what had their rulers done! Luke reports only the general impression that was made, for the thoughts and the feelings varied greatly among so many.

Did this feeling pass away and leave no fruit? Some think so. But, surely, with this feeling we may combine Peter's sermon at Pentecost, Acts 2:22-24, which drove at the consciences with the direct charge: "Him ye have taken, and by wicked hands have crucified and slain," and produced the effect that they were pricked in their hearts and cried: "Men and brethren, what shall we do?" The pilgrims scattered, but the people of Jerusalem, who were the very ones who had sanctioned the death of Jesus, remained, and many heard Peter's sermon.

49) Luke distinguishes sharply from the crowds "all those known to him" and uses the adversative δέ, and "all" suggests that they were a goodly company. "Also women" (no article) names these especially and then describes them as being "they who together used to follow him (present participle) from Galilee," which recalls 8:2, 3. Matthew and Mark name some of them and add the detail that they had ministered to Jesus just as Luke 8 reports. Matthew's "many" shows that the women, too, were quite a number. Luke paints the

scene with his imperfect tenses and present participles: the crowds were returning and striking their breasts, and the friends and the women were standing and looking on at these things. But he abuts the two imperfect verbs and draws more attention to the tenses; he also arranges them in the form of a chiasm with the subjects outside and the verbs inside.

Alas, only one of the eleven was there: John. Here would have been the place for Peter, but he had to crowd in where the devil could make him fall. The present participle ὁρῶσαι is feminine and gets its gender from γυναῖκες but belongs also to γνωστοί; all were seeing. Luke purposely changes the participle in both meaning and tense from the θεωρήσαντες that was used in v. 48. The crowds viewed a spectacle, these friends were seeing what was taking place with breaking hearts.

The crowds left, everything was over as far as they were concerned. These friends were still standing, could not leave, all was not over for them by any means. Love for the dead Jesus held them. What would become of his body? They were torn with grief, and a new dread wrings their hearts. The fact that they stood afar off (the Greek idiom is "from afar" and measures from Jesus) ought not to be attributed to their fear. John and Jesus' mother and Mary Magdalene had found an opportunity to go right up to the cross. This standing far off was due to necessity. The soldiers guarded the crosses, kept a wide space free about them, and would certainly not let a large company of friends of Jesus approach. Though Jesus was already dead, he might still hang on the cross for a long time. The others were not dead; so the guard remained. We know that later the order came to dispatch the victims, and Jesus was found to be already dead. Luke's imperfect tenses are more than descriptive, they hold the reader in suspense as to what will follow. And something most unexpected and remarkable did follow as Luke now tells with an exclamation.

Luke 23:50, 51

50) **And lo, a man by name Joseph, being a councillor, a man good and righteous (this one had not voted for their counsel and action) from Arimathaea, a city of the Jews, who was waiting for the kingdom of God: this one, having gone to Pilate, asked in due order for the body of Jesus.**

Jesus was dead; there stood his friends and the women, utterly helpless, utterly unprepared. No one had thought that matters would progress this far. Nor was there a leader who could take charge of things and know what to do. It seemed as if the sacred body would be dragged away by the soldiers and put out of sight in some pit together with the bodies of the malefactors. What else could be done? God took care of his Son's body in death. It is laid away in a most astonishing manner in fulfillment of Isa. 53:9: "And he made his grave . . . with the rich in his death." Help appeared suddenly, help such as no man would have dreamed possible. Joseph of Arimathaea came forward, took full charge, and attended to the proper burial.

Luke describes Joseph at length and yet leaves out the fact that he was rich and for this reason also a man of standing and influence. The dative ὀνόματι, "with name," is one of the common ways of introducing a person's name. It is astonishing to learn that he was a "councillor," one of the seventy that constituted the Council or Sanhedrin. But after all that Luke's Gospel has told us about this body it was quite necessary to say that Joseph was unlike the body to which he belonged, that he was "a man good and righteous." Δίκαιος is explained in 1:6, and "upright" is not an accurate translation.

51) Joseph's membership in the Sanhedrin necessitates a further explanation, which Luke places in parentheses: he had not voted for their counsel and action. The middle voice of the periphrastic past perfect means "to deposit a vote with." The counsel and the

action to which Luke refers were the first, when the Sanhedrin voted to have Jesus put out of the way. Luke states only that Joseph did not vote for these measures. Did he vote against them? We do not know. Matthew and John tell us that he was a disciple of Jesus, but John adds that he kept this fact secret for fear of his colleagues. This body had officially threatened to expel from the synagogue any man who dared to confess Jesus (John 9:22), and this meant complete cutting off from the Jewish religion and ostracism from official, social, and commercial intercourse. It was fear that sealed Joseph's lips. So it is no wonder that he remained away from the Sanhedrin or was not even summoned the night when it was voted to put Jesus to death.

"From Arimathaea" names his home town and not his present home, which was Jerusalem, for there he had his tomb made, one that was not yet quite finished. The mention of his home town serves to distinguish him from other Josephs. Arimathaea is the town of Rama, which was originally a part of Samaria but was later transferred to Judea so that Luke identifies it as "a city of the Jews." Instead of calling Joseph a disciple, Luke says that he was one of those who were "waiting for the kingdom of God" (Mark 15:43), in this respect he was like Simeon and Anna who are mentioned in 2:25, 38. He felt that the time was near for the coming of the Messiah and his royal rule, but he considered it a spiritual rule. He had turned to Jesus in this expectation.

52) This man, who has thus far been fearful and cowardly, does an astonishing thing. He casts his fears to the winds and boldly takes charge now that the great need has arisen. He must have stood among the spectators for a long while. Then, after his resolve had been made, he most likely first spoke to the centurion about going to Pilate and asked him to wait with the disposal of the body of Jesus. The centurion gladly assented to

the proposal of a man who was as important as this one was. So Joseph hurries to Pilate, and προσελθών means that he went right into the Prætorium to the governor himself.

But we should not suppose that he broke with the entire Jewish religion by thus entering a Gentile abode. All that he did was to incur ceremonial pollution for that day. The Sanhedrists had avoided this when they came to Pilate with Jesus, but only because they wanted to eat the *chagiga* in the afternoon. Joseph was not concerned about eating this sacrificial meal, he intended to bury Jesus and would be unclean anyway because of his handling Jesus' dead body.

Luke's aorist states only that he asked and obtained the body, he omits the fact that Pilate first made sure that Jesus was already dead. When R., W. P., says that the middle voice means that Joseph asked the grant of the body as a personal favor he contradicts his grammar, cf., R. 805. The middle of this verb is used in business transactions. The Romans quite generally allowed the relatives and the friends of men who had been executed to bury their bodies if they so desired. It was on this ground that Joseph based his request, which Pilate granted readily. Hence also Matthew writes ἀποδοθῆναι; Pilate commanded the body "to be duly given" even as Joseph had "asked in due order."

53) Joseph did not at once hurry from Pilate to Calvary. Mark tells us that he first bought fine linen for the body. He could easily buy this on his way back to the hill of crucifixion; linen for burial purposes was always available. But the great point to be noted is the fact that he bought only the linen and no spices. The synoptists say nothing whatever about Nicodemus, but John reports that he bought only the spices and no linen. We are compelled to conclude that these two men, both of whom were Sanhedrists, met early enough somewhere, somehow to confer with each other, to join in this task and thus to divide their purchases. Nico-

demus bought a hundred pounds of spices, a lavish amount; he must have engaged a couple of carriers to bring the load, being too old to manage it himself.

And having taken it down, he wrapped it in fine linen and placed him in a tomb, rock-hewn, where no one ever yet had been laid.

It is Joseph who "took down" the body, καθαιρέω, the regular verb to indicate this act. He is the actor throughout. This means that he took full charge, the others who helped permitted him to lead. That, too, may be the reason the synoptists say nothing about Nicodemus.

Joseph must have been a masterful man. He certainly had help, and we may think of Nicodemus, John, the centurion, and a number of women. It is possible that some of his men helped at the centurion's direction. It seems most probable that the body was lowered from the cross after the nails had been drawn out of it. Means to reach the crosspiece were at hand, they were the same that had been used in crucifying Jesus.

Like Matthew and Mark, Luke says only that the body was wrapped in σινδών, cloth of fine linen which was torn into long strips for the purpose of wrapping it around the limbs and the body. John speaks of these ὀθόνια or bands, between which the aromatic spices were sprinkled as they were being wrapped. Only the head was left free to be covered with a special cloth after the body had been deposited in the tomb. The bloodstains must have been removed from the body before this was done; perhaps the sour wine of the soldiers was used for this purpose with the centurion's permission. No anointing of the body was possible on Calvary; Mary of Bethany had attended to that in advance, John 12:7.

But where could the body of Jesus be taken now that a tomb so suddenly became a vital necessity? It is Joseph who meets also this need. All the evangelists tell about the tomb, and Matthew says "his own new tomb" and informs us that it belonged to Joseph. It was "rock-hewn," cut out of the solid rock of a cliffside. It was new, and Luke and John add the detail that it was so new that no one had as yet been laid in it.

Note the three negatives in the clause, each strengthens the other in Greek fashion. The form of the verb is the periphrastic imperfect, but it is regularly used as a past perfect and as a passive for τίθημι, "had been laid." "Was laid" (A. V.) is wrong in voice. Luke could have written ἦν τιθειμένος. R. 375, 906. John adds the note that this fine, new tomb was near Calvary, which made it especially available when the friends of Jesus were pressed for time—the Sabbath began with the setting of the sun. The body could hardly be carried away to any great distance. Here Joseph laid "him," Luke writes, αὐτόν, "him," whereas he just before wrote αὐτό, "it," the body. Joseph did not dissociate Jesus' person and his body.

A tomb "where no one ever yet had been laid," new and sweet, where no decay or odor of death had as yet entered, was a fitting place for the body of Jesus which no corruption or decomposition dared ever to touch (Acts 2:27). Here his holy body would have peaceful rest, all its dreadful, painful work being done. Yet Jesus was not intended for a tomb. He needed one only on our account and only until the third day. Luther writes: "As he has no tomb for the reason that he will not remain in death and the tomb; so we, too, are to be raised up from the tomb at the last day through his resurrection and are to live with him in eternity."

Quite recently, in a quiet spot just outside the walls of the present Jerusalem, at the foot of a skull-shaped hill (Golgotha, most likely), the so-called "Garden Tomb" has been discovered, which corresponds in every detail with the data that are furnished by the Gospels regarding Joseph's tomb. It must have belonged to a rich man, for it is an ample chamber, hewn out of the solid cliff, the face of which is smooth and perpendicular. The floor is not sunken, does not need to be. It has a vestibule and in the main chamber along the three sides only three places for bodies, the center being left unused. It is a new tomb, for only one place for a body is finished, the other two are not quite completed. The place toward the cliff has its floor hewn out a little in the shape of a human body. The three places for bodies along the sides of the three walls are cut out boxlike, the bottom of each being level with the floor. At the foot-end of the place that is finished for a body and likewise at the head-end, between this and the next place for a body, the stone is left thick enough to afford a seat so that an angel could sit, "one at the head, and the other at the feet, where the body of Jesus had lain," John 20:12, and the angel at the feet would also be "sitting on the right side," Mark 16:5, as one enters the vestibule. These heavier rock sections across the foot-end and on the left of the head-end are still intact whereas the thinner wall along the side where the body lay has mostly broken down. When the author viewed this tomb he was deeply impressed and compelled to say, "If this is not the actual tomb into which Jesus was laid it duplicates it in every respect." So many fake sites are shown in the Holy Land that to view a site like this leaves an unforgettable impression.

The great stone that was rolled before the door of the tomb was a flat, upright slab, circular like a great wheel. This moved in a groove that was next to the cliff and was wheeled back to the left to expose the door, forward to close it. The groove slanted upward from the door so that, when the stone was wheeled to the left, it had to be blocked to hold it in place. The bottom of the slant was just in front of the door, where the stone would come to rest on a level. After the body was duly placed into the tomb, the circular slab closed the entrance as indicated. This stone should not be called a "boulder." It is no boulder and is never called πέτρος but always λίθος; and no one can imagine how a rough boulder could do anything but merely block a rectangular door.

54) And it was Preparation Day, and Sabbath was dawning.

Mark calls this day the pro-Sabbath, the others "the Preparation," Luke "Preparation Day." This was, of course, Friday, but not in the sense that every Friday was "Preparation Day"; only one Sabbath had such a Friday, and that was the Sabbath of the Passover week. "Preparation" means that all things had to be prepared and arranged in such a way that this high and exceptional Sabbath could be spent in perfect quiet in the most solemn manner. Such was the day, and it was now almost over, for "Sabbath was dawning." The imperfect shows that it was coming gradually.

What sounds strange to us is the fact that it should "be dawning" when it began when the first star appeared in the sky in the late evening. A variety of explanations are given by the commentators, and the most probable seems to be that the verb is taken from the dawning of the natural day in the morning and was transferred to the evening with its first starlight. Luke describes the time and its character to show why the burial had to be hurried; yet he does not wish to say that it was finished a little before starlight, it had to be finished before that in order to leave time for other very important work that had to be done before the Sabbath actually set in.

55) Now after following behind, the women, those who had come together with him from Galilee, viewed the tomb and how his body was laid. Moreover, having returned, they prepared aromatic spices and perfumes. And for the Sabbath they rested according to the commandment.

The men of the little company carried the body— such was the funeral procession. The clause about the women who had followed him out of Galilee does more here than does the same reference in v. 49; αἵτινες = "since they were such as" and in addition to identifying the women again states the reason they were here. What had drawn them to follow Jesus from Galilee held them now even though he was dead. They could not tear themselves away. The men could have attended to the burial alone since all that was to be done was to lay the body gently down in the place that had been hewn out in the rock chamber and was ready to have a body placed there. Only the linen cloth needed to be placed around the head.

The women rendered no service at all. Yet they had business here. They viewed the tomb, also how the body was placed. They did all this, of course, because of their love and for themselves; but also because they intended to return on Sunday morning in order to anoint the body and thereby to complete what could not be attended to late on this Friday afternoon for lack of material, time, and facilities. It was the first time they had seen this tomb, its construction and its facilities, and so they viewed it all. The view that they did this from a distance is not tenable. They went in and saw just how the body was placed in its rock chamber. Sad, sad sight for their torn hearts!

56) Some of the women lingered after the tomb had been closed by the wheeling of the great round slab in place, which closes the door, and after the men and the other woman had returned to the city. But Luke speaks only of the return and that the women prepared the *aromata*, aromatic, costly spices in powdered form, and the *myra*, perfume liquids or extracts, which were to be used as early as possible on Sunday for making the burial as perfect as possible. This could not be put off for fear decay might make it impossible to handle the body. Even hours counted because they had to wait two whole nights and a day before they could possibly come to the body again, and corruption

starts quickly in that climate. So the women got everything ready on Friday so they could hasten out very early on Sunday.

Yes, some time was still left on Friday; we need not suppose, as some do, that this Preparation Day was extended into the early hours of the Sabbath after starlight, which made it possible to do work that needed to be done in preparation for the Sabbath. The main thing was to buy the materials and to arrange them in readiness for Sunday. On Saturday the Sanhedrists succeeded in having a Roman guard placed before the tomb after placing a seal on the stone and the rock wall, the breaking of which would betray any attempt to move the stone. Luke is careful to tell us that, despite all their need of preparing materials, the women strictly obeyed the Jewish commandment of complete rest on the Sabbath (the accusative to indicate the extent of time).

The holy body rested quietly in Joseph's tomb. Little had Joseph thought that he would use it so soon and for such a purpose. That body would presently arise, arise in a glorified state. The light of Easter would soon illumine Calvary.

CHAPTER XXIV

The record of the resurrection of the crucified dead body of Jesus constitutes the climax in all four Gospels. Yea, more than a climax. All that these Gospels record in the rest of their chapters heads straight for this final chapter on the risen and glorified Lord. Take away this chapter and the facts it records, and you cancel all else that is of any worth in all the previous chapters. Read I Cor. 15:12-20. The Christian religion stands and falls with the resurrection of the body that was laid into Joseph's tomb on Good Friday. Each evangelist tells the story in his own way with an eye to his readers for whom he has planned his entire record. When we try to trace the reasons each had for including just what he did we are on ground that is somewhat uncertain and should not be too insistent. Instead of becoming critical, we should be grateful for the records we have—most of us wish we had much more.

We have four records that stand as four witnesses. When one reads these Gospels, the one attitude of even the most critical reader must be that the reports are true in even every detail. This attitude is unaffected by text-criticism, which, however, belongs only in the hands of scholars who are fully competent for this type of work. Their approved results are most precious. What pertains to the body of each Gospel pertains in particular also to the section of each on the resurrection. No part of the testimony that is offered dare be discredited on any subjective or dogmatical grounds. Whether or not an individual reader is able to fit all the pieces in the records together means nothing as to the truth and the correctness of these pieces themselves. What one man cannot do proves nothing in regard to more competent men. We are also ready to wait until some points are cleared up and to content ourselves to leave some problems unsolved—few as they are at most. The faith of the church is based on these great chapters and continues triumphantly to confess: "The third day he rose again from the dead!"

1) **But on the first day with reference to the Sabbath, at deep dawn, they came to the tomb, bearing what aromatic spices they prepared.**

Δέ is to be construed with the μέν that occurs in the preceding sentence. This balance is ignored in our chapter division, see the R. V. The dative τῇ μιᾷ τῶν σαββάτων may be translated "on the first day of the week," but τὰ σάββατα does not mean "week" but only "Sabbath." Since they had no names for the weekdays the Jews designated them with reference to the Sabbath; thus "on the first (day) with reference to the Sabbath," i. e., following it. The plural is frequently used in the names for the festivals, and this same usage was applied to the Sabbath, the plural τὰ σάββατα means only the one Sabbath. Matthew's "very early in the morning" (A. V., the R. V. is incorrect); John's "when it was yet dark"; and Luke's "at deep dawn" (genitive of the time within) agree most perfectly and do not conflict with Mark's "at the rising of the sun." Since they started before dawn, while it was yet dark, the sun was rising about the time the women reached the tomb.

Why so early? For the best of reasons even as all the evangelists note the earliness. Jesus had been dead since Friday; bodies start to decompose very quickly in that climate, wherefore also the dead are buried the same day, or, if they die too late for sepulture, the next day. All haste was necessary in the minds of these women, even hours counted if they wanted to find Jesus' body in a condition that made it possible still to handle it. The subject continues from 23:55, "the women," as the feminine particple "bearing" shows. They came to the tomb laden with the aromatic spices they had prepared. The Greek aorist "did prepare" does not care to express the antecedence in time (R. 841) as does our past perfect "had prepared"; note also the incorporation of the antecedent *aromata* into the relative clause. Luke names some of the women in verse 10.

2, 3) And they did find the stone having been rolled away from the tomb. And they did not find the body of the Lord Jesus.

Luke writes about this stone as being something that was quite well known. Theophilus knew how tombs like that were usually closed and, when necessary, were opened. So Luke reports only the great, significant fact that the women found that the stone had been rolled away from the tomb, which means that it was not in its groove (see 23:53) so that it could be wheeled back again into its place before the door but had been rolled clear out of its groove, "away from the tomb" as if a mighty force had hurled it away. The great stone lay flat. Luke says nothing about the earthquake that had occurred while the women were on the way out to the tomb and nothing about the angel who had touched the great stone and thereby made it roll away from the tomb to lie flat on the ground.

Note that what "they did find" and what "they did not find" are placed side by side. The body was gone. The tomb was empty. Already these facts speak volumes. Before the angel opened the tomb, the body which had been reanimated by its spirit and in the same instant had become glorified, passed unseen out of the grave wrappings and through the solid stone and left the tomb empty save for the grave wrappings which now lay as they had been wrapped but were flat because the body had gone out of them. The angel removed the stone to show that the tomb was empty. No evangelist attempts to describe the resurrection proper; it had no witnesses. It is the direct opposite of the ascension. The apostles saw the beginning of

Luke 24:3, 4 1171

the latter but not the end when the cloud enfolded Jesus and he was transferred timelessly into heaven; no one saw the beginning of the former, but they all saw the end when the living, glorified body appeared to them again and again.

All those paintings which portray the glorious Savior coming out of the opened door of the tomb while the Roman guard flees in dismay at the sight of him are the artist's imagination, and the facts should be carefully taught. Silently, invisibly, wondrously, gloriously the living body passed out through the rock. This mode of being is well described in *Concordia Triglotta*, 1004, 100: "The incomprehensible, spiritual mode, according to which he neither occupies nor vacates space, but penetrates all creatures, wherever he pleases; as, to make an imperfect comparison, my sight penetrates and is in air, light, or water, and does not occupy or vacate space; as a sound or tone penetrates and is in air or water or board or wall, and also does not occupy or vacate space; likewise, as light and heat penetrate and are in air, water, glass, crystal, and the like; and much more of the like. This mode he used when he rose from the closed sepulcher, and passed through the closed door, and in the bread and wine in the Holy Supper."

The resurrection marks a new era. Heaven and earth are now joined, for Christ, our Savior, is risen. The wall of separation has fallen; God is reconciled to men; the sacrifice of the Son has been accepted by the Father. This is the supreme Easter reality. The genitive "of the Lord Jesus" is lacking in so few texts that the R. V. should not have added its marginal note. In Luke's Gospel Κύριος occurs repeatedly as a title for Jesus from 7:13 onward (see this passage), and the only new feature is that "Jesus" is added.

4) And it came to pass while they were perplexed about this, lo, two men suddenly stood beside them in dazzling apparel. And they having become

frightened and bowing their faces to the ground, they said to them: **Why are you seeking the living one with the dead? He is not here but did arise! Remember how he made utterance to you, yet being in Galilee, saying that it is necessary that the Son of man be delivered into the hands of sinful men and be crucified and on the third day rise again.**

See 1:8 on ἐγένετο καί to mark an important event, likewise on ἐν τῷ with an infinitive for "while." Luke alone testifies that the women were first allowed to see that the body was gone, that the wrappings were lying flat. Compare John 20:5-7 and note how in Mark the angel bids the women to look at the place where they laid him—there was something that was most astonishing to see, namely those empty, eloquent gravebands. Then there arose the great perplexity of the women; notice how soon after this Peter and John were affected by the same sight. Matthew and Mark say only that the angel spoke to the women and mention only one angel because they are thinking of the speaker alone. With an exclamation, "lo," Luke tells us more, namely that there were two angels (John 20:12), and that they suddenly stood beside the women in the tomb, ἐπέστησαν, which is used with reference to the unexpected coming upon someone. We take it that they were there all the time, and that their presence was now all at once made visible to the perplexed women.

Why anyone should find a discrepancy in the number of the angels is hard to see. Even in Luke's account the plural "they said" does not mean that both recited the words, but that one spoke for both. Luke has "men," ἄνδρες; Mark, "a young man," νεανίσκος; the others, "angels," ἄγγελοι. This point should not be overlooked; these angels appeared in the form of men, of men in the full vigor of youth. Though they are sexless, this is the form they took. The Scriptures know of no lady angels or baby angels. When God sends angels in this form, men instantly recognize them as what they are. How could it be otherwise! When God wants to reveal he reveals. "In dazzling or flashing apparel" at once brings out the heavenly character of these messengers; look at 9:29, the best analogy, which has the same word for dazzling.

5) No wonder that fear came over the women (aorist participle, the fear set in), and that they kept inclining their faces to the ground (present participle to indicate what they did again and again, every time they tried to look up). The angels deliver their message. Luke omits "stop fearing!" and at once reports the Easter news itself. "Why are you seeking the living one as in company with ($\mu\epsilon\tau\acute{a}$) the dead?" This is not a rebuke; it reveals what the women are doing in their great, blind ignorance, brings this home to them. The question stresses the very thoughts of these women, all their heaviness of heart about the dead body of Jesus, their desire to finish the burying with spices and perfumes, the tears they expected to shed when they left him as dead and in company with all the dead —and through all this murk flashes the one word "the living one," one intense Easter ray. "Living one, living one!"—unbelievable, yet angels attest the word. And they had spices, etc., for one who was dead! One of the strange facts is that no evangelist ever mentions what became of those spices on which so much care and love were spent, those spices but for which the women would not be here.

6) The texts already mentioned omit: "he is not here, but did rise," but on insufficient authority to cast doubt on the genuineness of these words. "He is not here" points to the obvious fact. Mark reports that all the women were bidden to look at the place that was now empty. But this negative is intended only to make the positive stand out, the simple aorist to express the fact as a fact: "on the contrary ($\dot{a}\lambda\lambda\acute{a}$), he did arise." The form $\dot{\eta}\gamma\acute{\epsilon}\rho\theta\eta$ is passive, "he was raised," but many such passives are used without having the passive

sense (R. 817). This is generally assumed here although the passive of this verb occurs also in the purely passive sense. Note the active sense of ἀναστῆναι, "to rise again," in v. 7. If one should insist on translating ἠγέρθη "he was raised," we know of no way to refute him. Both are possible, and either would be in place here. The resurrection is called an act of God: "raised up from the dead by the glory of the Father" (ἠγέρθη), Rom. 6:4; 8:11; Matt. 16:21; 17:23; 26:32; it is also called an act of Jesus himself, Mark 9:31; Luke 18:33 (ἀναστήσεται). Both are true even as all the *opera ad extra* are *communa*. The Greek uses the aorist to express a very recent past act, "did arise," whereas we require the perfect "has arisen" (R. 845).

Luke has the fullest account as to how the angel reminded the women of the words that Jesus had uttered in Galilee. "Yet being in Galilee" means as early as that and, of course, thus refers to all the utterances that were made since that time. Those were true prophetic utterances, and their truth is now attested by the literal fulfillment. But the women as well as the apostles themselves had not understood those utterances literally and had allowed them to pass from their minds.

7) The angel quotes them in indirect discourse from 9:22, 44; Matt. 16:21; 17:22, 23; Mark 8:31; 9:31. See 5:24 on Son of man; and δεῖ indicates the divine necessity of love that is back of the plan of redemption. The angel recalls the three essential acts: the deliverance into the hands of men, the death by crucifixion, and what the women now see with their eyes, "and on the third day rise again," i. e., rise up to life again. But not to the former life in lowliness, those linen wrappings speak of a miraculous passing out of the body—rise again glorified and in the state we call that of exaltation.

8, 9) And they remembered his utterances, and having returned from the tomb, they reported all

these things to the Eleven and to all the rest. Now they were Mary Magdalene and Joanna and Mary of James, and the others with them kept telling these things to the apostles. And these utterances appeared in their sight as silly talk, and they were disbelieving them.

This flood of remembering was far more than merely a recalling of those utterances; it was a recalling of them and a combining them with the realities. They had seen Jesus being delivered into the hands of men and all that this meant, they had seen Jesus die on the cross, and they were now with the same actuality and reality seeing on this the third day that he had indeed arisen. Since they had all this literal fulfillment before them, the prophecy stood out wondrously in their minds. Matthew describes how they met Jesus himself on their return, but Luke hastens to add at once that the women made report to the Eleven and to the rest, i. e., to all the other disciples. We should not imagine that all these were assembled together and received this report in a body. We know that Mary Magdalene found only Peter and John, and that Thomas was absent from the group for a week. The report reached all those who are mentioned as the news could be carried to them, and we may well suppose that it brought about a gradual gathering, at least for the discussion of this report.

10) Not until this high point in the story is reached does Luke record the names of some of the women. In 23:55 and in all that follows we learn only that these women were "out of Galilee." We now hear that the foremost among them was Mary Magdalene. As Peter was the leader among the Twelve, the men, so "Magdalene Mary" was the leader among the women. In regard to prominence she stands out like Peter, in her love she is like John. See 8:2, 3 on her and on Joanna. The second Mary in Luke's record is identified by a reference to her husband Clopas or to her sons

James and Joses, Luke uses only James for this purpose. She was the Virgin's sister or half-sister (John 19:25). When Luke writes, "and the rest with them kept telling," etc., he uses brevity by telling us about the presence of these other women and how they joined with the ones who are named in a repeated telling of these things. The news was so astounding, the things they had seen and heard so mighty and true, that they would of their own accord go over the story again and again; but they were surely also questioned most closely and thus had to relate the occurrences again and again.

The evangelists are always brief, Luke very much so in this account. But that fact draws attention to every repetition that may appear in such a succinct record. Luke states with an aorist that the women made a report to the Eleven and then with an imperfect states once more that they kept telling the apostles these things. Why the double statement? Because the Eleven were the apostles, and because as the apostles they should have been most ready to believe. They had heard the detailed prophecies from Jesus' lips more often than the others; John relates at length what Jesus said to them on Thursday night. Yes, if anyone, these eleven apostles should have believed. On them the women centered their message as the angel and Jesus, too, had told them to do.

11) This is a case where καί adds an adversative fact coordinately. All these utterances seemed in their eyes ("before them" as judges) as λῆρος, nonsense, the wild talk of a pack of hysterical women. In this instance the neuter plural subject is construed with a plural verb in the Greek. This usually means more than that the writer may choose either a singular or a plural verb. These were utterances of so many individual witnesses, each testimony counted for itself, and thus all the testimonies formed a true plural and not merely an aggregate. This plural verb quietly re-

minds us also that in the case of the Jews creditable testimony required at least two or three corroborating witnesses. And we may take it that for this reason, too, Luke actually named three such witnesses in v. 10.

But it was all in vain as far as the apostles were concerned: "they were disbelieving them" (αὐταῖς, feminine, the women), the imperfect expresses continuous disbelief. Do we feel like chiding the apostles for this long disbelief in the face of such witnesses? Let us note rather that the claim that they were common, credulous people who were ready to believe what careful men would today not think of believing, breaks down completely. These men were quite the opposite. Whereas they should have believed they disbelieved. They held out until the last. Even John must be included, for his believing which is stated in John 20:8 is heavily qualified in v. 9 so that Luke cannot register him as an exception.

12) The texts which have the two omissions that were already noted (in v. 3 and 6) and a few others of no consequence omit also this entire verse. Text critics are inclined to reject this verse as not being genuine, not, however, because of the lack of textual evidence, which is quite too favorable for that, but because of the presence of words in this verse which appear also in John 20:2-10. They think it more probable that this verse was interpolated from John's account than that John should have borrowed expressions from this verse in Luke. On textual grounds this verse must therefore remain. As to the verbal agreements it should be noted that in a number of instances in these last chapters Luke plainly matches statements that are made in John, statements that are not found in Matthew and in Mark. The view that the agreement with John is too close in this verse is in our judgment too subjective. John did have Luke before him, and no one will be able to prove why he should not have appropri-

ated words from Luke in his own far fuller account, especially also since in so many instances John supplements the synoptists and makes it plain that he does so by using some of the very words which they used in their more fragmentary accounts.

Moreover, Peter having arisen, ran to the tomb and, having stooped down, sees the linen bands alone; and went away to himself, wondering at what had occurred.

Luke's appended statement which disregards the connection of time is precisely one of the incidents that John would want to relate in full, the more so since he himself ran out to the tomb together with Peter. So we learn that this happened at once after Mary Magdalene hastened back from the tomb to bring help because she thought that the prostrate position of the stone indicated a rifling of the tomb. She found only Peter and John, and both ran to the garden as John relates. But all that Luke wants to report is that Peter, when he stooped and looked into the open tomb, with his own eyes saw the linen bands—"alone," emptied of the body, the undisturbed windings lying flat. Astounding sight!

Luke uses the vivid present tense: "he sees," yes, sees and sees. How could the body have left those bands except through a miracle? What was the miracle— what was it? But even this direct, visual evidence made Peter only wonder and wonder as he went away by himself "at the thing that has happened" in the tomb. So slow was even a Peter to believe. It is Luke's intention to make this plain. The phrase πρὸς ἑαυτόν causes trouble. It does not mean "to his home" (R. V.) although the construction with ἀπῆλθε is correct; "in himself" (A. V.) regards the phrase as modifying "wondering," which would make it too emphatic in the Greek because it would then have the forward position. It simply means: "he went away to or by himself, wondering," etc., B.-P. 1140.

13) **And lo, two of them on that day were going to a village distant sixty stadia from Jerusalem, for which as a name Emmaus.**

This interjection "lo" pertains to the entire account which is so astonishing in many ways, for it was not at all wonderful that two of them should be going to Emmaus on that Sunday. The periphrastic imperfect pictures the two on their way. Luke is precise regarding the name of the village and its distance from Jerusalem. Both points have precipitated much discussion and research which is complicated by the insertion of ἑκατόν, "a hundred," in important texts, which makes the distance 160 stadia. The details of this discussion need not occupy us here. The reading "60 stadia" is correct. Nicopolis cannot be the village intended, for it was not a "village" (Luke) but a considerable city prior even to Christ's time and was located 176 stadia from Jerusalem, which figure exceeds even the 160 stadia that are found in some of the texts, to say nothing about the assured 60. It seems that "a hundred" was inserted on the supposition that Luke had in mind Nicopolis, the old *Amwas*. To go to and to return to this city would require over twelve hours, a journey that cannot be fitted into Luke's account. Several places bore the name Emmaus. Many have thought of the 'Ammaous mentioned in Josephus, *Wars*, 7, 6, 6, but the correct reading in Josephus is 30 and not 60 stadia. We thus cannot locate the place. A Greek στάδιον=600 feet, and this word is declined also as a masculine, B.-D. 49. The supposition seems warranted that the two disciples had their home in Emmaus and were returning to it toward evening.

14) **And they were conversing with each other concerning all these things that had happened. And it came to pass while they were conversing and questioning together, Jesus himself having drawn near, began to go with them. But their eyes were held not to recognize him.**

Ὁμιλεῖν is the regular verb for "to converse," and the subject that occupied these two was not merely the report of the resurrection but all that had occurred in these days (v. 18).

15) On "it came to pass" and "while," as Lukan favorite expressions, see 1:8. The former marks the importance of what came to pass. We see that the two disciples were also questioning together besides conversing, neither of them was able to get any farther. Then, from a few paces to the rear of them, Jesus himself drew up and began to walk together with them in the most natural way as one traveller joins a pair of others on the road. This is the first appearance of the risen Savior that Luke records. During these forty days after the resurrection Jesus came and went as he desired. So he was here on the road where he wished to be and with a few strides easily caught up with these travellers.

16) Luke explains that the eyes of the two disciples "were held" so that they did not recognize Jesus. The passive verb connotes an agent, namely God, just as the passive does in v. 31: their eyes "were completely opened." In Mark 16:12 it is stated that Jesus appeared "in a different form" (μορφή), which means different from the form in which he appeared to Mary Magdalene in the garden of the tomb (Mark 16:9). Throughout these forty days each appearance was naturally made in such a way as to fit the time, the place, and the persons concerned. In the present instance Jesus must have appeared as another traveller. But even then he would have been recognized quickly had the eyes of the two disciples not been held. The recognition was instantaneous in v. 31. The infinitive with τοῦ may be regarded in three ways: to express purpose: "that they should not know him" (our versions); to express result: "so that they did not know him"; or as an ablative: were held "from knowing him," R. 1171 makes μή redundant. We regard it as expressing "re-

sult" and consider the ablative the least likely construction.

17) **And he said to them, What are these statements which you are exchanging with each other as you are walking? And they stopped, sullen. And answering, one, by name Cleopas, said to him, Thou, dost thou dwell as an outsider all alone in Jerusalem and didst not come to know the things that took place in her in these days?**

The question of Jesus seems to imply that it was put after Jesus had for a while listened to the animated discussion that continued after he drew up with the two. They were in the midst of it, and both "questioning" (v. 15) and "exchanging" imply that each disciple was putting questions at the other which neither could answer. So the inquiry of Jesus was most natural when he at a convenient moment asked what these λόγοι or statements were about. We should not regard this as pretense on the part of Jesus. As is the case in other instances when he asked about things that he himself knew well, so this question had the simple purpose of making these disciples state their problem to him as directly as possible in order that he might solve it for them in a perfectly objective way. His question looked forward to what he intended to say after he had received the answer.

But its first effect was that the two disciples stopped in their tracks and looked at Jesus with displeased surprise and astonishment: σκυθρωποί means with darkened faces, hence "sullen." "Sad" is not enough, and "perplexed" (R., *Tr.*) is incorrect; M.-M. 580 have "of a gloomy countenance." The A. V. translates the reading "are" in place of "they stopped" and so draws the adjective into the question: "as ye walk and are sad." The better reading is "they stood," i. e., stopped. It is this stopping that lends force to the adjective "sullen."

18) This interpretation helps us to understand the answer which was given by Cleopas, which was

really not an answer to Jesus' question but an incredulous, exclamatory question because of what appeared like impossible ignorance on Jesus' part. The verb παροικεῖς means to dwell as a πάροικος, as one who is not a native but has come in from the outside, and is followed by the accusative of the place: "to inhabit Jerusalem as one having come from the outside." A Gentile might be referred to thus, but the verb here refers to a Jew who had been born and reared elsewhere but was now residing in the Holy City. Mere temporary sojourn (M.-M.) is not necessarily implied.

The adjective μόνος, "alone," helps to bring out the idea: an outsider living in Jerusalem so entirely off to himself and "all alone," without contact with anybody who might keep him posted on the big things that were going on in the city. Cleopas intends to ask whether it was possible that Jerusalem had harbored such a person. Σύ is emphatic: "Thou, art thou" such a person? The aorist ἔγνως is ingressive: "not come to know" all that occurred in the city during these last days. So completely are Cleopas and his companion taken up with these occurrences that he thinks that everybody who is living in Jerusalem must know all about them and could not be living so alone as to escape this knowledge.

We can only guess how Jesus made the impression on Cleopas that he was not a native Jerusalemite. Many foreign-born Jews gravitated to the Holy City and became permanent residents there. Jesus perhaps retained his Galilean accent. Is Cleopas to be identified with the Clopas who is mentioned in John 19:25? We hear "yes" and "no" and receive nothing decisive either way even if the names are only variant pronunciations, which is most likely the case. Luke mentions the name so incidentally that we cannot safely conclude anything in regard to the importance of the man. The view that these two disciples belonged to the Seventy is a guess, likewise that the other was Nathanael, Bartholomew,

Peter, some other Simon, or James the less, that father and son were thus going to their home in Emmaus, and that the father answered and not the son.

19) With perfect calmness Jesus persists in eliciting the statement he wants made. **And he said to them, What things? And they said to him: Those about Jesus, the Nazarene, who was a prophet powerful in deed and word before God and all the people; also how our high priests and rulers delivered him up to a death judgment and crucified him. But we were hoping that he was the one about to ransom Israel. Yes, and along with all these things he is spending the third day since these things occurred. And another thing, some women from among us dumbfounded us, having gone early to the tomb and not finding his body, they came saying that they had seen also a vision of angels who declared him to be living. And some of those with us went away to the tomb and found it thus even as the women said; but him they did not see.**

The word ποῖος is sometimes qualitative, sometimes it is not; it need not here be "what kind of things" but simply "what things," being noncommittal. Between them or with one of them acting as the speaker they report the entire story of Jesus to Jesus himself simply, directly, and quite exactly but from the standpoint of the disciples who were simply at sea in regard to the final outcome that had been reported to them by the women that very morning. It was just what Jesus wanted, namely that these two should express themselves fully and thus enable Jesus to clear up the very things that were so dark and perplexing to them and to all the rest of the men. Jesus chose these two because they were two and could serve as two witnesses, not only to testify that they had seen him, but to testify to all that he was telling them about the Scripture prophecies regarding his death and his resurrection.

The theme is "the things concerning Jesus, the Nazarene," which names him in the usual way as one would speak to a stranger who knew nothing about him. "Jesus" was a name that was found frequently among Jews, and "the Nazarene" thus distinguished him by naming the town from which he came. The relative clause begins the story under this theme and at once draws a brief but very adequate picture of this Jesus. We need not have ἐγένετο mean "who became" as though Jesus grew to be a prophet; it is the constative historical aorist which states summarily what Jesus "was."

We have no idiom for ἀνὴρ προφήτης, so we say only "a prophet," but the two nouns are intended to mean "a notable man who was a prophet." But "prophet" is a broad word, which is quite properly applied to Jesus as the Messiah. It is not restrictive as making Jesus only another one of the great prophets whom the Jews knew, a sort of second to the Baptist; for Deut. 18:15-19 made "prophet" a title for the promised Messiah, and the Jews used this word with reference to him. The fact that the title is meant in this exalted sense is clear from the addition: "powerful in work and word in the presence of God and of all the people" (λαός, Israel). This phrase conveys the thought that God himself approved of this powerful prophet, likewise that the people as a whole did so.

20) The picture is grand and impressive: this powerful prophet moving before God and all the people with word and deed. With the close connective τε and with the conjunction that denotes manner the terrible end of his career are summarily but adequately added: "also how our high priests," etc. "Delivered him up unto a death judgment" states the precise fact that the Sanhedrin itself handed Jesus over to Pilate to have a judgment pronounced on him that would remand him to death (the genitive is qualitative, and the two nouns form one concept: *Todesurteil*.) And thus the

Sanhedrin "crucified him," it was the real agent in this awful act. The two are correlative, "delivered him up" and "crucified him." That is how he came to be crucified and was not stoned or killed in some other way.

21) Deep feeling runs through the entire recital but reaches its full intensity in the parenthetical statement (marked as such by δέ) about "we," meaning all those who were most closely attached to Jesus: "we, however," in contrast to our rulers, "we were hoping (the imperfect, hoping all along) that he (emphatic αὐτός) was the one about to be ransoming Israel." The substance of this hoping is retained in the tense of the direct discourse in which it was originally expressed: "He is the one," etc.; the English has to use "was." The hope was national, the thinking of "Israel," the sacred, honored name of the chosen people.

The verb λυτροῦσθαι calls for attention; we may translate "to redeem," but when we do so we must hold fast the original meaning of redeem, namely "to ransom," to set free by the payment of a λύτρον or ransom price. The treatment of the verb and of the corresponding nouns in the dictionaries is not satisfactory as Warfield, *Christian Doctrine*, has shown. The idea of a λύτρον never disappears; the verb never means merely "to save" or "to deliver," for the saving act always costs something that corresponds to the saving that is effected. If it is deliverance from sin, the price is blood-sacrifice; if from danger or evils, the price is the strain, effort, etc. But the price always lies in the verb. The active voice means to receive the price and then to free; the middle, to pay the ransom or price and thus to free, and the passive, to have the price paid and thus to be set free. The infinitive is used here: "the one about to pay the ransom or price and thus deliver Israel."

It is unfair to say that this meant political deliverance in the minds of the speakers. The statement appears *after* the one about the death and *before* the one that voices the complaint that Jesus has already spent three days in the tomb. This means that these disciples thought that Jesus would ransom Israel in spite of his death and perhaps through his death. The verb "to ransom" is perfectly in place. Just how the ransoming would be effected, and just what release it would buy for Israel were not clear to the two disciples, could not be. But they were correct in thinking that it would be a ransoming, but their hope was dying because Jesus lay dead and would remain dead.

The two ἀλλὰ καί are not adversative but affirmative. The first is climacteric with strong ascensive force which is increased by the addition of γέ, all of which we try to convey by translating: "yea, and," etc. The subject of ἄγει is "he" (Jesus); the verb is not impersonal, could not be when an object follows. What perplexes and upsets these disciples and causes all their questioning is the fact that "along with these things" that brought on the death of Jesus he is now spending already the third day since these things occurred (meaning his trial and death), and not a thing has as yet happened.

22) The ἀλλὰ καί is here continuation: "and another thing." See R. 1148 and 1185. This thing about the women is simply upsetting to these disciples, ἐξέστησαν, they dumbfounded us. The Greek uses the adjective in preference to the adverb: "having gone as early ones."

23) Instead of finding the body as they had expected they brought back the incredible report that they had seen a vision of angels who declared Jesus to be living.

24) They add the detail about the two disciples who had run out to the tomb (v. 12: John 20:3) and found just what the women said—"but him they saw not." This is the sad ending. The fact that the women had seen him (Matt. 28:9, 10), also Mary Magdalene (John 20:18), apparently failed to satisfy the men.

The very excitement with which the women reported what they had seen made the men think that they were nervously upset, had imagined things, and ought not to be believed beyond the verifiable fact that the body was indeed gone.

25) The disciples had spoken, had put the whole story into words, and had thus stated their entire problem. That is what Jesus had asked them to do, and he now presents to them the full solution of their problem and of all its perplexities.

And he said to them: O dullards and slow of heart to believe on all the things which the prophets did utter! Was it not necessary that the Christ suffer, and that he enter into his glory? And having begun with Moses and with all the prophets, he interpreted to them in all the Scriptures the things concerning himself.

The very tone with which Jesus begins, one of pained surprise and plain rebuke, shows that the same great person is speaking with authority and convincing power although he is unrecognized at the time. "O dullards" reproves their intellect and intelligence. Unbelief often lays claim to great intellectual powers and penetration; it is in reality the most pitiful and painful ignorance. These two Jews should have *known* their Scriptures better.

But we should not separate the terms; "slow of heart" (dative of relation after an adjective) is connected with "dullards" even as the infinitive modifies both: "dull and slow to believe on all the things which (the relative accusative drawn to the dative antecedent) the prophets did utter" (their spoken utterance being identical with their written records). They believe some of the things that had been written by the prophets, e. g., that the Messiah would come and establish his kingdom; but they did not believe all that had been written, they overlooked the very things that were so essential to this Messiah and his kingdom, the things which Jesus now expounds. That was their great inconsistency, their great lack of intelligence.

But the real trouble is in the heart, of which the intelligence is only one faculty. In the Scriptures καρδία is the seat of the personality, of the ἐγώ, and thus of the thinking, the feeling, and especially also the willing. The avenue into the heart is, indeed, through the intelligence, but the intelligence will see or not see what the inner personality desires. So both are here rebuked, but the full weight of the rebuke falls on these hearts that are so "slow to be believing," etc., ἐπί with the dative stating "on" what the confidence of faith should rest. "Slow," sluggish, means unresponsive to the prophetic words that ought to awaken faith. This is the resistance to the gracious power in the divine words. See how Jerusalem resisted to the last, and now hear the Savior's complaint regarding even his disciples.

26) The interrogative word οὐχί, which implies a decided affirmative answer, at once illumines the intelligence and appeals to the heart and the will. Why, it could not have been otherwise than that, when the Christ should come, he had to suffer and to enter into his glory. Δεῖ expresses all kinds of necessity; here the imperfect ἔδει expresses the necessity that is involved in prophecy, a necessity that reaches back to the very first prophecy that was uttered about the Messiah and continues through the centuries until now, R. 887. No divine prophecy can possibly fail. Neither can all these prophets' utterances about the suffering of the Messiah and about his then entering into his glory. To know those prophecies at all is to know that they must necessarily come to fulfillment. The question that Jesus thus puts is one that both of these disciples would answer with "yes." As Jews they had always believed that about the divine prophecies. So Jesus opens the way for the rest of his task which is now once more with

full vividness and clarity to unroll the ancient prophecies before the minds of these disciples and let the power of their truth fall on their hearts in order finally to produce faith.

In this instance the necessity goes back only to the prophets whose inspired words of revelation cannot possibly fail since they come from God. But back of this necessity there lies another, one that is found in God himself, the necessity of his love and his resolve to save the world. This is not an abstract necessity, nor can we speak of it in a philosophical sense as some do. It is not a metaphysical part of God's being which he acts on because he cannot help but do so. This ultimate necessity rests on the free volition of God and on his unfathomable love to send his own Son for our redemption. This much is revealed, and no finite mind can penetrate farther back into the being of God.

The two acts of this necessity that are revealed through the prophets are: "to suffer and to enter into his glory." They constitute a unit, and a misunderstanding results when a subordination is made: "to suffer in order to enter (or so as to enter) his glory." To suffer means to expiate the world's guilt by a bloody death; and with this there goes the other half, to enter his glory, to lay this sacrifice before God, which means that God is to accept it for the whole world's guilt. As it was necessary that the price be paid, so it was necessary that God accept the payment, accept it by glorifying him who died for us and by seating him at his right hand. Both parts were revealed, and both were fulfilled, and our faith rests on both. On the part in glory read Ps. 110 and Luke 20:42-44. It is debated whether this second part about the glory was fulfilled in the resurrection or in the ascension. That is one of those useless questions which presents an alternative where none exists. The two belong together even as they are often called the glorification. John 17:1, 5; 12:23, 28; 13:32; Phil. 2:9-11; Acts 3:21; 5:31. "His glory" is that which the Son had "before the world was" (John 17:5); and "to enter" that glory meant that the human nature of Jesus was to receive its full and eternal exercise.

27) All that remained to Jesus was to go through the prophets, state what they had uttered, and bring out just what that utterance had declared in advance. The wording has been called careless because of the use of the two prepositions: "having begun from Moses and from all the prophets," etc. But whether we prefer the aorist "he did interpret" or the imperfect "he was interpreting" (but did not finish), the two prepositions are in place. Jesus made two beginnings, one with Moses and another with the rest of the prophets. The thought is that Moses stands alone, is higher than the prophets, that he is no less than the mediator of the old covenant even also as the Pentateuch stands out by itself. "All the prophets" are the rest of the Old Testament, the old name for which is "the Law and the Prophets," the very distinction that Luke has in mind. We prefer the aorist, for we cannot think that Jesus failed to finish this task. He surely timed his walk in such a way as to complete this task.

Yes, Jesus finds himself in "all" the prophets. We should give much for even a record of the passages he used, give more for his exegesis of those passages; but we are left to search for ourselves. "Jesus found himself in the Old Testament, a thing that some modern scholars do not seem able to do," R., W. P. "O dullards and slow in heart!" Some object to the reflexive "the things concerning himself" and think that the reading should be "concerning him." Luke could have written either. Having told us that this was Jesus, "himself" is even better than the distant "him" would be.

28) **And they drew near to the village where they were going, and he made the appearance of going farther. And they constrained him, saying, Abide together with us because it is toward evening,**

and the day has already declined. And he went in to abide with them.

The Greeks use "where" for "whither" much as we do. When προσποιέω is used in the middle voice it means *Miene machen*. It is to be understood in the good sense here: "he made as if," and he would certainly have gone on if he had not been urged to stay. Jesus forces himself into no one's home.

29) But these two disciples not only invite but also constrain him to remain with them. This reads so much as if the house to which they had come was their own home that we discard the idea of an inn or of some friend's house. Their words are preserved. "Abide together with us," in our company, etc. It is easy to see why. They voice exactly the feeling of all sincere disciples toward Jesus to this day. We also feel the need of Jesus, of his invisible yet no less real presence, especially when we think of the nearness of the night of death. We need not allegorize the text but apply it to our own heart. The aorist "they constrained" implies success, but Luke adds the statement that he went in with them. It is grammatical stickling to say, "Only into the village because no house has been mentioned"; but Jesus reclines in the next verse, and that does not occur on the street.

30) **And it came to pass on his having reclined together with them, having taken the bread, he blessed it and, having broken it, he was in the act of giving it over to them. And their eyes were opened, and they recognized him; and he became hidden from them.**

Ἐγένετο plus a finite verb is used as it was in 1:8, and ἐν τῷ with an aorist infinitive as it was in 2:27; 3:21. The former marks the importance of what follows. The table was set for an evening meal, and Jesus had reclined for dining in the Jewish fashion. The two reclined with him. The strange fact is that Jesus did not act as a guest but as the host, for he took the bread in his hands and pronounced the blessing. This was the regular table prayer just as we still say grace before eating. It was all perfectly natural, the result of the relation that had been established on the journey when Jesus acted as the teacher and the two disciples as his pupils. Neither of them thought it odd that Jesus should proceed as he did. After the blessing had been pronounced (aorist), Jesus broke the bread (aorist), the flat, unleavened cake that was always divided by breaking and never by cutting. But in the act of giving it over to them, as they were taking it from his hands (significant imperfect), their eyes were opened, etc. The description is exact and beautiful. Imagination has made this the Sacrament. A strange sacrament, indeed—broken off in the very first act of it and never completed.

31) This is the reverse of v. 16, the one verse helps to interpret the other. The aorist suggests an instantaneous opening of the eyes. The disciples had looked upon Jesus, but they had not recognized him up to this moment. As if a veil had fallen from their eyes, they now saw that it was Jesus. In v. 25 they complained of a fatal lack in the evidence of the news that he was alive: "but him they did not see," namely Peter and John, witnesses that were far more creditable than the women. They themselves had seen him all this time, had realized it at this wonderful moment, and had recognized him fully (ἐπί in the verb intensifies). It was all so certain that not the shadow of a doubt was possible. But in that same instant, when their hands almost touched his as they took the bread, he became ἄφαντος, "nonappearing," "hidden from them." The place where he lay a moment ago was empty. This, too, was highly necessary for these disciples. They must realize that while Jesus was alive after his soul and his body had been reunited he was not to enter and to continue the old, earthly life in which they had known him so long. He had entered a new state in which he

appeared and disappeared at will. As he had left the
sealed tomb, so he now left the closed house. The
thought was overwhelming—incomprehensible, yet infinitely blessed.

32) **And they said to each other, Was not our
heart burning in us as he was talking to us on the
way, as he was opening to us the Scriptures? And
having arisen in that same hour, they returned to
Jerusalem, and they found gathered together the
Eleven and those with them, saying, Certainly the
Lord did rise up and did appear to Simon! And they
for their part began to rehearse the things on the
way, and how he was made known to them in connection with the breaking of the bread.**

From the immediate effect that was produced upon
the two disciples Luke reports only the exclamatory
question: "Was not our heart burning," etc.? Why the
word "burning" should have caused textual emendation
is hard to see. It expressed the effect which the exposi-
tions of Jesus had produced on these two disciples, on
both equally, that caused their heart to warm and to
glow within them when they heard what the Scriptures
said about the blessed suffering and the glorification of
the Messiah. They saw that Jesus was this Messiah,
and that what had been reported to them by the women
must be true.

One should not, however, think that the two say
this and mean that they should have known Jesus when
he spoke to them since no one could speak like that but
he. Any thought of that nature was a minor one. Their
question intends to say that the way in which he spoke
to them and that the effect of his words on their hearts
are mighty corroborative evidence for what they realized just now, that they had indeed seen Jesus. It was
now all as plain as day. The two clauses are parallel,
the second being an apposition to the first: "how he
was talking," and: "how he was fully opening." Not
his λαλεῖν, mere utterance (the opposite of being silent),

but this talking as opening up the Scriptures in such a wonderful way made their hearts glow and burn with new faith, assurance, and joy.

33) So they returned to Jerusalem at once. We now see why Luke reported the distance. It was not so far but what the two could easily retrace their steps. We take it that they got back to Jerusalem by about nine o'clock. Two facts are notable: they knew just where to go, and they found not only the apostles but also others together in one place. This is what the morning's news of the resurrection had done in spite of the disbelief with which it was received. When Mary Magdalene rushed back to the city early in the morning she found only Peter and John, these two friends were still together. The rest were scattered. But all are now together again. Since Jesus was dead, the bond was broken, nothing could hold even the Eleven together; but when the possibility that Jesus had risen from the dead became known, the old bond began to hold again. The perfect participle "having been gathered together" implies "and still gathered thus" when the two came. John 20:24 states that Thomas was absent, yet Luke writes that the two disciples from Emmaus found "the Eleven." As they were formerly called "the Twelve," so they are now called "the Eleven" whether the full number was actually present or not. Note I Cor. 15:5 on "the Twelve." Luke did not care to explain the absence of the one about whom he intends to say nothing in his record.

34) Jubilant shouts greet the two late arrivals: "The Lord truly arose!" $\dot{\eta}\gamma\dot{\epsilon}\rho\theta\eta$ is explained in v. 6, the aorist to designate the past fact. Κύριος (see 7:13) is surely the proper name, for it means "divine Lord" and was soon to be used in the full designation "our Lord Jesus Christ." The decisive evidence on which this jubilant shout rests is added: "and did appear to Simon," the aorist again expresses the past fact. This Simon is Peter, his old name was commonly used

among his friends. Him the men believed. It is a bit inconsistent, for he was only one witness, the testimony of the women was set aside. But men are strange. Think of Thomas despite a dozen men who were witnesses.

When and where did Jesus appear to Peter, and what are the details? We know only the fact which Paul corroborates in I Cor. 15:5 and even regards the appearance to Simon (Cephas) as being one of the great evidences for the resurrection. And let us note that Paul, too, fails to mention the testimony of the women. Just why he did this is hard to say. Although Peter was the first man to see the risen Lord, this does not give him a papal distinction. All details are, it seems, purposely withheld, not because the church would have made much of them in elevating Peter above the other apostles, but for the opposite reason, because Peter had denied Jesus, and this appearance to him was in the nature of a private absolution. Hence a veil is in place.

35) The αὐτοί has emphasis, for it places the two over against all the others whom they found. They told their wonderful story, which certainly surpassed that of Peter. The phrase ἐν τῇ κλάσει is often translated and also interpreted as though it indicated the means by which Jesus was made known. This puts into the phrase what is not in it, for the making known occurred as v. 30 describes it: "in connection with the breaking of the bread," right after the breaking, when the bread was being handed over to them. The supposition that they had often seen Jesus do this act and that, when they now see it once more, this revealed his person to them is untenable.

36) **Now, while they were telling these things, he himself stood in their midst and says to them, Peace to you!**

When we reconstruct this scene we add from John the detail that the doors were locked for fear of the

Jews, so that no one could enter the room without first knocking and being admitted. From Mark we learn that the disciples were reclining on their couches at supper, and that the meal was apparently about ended. All those who are in the room are engaged in animated conversation about "these things" that had been reported by Simon and by the two disciples from Emmaus. Then all in an instant Jesus himself (emphatic αὐτός) "stood in their midst," ἔστη, the aorist to indicate the fact. John writes "came and stood," which marks the arrival as well as the standing.

Among the ridiculous ideas that are connected with this statement are these: Jesus climbed up a ladder and through a window; he descended on a stairway from the roof; he entered into the house before the doors were locked; he slipped in when the two disciples from Emmaus were admitted; he was allowed to come in through connivance on the part of the doorkeeper. They all agree in denying the miracle. Others have the doors open of themselves to let Jesus walk in; or they leave them locked while Jesus walks through them as if they were not there; or they have him walk right through the walls of the house and of the room. This latter is a miracle, indeed, but it is crudely conceived. Acts 12:10 is useless in this connection, for the body of Peter was not in the same state as that of the risen Lord.

Since he is in his risen and glorified state, time, space, the rock of the tomb, the walls and the doors of buildings no longer hamper the body of Jesus. He appears where he desires to appear, and his visible presence disappears when he desires to have it so. This is wholly supernatural, wholly incomprehensible to our minds. Nor may we ask or seek to comprehend where Jesus stayed during the intervals between his appearances during the forty days. When our bodies shall eventually enter the heavenly mode of existence, we may know something of these supreme mysteries, but we doubt that we shall even then really comprehend the profundities of the divine omnipresence of which the human nature of Jesus partakes, and which he exercised since his vivification in the tomb as he did in these wondrous appearances.

Jesus did not walk through anything. The disciples did not see him take so many steps from the doors or the wall to their midst. He was there, and that was all. Luther is right over against the Zwinglians: "By this coming through locked doors is shown that since his resurrection in his kingdom on earth he is no longer bound to bodily, visible, tangible, mundane substance, *time, place, space, and the like*, but wants to be known and believed as ruling by his power everywhere present, having the will to be with us and help us in all places and at all times, when and where we need it, unfettered and unhindered by the world and all its might."

Jesus says at once: "Peace to you!" But this common Oriental form of greeting, which implies only a kindly human wish when it is spoken by ordinary lips, means infinitely more when it is spoken by him who died and rose for us. As is the person, so is the word. When Jesus says "peace" he actually gives what the word says. It is not a lovely-looking package that is empty inside but one that is filled with heavenly reality that is far more beautiful than the covering in which it is wrapped. The concept $εἰρήνη$, the condition of peace and the feeling that results from the condition, are treated in 7:50. We must add here the seals of this divine peace, the death and the resurrection. A peace that is so sealed he conveys to the disciples. We do not know that anyone present, even Peter who had already seen the risen Lord (v. 34), made any response to the greeting; responses were always made. We see why none was made in this instance.

37) But terrified and become afraid, they were thinking they were beholding a spirit.

The disciples believed that Jesus had risen from the dead (v. 34, 35). But when the living Lord suddenly stood in the room before their very eyes, the effect of this appearance terrified them. Luke uses two words to describe this reaction in order to show how completely they were struck with fear. The disciples recognized the powers of the resurrection of Jesus only gradually. Terror arouses all the superstition that is latent in men's minds. We see it when the Twelve were out on the sea in the raging storm; were physically exhausted and cried that they saw a phantom (Matt. 14:26). The same thing occurs here, save that no one cried out, but they were thinking that they were beholding a πνεῦμα, "a spirit," i. e., seeing a ghost. No one had ever seen one, nor had they; it was what they thought a spirit, an unsubstantial appearance without a solid material body of actual flesh, must be like.

One thing may be noted here: we do not know by how much the glorified form of Jesus differed from his appearance in his earthly life, and not even whether he always appeared in the same form during the forty days. May we say that a majesty and an exaltation were now evident in the old familiar form and face, such as the disciples had not seen before? Simon and the two Emmaus disciples had seen him, but we have no details about the former case and know that in the other Jesus became invisible just as he was recognized. When fear set in in a company like the present one, its contagion was hard to resist. Men are strange, indeed—so joyful a moment ago because Jesus had arisen, so frightened now on beholding him in his risen form.

38) And he said to them: Why are you agitated, and because of what are thoughts going up in your hearts? See my hands and my feet, that it is I myself! Handle me and see! For a spirit does not have flesh and bones even as you behold me

having. And on saying this he showed to them the feet and the hands.

John says that he showed them also his side, namely the wound that had been left by the gash of the spear. The perfect participle is used as an adjective in the predicate after the copula, and the perfect tense of the participle has its usual strong present connotation. The disciples "are" in a shaken condition. The effect of this is that all kinds of foolish thoughts are coming up in their hearts. "Why" does not specify, but "because of what" asks for a reason. No rational reason can be assigned for their agitation or for the wild ideas that were shooting up in their minds. Jesus knows what they are thinking, and his double question aims to dispel those frantic thoughts and to put something sensible in their place.

They thought of "a spirit." Did they mean an evil spirit that was impersonating Jesus and trying to terrify them? If so, the questions dispelled that notion. Or did they think that only the spirit of Jesus had returned to them from the other world? That notion, too, Jesus dispels at once. Luther takes occasion in this connection to explode the spiritistic superstitions as though the spirits of the dead are able to return from the other world and are able to communicate with us in some way. The Bible denies this throughout. God refuses to send one from the dead to warn us or to preach to us, 16:31, and has forbidden us to try to talk with the dead, Deut. 18:11; Isa. 8:19. Jesus calls the disciples to calm, sensible consideration.

39) He holds out his hands and his feet, John adds his side. Two purposes are thus met. These bodily members are solid flesh and bone. Jesus demands that they be handled, and the aorist implies that his command was obeyed. Jesus adds what they themselves know, that a spirit has no flesh and bones "even as you behold me having." Let no one say that awe restrained

the disciples from touching the glorified body. Do you
suppose that Jesus would take the risk that the old
doubts should again appear afterward? He was here
to convince every one of these men of the reality of
his human body, "flesh and bones," and he convinced
them by their actually handling him.

The first ὅτι=that, the clause is an object after
ἴδετε; the second ὅτι is just as plainly "because," it states
an acknowledged reason. But a good purpose accompanies the first clause, "that it is I myself," the Jesus
you have known so long. He establishes his personal
identity by means of his body. Hands, feet, side—these
bear the five holy wounds of his crucifixion. By them
they know him to the exclusion of the least doubt. Jesus
makes the disciples learn what a resurrection body is
like: it is the body of the same person, the same body
of that person, and yet both the person and the body
are in a new and wonderful state.

Many seem to be afraid that we may think that the
body of Jesus retained permanently the gaping wounds
that had been made at the crucifixion, and so they assure us that these wounds were not permanent, and
others turn them into stigmata, marks that indicate
where the wounds had been. It is best never to pronounce on matters that are quite unknown to us. If
Jesus wished to retain his wounds he could certainly
do so, and they would certainly always appear as the
evidence in his very body and of his glorious work of
redemption. But the view is untenable that Jesus
speaks of his flesh and bones, not of his blood, because
the circulation of the blood could be felt less easily, and
because what was in his veins might be something else
than blood.

Modernists grant the death of Jesus but certainly
not his bodily resurrection, the latter is a *priori* impossible. But how account for the empty tomb? What
became of the dead body that had been placed under
guard by a detachment of Roman soldiers? No denier

cf the resurrection is able to give even a plausible answer. Here we have the answer of Jesus as to what became of his body. That body arose—and there is no resurrection except that of the dead body.

40) Jesus showed the disciples his bodily members, not merely to see them but to handle them. The texts that shorten v. 3, 6, 9 and omit v. 12 and also from καί in v. 36, omit also v. 40; but they are too few to warrant even the marginal notes that are added in the R. V.

41) **But they still disbelieving from joy and wondering, he said to them, Have you something eatable here? And they gave over to him a piece of broiled fish. And having taken it, he ate it before them.**

It is one thing to disbelieve, it is quite another to disbelieve because of joy. The heart is too small to take in the great joy all at once. There is a flutter as if the reality might after all not be real. Luther calls this a curious statement—fear and fright at first hold up faith, it is then held up by the very opposite, joy. He calls it one of the Christian's afflictions that grace is altogether too great and glorious for us promptly to take it all in. While the joy and the wonder were at their height, Jesus asked for τι βρώσιμον, "something eatable." This was done because the disciples had been dining. The food must have been eaten, the tables, too, had perhaps already been cleared.

42) They promptly hand Jesus a piece of broiled fish (ὀπτός is the verbal from ὀπτάω, to cook, roast, or broil, and is used as an adjective). Note that ἐπέδωκαν is the same verb that was used in v. 30, where Jesus hands out the bread in Emmaus. The addition "and of an honeycomb," literally, "of honeycomb from bees" (μελισσίου), like the addition "bread," and like other expansions of the text, lack authority to such an extent as to be hardly worthy of attention save by text critics.

43) Jesus took this fish and ate it before them, i. e., for them to see. He ate, not for his own sake, but to add this new proof that it was, indeed, his own physical body that stood before them. This eating is cumulative proof which is strong in itself but stronger because of what precedes and makes that, too, stronger. Compare Gen. 18:6-8; 19:3 on the eating of God and of angels. To call it impossible is to pretend to have knowledge that no man possesses; and to go beyond the fact of eating is to do the same unwarranted thing. Why discourse about glorified bodies, their capabilities and incapabilities, when we know nothing on the subject? Jesus was wise. The great joy (John 20:20) of the disciples was not an entirely safe symptom, nor was the wondering that was connected with it; presently, after Jesus would be gone, and sober thought would once more come back, the old doubts and new ones might return. So Jesus does this physical eating and brings back the question of his actual and bodily resurrection and furnishes another decisive proof for all sober minds.

44) After these incontrovertible proofs are in their possession, Jesus repeats what he had done for the two Emmaus disciples (v. 25-27): he takes all these disciples into the Scriptures. Note the connecting thought that runs through this chapter and that most likely influenced Luke in choosing his material: the angels quote the prophecy of Jesus which itself rested on the Old Testament; the Emmaus disciples hear the Scriptures expounded at length, so Jesus now explains them to the disciples here in the city.

Moreover, he said to them, These are my words which I did utter to you, yet being with you, that it is necessary that there be fulfilled all the things that have been written in the law of Moses and the Prophets and the Psalms concerning me. Then he opened their mind to understand the Scriptures.

We acknowledge that "moreover he said to them" neither affirms nor denies the immediate connection with the preceding. We admit more, that especially in Luke an interval might be supposed, that v. 44 might place us elsewhere at a later time. So we meet the opinion that in v. 44-49 Luke intends to offer a summary of what Jesus said to his disciples during the forty days—but nobody who is just reading these verses would see a summary in them.

There is another opinion which thinks that these verses were spoken on the day of Christ's ascension, an idea, however, that is without supporting evidence. Our conviction that v. 44-49 belong to the appearance on Easter evening and continue the narrative from v. 43 rests, not on the opening words "he said to them," but on the correspondence of John 20:21-23 with this passage in Luke. Both deal with the commission of the apostles, both with the forgiveness of sin. John 20:19-23 records the appearance on Easter evening and intends to supplement what Luke wrote in 24:44-49. John shows that on that evening Jesus said far more than is found in Luke 24:36-43; we must include what he said in 44-49. The reason these verses should be dated later has yet to be shown.

"These the words" refers back (not forward as has been supposed), but hardly to a previous discourse, the closing sentence of which Luke now records. The λόγοι are statements, certain facts that were uttered in words, the substance that was spoken. They are dated: Jesus uttered them while he was yet with his disciples, namely before his death. Οὗτοι is masculine only because of the predicate οἱ λόγοι; it stands for ταῦτα, "these things," the ones that involved and are evident in what v. 36-43 record. Jesus stated these things to his disciples during past days in *logoi*. Luke has told us that they failed completely to understand them at the time (9:44). But those words were not spoken in vain by any means. The disciples remembered them and now see them fulfilled and are at last able to understand them. They now stand out for the disciples as being the mighty prophecies of Jesus.

He summarizes those *logoi*: "that it is necessary," etc. Compare v. 26 on the necessity. The perfect "the things that have been written" is the Greek way of saying that those written records still stand. Jesus again asserts that the whole Old Testament wrote concerning him. He even names the three parts of the Old Testament, and does that under one article: "the Law of Moses (Pentateuch) and Prophets and Psalms"; in v. 27 the briefer designation is used which includes all except the Law under the term "the Prophets." In this Jewish division Prophets includes Joshua, Judges, Samuel, Kings, and all the actual prophets save Daniel. The common term for the rest of the books was the Hagiographa, which included Daniel. Jesus calls this part of the Old Testament "Psalms," which is out of the ordinary yet does not intend to stress the Psalms in a special way or to leave out Daniel, for instance. Jesus views the Old Testament as a unit, and its prophecy concerning him is not confined to a few incidental passages. These only stand out like Isa. 53 and Ps. 22. The entire Old Testament economy centers in Christ; none of it would have existed without him or can now be properly understood without him. This was all so clear to the mind of Jesus that he could dip into these writings at a thousand points and show how they spoke περὶ ἐμοῦ.

45) Jesus then went into the Scriptures at length, much as he did in v. 27, and opened the mind of the disciples to a real understanding of them. The present infinitive points to a continuous and thus lasting understanding. This means that the disciples now saw that the Old Testament stated prophetically the very things they had witnessed and were now witnessing. Prophecy becomes wonderfully clear when we can place the ful-

fillment beside it, especially when we can do it in the way in which Jesus did.

46) "And he said to them" by no means indicates that what is now quoted was spoken at a later time. The connection with what is spoken is too close. We have the precedent for this connection in v. 25, 26, plus the parallel passage John 20:21-23 for a part of what Luke now quotes. It took some time to open the minds of the disciples, and so Luke now states that Jesus spoke the following.

And he said to them: Thus it has been written, that the Christ suffer and arise from the dead on the third day, and that repentance be proclaimed on the basis of his name and remission of sins unto all the nations beginning from Jerusalem. You are witnesses of these things. And lo, I myself am sending forth the promise of my Father upon you. But you, you sit in the city until you become clothed from on high with power.

We cancel "and thus it behooved" after "thus it has been written" as lacking textual authority. When he comes to the conclusion of the opening of the mind of the disciples to the Scriptures Jesus emphasizes once more that it stands written thus in a permanent divine record. The three infinitives state the substance of what has been written: suffer—arise—be proclaimed. R. 858 calls these aorists timeless, we regard them as being constative. This is especially true of a proclaiming which runs through the ages but is here summed up in one aoristic point. The suffering and the rising had been accomplished, the proclaiming was yet to begin; but as they were recorded in the Old Testament— and of that Jesus speaks here—all three acts were future, each was viewed in a punctiliar way.

The verb is active here: that the Christ "arise." The Scriptures say both, that he himself arose, and that he was raised by the Father; see v. 6. The phrase $\dot{\epsilon}\kappa\ \nu\epsilon\kappa\rho\tilde{\omega}\nu$ is treated in 9:7.

47) "To enter into his glory" is comprehensive in v. 26; the disciples now hear what this involves, namely their preaching and their being clothed with power. This, too, "has been written." The verb κηρύσσειν, to act as a κῆρυξ, to proclaim in public as a herald, is the standard verb for preaching. The herald gets his message from the man who sends him, and all he does is to announce that message. He dare not change it in any way. Men may say and think of it what they please, his business is only the loud, public heralding. The passive hides the agents, the heralds, for the moment but Jesus at once names them. This heralding is to be done "on the basis of his (the Christ's) name"; it is to rest on the revelation that he has made of himself. See 9:48 on this important phrase. Μετάνοια, "repentance," is treated in 3:3; and ἄφεσις, "remission of sins," in 1:77. They are to be understood in the same sense here and throughout the Scriptures. The reading is: "repentance and (not: for) remission." The great news is to be proclaimed that on the name of the Christ, on the basis of his revelation, a complete change of heart and riddance from all sins are to be obtained.

The proclamation is to be made "unto all the nations," πάντα τὰ ἔθνη (the same term that is used in Matt. 28:19 and is expanded fully in Acts 1:8). Let no one say that Jesus did not say this about all nations so often during these forty days. He had to say it often in order to impress it upon the disciples who clung so tenaciously to their narrow Judaism (Acts 1:6). Judaism is included in "all nations" as being one nation, but only as being one among many. The reading ἀρξάμενοι, a nominative plural participle after a passive aorist infinitive, has caused textual changes, grammatical perplexity, and resort to a punctuation which makes the participle a part of the following sentence. R. 1203 speaks about an anacoluthon or a use of the participle as a principal verb and in 946 is willing to change the punctuation and to give this form an imperative sense.

But there is a simpler solution. The Greek freely adds either an apposition or a participle in the nominative case, where a pedant would insist on an oblique case (here the accusative). When it is doing this the Greek is conscious of no grammatical irregularity whatever. B.-D. 137, 3. This pertains especially to the participle we have here with its idea of *von—an, anfangend von*, B.-D. 419, 3. These Galileans are not to start their world-wide preaching from Galilee even though Jesus did a good deal of work there, and even though the Sanhedrin would offer the strongest opposition. "Starting from Jerusalem" is the Lord's order. Not because salvation is of the Jews; it could be of the Jews even if the disciples started in Galilee. Jerusalem is the heart of the Jewish nation; Jesus will win his first victories there.

48) Jesus does not need to say outright that these disciples to whom he is speaking are to be the preachers that were foretold in the Scriptures as going out to all nations. All he says is: "*You* are witnesses of these things." They saw the fulfillment of the Scripture prophecies concerning the Christ in Jesus, are seeing it at the moment of Jesus' speaking. They are to be the witness-heralds. Their proclamation is to be testimony. They therefore lead all other heralds, who, because they are not themselves witnesses, can only take up the testimony of these witnesses and keep on heralding it. Acts 1:8; 2:32; 3:15, "witnesses."

49) The disciples need have no fears regarding this coming task. The great thing that Jesus will do for them, which is ushered in with the exclamation "lo," is that he himself (ἐγώ, emphatic) will send forth (so soon that he uses the present tense) the promise of his Father upon them, the Holy Spirit, the other Paraclete, who had been promised by the Father and is therefore called "the Father's promise"—see Peter's sermon which expounds this promise on the basis of Joel, Acts 2:16, etc. In view of the fulfillment of this

promise by the risen Jesus he already now orders them to sit, i. e., stay, in the city until that day should come, which would not be long as he told them in Acts 1:5. It is pedantic to say that the disciples were not to step out of the city until Pentecost, and that this is in contradiction to Matt. 28:7, 16, etc.; Mark 16:7; John 21:1. Complying with further orders of Jesus that were given already before his death (Matt. 26:32), the whole host of his disciples, about 500, met for a specific purpose and at a designated place in Galilee (I Cor. 15:5; Matt. 28:16); but on Pentecost these witnesses were found waiting in Jerusalem.

What they were to wait for Jesus explains further: "until you become clothed from on high with power." The verb is the middle voice, "become clothed with," but not, "put on yourselves" as R., W. P. thinks. The figure of being clothed with authority or with power in the sense of receiving it in order to exercise it is common. It denotes that the power is a gift, and its source is "from on high," from the Father and from Jesus who will presently ascend on high. The gift of the Spirit will fill the disciples with power that is fully and completely adequate to perform their task in Jerusalem and among the nations.

50) **Now he led them out till over against Bethany. And having lifted up his hands, he blessed them. And it came to pass while he was blessing them he separated from them and was being borne into the heaven. And they, having bowed in worship to him, returned to Jerusalem with great joy. And they were continually in the Temple praising God.**

In this section, too, we find omissions as these are noted in the R. V. margin, but they have very minor textual evidence so that we need say no more. The claim is unwarranted that Luke tells us in his Gospel that Jesus ascended to heaven on the very day of his resurrection whereas the same Luke tells us in the

Acts that Jesus ascended forty days later. This claim says that "he led them out" means that very Easter night. So the ascension took place at night, in the moonlight. Luke first got hold of one tradition and followed it, he then discovered another and again followed it without a word of explanation—and he sent both documents to the same man, Theophilus!

In his Gospel, let us understand it well, Luke offers no date for the ascension. He furnishes only a brief account because he intends to open the Acts with a full account of this act and there furnishes us the exact date. This proceeding on the part of Luke explains fully why the other Gospels stop with the resurrection. The resurrection constitutes the climax throughout apostolic preaching. That was the apostolic view. It is also Luke's view. What he adds about the ascension in his Gospel is given only for good measure. He has Pentecost in mind in v. 49 and so writes a few sentences about the ascension. But both the ascension and Pentecost really belong in Acts.

The place from which Jesus led his disciples out is not mentioned, but the context points to Jerusalem. "He led them out" reminds us of his walk with the two Emmaus disciples. He was in his glorified body, and we assume that he was seen only by the disciples as being those by whom alone he wished to be seen. Ἕως πρός="till over against," or "till toward," and does not, of course, mean that Jesus went to Bethany but only to that point on the Mount of Olives where the road forks, one branch going on to Jericho, the other to Bethany. It is noteworthy that both the agony and the ascension took place on the Mount of Olives; the places are located some distance apart but are still on the same ridge. Our humiliations and our exaltations often lie close together. Jesus and the disciples had often walked over this piece of road during these past days —think how they were walking it now!

When Jesus had reached the spot he had chosen, as the Acts show, he and the disciples spoke once more. Then a hush fell, he raised up his hands and blessed them, spoke a word of divine benediction over them. Luke states only the fact. The great moment had come, and it was sanctified by this blessing.

51) Luke again uses his two favorite idioms: "it came to pass" followed by a finite verb and ἐν τῷ with an infinitive. The former marks the importance of the event. As the words of blessing were being spoken, he separated from them, slowly, visibly, and their eyes followed him (Acts 1:10). Luke adds a descriptive imperfect: "and was being borne into heaven," which shows how his visible body rose higher and higher in a wondrous manner. The ascension pertains only to the body and human nature of Jesus.

What a majestic act! How perfectly it completed and rounded out the earthly career of Jesus! No other mode of departure would have left the impression that this one left. During the forty days he had merely vanished whenever he left the disciples; but he now ascends visibly, and the disciples understand that no further appearances are to follow. They are granted the privilege of seeing his final going to the Father, and they know that the Comforter will soon come down upon them, and that their great work will then begin. The Acts relate that a cloud enveloped him, and so they saw him no more. No; he did not continue rising physically into upper space, hidden by the cloud. Timelessly his glorified body was in heaven, in the glorious abode of God, the angels, and the spirits of the blessed.

Read Acts 1:9; John 6:62; Heb. 4:14; 9:24; John 14:1-6. These speak of the place. The ascension was also the exaltation, Dan. 7:14; Ps. 110:1; Matt. 22:44; Acts 2:34; Heb. 1:13. Both the ascension and the exaltation are full of saving power. Acts 2:33; Rom. 8:34; Eph. 2:6; Heb. 6:19, 20; 9:24. Jesus now entered upon his kingly work. His prophetic and his high-priestly work he completed on earth and only continues in heaven; but his kingly work he only began on earth and really entered upon in heaven. Read Ps. 47:5-9; 68:18. Not merely as a saint did Jesus ascend to heaven, "above all heavens" as the apostle says; not merely to be in heaven as Elijah is in heaven; but in his human nature to be exalted in the glory of the divine majesty forever. Yes, in heaven the saints see the man Jesus, but those who think that he is confined in heaven so that in his human nature he is there only and cannot at the same time be where he promised to be here on earth, have to learn what his ascension and his glorification really mean. The disciples witnessed the end of the resurrection, not its beginning in the secret tomb; they witnessed the beginning of the ascension, not its end when Jesus was enthroned. Luke lets the imperfect ἀνεφέρετο stand without bringing its motion to rest in an aorist, which is highly expressive of the actual act as the disciples saw it, their eyes noted no rest.

52) The disciples were overcome by the glorious act which they witnessed and bowed to the earth in worship. *Christus est Deus* is Bengel's brief comment. Matt. 28:9. This worship of Jesus, in whom we see the deity, and who is deity in his person, will continue to all eternity. The visible presence of Jesus was gone, not to appear again as before, but when the disciples returned to Jerusalem, their hearts sang "with great joy." They were not bereaved but enriched. Their fear was gone; they no longer hid behind locked doors. They had a Lord and Savior in heaven, who ruled all things with his omnipotent and omnipresent power and would make good all his promises.

53) That is why Luke adds the statement that these disciples were continually in the Temple, blessing God. Their hearts were so full of gratitude that they naturally sought this outlet in their great place of worship, the Temple. Prudence would have hurried them

off to their homes in Galilee. But Another directed them to stay right here in Jerusalem. No Sanhedrin frightened them; they went regularly and in public to the Temple—all men could see them. But they only worshipped, they did not preach—they waited. "Praising God" is Luke's last word. It is fitting, indeed, as the final note. Close the book and also praise God!

Soli Deo Gloria

www.ingramcontent.com/pod-product-compliance
Lightning Source LLC
Chambersburg PA
CBHW071849290426
44110CB00013B/1083